FIFTH EDITION

EXPLORING THE PHILOSOPHY OF RELIGION

David Stewart

Ohio University

Prentice
Hall

Upper Saddle River, New Jersey 07458

Library of Congress Cataloging-in-Publication Data

STEWART, DAVID.
  Exploring the philosophy of religion / DAVID STEWART.—5th ed.
    p. cm.
  Includes bibliographical references and index.
    ISBN 0-13-019519-7
  1. Religion—Philosophy.   I. Title.
  BL51.S658 2001
  210—dc21   00-028474

VP, Editorial Director: *Charlyce Jones Owen*
Acquisitions Editor: *Ross Miller*
Assistant Editor: *Katie Janssen*
Editorial/Production Supervision: *Joanne Riker*
Manufacturing and Prepress Buyer: *Sherry Lewis*
Marketing Manager: *Gina Sluss*
Cover Director: *Jayne Conte*
Cover Designer: *Bruce Kenselaar*

This book was set in 10/12 Goudy by East End Publishing Services, Inc.
and was printed and bound by RR Donnelly & Sons, Company. The cover
was printed by Phoenix Color Corp.

© 2001, 1998, 1992, 1988, 1980 by Prentice-Hall, Inc.
A Division of Pearson Education
Upper Saddle River, New Jersey 07458

Printed in the United States of America

10 9 8 7 6 5 4 3 2 1

ISBN 0-13-019519-7

PRENTICE-HALL INTERNATIONAL (UK) LIMITED, *London*
PRENTICE-HALL OF AUSTRALIA PTY. LIMITED, *Sydney*
PRENTICE-HALL CANADA INC., *Toronto*
PRENTICE-HALL HISPANOAMERICANA, S. A., *Mexico*
PRENTICE-HALL OF INDIA PRIVATE LIMITED, *New Delhi*
PRENTICE-HALL OF JAPAN, INC., *Tokyo*
SIMON & SCHUSTER ASIA PTE. LTD., *Singapore*
EDITORA PRENTICE-HALL DO BRASIL, LTDA., *Rio de Janeiro*

CONTENTS

EXPLORING THE PHILOSOPHY OF RELIGION

CHAPTER FOUR
ARGUMENTS FOR GOD'S EXISTENCE   117

CHAPTER FIVE
THE PROBLEM OF EVIL   165

CHAPTER SIX
FAITH AND REASON   215

PREFACE

A new edition of a textbook provides the occasion for correcting some of the deficiencies of the former edition as well as responding to the needs of the book's users. I have incorporated suggestions of several reviewers by changing the order of the selections, beginning with the more "existential" topics and then going on to the more abstract issues. The first chapter, now entitled "The Varieties of Religious Experience" might have been headed the "phenomenon" of religion, though I feared that this would impose too great an expectation on the offerings of that section. The readings address the question of how the religious impulse arises, whether in religious experience, the feelings of the numinous, or the encounter with the Eternal Thou. Also, in an increasingly global marketplace both for the exchange of goods and services as well as the exchange of ideas, it seemed necessary to address the pluralistic nature of religious faith, and the new selection by John Hick—*The Pluralistic Hypothesis*—does precisely that.

The readings in the chapter on religion and human destiny also respond to readers' requests for more classic sources. New in this section are excerpts from Epicurus, Plato, and the New Testament. This return to classics is found also in the chapter detailing arguments for God's existence with selections from Paley on the design argument and Kant on the moral argument. In teaching this course I find that students are intensely interested in the divine attributes and with such questions as divine foreknowledge and human freedom. The new selection from J. S. Mill on the divine attributes provides an opportunity to discuss this topic in the context of a theodicy derived solely from natural theology.

The following chapter dealing with faith and reason is supplemented by an extract from Paul Tillich's *Dynamics of Faith* detailing his view of faith as ultimate concern. This topic is not only important in showing a possible way of understanding faith but also in providing students with a vocabulary to discuss this important issue.

New to the chapter on religious language is Rosemary Ruether's important paper on The Female Nature of God. Coming at the end of the section analyzing the nonliteral use of language when speaking of the divine, this piece shows how our understanding of the divine nature can be enhanced by the feminine imagery found in traditional God talk. All the new readings in this edition respond to users' requests for lengthier selections with shorter introductory summaries.

This edition continues to include selections from Eastern as well as Western religious traditions and follows the general plan of this text to combine the best features of a text and a reader. The book attempts to provide both clear and understandable analysis, coupled with important primary-source readings. The topics chosen have a permanent place in the philosophy of religion, but users of the book do not need to use the chapters in the order in which they are presented here.

I am also indebted to David Bruce for his help with research, proofreading, and indexing. Immense support was given to this project by my Prentice Hall editors Karita France dos Santos and Ross Miller with additional support from Jennifer Ackerman and assistant editor Katie Janssen, without whose help this new edition would have been impossible.

David Stewart
Ohio University

Exploring the Philosophy of Religion

CHAPTER ONE

THE VARIETIES OF RELIGIOUS EXPERIENCE

INTRODUCTION

Philosophy and Religion

Both *philosophy* and *religion* are common terms, although defining them precisely is difficult due to the diversity of meanings each has acquired. The word *religion* derives from a Latin term that referred to the bond between man and the gods, and in the view of most persons religion implies a belief in some kind of supernatural being or beings. This is the definition of religion usually offered by dictionaries, but such an understanding of religion would exclude some religious traditions; for example, in Confucianism the question of the existence of supernatural beings never arises. The term *religion* has even been extended to such secular movements as communism or various nationalisms that, even while denying the existence of God, demand a total, "religious" commitment from their adherents.[1]

Further complicating the problem of arriving at a satisfactory definition of religion is the wide diversity of religious traditions. Every culture has a religious tradition of some sort, and these are as varied as the cultures that gave them birth. Many religious traditions are thoroughly bound up with cultic and ritual practices, but others are not. Some religions are tied to a priesthood, but this is not true of all. Divine revelation plays an important role in some traditions, but the relative importance of revelation in contrast with what can be known by reason alone is itself often a matter of disagreement.

In the study of religion, one response to this diversity of meanings is to adopt a neutral, descriptive approach. That is, one simply investigates a religion in its various cultural manifestations, describing religious phenomena, whatever

[1] For example, see Hans Mol, *Identity and the Sacred: A Sketch for a New Social-Scientific Theory of Religion* (New York: Free Press, 1977).

they may be. Such descriptive study concentrates on comparing or contrasting the various modes of religious awareness that are encountered, and perhaps deriving from this descriptive analysis certain conclusions about the nature of the religion under study. Whatever the merits of this approach may be, it cannot be considered a philosophical study of religion, for philosophy is the *critical* examination of human life and thought.

The study of religion, like the study of any other organized human activity, can be approached from a variety of standpoints. The historian, sociologist, and psychologist each approach religion with a unique concern. The historian will be interested in the development over time of a religious tradition, its similarities to other traditions, and the influence that a religion has on the economic, political, and social affairs of a particular society. The sociologist is concerned with discovering what societal values are expressed in a religious tradition, how the religious beliefs of a group provide cohesiveness in a society, and how stratifications within the society are affected by its religious traditions. The psychologist will focus on belief structures themselves as indicative of a particular kind of self-understanding. Of course, the concerns of historians, sociologists, and psychologists will overlap, for the borderline between disciplines is not always sharply defined.

Besides the differences among the interests of the various academic disciplines, there is also the difference between being a student *of* a religion and being a believer *in* that religion. A student might investigate Islam and try to understand what Moslems believe, how those beliefs are incorporated into ritual and cultic practices, what the various Moslem sects are, and how the beliefs of Islam relate to other religions in the Near East—all without accepting the tenets of Islam as true. A believer, on the other hand, may adopt the neutral stance of a student of religion, but the believer's attitude toward a religion will inevitably be influenced by personal religious commitments, particularly if the religion under scrutiny is the believer's own. The believer's attitude is a much more existential one, since the religion under scrutiny is not just a subject for academic study, but also a matter of personal commitment. The principal difficulty encountered in studying one's own religious tradition is in adopting an objective viewpoint (insofar as any objectivity is possible in religious study).

The philosophical study of religion, by virtue of the critical task of philosophy, demands detachment from personal beliefs in order to examine critically the fundamental questions raised by religion. This detachment is a necessary first step if one is to conduct a truly philosophical study of religion. This does not mean that an individual committed to a particular religious tradition cannot philosophize about that tradition; that would imply that a person could not believe religiously what had been discovered philosophically, a strange state of affairs indeed! The point is that the philosophical study of religion demands a degree of detachment from personal religious beliefs. In turn, a philosophical approach to religion may well produce fresh understanding and increased clarity, upon which an even deeper commitment can be based. In a philosophical analysis of a religion, the student will be enriched by contact with the work of historians, sociologists, psychologists, and scholars of comparative religion. But encounters with these disciplines merely prepare the student for the philosophical task, which is to analyze critically the fundamental issues raised by religion and to subject these issues to rigorous scrutiny.

If, however, as we have seen, even the task of discovering an essential nature of religion seems impossible, how can the philosopher begin? One answer to this question is to recognize that there is no such thing as religion, only religions. Religions can be grouped into various traditions, and within these traditions certain fundamental and common questions will emerge. This means that, for example, a philosopher analyzing a family of Eastern religions would discover a different set of questions than would emerge from the study of an ancient animistic religion. In other words, each religion raises its own set of questions, and part of the philosopher's job is to ferret out these fundamental issues and submit them to as thorough an examination as possible.

One of the challenges in approaching the study of religion in a college course is defining the scope of what will be covered. One method or type of course is the history-of-religions approach, which looks at the content of specific religious traditions, examines the growth and development of that content, and compares it with the content of other religions. While interesting and important, and even when including some treatment of the philosophical themes of various religions, this approach is a descriptive survey method, not a philosophical one. Sometimes, courses or books based on the comparative approach to the study of religion can become a little like the commercial recordings of "One Hundred of the World's Best-loved Melodies" or "Mozart's Greatest Hits." While providing breadth, such broad comparative study of religion risks losing the depth of analysis that is important to philosophy and appropriate to major themes such as God, evil, death, and faith. Some persons coming to a philosophy class on religion may therefore be disappointed to discover that it does not offer thumbnail sketches of the beliefs of Islam, Taoism, Confucianism, Hinduism, and other of the world's great religions. As interesting as such a comparative study would be, it would not focus on the themes that are the primary concern of a philosophical study.

A philosophical study of religion is also affected by the meaning of the term *philosophy* itself. With its beginnings in Greece, philosophy as a discipline has become identified with a particular way of thinking. Western philosophy places great emphasis on the human faculty of rationality and the role played by reason and argument in discovering truth. Its methods are argument, analysis, dialectical reasoning, and discursive thought. Consequently, of prime interest to philosophy are such religious questions as Is faith rational? Can the claims of the Judaeo-Christian tradition about God be proved? How can we harmonize belief in a benevolent God with the fact of evil and suffering in the world? and What language should we use when speaking of God? Western religions are not the only traditions to raise such questions, but because of the interplay between philosophy and religion in the West, philosophy of religion as a discipline has taken on a decidedly Western cast. But, as we will see in the selections that follow, non-Western religious traditions also deal with some of the same issues. Given the increasingly global nature of trade and the growing interplay among cultures, it is important that the perennial questions not be dealt with in an exclusively Western frame of reference, but that, where possible, they be seen in both their Western and Eastern forms. In doing so, however, it is important not to treat Eastern approaches as simply Western responses in different terminology, but to recognize the distinctive contributions they make to our understanding of philosophical themes.

In general, we can say with the contemporary philosopher John Hick that philosophy of religion is philosophical thinking about religion. But we must understand this as philosophical thinking not about religion in general, but about the *problems* raised by a particular religious tradition. To quote Hick, the philosophy of religion "seeks to analyze concepts such as God, holy, salvation, worship, creation, sacrifice, eternal life, etc., and to determine the nature of religious utterances in comparison with those of everyday life, scientific discovery, morality, and the imaginative expressions of the arts."[2] We must emphasize, however, that these concepts, while central to the Judaeo-Christian tradition, are not universal to all religions. When we look at what philosophers in both the Jewish and Christian traditions have pointed to as central concerns, we find a cluster of problems—the nature and existence of God, the problem of evil, the relation between faith and reason, the nature of religious language, the meaning of death, the relationship between morality and religion, and the question of human destiny. It is to these concepts, therefore, that we will seek to apply the rigors of philosophical analysis.

THE RELATION OF PHILOSOPHY AND RELIGION

The philosophy of religion, in the sense just defined, can be a useful tool in understanding religion, but the two are distinct. As has already been mentioned, philosophy can concern itself with varied religions—the religions of the East, ancient religions, contemporary religions, religions of the Middle Ages, and so forth. In each case, the philosopher's task is to determine the central issues and analyze them through careful scrutiny and investigation. In this sense, philosophy of religion is analogous to similar philosophical efforts aimed at other human disciplines. There can be philosophy of science, philosophy of education, philosophy of law, philosophy of art, philosophy of culture, and philosophy of psychology, to name just a few possibilities. In each case, the philosophical study of the discipline is distinct from the discipline itself. A philosophical study of law would raise such fundamental notions as the nature of justice, the meaning of *rights*, the nature of equality, and the status of law itself. The philosopher dealing with science would probe beneath the methods of scientists and question the meaning of *proof* and

---

[2] John Hick, *Philosophy of Religion*, 2d ed., Foundations of Philosophy Series (Englewood Cliffs, NJ: Prentice Hall, 1973), p. 2.

such assumptions made by scientists as their belief in the uniformity and regularity of nature, the dependability of inductive reasoning, and the meaning of such fundamental concepts as cause and effect. In both cases, the philosopher is not practicing law or doing science, but is forcing to the forefront the fundamental questions raised by these activities. Lawyers may talk a lot about justice, but what do they mean by it? Scientists may believe that the present laws of physics will hold true in the future, but on what basis do they accept the conviction?

Similarly, philosophy of religion is different from the practice of religion. Philosophy of religion is not a systematic statement of religious beliefs (which would be theology or dogmatics), but a second-order activity focused on the fundamental issues of a given religion. Christians, for example, talk a lot about God, but what is the evidence that God exists? If God's existence can be proved, how does one go about proving it? And if God exists, how can one account for the presence of evil in the world? Such questions are philosophical in nature, and the philosopher will not be content to let them go unexamined. The task of philosophy, at least as it is conceived of in the West, is to submit claims such as those made by religions to a thoroughgoing rational investigation.

There are philosophers, however, who question Western philosophy's focus on rational analysis. They point out that this emphasis on rationality is one-sided, for human beings are not just creatures of reason, but function through a complex unity of reason, emotion, will, appetites, and feelings. Religion, they insist, makes an appeal not just to human reason, but to emotion and feelings as well; therefore, any philosophical investigation of religion must include its nonrational as well as rational aspects. Indeed, though religion has rational elements, it appeals as well to the heart. Are people religious because they have felt the force of a powerful rational argument? Probably not. There are grounds for saying that religion seems to arise not so much from rational insight as from a powerful nonrational experience of something ultimate that demands allegiance and loyalty. How such experience arises and how it can be accounted for is the concern of the first group of readings.

Mystical Experience

Religious experience is as hard to define as is religion. If we understand religion to be that which demands our ultimate allegiance, or that which involves our beliefs about God or what we consider sacred, then we can better understand religious *experience*. It can take many different forms, but central to it is the direct encounter with what one considers the divine, the sacred, or the ultimately important. The exploration of some of these varieties of religious experience is the task of this first collection of readings.

Ambiguity also surrounds the use of the term *mysticism*, which is used to describe anything from an encounter resulting in unification with the divine to any experience slightly out of the ordinary. As we are using the term in this chapter, basic to all types of mystical experience is an encounter with the divine or the sacred. Mystical experience in this sense is not confined to any particular religious tradition. No single set of doctrines is associated with it, and not all mystics are even in agreement as to precisely what constitutes a mystical experience. Some mystics have found the experience to be a spontaneous and unexpected joy; others have found the experience only after a long and tortuous ascetic life. Aldous Huxley, in his book *The Doors of Perception*, claims to have undergone heightened experiences not unlike those of the mystics through the use of hallucinogenic drugs.

Although not every religious experience is mystical in the strict sense of the term, there are mystical elements in many different kinds of religious experience, and mystical types of religious experience seem to be found in all religious traditions. One type of mystical experience, a kind that can be called *union mysticism*, is the experience of complete union with the divine involving complete loss of self-identity. How the divine with which one is united is understood varies, depending on the religious tradition of the one having the experience. For Hindus, this union is with Brahman, or the One, and involves the complete loss of self or self-identity.

W. T. Stace further distinguishes between what he calls *introvertive* (inward-looking) and *extrovertive* (outward-looking) mysticism.[1] Introvertive mysticism,

---

[1] See W. T. Stace, ed., *The Teachings of the Mystics* (New York: New American Library, 1960).

as in the example from Hinduism just given, offers an experience of complete withdrawal from the world and a union with the transcendent characterized variously as the One, God, or, paradoxically, the Abyss or sheer Nothingness. Extrovertive forms of union, in contrast, produce a sense of unity with nature in which all distinctions between the self and nature disappear, and an experience of overwhelming totality and oneness occurs. For both types of mystical experience, the sense of union and loss of self-identity is important. In such experiences of union, mystics almost uniformly claim to have risen above the limitations of space and time, and to have experienced a loss of individuality in union with something greater than themselves. A mystical experience is intensely private, beyond words, beyond reason and emotion, and essentially indescribable.

Another form of mysticism, found more frequently in Christianity than is union mysticism, could be referred to as *communion mysticism*. Here the experience is not that of union with the divine, but the sense of the presence of God within one's life, or communion with God, or the sense that in prayer someone is listening. References to this type of religious experience are found throughout the New Testament. Jesus said, "Abide in me, and I in you" (John 15:4). Paul spoke of "Christ in you, the hope of glory" (Colossians 1:27) and said of the body that it is "God's temple and that God's Spirit dwells in you" (1 Corinthians 3:16). The English theologian W. D. Davis speaks of this as "Christ-mysticism."[2] In such experiences one has, not a loss of self, but rather a transformed self, a new self arising from the old. Spoken of variously as new life or a new birth, this experience of God brings about a renewed sense of purpose. Paul's experience of Christ led him to say, "I have been crucified with Christ; it is no longer I who live, but Christ who lives in me" (Galatians 2:20).

Although mysticism, understood as communion mysticism, is not an unusual feature of Christianity, there have been Christian mystics whose experiences seemed more intense and involved visions, ecstatic experiences, the hearing of voices, and other phenomena that are not the usual expectations of Christians. Roman Catholic Christianity has been able to incorporate such persons more willing than has Protestant Christianity. Among Catholic mystics are Bernard of Clairvaux (twelfth century), St. Bonaventure (thirteenth century), and St. Teresa and St. John of the Cross (sixteenth century). In spite of its skepticism of such experiences with their intense emotion and anitrational auras, Protestant Christianity has nonetheless included such mystics as Jakob Böhme (seventeenth century), George Fox (seventeenth century), and William Law (eighteenth century).

Judaism has likewise had its mystics. Hasidic Judaism, with its roots going back to the twelfth century, has emphasized the importance of the mystical life, and in the later Middle Ages a mystical minority movement known as Cabalism arose in Judaism. Its influence was principally in Spain and southern France, and it has no continuity with modern Judaism (whereas Hasidism does). Later

[2] See W. D. Davis, *Invitation to the New Testament* (Garden City, NY: Doubleday Anchor Books, 1969), pp. 347–350.

in this chapter there are selections from the writings of Martin Buber, who was profoundly influenced by the Hasidic movement. But it is clear that Buber's mysticism is the communion type, not union mysticism, for basic to Buber's description of the divine-human encounter is the notion of an I-Thou relationship. If the self, or the I, were absorbed and united with the Thou, there could be no relationship. More on the I-Thou relationship later in this chapter.

However we define it, mystical experience is not rare. National surveys reveal that a sizable percentage of Americans report having had an experience involving religious insight or awakening, or an encounter with the divine. The sociologist and priest Andrew Greeley observes that "a full 35% of Americans reported they had had a mystical experience: feeling 'very close to a powerful, spiritual force that seems to lift you out of yourself.' And one-seventh of those who have had such experiences—5% of the whole population—have literally been 'bathed in light' like the Apostle Paul."[3]

That people today report having had religious experiences is an empirical fact, and such experiences immediately raise a host of questions for philosophers. Among the first would be the question of how we can know whether the reports of mystical experience are different in kind from the reports of those having delusions. One answer is given by the British philosopher C. D. Broad, who, throughout his philosophic career, was interested in paranormal experiences, including the experiences of mystics. How are we to tell whether they are analogous to the delusions of someone who has had too much drink or are like the insights of a person with sight in a kingdom of the blind?

Broad, who has a rather sympathetic approach to the claims of mystics, offers the following argument: The delusions of an alcoholic suffering from delirium tremens are perceptions of things not unlike the objects we perceive in our everyday life. The alcoholic may see pink rats or snakes on the bed, and since we would be able to see these things if they were there, that we don't see them is a strong argument for the view that the drunk is suffering from delusions. Broad suggests that the case with the mystic may be more aptly compared with the perceptions of a person with sight in a land of the blind. Here is how Broad puts it:

> When there is a nucleus of agreement between the experiences of men in different places, times, and traditions, and when they all tend to put much the same kind of interpretation on the cognitive content of these experiences, it is reasonable to ascribe this agreement to their all being in contact with a certain objective aspect of reality *unless* there is some positive reason to think otherwise. The practical postulate which we go upon everywhere else is to treat cognitive claims as veridical unless there be some positive reason to think them delusive. This, after all, is our only guarantee for believing that ordinary sense-perception is veridical. We cannot *prove* that what people agree in perceiving really exists independently of them; but we do always assume that ordinary waking sense-perception

---

[3] Andrew Greeley, "Mysticism Goes Mainstream," *American Health*, January–February 1987, p. 47

is veridical unless we can produce some positive ground for thinking that it is delusive in any given case. I think it would be inconsistent to treat the experiences of religious mystics on different principles.[4]

What basis do we have for accepting the claims of mystics as veridical, that is, as truthful and dependable insights into the nature of things? Like the arguments for the existence of God, we will see that the issue is inconclusive. Reasonable people can refuse to accept the veridical nature of mystical experience and still be religious. Others who have such experiences find themselves driven to religion. Still others apparently have had experiences similar to mystical experience completely apart from a commitment to any religion.

The reading that follows, a selection from the philosopher William James, is a discussion of mystical experience more relevant to union mysticism than to communion mysticism. After giving a definition of mystical experiences, James offers several examples, a description of some of the disciplines used by mystics to induce the experiences, and the vocabulary they develop to describe them. He ends with an analysis of mystics' claims that they have a special and privileged way of knowing religious truth.

Mysticism

WILLIAM JAMES

What does the expression 'mystical states of consciousness' mean? How do we part off mystical states from other states?

The words 'mysticism' and 'mystical' are often used as terms of mere reproach, to throw at any opinion which we regard as vague and vast and sentimental, and without a base in either facts or logic. For some writers a 'mystic' is any person who believes in thought-transference, or spirit-return. Employed in this way, the word has little value: there are too many less ambiguous synonyms. So, to keep it useful by restricting it, I will . . . propose to you four marks which,

[4]C. D. Broad, *Religion, Philosophy and Psychical Research* (New York: Harcourt, Brace & Company, 1953), p. 197.

Source: William James, *The Varieties of Religious Experience* (New York: Longmans, Green, 1902).

when an experience has them, may justify us in calling it mystical. . . . In this way we shall save verbal disputation, and the recriminations that generally go therewith.

1. Ineffability.—The handiest of the marks by which I classify a state of mind as mystical is negative. The subject of it immediately says that it defies expression, that no adequate report of its contents can be given in words. It follows from this that its quality must be directly experienced; it cannot be imparted or transferred to others. In this peculiarity mystical states are more like states of feeling than like states of intellect. No one can make clear to another who has never had a certain feeling, in what the quality or worth of it consists. One must have musical ears to know the value of a symphony; one must have been in love one's self to understand a lover's state of mind. Lacking the heart or ear, we cannot interpret the musician or the lover justly, and are even likely to consider him weak-minded or absurd. The mystic finds that most of us accord to his experiences an equally incompetent treatment.

2. Noetic quality.—Although so similar to states of feeling, mystical states seem to those who experience them to be also states of knowledge. They are states of insight into depths of truth unplumbed by the discursive intellect. They are illuminations, revelations, full of significance and importance, all inarticulate though they remain; and as a rule they carry with them a curious sense of authority for after-time.

These two characters will entitle any state to be called mystical, in the sense in which I use the word. Two other qualities are less sharply marked, but are usually found. These are:—

3. Transiency.—Mystical states cannot be sustained for long. Except in rare instances, half an hour, or at most an hour or two, seems to be the limit beyond which they fade into the light of common day. Often, when faded, their quality can but imperfectly be reproduced in memory; but when they recur it is recognized; and from one recurrence to another it is susceptible of continuous development in what is felt as inner richness and importance.

4. Passivity.—Although the oncoming of mystical states may be facilitated by preliminary voluntary operations, as by fixing the attention, or going through certain bodily performances, or in other ways which manuals of mysticism prescribe; yet when the characteristic sort of consciousness once has set in, the mystic feels as if his own will were in abeyance, and indeed sometimes as if he were grasped and held by a superior power. This latter peculiarity connects mystical states with certain definite phenomena of secondary or alternative personality, such as prophetic speech, automatic writing, or the mediumistic trance. When these latter conditions are well pronounced, however, there may be no recollection whatever of the phenomenon, and it may have no significance for the subject's usual inner life, to which, as it were, it makes a mere interruption. Mystical states, strictly so called, are never merely interruptive. Some memory of their content always remains, and a profound sense of their importance. They modify the inner life of the subject between the times of

their recurrence. Sharp divisions in this region are, however, difficult to make, and we find all sorts of gradations and mixtures.

These four characteristics are sufficient to mark out a group of states of consciousness peculiar enough to deserve a special name and to call for careful study. Let it then be called the mystical group.

Our next step should be to gain acquaintance with some typical examples. . . . .

In India, training in mystical insight has been known from time immemorial under the name of yoga. Yoga means the experimental union of the individual with the divine. It is based on persevering exercise; and the diet, posture, breathing, intellectual concentration, and moral discipline vary slightly in the different systems which teach it. The yogi, or disciple, who has by these means overcome the obscurations of his lower nature sufficiently, enters into the condition termed *samâdhi*, "and comes face to face with facts which no instinct or reason can ever know."

The Buddhists use the word 'samâdhi' as well as the Hindus; but 'dhyâna' is their special word for higher states of contemplation. There seem to be four stages recognized in dhyâna. The first stage comes through concentration of the mind upon one point. It excludes desire, but not discernment or judgment: it is still intellectual. In the second stage the intellectual functions drop off, and the satisfied sense of unity remains. In the third stage the satisfaction departs, and indifference begins, along with memory and self-consciousness. In the fourth stage the indifference, memory, and self-consciousness are perfected. [Just what 'memory' and 'self-consciousness' mean in this connection is doubtful. They cannot be the faculties familiar to us in the lower life.] Higher stages still of contemplation are mentioned—a region where there exists nothing, and where the mediator says: "There exists absolutely nothing," and stops. Then he reaches another region where he says: "There are neither ideas nor the absence of ideas," and stops again. Then another region where, "having reached the end of both idea and perception, he stops finally." This would seem to be, not yet Nirvâna, but as close an approach to it as this life affords.

In the Mohammedan world the Sufi sect and various dervish bodies are the possessors of the mystical tradition. The Sufis have existed in Persia from the earliest times, and as their pantheism is so at variance with the hot and rigid monotheism of the Arab mind, it has been suggested that Sufism must have been inoculated into Islam by Hindu influences. Christians know little of Sufism, for its secrets are disclosed only to those initiated. . . .

In the Christian church there have always been mystics. Although many of them have been viewed with suspicion, some have gained favor in the eyes of the authorities. The experiences of these have been treated as precedents, and a codified system of mystical theology has been based upon them, in which everything legitimate finds its place. The basis of the system is 'orison' or meditation, the methodical elevation of the soul towards God. Through the practice of orison the higher levels of mystical experience may be attained. It is odd that Protestantism, especially evangelical Protestantism, should seemingly have abandoned everything methodical in this line. Apart from what prayer may lead to, Protestant mystical experience appears to have been almost exclusively sporadic. It has been left to our mind-curers to reintroduce methodical meditation into our religious life.

The first thing to be aimed at in orison is the mind's detachment from outer sensations, for these interfere with its concentration upon ideal things. Such manuals as Saint Ignatius's Spiritual Exercises recommend the disciple to expel sensation by a graduated series of efforts to imagine holy scenes. The acme of this kind of discipline would be a semi-hallucinatory mono-ideism—an imaginary figure of Christ, for example, coming fully to occupy the mind. Sensorial images of this sort, whether literal or symbolic, play an enormous part in mysticism. But in certain cases imagery may fall away entirely, and in the very highest raptures it tends to do so. The state of consciousness becomes then insusceptible of any verbal description. Mystical teachers are unanimous as to this. Saint John of the Cross, for instance, one of the best of them, thus describes the condition called the 'union of love,' which, he says, is reached by 'dark contemplation.'

My next task is to inquire whether we can invoke [mystical experience] as authoritative. Does it furnish any *warrant for the truth* of the twice-bornness and supernaturality and pantheism which it favors? I must give my answer to this question as concisely as I can.

In brief my answer is this—and I will divide it into three parts:—

1. Mystical states, when well developed, usually are, and have the right to be, absolutely authoritative over the individuals to whom they come.
2. No authority emanates from them which should make it a duty for those who stand outside of them to accept their revelations uncritically.
3. They break down the authority of the non-mystical or rationalistic consciousness, based upon the understanding and the senses alone. They show it to be only one kind of consciousness. They open out the possibility of other orders of truth, in which, so far as anything in us vitally responds to them, we may freely continue to have faith.

I will take up these points one by one.

1.

As a matter of psychological fact, mystical states of a well-pronounced and emphatic sort *are* usually authoritative over those who have them. They have been 'there,' and know. It is vain for rationalism to grumble about this. If the mystical truth that comes to a man proves to be a force that he can live by, what mandate have we of the majority to order him to live in another way? We can throw him into a prison or a madhouse, but we cannot change his mind—we commonly attach it only the more stubbornly to its beliefs. It mocks our utmost efforts, as a matter of fact, and in point of logic it absolutely escapes our jurisdiction. Our own more 'rational' beliefs are based on evidence exactly similar in nature to that which mystics quote for theirs. Our senses, namely, have assured us of certain states of fact; but mystical experiences are as direct perceptions of fact for those who have them as any sensations ever were for us. The records show that even though the five senses be in abeyance in them, they are absolutely sensational in their epistemological quality, if I may be pardoned the barbarous expression,—that is, they are face to face presentations of what seems immediately to exist.

The mystic is, in short, *invulnerable*, and must be left, whether we relish it or not, in undisturbed enjoyment of his creed. Faith, says Tolstoy, is that by which men live. And faith-state and mystic state are practically convertible terms.

2.

But I now proceed to add that mystics have no right to claim that we ought to accept the deliverance of their peculiar experiences, if we are ourselves outsiders and feel no private call thereto. The utmost they can ever ask of us in this life is to admit that they establish a presumption. They form a consensus and have an unequivocal outcome; and it would be odd, mystics might say, if such a unanimous type of experience should prove to be altogether wrong. At bottom, however, this would only be an appeal to numbers, like the appeal of rationalism the other way; and the appeal to numbers has no logical force. If we acknowledge it, it is for 'suggestive,' not for logical reasons: we follow the majority because to do so suits our life.

But even this presumption from the unanimity of mystics is far from being strong. . . . The classic religious mysticism, it now must be confessed, is only a 'privileged case.' It is an *extract*, kept true to type by the selection of the fittest specimens and their preservation in 'schools.' It is carved out from a much larger mass; and if we take the larger mass as seriously as religious mysticism has historically taken itself, we find that the supposed unanimity largely disappears. To begin with, even religious mysticism itself, the kind that accumulates traditions and makes schools, is much less unanimous than I have allowed. It has been both ascetic and antinomianly self-indulgent within the Christian church. It is dualistic in Sankhya, and monistic in Vedanta philosophy. I called it pantheistic; but the great Spanish mystics are anything but pantheists. They are with few exceptions non-metaphysical minds, for whom 'the category of personality' is absolute. The 'union' of man with God is for them much more like an occasional miracle than like an original identity. How different again, apart from the happiness common to all, is the mysticism of Walt Whitman, Edward Carpenter, Richard Jefferies, and other naturalistic pantheists, from the more distinctively Christian sort. The fact is that the mystical feeling of enlargement, union, and emancipation has no specific intellectual content whatever of its own. It is capable of forming matrimonial alliances with material furnished by the most diverse philosophies and theologies, provided only they can find a place in their framework for its peculiar emotional mood. We have no right, therefore, to invoke its prestige as distinctively in favor of any special belief, such as that in absolute idealism, or in the absolute monistic identity, or in the absolute goodness, of the world. It is only relatively in favor of all these things—it passes out of common human consciousness in the direction in which they lie.

So much for religious mysticism proper. But more remains to be told, for religious mysticism is only one half of mysticism. The other half has no accumulated traditions except those which the textbooks on insanity supply. Open any one of these, and you will find abundant cases in which 'mystical ideas' are cited as characteristic symptoms of enfeebled or deluded states of mind. In delusional insanity, paranoia, as they sometimes call it, we may have a *diabolical* mysticism, a sort of religious mysticism turned upside down. The same sense of ineffable importance in the smallest events, the same texts and words coming with new meanings, the same voices and visions and leadings and missions, the same controlling by extraneous powers; only this time the emotion is pessimistic: instead of consolations we have desolations; the meanings are dreadful; and the powers are enemies to life. It is evident that from the point of view of their psychological mechanism, the classic mysticism and these lower mysticisms spring from the same mental level, from that great subliminal or transmarginal region of which science is beginning to admit the existence, but of which so little is really known. That region contains every kind of matter: 'seraph and snake' abide there side by side. To come from thence is no infallible credential. What comes must be sifted and tested, and run the gauntlet of confrontation with the total context of experience, just like what comes from the outer world of sense. Its value must be ascertained by empirical methods, so long as we are not mystics ourselves.

Once more, then, I repeat that non-mystics are under no obligation to acknowledge in mystical states a superior authority conferred on them by their intrinsic nature.

3.

Yet, I repeat once more, the existence of mystical states absolutely overthrows the pretension of non-mystical states to be the sole and ultimate dictators of what we may believe. As a rule, mystical states merely add a supersensuous meaning to the ordinary outward data of consciousness. They are excitements like the emotions of love or ambition, gifts to our spirit by means of which facts already objectively before us fall into a new expressiveness and make a new connection with our active life. They do not contradict these facts as such, or deny anything that our senses have immediately seized. It is the rationalistic critic rather who plays the part of denier in the controversy, and his denials have no strength, for there never can be a state of facts to which new meaning may not truthfully be added, provided the mind ascend to a more enveloping point of view. It must always remain an open question whether mystical states may not possibly be such superior points of view, windows through which the mind looks out upon a more extensive and inclusive world. The difference of the views seen from the different mystical windows need not prevent us from entertaining this supposition. The wider world would in that case prove to have a mixed constitution like that of this world, that is all. It would have its celestial and its infernal regions, its tempting and its saving moments, its valid experiences and its counterfeit ones, just as our world has them; but it would be a wider world all the same. We should have to use its experiences by selecting and subordinating and substituting just as is our custom in this ordinary naturalistic world; we should be liable to error just as we are now; yet the counting in of that wider world of meanings, and the serious dealing with it, might, in spite of all the perplexity, be indispensable stages in our approach to the final fullness of truth.

Discussion Questions

1. Even though national surveys reveal that many people have had intense religious experiences, such experiences do not seem to be widely talked about. Why do you think this is the case?

2. Do you agree with C. D. Broad's view that mystics should be compared to persons with sight in the land of the blind? Why or why not?

3. William James gives examples of mystical experiences in different religious traditions. What conclusion can you draw from this about the relation between mysticism and religion?

4. Explain in your own words the difference between *communion mysticism* and *union mysticism*.

5. James concludes, "non-mystics are under no obligation to acknowledge in mystical states a superior authority conferred on them by their intrinsic nature." What reasons does he advance for this conclusion? Do you agree?

The Experience of the Holy

The preceding discussion of mysticism emphasized the importance of including the nonrational element in any account of religious experience. Even though there is a place for the rational and the cognitive in religion, many philosophers have protested against the somewhat one-sided emphasis, at least in Christian thought, on the rational arguments for elements of religious beliefs.

One of the most eloquent spokesmen for the significance of the nonrational in religion was Friedrich Schleiermacher, who in the eighteenth century proposed an alternative way of viewing the sources of religion. The eighteenth-century mechanistic world view left little room for God. Advances in physics, mathematics, astronomy, and the geological sciences all posed threats to the traditional arguments for the existence of God and the truth of the Christian religion. In response to these attacks, Schleiermacher proposed in a book written in 1799 to explore the nonrational aspect of religion. This book, *On Religion: Speeches to Its Cultured Despisers*, suggests that religion arises not in our intellectual faculties, but in the feelings of utter dependence that a finite creature experiences when faced with its own finitude and contingency. Although influential in his own day, Schleiermacher was rediscovered in the twentieth century, which witnessed some of the same attitudes toward religion that had been prevalent in Schleiermacher's century. In a 1926 reprint of the first edition of Schleiermacher's book, the German theologian Rudolf Otto made the following assessment of the importance of Schleiermacher's work:

> He wished to show that man is not wholly confined to knowledge and action, that the relationship of men to their environment—the world, being, mankind, events—is not exhausted in the mere perception or shaping of it. He sought to prove that if one experienced the envisioning world in a state of deep emotion, as intuition and feeling, and that if one were deeply affected by a sense of its eternal and abiding essence to the point where one was moved to feelings of devotion, awe, and reverence—then such an affective state was worth more than knowledge and action put together. And this was what the cultured had to learn from the beginning.[1]

[1] Rudolf Otto, "Introduction" to Friedrich Schleiermacher, *On Religion: Speeches to Its Cultured Despisers*, trans. John Oman (New York: Harper & Row, 1958), p. xix.

There is, however, a major flaw in Schleiermacher's proposal: It is an entirely subjective account of religion. Religion arises in feelings, but feelings of what? When Schleiermacher describes these feelings, he does so solely in terms of their subjectivity—utter dependence, devotion, awe, and so forth. There can be no feelings worthy of the name *faith* without a content. What, indeed, is the content of the feelings of "creature consciousness" to which Schleiermacher points?

It is, in part, to answer this question that Rudolf Otto proposes to describe that to which the feelings of dependence and devotion are directed. He uses the term *holy* (*das Heilige* in German) and offers a synonym for the word *holy* in the term *numinous*. Like Schleiermacher, Otto rejects the excessive emphasis on rational approaches to religion, which he thinks have dominated theological thought and constituted a bias against discovering the origins of religion in feelings not unlike those that Schleiermacher had described a century and a half earlier. But unlike Schleiermacher, Otto is more interested in the content of this experience than in the subjective side of the experience itself. By using the term *holy* to describe the experience, Otto is aware that he is open to misunderstanding, for *holy* has taken on the meaning of moral perfection and ethical purity. This was not its original meaning, however; it first signified that which was separate and unapproachable, set apart and distinct from human beings. When the ancient Hebrews spoke of the holiness of God, they were thinking not only of God's moral perfection, but of God's distinct otherness as a being completely different and separate from sinful humankind.

Since the term *holy* has these moral connotations, Otto coins a new term, *numinous*, from the Latin *numen*, signifying divine power or divine will. The experience of the numinous is difficult to describe, yet Otto insists that it is an experience basic to all religions. Being a student of world religions, Otto is convinced that religion arises not from rational argumentation, but from a profound experience of divine power that can take many forms, although there are common features in all its manifestations. As Otto describes this experience,

> The feeling of it may at times come sweeping like a gentle tide, pervading the mind with a tranquil mood of deepest worship. It may pass over into a more set and lasting attitude of the soul, continuing, as it were, thrillingly vibrant and resonant, until at last it dies away and the soul resumes its "profane," non-religious mood of everyday experience. It may burst in sudden eruption up from the depths of the soul with spasms and convulsions, or lead to the strangest excitements, to intoxicated frenzy, to transport, and to ecstasy. It has its wild and demonic forms and can sink to an almost grisly horror and shuddering. It has its crude, barbaric antecedents and early manifestations, and again it may be developed into something beautiful and pure and glorious. It may become hushed, trembling, and speechless humility of the creature in the presence of—whom or what? In the presence of that which is a *mystery* inexpressible and above all creatures.[2]

---

[2] Rudolf Otto, *The Idea of the Holy*, 2d ed., trans. John W. Harvey (London: Oxford University Press, 1950), pp. 12–13.

As you read through the selection from Otto, notice that he uses various descriptive phrases for the experience of the numinous. These differing descriptions should not be taken as different experiences, but as various aspects of the same experience of the numinous. The descriptions must vary because the experience itself may be articulated differently, depending on whether the religious consciousness undergoing the experience is primitive or well developed. A central descriptive phrase Otto uses to describe the experience of the numinous is *mysterium tremendum*. *Tremendum*, as its English derivative, *tremendous*, suggests, involves the notions of power and might. Otto further analyzes the sense of *tremendum* as involving elements of awe, overpoweringness, and energy. Corresponding to these qualities (or *quale*) are the subjective responses of dread, insignificance, and impotence. All these feelings are reflected in the description given by the Hebrew prophet Isaiah of an experience that qualifies in every way as an experience of the holy:

> And the foundations of the thresholds shook at the voice of him who called, and the house was filled with smoke. And I said: "Woe is me! For I am lost; for I am a man of unclean lips, and I dwell in the midst of a people of unclean lips; for my eyes have seen the King, the Lord of hosts." (Isaiah 6:4–5, RSV)

If all this is difficult to understand, it should only be expected, for as the term *mysterium* suggests, there is something "wholly other" about the numinous, something that reason with its limited powers can never grasp. It is clear that scientifically educated people do not like mystery; they think more in terms of problems and difficulties that can be dispelled by an increase in human knowledge. A mystery, as Otto points out, is entirely different from a problem. There is within a mystery something that will forever elude attempts to comprehend it. "The truly 'mysterious' object," Otto says, "is beyond our apprehension and comprehension, because in it we come upon something inherently 'wholly other.' . . . "

If Otto's description of the experience of the numinous still seems remote and difficult, perhaps C. S. Lewis's description of an analogous experience will help:

> Suppose you were told there was a tiger in the next room; you would know that you were in danger and would probably feel fear. But if you were told "There is a ghost in the next room," and believed it, you would feel, indeed, what is often called fear, but of a different kind. It would not be based on that knowledge of danger, for no one is primarily afraid of what a ghost may do to him, but of the mere fact that it is a ghost. It is "uncanny" rather than dangerous, and the special kind of fear it excites may be called Dread. With the Uncanny one has reached the fringes of the Numinous. Now suppose that you were told simply, "There is a mighty spirit in the room," and believed it. Your feelings would then be even less like the mere fear of danger: but the disturbance would be profound. You would feel wonder and a certain shrinking—a sense of inadequacy to cope with such a visitant and of prostration before it—an emotion which might be expressed in Shakespeare's words "Under it my genius is

rebuked." This feeling may be described as awe, and the object which excites it
as the Numinous.[3]

Lewis's analogy also points up the other aspect of the experience of the numinous as Otto describes it: the feeling of fascination and attraction. Who has not
had an experience of being around a campfire swapping ghost stories? Each person attempts to outdo the other in piling horrible detail upon grisly fact. While
all this should be repelling, there is something fascinating and compelling about
the tales of the preternatural. And so it is with the numinous. While there is
within the experience of the numinous that which repels, the awe-fulness, power,
and urgency of the numinous also fascinate and attract and give rise to feelings
that in their more developed forms are the basis of religion. Experiencing the presence of God in a thirteenth-century cathedral may be a far cry from the more ro-
bust forms that the experience of the numinous has taken, but however the
numinous is experienced, it defies conceptual analysis and will forever elude attempts to understand it completely.

The Idea of the Holy

RUDOLF OTTO

"NUMEN" AND THE "NUMINOUS"

"Holiness"—"the holy"—is a category of interpretation and valuation peculiar to
the sphere of religion. It is, indeed, applied by transference to another sphere—
that of ethics—but it is not itself derived from this. While it is complex, it contains a quite specific element or "moment," which sets it apart from "the rational"
in the meaning we gave to that word above, and which remains inexpressible—
an 'άρρητον or *ineffabile*—in the sense that it completely eludes apprehension in
terms of concepts. The same thing is true (to take a quite different region of experience) of the category of the beautiful.

Source: Reprinted from *The Idea of the Holy* by Rudolf Otto, trans. John W. Harvey, 2d ed.
(1950), by permission of Oxford University Press.

[3] C. S. Lewis, *The Problem of Pain* (London: Geoffrey Bles, 1956), p. 5.

Now these statements would be untrue from the outset if "the holy" were merely what is meant by the word, not only in common parlance, but in philosophical, and generally even in theological usage. The fact is we have come to use the words, "holy," "sacred" (*heilig*) in an entirely derivative sense, quite different from that which they originally bore. We generally take "holy" as meaning "completely good"; it is the absolute moral attribute, denoting the consummation of moral goodness. In this sense Kant calls the will which remains unwaveringly obedient to the moral law from the motive of duty a "holy" will; here clearly we have simply the *perfectly moral* will. In the same way we may speak of the holiness or sanctity of duty or law, meaning merely that they are imperative upon conduct and universally obligatory.

But this common usage of the term is inaccurate. It is true that all this moral significance is contained in the word "holy," but it included in addition—as even we cannot but feel—a clear overplus of meaning, and this it is now our task to isolate. Nor is this merely a later or acquired meaning; rather, "holy," or at least the equivalent words in Latin and Greek, in Semitic and other ancient languages, denoted first and foremost *only* this overplus: if the ethical element was present at all, at any rate it was not original and never constituted the whole meaning of the word. Any one who uses it today does undoubtedly always feel "the morally good" to be implied in "holy"; and accordingly in our inquiry into that element which is separate and peculiar to the idea of the holy it will be useful, at least for the temporary purpose of the investigation, to invent a special term to stand for "the holy" *minus* its moral factor or "moment," and, as we can now add, minus its "rational" aspect altogether. . . .

Accordingly, it is worthwhile, as we have said, to find a word to stand for this element in isolation, this "extra" in the meaning of "holy" above and beyond the meaning of goodness. By means of a special term we shall the better be able, first, to keep the meaning clearly apart and distinct, and second, to apprehend and classify connectedly whatever subordinate forms or stages of development it may show. For this purpose I adopt a word coined from the Latin *numen*. *Omen* has given us "ominous," and there is no reason why from *numen* we should not similarly form a word "numinous." I shall speak, then, of a unique "numinous" category of value and of a definitely "numinous" state of mind, which is always found wherever the category is applied. This mental state is perfectly *sui generis* and irreducible to any other; and therefore, like every absolutely primary and elementary datum, while it admits of being discussed, it cannot be strictly defined. There is only one way to help another to an understanding of it. He must be guided and led on by consideration and discussion of the matter through the ways of his own mind, until he reaches the point at which "the numinous" in him perforce begins to stir, to start into life and into consciousness. We can cooperate in this process by bringing before his notice all that can be found in other regions of the mind, already known and familiar, to resemble, or again to afford some special contrast to, the particular experience we wish to elucidate. Then we must add: "This X of ours is not precisely *this* experience, but akin to this one and the opposite of that other. Cannot you now realize for yourself what it is?" In other words our X cannot, strictly speaking, be taught, it can only be evoked, awakened in the mind; as everything that comes "of the spirit" must be awakened.

"MYSTERIUM TREMENDUM"

The Analysis of "Tremendum"

We said above that the nature of the numinous can only be suggested by means of the special way in which it is reflected in the mind in terms of feeling. "Its nature is such that it grips or stirs the human mind with this and that determinate affective state." We have now to attempt to give a further indication of these determinate states. We must once again endeavor, by adducing feelings akin to them for the purpose of analogy or contrast, and by the use of metaphor and symbolic expressions, to make the states of mind we are investigating ring out, as it were, of themselves.

Let us consider the deepest and most fundamental element in all strong and sincerely felt religious emotion. Faith unto salvation, trust, love—all these are there. But over and above these is an element which may also on occasion, quite apart from them, profoundly affect us and occupy the mind with a wellnigh bewildering strength. Let us follow it up with every effort of sympathy and imaginative intuition wherever it is to be found, in the lives of those around us, in sudden, strong ebullitions of personal piety and the frames of mind such ebullitions evince, in the fixed and ordered solemnities of rites and liturgies, and again in the atmosphere that clings to old religious monuments and buildings, to temples and to churches. If we do so we shall find we are dealing with something for which there is only one appropriate expression, *"mysterium tremendum."* The feeling of it may at times come sweeping like a gentle tide, pervading the mind with a tranquil mood of deepest worship. It may pass over into a more set and lasting attitude of the soul, continuing, as it were, thrillingly vibrant and resonant, until at last it dies away and the soul resumes its "profane," non-religious mood of everyday experience. It may burst in sudden eruption up from the depths of the soul with spasms and convulsions, or lead to the strangest excitements, to intoxicated frenzy, to transport, and to ecstasy. It has its wild and demonic forms and can sink to an almost grisly horror and shuddering. It has its crude, barbaric antecedents and early manifestations, and again it may be developed into something beautiful and pure and glorious. It may become the hushed, trembling, and speechless humility of the creature in the presence of—whom or what? In the presence of that which is a *mystery* inexpressible and above all creatures.

It is again evident at once that here too our attempted formulation by means of a concept is once more a merely negative one. Conceptually *mysterium* denotes merely that which is hidden and esoteric, that which is beyond conception of understanding, extraordinary and unfamiliar. The term does not define the object more positively in its qualitative character. But though what is enunciated in the word is negative, what is meant is something absolutely and intensely positive.

This pure positive we can experience in feelings, feelings which our discussion can help to make clear to us, in so far as it arouses them actually in our hearts.

The Element of Awefulness

To get light upon the positive *"quale"* of the object of these feelings, we must analyze more closely our phrase *mysterium tremendum*, and we will begin first with the adjective.

Tremor is in itself merely the perfectly familiar and "natural" emotion of *fear*. But here the term is taken, aptly enough but still only by analogy, to denote a quite specific kind of emotional response, wholly distinct from that of being afraid, though it so far resembles it that the analogy of fear may be used to throw light upon its nature. There are in some languages special expressions which denote, either exclusively or in the first instance, this "fear" that is more than fear proper. The Hebrew *hiqdīsh* (hallow) is an example. To "keep a thing holy in the heart" means to mark it off by a feeling of peculiar dread, not to be mistaken for any ordinary dread, that is, to appraise it by the category of the numinous. But the Old Testament throughout is rich in parallel expressions for this feeling. Specially noticeable is the *'ēmāh* of Yahweh ("fear of God"), which Yahweh can pour forth, dispatching almost like a demon, and which seizes upon a man with paralyzing effect. It is closely related to the δεῖνα πανικόν of the Greeks. Compare Exod. xxiii. 27: "I will send my fear before thee, and will destroy all the people to whom thou shalt come . . . "; also Job ix. 34; xiii. 21 ("let not his fear terrify me"; "let not thy dread make me afraid"). Here we have a terror fraught with an inward shuddering such as not even the most menacing and overpowering created thing can instill. It has something spectral in it. . . .

The Element of "Overpoweringness" ("majestas")

We have been attempting to unfold the implications of that aspect of the *mysterium tremendum* indicated by the adjective, and the result so far may be summarized in two words, constituting, as before, what may be called an "ideogram," rather than a concept proper, viz. "absolute unapproachability."

It will be felt at once that there is yet a further element which must be added, that namely, of "might," "power," "absolute overpoweringness." We will take to represent this the term *majestas*, majesty—the more readily because anyone with a feeling for language must detect a last faint trace of the numinous still clinging to the world. The *tremendum* may then be rendered more adequately *tremenda majestas*, or "aweful majesty." This second element of majesty may continue to be vividly preserved, where the first, that of unapproachability, recedes and dies away as may be seen, for example, in mysticism. It is especially in relation to this element of majesty or absolute overpoweringness that the creature-consciousness, of which we have already spoken, comes upon the scene, as a sort of shadow or subjective reflection of it. Thus, in contrast to "the overpowering" of which we are conscious as an object over against the self, there is the feeling of one's own submergence, of being but "dust and ashes" and nothingness. And this forms the numinous raw material for the feeling of religious humility.[1]

The Element of "Energy" or Urgency

There is, finally, a third element comprised in those of *tremendum* and *majestas*, awefulness and majesty, and this I venture to call the "urgency" or "energy" of the numinous object. It is particularly vividly perceptible in the ὀργή or "wrath"; and it everywhere clothes itself in symbolical expressions—vitality, passion, emotional temper, will, force, movement,[2] excitement, activity, impetus. These features are typical and recur again and again from the daemonic level up to the idea of the "living" God. We have here the factor that has everywhere more than any other prompted the fiercest opposition to the "philosophic" God of mere rational speculation, who can be put into a definition. And for their part the philosophers have condemned these expressions of the energy of the numen, whenever they are brought on to the scene, as sheer anthropomorphism. In so far as their opponents have for the most part themselves failed to recognize that the terms they have borrowed from the sphere of human cognitive and affective life have merely value as analogies, the philosophers are right to condemn them. But they are wrong, in so far as, this error notwithstanding, these terms stood for a genuine aspect of the divine nature—its nonrational aspect—a due consciousness of which served to protect religion itself from being "rationalized" away.

For wherever men have been contending for the "living" God or for voluntarism, there, we may be sure, have been nonrationalists fighting rationalists and rationalism. It was so with Luther in his controversy with Erasmus; and Luther's *omnipotentia Dei* in his *De Servo Arbitrio* is nothing but the union of "majesty"—in the sense of absolute supremacy—with this "energy," in the sense of a force that knows not stint nor stay, which is urgent, active, compelling, and alive. In mysticism, too, this element of "energy" is a very living and vigorous factor, at any rate in the "voluntaristic" mysticism, the mysticism of love, where it is very forcibly seen in that "consuming fire" of love whose burning strength the mystic can hardly bear, but begs that the heat that has scorched him may be mitigated, lest he be himself destroyed by it. And in this urgency and pressure the mystic's "love" claims a perceptible kinship with the ὀργή itself, the scorching and consuming wrath of God; it is the same "energy," only differently directed. "Love," says one of the mystics, "is nothing else than quenched wrath."

The element of "energy" reappears in Fichte's speculations on the Absolute as the gigantic, never-resting, active world-stress, and in Schopenhauer's daemonic "Will." At the same time both these writers are guilty of the same error

---

[1] Cf. R. R. Marett, "The Birth of Humility," in *The Threshold of Religion*, 2d ed., 1914. [Tr.]
[2] The "mobilitas Dei" of Lactantius.

that is already found in myth; they transfer "natural" attributes, which ought only to be used as "ideograms" for what is itself properly beyond utterance, to the nonrational as real qualifications of it, and they mistake symbolic expressions of feelings for adequate concepts upon which a "scientific" structure of knowledge may be based.

In Goethe . . . the same element of energy is emphasized in a quite unique way in his strange descriptions of the experience he calls "daemonic."

THE ANALYSIS OF "MYSTERIUM"

Ein begriffener Gott ist kein Gott.
"A God comprehended is no God."

Tersteegen

We gave to the object to which the numinous consciousness is directed the name *mysterium tremendum*, and we then set ourselves first to determine the meaning of the adjective *tremendum*—which we found to be itself only justified by analogy—because it is more easily analyzed than the substantive idea *mysterium*. We have now to turn to this, and try, as best we may, by hint and suggestion, to get to a clearer apprehension of what it implies.

The "Wholly Other"

It might be thought that the adjective itself gives an explanation of the substantive; but this is not so. It is not merely analytical; it is a synthetic attribute to it; i.e., *tremendum* adds something not necessarily inherent in *mysterium*. It is true that the reactions in consciousness that correspond to the one readily and spontaneously overflow into those that correspond to the other; in fact, anyone sensitive to the use of words would commonly feel that the idea of "mystery" (*mysterium*) is so closely bound up with its synthetic qualifying attribute "aweful" (*tremendum*) that one can hardly say the former without catching an echo of the latter, "mystery" almost of itself becoming "aweful mystery" to us. But the passage from the one idea to the other need not by any means be always so easy. The elements of meaning implied in "awefulness" and "mysteriousness" are in themselves definitely different. The latter may so far preponderate in the religious consciousness, may stand out so vividly, that in comparison with it the former almost sinks out of sight; a case which again could be clearly exemplified from some forms of mysticism. Occasionally, on the other hand, the reverse happens, and the *tremendum* may in turn occupy the mind without the *mysterium*.

This latter, then, needs special consideration on its own account. We need an expression for the mental reaction peculiar to it; and here, too, only one word seems appropriate, though, as it is strictly applicable only to a "natural" state of mind, it has here meaning only by analogy: it is the word "stupor." *Stupor* is plainly a different thing from *tremor*; it signifies blank wonder, an astonishment that strikes us dumb, amazement absolute.[3] Taken, indeed, in its purely natural sense, *mysterium* would first mean merely a secret or a mystery in the sense of that which is alien to us, uncomprehended and unexplained; and so far *mysterium* is merely an ideogram, an analogical notion taken from the natural sphere, illustrating, but incapable of exhaustively rendering, our real meaning. Taken in the religious sense, that which is "mysterious" is—to give it perhaps the most striking expression—the "wholly other" (θάτερον, *anyad*, *alienum*), that which is quite beyond the sphere of the usual, the intelligible, and the familiar, which therefore falls quite outside the limits of the "canny," and is contrasted with it, filling the mind with blank wonder and astonishment. . . .

In accordance with laws of which we shall have to speak again later, this feeling or consciousness of the "wholly other" will attach itself to, or sometimes be indirectly aroused by means of, objects which are already puzzling upon the "natural" plane, or are of a surprising or astounding character; such as extraordinary phenomena or astonishing occurrences or things in inanimate nature, in the animal world, or among men. But here once more we are dealing with a case of association between things specifically different—the "numinous" and the "natural" moments of consciousness—and not merely with the gradual enhancement of one of them—the "natural"—till it becomes the other. As in the case of "natural fear" and "daemonic dread" already considered, so here the transition from natural to daemonic amazement is not a mere matter of degree. But it is only with the latter that the complementary expression *mysterium* perfectly harmonizes, as will be felt perhaps more clearly in the case of the adjectival form "mysterious." No one says, strictly and in earnest, of a piece of clockwork that is beyond his grasp, or of a science that he cannot understand: "That is 'mysterious' to me."

It might be objected that the mysterious is something which is and remains absolutely and invariably beyond our understanding, whereas that which merely eludes our understanding for a time but is perfectly intelligible in principle should be called, not a "mystery," but merely a "problem." But this is by no means an adequate account of the matter. The truly "mysterious" object is beyond our apprehension and comprehension, not only because our knowledge has certain irremovable limits, but because in it we come upon something inherently "wholly other," whose kind and character are incommensurable with

---

[3] Compare also *obstupefacere*. Still more exact equivalents are the Greek θάμβος and θαμ–βεῖν. The sound θ α μ β (*thamb*) excellently depicts this state of mind of blank, staring wonder. And the difference between the moments of *stupor* and *tremor* is very finely suggested by the passage, Mark x.32. . . . On the other hand, what was said above of the facility and rapidity with which the two moments merge and blend is also markedly true of θάμβος, which then becomes a classical term for the (ennobled) awe of the numinous in general. So Mark xvi.5 is rightly translated by Luther "und sie entsetzten sich," and by the English Authorized Version "and they were affrighted."

our own, and before which we therefore recoil in a wonder that strikes us chill and numb.[4]

This may be made still clearer by a consideration of that degraded offshoot and travesty of the genuine "numinous" dread or awe, the fear of ghosts. Let us try to analyze this experience. We have already specified the peculiar feeling-element of "dread" aroused by the ghost as that of "grue," grisly horror.[5] Now this "grue" obviously contributes something to the attraction which ghost-stories exercise, in so far, namely, as the relaxation of tension ensuing upon our release from it relieves the mind in a pleasant and agreeable way. So far, however, it is not really the ghost itself that gives us pleasure, but the fact that we are rid of it. But obviously this is quite insufficient to explain the ensnaring attraction of the ghost-story. The ghost's real attraction rather consists in this, that of itself and in an uncommon degree it entices the imagination, awakening strong interest and curiosity; it is the weird thing itself that allures the fancy. But it does this, not because it is "something long and white" (as someone once defined a ghost), nor yet through any of the positive and conceptual attributes which fancies about ghosts have invented, but because it is a thing that "doesn't really exist at all," the "wholly other," something which has no place in our scheme of reality but belongs to an absolutely different one, and which at the same time arouses an irrepressible interest in the mind.

But that which is perceptibly true in the fear of ghosts, which is, after all, only a caricature of the genuine thing, is in a far stronger sense true of the "daemonic" experience itself, of which the fear of ghosts is a mere off-shoot. And while, following this main line of development, this element in the numinous consciousness, the feeling of the "wholly other," is heightened and clarified, its higher modes of manifestation come into being, which set the numinous object in contrast not only to everything wonted and familiar (i.e., in the end, to nature in general), thereby turning it into the "supernatural," but finally to the world itself, and thereby exalt it to the "supramundane," that which is above the whole world order. . . .

Let us look back once more from the point we have reached over the course our inquiry has so far taken. As the subtitle of this book suggests, we were to investigate the nonrational element in the idea of the divine. The words "nonrational" and "irrational" are today used almost at random. The nonrational is sought over the most widely different regions, and writers generally

---

[4] In *Confessions*, ii.9.1, Augustine very strikingly suggests this stiffening, benumbing element of the "wholly other" and its contrast to the rational aspect of the numen; the *dissimile* and the *simile*:

"Quid est illud, quod interlucet mihi et percutit cor meum sine laesione? Et inhorresco et inardesco. *Inhorresco, in quantum dissimilis ei sum. Inardesco, in quantum similis ei sum.*"

("What is that which gleams through me and smites my heart without wounding it? I am both a-shudder and a-glow. A-shudder, in so far as I am unlike it, a-glow in so far as I am like it.")

[5] *gruseln, gräsen.*

shirk the trouble of putting down precisely what they intend by the term, giving it often the most multifarious meanings or applying it with such vague generality that it admits of the most diverse interpretations. Pure fact in contrast to law, the empirical in contrast to reason, the contingent in contrast to the necessary, the psychological in contrast to transcendental fact, that which is known *a posteriori* in contrast to that which is determinable *a priori*; power, will, and arbitrary choice in contrast to reason, knowledge, and determination by value; impulse, instinct, and the obscure forces of the subconscious in contrast to insight, reflection, and intelligible plan; mystical depths and stirrings in the soul, surmise, presentiment, intuition, prophecy, and finally the "occult" powers also; or, in general, the uneasy stress and universal fermentation of the time, with its groping after the thing never yet heard or seen in poetry or the plastic arts—all these and more may claim the names "nonrational," "irrational," and according to circumstances are extolled or condemned as modern "irrationalism." Whoever makes use of the word "nonrational" today ought to say what he actually means by it. This we did in our introductory chapter. We began with the "rational" in the idea of God and the divine, meaning by the term that in it which is clearly to be grasped by our power of conceiving, and enters the domain of familiar and definable conceptions. We went on to maintain that beneath this sphere of clarity and lucidity lies a hidden depth, inaccessible to our conceptual thought, which we in so far call the "nonrational."

The meaning of the two contrasted terms may be made plainer by an illustration. A deep joy may fill our minds without any clear realization upon our part of its source and object to which it refers, though some such objective reference there must always be. But as attention is directed to it the obscure object becomes clearly identified in precise conceptual terms. Such an object cannot, then, be called, in our sense of the word, "nonrational." But it is quite otherwise with religious "bliss" and its essentially numinous aspect, the *fascinans*. Not the most concentrated attention can elucidate the object to which this state of mind refers, bringing it out of the impenetrable obscurity of feeling into the domain of the conceptual understanding. It remains purely a felt experience, only to be indicated symbolically by "ideograms." That is what we mean by saying it is nonrational.

And the same is true of all the moments of the numinous experience. The consciousness of a "wholly other" evades precise formulation in words, and we have to employ symbolic phrases which seem sometimes sheer paradox, that is, *irrational*, not merely nonrational, in import. So with religious awe and reverence. In ordinary fear and in moral reverence I can indicate in conceptual terms what it is that I fear and revere; injury, e.g., or ruin in the one case, heroism or strength of character in the other. But the object of *religious* awe or reverence—the *tremendum* and *augustum*, cannot be fully determined conceptually: it is nonrational, as is the beauty of a musical composition, which no less eludes complete conceptual analysis.

Discussion Questions

1. Do you agree with Schleiermacher's claim that religion arises out of the experience of a feeling of utter dependence, awe, and finitude? Why or why not?

2. Do you think it makes sense to speak of the experience of the numinous as nonrational? Give reasons for your answer.

3. Is the term *numinous* a good substitute for what Rudolf Otto wants to describe as the "holy"? Can you think of a better term?

4. Have you ever had an experience of the numinous? If so, can you describe it?

5. What aspects of the numinous does Otto try to capture in the terms *mysterium tremendum*, *majestas*, and *urgency*?

6. What is the relationship between mystery and the Wholly Other? That is, can the Wholly Other be experienced and present itself in a nonmysterious way? And how would you relate mystery and the nonrational element in religion?

The Eternal Thou

Thus far, we have examined two types of religious experience. Mystical experience is intensely private and, while perhaps leading to faith, concentrates not on the content of that faith, but rather, on a relationship with the transcendent. Rudolf Otto gives more attention to the content of such faith when he focuses on the experience of the numinous, the divine experienced as wholly other, majestic, and powerful. Although Otto undoubtedly pinpoints an important phenomenon in religion, the numinous may not be a part of the experience of most persons reading this book. To be sure, there are many experiences that have a numinous quality to them, but to build a satisfying analysis of religion based on the analysis of *mysterium tremendum*, *majestas*, and *fascinans* may seem remote to those for whom religion is a much more inward affair of the heart.

It is to such persons that another German philosopher, Martin Buber, may appeal. Buber, whose own religious tradition was that of Judaism, emphasizes a side of religious experience that is faithful to both the Jewish and Christian religions, namely, that without meaningful relations to other persons, no one can have a meaningful relation to God. Because he underscores the interpersonal aspect of religion, Buber has frequently been classified with the existentialist theologians, who, among other things, are known for their emphasis on personal encounter. For existentialists, the point of departure for philosophy is the question of what it means to be an existing, human being, and central to this question is our relationship to other people. Although one does not find in Buber the usual vocabulary of existential philosophy, the central emphases of his work are certainly compatible with existentialism. It is with the central question of the meaning of humanness that Buber begins.

Before turning to the selection from Buber, a bit of background on the terms he uses is required. The citation is from his book originally published in German under the title *Ich und Du*, which in its English translation can be rendered either *I and Thou* or *I and You*. The fact that either English translation is possible is due to the lack in English of a distinction between formal and informal pronouns. German, as well as French, has two forms for the personal pronoun that are collapsed into the single English pronoun *you*. In German, the formal pronoun is *Sie*; in French, *vous*. One always uses the formal pronoun when addressing casual acquaintances or in formal settings. The informal pronouns, *du* in German and *tu* in French, are reserved for intimate friends, members of one's family, small children, and animals.

At one time, speakers of English were able to make a similar distinction. The pronoun *you* was used in situations requiring formal language; the familiar pronoun *thou* was used only in situations of the most intimate familiarity. Through the passage of time this distinction has been lost, and if anything, the word *thou* has taken on a formal significance by its use almost exclusively in liturgical language. This was probably the result of the continued widespread use of the King James Version of the Bible, in which *thee, thine,* and *thou,* as well as the verb forms that went with them (*art, hast,* and *wilt*) were used throughout. In 1611, the year in which the King James Version appeared, the distinction between formal and familiar pronouns was still recognized. It is significant to note that the translators of that day chose the familiar pronouns for the language of Scripture. As mentioned, *thee, thou,* etc., have since taken on a formal meaning. In fact, when the translators of the 1946 Revised Standard Version of the Bible omitted the archaic pronouns, many persons actually considered it an act of irreverence. The original Greek of the New Testament knows of no such distinctions, and the current use of the pronouns *you, yours,* etc., is in keeping with the meanings of *thee* and *thou* when they were current in the seventeenth century.

Today, however, English does not allow a distinction between the formal and familiar second-person pronouns the way German does, but the choice of *I and Thou* as a translation for the German *Ich und Du* does serve as a reminder that Buber's use of the familiar pronoun is intended to signify a relationship based on the most intimate kind of personal relationship.

Buber begins by suggesting that there are two primary words: "I-Thou" and "I-It." By calling these the two *primary* or *basic* words, Buber emphasizes that there are two ways of becoming a self or an "I," for there are two primary ways of relating. In short, I-Thou and I-It denote two modes of human existence. Although the vocabulary Buber uses is unique, the ideas are not, for it was an insight of the ancient Greek philosophers that human beings are indisputably social creatures. Aristotle observed that a person who had no need of human society was either a beast or a god, not a human being. The Greek language also gives us the term *idiot* from the word *idios,* meaning *one's own* or *personal.* A person who avoids human society and shuns personal relationships by insisting on being alone is truly "idiotic" in the Greek way of thinking. This is echoed by Buber, who sees two modes of human existence, characterized by the pair of terms I-Thou and I-It. A person becomes human only in relationships, and these paired terms describe two possible ways of relating.

The I-Thou relationship is one of intimacy, mutuality, sharing, and trust. The I-It relationship is one of having, using, exploiting. To put it in different terms, the I-It relationship is one-way, from subject to object, from I to thing.

The I-Thou relationship is a two-way form of relating in which the I gives to and receives from the Thou. Examples of these two types of relationships are easy to find. Anyone who has ever dealt with a large bureaucracy, a huge organization, or perhaps even registered for college courses knows what it is like to be treated as a thing. When one is treated as an "it," there is no mutuality; the one so treating you has only an interest in getting something from you and is totally unconcerned about relating to you as a person.

When we relate to another person as a Thou, we do not treat that person as a thing or an object. This is what Buber means when he says, "When I face a human being as my Thou and say the primary word I-Thou to him, then he is not a thing among things and does not consist of things." There is nothing wrong with the I-It relationship per se as long as it is limited to things, to objects. But to treat a person as a thing, as an It, is not only to debase the other person, but also to sacrifice one's own humanity. Buber's point is that we become human only through genuinely human relationships, I-Thou relationships, and when we treat a Thou as an It, we lose something of our own humanness. This can be applied to many situations: In the master-slave relationship, the master treats the slave as an It, and the master is dehumanized just as surely as the slave. We should not possess another person or exploit another person. Our vocabulary, if we follow Buber's lead, would have to be changed. We could speak of owning ("having") a car, having a house, or having a stereo, for all these are in the sphere of the I-It, and we do relate ourselves to objects in the sphere of "having" in the sense of possessing. It would, however, debase the relationship between husband and wife or parent and child to say that we *have* a wife, or *have* children. It would be better to say that we are married (a relationship) and are parents (a relationship).

This might seem highly abstract until we realize that Buber has pointed out an extremely important issue. The I-Thou relationship is one involving our whole being that calls for a response of the whole being of the other. If we establish an I-Thou relationship with another person, we will not be able to hate that person, for hate can arise only in an I-It relationship. We see this vividly in wartime when the powerful forces of public propaganda are brought to bear against the "enemy," whom we are taught to hate. We devise a whole arsenal of epithets to depersonalize the "enemy": Wartime propaganda speaks of the Reds, gooks, Nips, Huns, Krauts, and so forth. We can hate an abstract "enemy" but not a person to whom we are related in an I-Thou way.

It is easy to misread Buber and think that the I-Thou relationship can only be between persons. Buber suggests, however, that it is possible to sustain an I-Thou relationship with animals, trees, flowers, and even inanimate objects. A logger surveying a stand of timber and calculating the number of board feet that will result when the trees are harvested has only an I-It relationship with the forest. The logger is concerned only with exploiting the resources of the forest and marketing the lumber successfully to make the largest possible profit. This is not the only way to relate to a tree or to a forest. Basking in the shade of a tree, contemplating it, writing a poem about it, marveling at its wonder and complexity—all these signal an I-Thou relationship. And who has not experienced an I-Thou relationship with a family pet whose whole life is focused on the relationship with the family?

Again, this might sound like the abstract meditations of a philosopher until one realizes that it meshes perfectly with the current ecological emphasis on the symbiotic relationship we must establish with nature. We have come to, or are at least rapidly approaching, the end of the era when we can look at nature as an unlimited source of material to be exploited at our whim. The biosphere is a fragile thing, and only if we can place ourselves in a relationship in which we see our interdependence—us on nature, nature on us—can we hope to avoid ecological disaster.

When we think of God, a word that Buber says is "the most heavily laden of all the words used by men," it is possible to have either an I-It or an I-Thou relationship with God. For many persons God is an abstraction to be argued about, proved by rational argument, or discussed with the same intensity one devotes to an examination of the current state of the weather. The philosopher who attempts to prove the existence of God, according to Buber, is relating to God in an I-It way. To treat God as a problem to be solved by rationalistic exercises is to relate to God as an object, a thing, an It. The only satisfying relationship with God is one of mutuality and inward intensity in an I-Thou relationship. We relate to God not only as a Thou, but also as the Eternal Thou. But where, we might ask, is such a relationship to be discovered?

Buber's answer is that God, the Eternal Thou, is ever present. God is present in every genuine I-Thou relationship, and each genuine I-Thou relationship whets the appetite for a relationship with God as the Eternal Thou. Buber would demur at Otto's insistence that God is the wholly Other. God is that, to be sure, but Buber insists that God is also the wholly Present. The proper relationship to God is not one of argumentation and debate over God's existence and attributes, but one based on prayer and sacrifice. It is for this reason that the most widely used analogy in terms of which we speak of God is as a person. This way of referring to God is an attempt to capture the sense of God as the Eternal Thou while recognizing that the analogy of God as a person cannot exhaust the nature and essence of God.

As was the case with Rudolf Otto, reading Martin Buber is less like analyzing a traditional philosophical argument than it is like reading a poem. The comparison is proper, for Buber is something of a philosophical poet. He is not so much attempting to prove something to you as he is calling to your attention aspects of human experience that might otherwise be overlooked. Like all great poets, he sometimes creates his own vocabulary, but in this creation lies the richness of his thought.

I and Thou

MARTIN BUBER

TO MAN THE WORLD IS TWOFOLD, in accordance with his twofold attitude.

The attitude of man is twofold, in accordance with the twofold nature of the primary words which he speaks.

The primary words are not isolated words, but combined words.

The one primary word is the combination *I-Thou*.

The other primary word is the combination *I-It*; wherein, without a change in the primary word, one of the words *He* and *She* can replace *It*.

Hence the *I* of man is also twofold.

For the *I* of the primary word *I-Thou* is a different *I* from that of the primary word *I-It*.

❦

PRIMARY WORDS DO NOT SIGNIFY THINGS, but they intimate relations.

Primary words do not describe something that might exist independently of them, but being spoken they bring about existence.

Primary words are spoken from the being.

If *Thou* is said, the *I* of the combination *I-Thou* is said along with it.

If *It* is said, the *I* of the combination *I-It* is said along with it.

The primary word *I-Thou* can only be spoken with the whole being.

The primary word *I-It* can never be spoken with the whole being.

❦

THERE IS NO *I* TAKEN IN ITSELF, but only the *I* of the primary word *I-Thou* and the *I* of the primary word *I-It*.

When a man says *I* he refers to one or other of these. The *I* to which he refers is present when he says *I*. Further, when he says *Thou* or *It*, the *I* of one of the two primary words is present.

Source: Reprinted with the permission of Scribner, a division of Simon & Schuster, from *I and Thou* by Martin Buber, trans. Ronald Gregor Smith. Copyright © 1958 by Charles Scribner's Sons.

The existence of *I* and the speaking of *I* are one and the same thing.

When a primary word is spoken the speaker enters the word and takes his stand in it.

❦

THE LIFE OF HUMAN BEINGS is not passed in the sphere of transitive verbs alone. It does not exist in virtue of activities alone which have some *thing* for their object.

I perceive something. I am sensible of something. I imagine something. I will something. I feel something. I think something. The life of human beings does not consist of all this and the like alone.

This and the like together establish the realm of *It*.

But the realm of *Thou* has a different basis.

When *Thou* is spoken, the speaker has no thing for his object. For where there is a thing there is another thing. Every *It* is bounded by others; *It* exists only through being bounded by others. But when *Thou* is spoken, there is no thing. *Thou* has no bounds.

When *Thou* is spoken, the speaker has no *thing*; he has indeed nothing. But he takes his stand in relation.

❦

THE *THOU* MEETS ME THROUGH GRACE—it is not found by seeking. But my speaking of the primary word to it is an act of my being, is indeed *the* act of my being.

The *Thou* meets me. But I step into direct relation with it. Hence the relation means being chosen and choosing, suffering and action in one; just as any action of the whole being, which means the suspension of all partial actions and consequently of all sensations of actions grounded only in their particular limitation, is bound to resemble suffering.

The primary word *I-Thou* can be spoken only with the whole being. Concentration and fusion into the whole being can never take place through my agency, nor can it ever take place without me. I become through my relation to the *Thou*; as I become *I*, I say *Thou*.

All real living is meeting.

❦

THE EXTENDED LINES OF RELATIONS meet in the eternal *Thou*.

Every particular *Thou* is a glimpse through to the eternal *Thou*; by means of every particular *Thou* the primary word addresses the eternal *Thou*. Through this mediation of the *Thou* of all beings fulfillment, and non-fulfillment, of relations comes to them: the inborn *Thou* is realized in each relation and consummated in none. It is consummated only in the direct relation with the *Thou* that by its nature cannot become *It*.

❧

MEN HAVE ADDRESSED THEIR ETERNAL *THOU* with many names. In singing of Him who was thus named they always had the *Thou* in mind: the first myths were hymns of praise. Then the names took refuge in the language of *It*; men were more and more strongly moved to think of and to address their eternal *Thou* as an *It*. But all God's names are hallowed, for in them He is not merely spoken about, but also spoken to.

Many men wish to reject the word God as a legitimate usage, because it is so misused. It is indeed the most heavily laden of all the words used by men. For that very reason it is the most imperishable and most indispensable. What does all mistaken talk about God's being and works (though there has been, and can be, no other talk about these) matter in comparison with the one truth that all men who have addressed God had God Himself in mind? For he who speaks the word God and really has *Thou* in mind (whatever the illusion by which he is held), addresses the true *Thou* of his life, which cannot be limited by another *Thou*, and to which he stands in a relation that gathers up and includes all others.

But when he, too, who abhors the name, and believes himself to be godless, gives his whole being to addressing the *Thou* of his life, as a *Thou* that cannot be limited by another, he addresses God.

❧

EVERY REAL RELATION with a being or life in the world is exclusive. Its *Thou* is freed, steps forth, is single, and confronts you. It fills the heavens. This does not mean that nothing else exists; but all else lives in *its* light. As long as the presence of the relation continues, this its cosmic range is inviolable. But as soon as a *Thou* becomes *It*, the cosmic range of the relation appears as an offense to the world, its exclusiveness as an exclusion of the universe.

In the relation with God unconditional exclusiveness and unconditional inclusiveness are one. He who enters on the absolute relation is concerned with nothing isolated any more, neither things nor beings, neither earth nor heaven; but everything is gathered up in the relation. For to step into pure relation is not to disregard everything but to see everything in the *Thou*, not to renounce the world but to establish it on its true basis. To look away from the world, or to stare at it, does not help a man to reach God; but he who sees the world in Him stands in His presence. "Here world, there God" is the language of *It*; "God in the world" is another language of *It*; but to eliminate or leave behind nothing at all, to include the whole world in the *Thou*, to give the world its due and its truth, to include nothing beside God but everything in him—this is full and complete relation.

Men do not find God if they stay in the world. They do not find Him if they leave the world. He who goes out with his whole being to meet his *Thou* and carries to it all being that is in the world, finds Him who cannot be sought.

Of course God is the "wholly Other"; but He is also the wholly Same, the wholly Present. Of course He is the *Mysterium Tremendum* that appears and overthrows; but He is also the mystery of the self-evident, nearer to me than my *I*.

If you explore the life of things and of conditioned being you come to the unfathomable, if you deny the life of things and of conditioned being you stand before nothingness, if you hallow this life you meet the living God.

Discussion Questions

1. Whereas Rudolf Otto suggests that we view God as wholly Other, Martin Buber urges that we understand God as both wholly Other and wholly Same. Do you think this is a contradiction? Give reasons for your answer.

2. Does the phrase I-Thou capture the sense of intimacy that Buber intended?

3. What would be the practical difference in establishing an I-Thou relationship with God rather than an I-It relationship with God?

4. Do you agree with the implication of Buber's view that we encounter God in every meaningful I-Thou relationship with other people? If so, what does this do to attempt to prove that God exists by means of rational arguments and proofs?

5. "All real living is meeting," Buber says. In what sort of encounter does the religious dimension of life arise?

Religious Pluralism

Today, with the increases in communication, travel, immigration patterns, and the generally enhanced knowledge of the world and its peoples, it is scarcely possible to adhere to one's own religion without encountering those with differing religions. We are speaking here not of different denominations or groups *within* a religion but of totally different religious traditions. This would not pose any particularly philosophical problems were it not for the fact that some religions claim that theirs is the only way to salvation and anyone outside of that religious tradition is damned. Close to this claim of exclusivity is the logical difficulty of dealing with religious truth claims. If religion A has the truth, and religion B differs from it, then how is it possible to avoid saying that religion B is false? And if religion C claims that it has the only way to salvation, how can it then accept the salvation claims of religions A and B?

In the selection that follows, John Hick deals with the conceptual difficulties that must be overcome if one is to have what he refers to as a pluralistic view of religions. Without repeating his discussion of the issues here, it is important to understand that Hick deals with the issues on several levels. Initially he looks at what might be called the moral imperatives of various religions or what he, using the terminology of the Christian faith, refers to as the "fruits of the Spirit." He notes that there is a consistency among the world's great religions in the kind of behavior they espouse and that judged on this basis no single tradition can claim moral superiority.[1] It is, of course, possible to point out major failings within each civilization and the religion it espouses. But no religious tradition seems to be any worse in this regard; people are often not as good as their religion demands or may even attempt to justify their monstrous acts by appealing to their religion for approval. In this regard, Hick says, "it is not possible to establish the unique moral superiority of any one of the great world faiths" and that "both the virtues and the vices are, so far as we can tell, more or less equally spread among the population, of whatever major faith. . . ."

[1] In an appendix to his book The Abolition of Man, C.S. Lewis offers a summary of the teachings of the world's religions that shows their consistency in moral demands. He refers to this, using the traditional terms, as Natural Law or the Tao, or Way. See C.S. Lewis, *The Abolition of Man* (New York: Macmillan, 1947), pp. 95–121.

The conclusion of Hick's selection focuses on the conceptual difficulty of accepting different religious traditions as equally true, for this at first appears to be a manifest contradiction. Appealing to three analogies, Hick first argues that people can perceive reality differently depending on their own perceptual experience, and he uses as an example the well-known duck-rabbit picture from psychologist Jastrow, an example also referred to by Ludwig Wittgenstein in *Philosophical Investigations.* Secondly, Hick points out that the epistemological difficulty inherent in the wave/particle complementarity in physics shows how we have come to accept dual accounts of a physical phenomenon as both true, depending on the observational context. This, he suggests, might provide an analogous way of thinking about different experiences of the Sacred. His final analogy is from cartography that allows a three-dimensional reality—the earth—to be portrayed variously in different projections, all of which have their purposes and none of which can be considered privileged. He concludes that "it could be that the conceptual maps drawn by the great traditions. . . are all more or less equally reliable within their different projections, and more or less equally useful for guiding us on our journey through life."

Though he does not mention this issue in the selection that follows, there are important issues in addition to the philosophical difficulties posed by claims of religious exclusivity. A religion's claim to have the only viable hold on the truth can lead to absolutism and intolerance. It is only a short step from absolutism to the view that anyone differing in their religious beliefs should not be allowed to hold those beliefs and should either be forced to change them or prevented from acting on them. Denial of religious freedom, repression, persecutions, pogroms, and wars of extermination too often follow absolutist claims about religious truth. This need not be the case, and it is not necessary for a religion to abandon its sense of uniqueness; the approach Hick suggests does not require that one give up traditional beliefs but only understand them in a new light. The issues he raises are important ones and are likely to become more so as the dynamics of contemporary life force the adherents of major religious traditions into even more direct contact with each other.

The Pluralistic Hypothesis

JOHN HICK

The new conditions affecting our understanding of the world religions have been gradually forming during the last three centuries. During what is called the European Enlightenment of the seventeenth and eighteenth centuries there developed a Western realization that Christendom is part of a much larger human world, with great civilizations having existed outside it, above all in China and India as well as the Islamic world; and along with this the realization that Christianity is one world religion amongst others. It was then that the generic idea of religion became established in educated circles, with Christianity seen as one particular form. But now, and particularly since the end of the Second World War, this awareness has become prominent in public consciousness. At least three developments have contributed to this. One has been an explosion of information in the West about the religions of the world. First rate scholarship, published in reasonably cheap paperbacks, is now readily available concerning—taking them in order of antiquity—Hinduism, Judaism, Buddhism, Jainism, Taoism, Confucianism, Islam, Sikhism, Baha'i, as well as the primal or indigenous religions of Africa, North and South America, Australasia, and elsewhere. Secondly, travel opportunities have multiplied and great numbers of Westerners have spent time in India, Turkey, Egypt, Thailand, Sri Lanka and other non-Christian countries, and have seen something of the peaceful influence of Buddhism among the Thai people, something of the ecstatic devotion and the powerful sense of the divine among Hindus, something of the marvels of Islamic civilization as expressed architecturally in, for example, the Taj Mahal at Agra or the great mosques of Istanbul; and many Westerners have also made their own mind-expanding and consciousness-altering inner journeys in the practice of Eastern methods of meditation. And third, and perhaps most important of all, there has been massive immigration from East to West, bringing Muslims, Sikhs, Hindus, Buddhists to settle in Europe and North America. There are, for example, between four and five million Muslims in North America, and about five million in Europe; and there are also in the West smaller but still quite large numbers of Hindus, Sikhs, and Buddhists, as well of course as the long-established Jewish communities, tragically reduced by a third in the Nazi Holocaust of the 1940s. As a result of this post-war

Source: From John Hick, *A Christian Theology of Religions*. © 1995 John Hick. Used by permission of Westminster John Knox Press.

immigration we are now familiar in many major cities of the Western world—including my own city of Birmingham, England—not only with churches and synagogues but also with mosques, gurudwaras, meditation centres, and temples of many kinds; and may have worshippers in these places as neighbours.

A further result, making an even deeper and more significant impression on many people is the fact that by coming to know individuals and families of these various faiths it has become a fairly common discovery that our Muslim or Jewish or Hindu or Sikh or Buddhist fellow citizens are in general no less kindly, honest, thoughtful for others, no less truthful, honourable, loving and compassionate, than are in general our Christian fellow citizens. People of other faiths are not on average noticeably better human beings than Christians, but nor on the other hand are they on average noticeably worse human beings. We find that both the virtues and the vices are, so far as we can tell, more or less equally spread among the population, of whatever major faith—and here I include Humanism and Marxism as major (though secular rather than religious) faiths. At any rate I have to record the fact that my own inevitably limited experience of knowing people who are Jews, Muslims, Hindus and Buddhists, including a few remarkable individuals of these religions as well as more ordinary individuals and families, both in the United States and Europe and also in India, Africa, Sri Lanka, and Japan, has led me to think that the spiritual and moral fruits of these faiths, although different, are more or less on a par with the fruits of Christianity; and reading some of the literature of the different traditions, both some of their scriptures and philosophies and also some of their novels and poetry portraying ordinary life, has reinforced this impression.

And again, when we look at the great civilizations of the earth, informed as they have been by different religious faiths, we see both great goods and great evils in each. But it doesn't seem possible to make a comparative assessment of these goods and evils in any acceptable way so as to establish the moral superiority of Christian civilization. For the goods and evils are so often incommensurate. How do you weigh the evils of the Indian caste system over the centuries against the evils of the European class system over the same centuries; or the poverty of so many Buddhist, Hindu and Muslim countries against the greedy use of the earth's non-renewable resources and the selfish destruction of the environment by so many Christian countries; or the social problems of Calcutta or Bangkok or Cairo against the poverty, drugs, violence, crime and despair in many of our own inner cities; or the cruelties of some Eastern regimes against the virulent anti-Semitism of Christian Europe? It is easy, of course, to pick out some manifest evil within another tradition and compare it with some manifest good within one's own. But this is not a truthful way of proceeding. The fact is that for every evil that you can quite rightly point to in another strand of history, it is possible with equal justification to point to a different but more or less equally reprehensible feature of one's own. We have to see the world religions as vast complex religio-cultural totalities, each a bewildering mixture of varied goods and evils. And when we do so we find that we have no way of objectively calibrating their respective values, adding so many points for this feature and deducting so many for that. We can, I suggest, only come to the negative conclusion that it is not possible to establish the unique moral superiority of any one of the great world faiths. It may be that in the sight of God one of them has in fact been, as an historical reality, superior to the others, but I don't think that from our human point of view we can claim to know this. . . .

SALVATION

Let's now look at the situation again from a slightly different angle. Let's concentrate on the idea of salvation, an idea that is absolutely central to Christian thought, both traditional and revisionary. If we define salvation as being forgiven and accepted by God because of the atoning death of Jesus, then it is a tautology that Christianity alone knows and teaches the saving truth that we must take Jesus as our lord and saviour, plead his atoning death, and enter into the church as the community of the redeemed, in which the fruits of the Spirit abound. But we've seen that this circle of ideas contradicts our observation that the fruits of the Spirit seem to be as much (and as little) evident outside the church as within it. I suggest that we should continue to follow the clue provided by these fruits; for Jesus was clearly more concerned with men's and women's lives than with any body of theological propositions that they might have in their minds. Indeed in his parable of the sheep and the goats the criterion of divine judgment is simply whether we have fed the hungry, welcomed the stranger, clothed the naked, and visited the sick and the imprisoned (Matt. 25.31–46)—in other words, whether our lives have shown the fruits of the Spirit. Suppose, then, we define salvation in a very concrete way, as an actual change in human beings, a change which can be identified when it *can* be identified—by its moral fruits. We then find that we are talking about something that is of central concern to each of the great world faiths. Each in its different way calls us to transcend the ego point of view, which is the source of all selfishness, greed, exploitation, cruelty, and injustice, and to become re-centered in that ultimate mystery for which we, in our Christian language, use the term God. We are, in the words (transposed into inclusive language) of the *Theologia Germanica*, to be to the Eternal Goodness what our own hands are to ourselves.[1] In Muslim terms, we are to submit absolutely to God, doing God's will and finding in this the fulfillment of our humanity. In Jewish terms, we are to live with joy and responsibility in accordance with God's Torah, finding in this, once again, the fulfillment of our humanity. In Hindu terms, to quote Radhadkrishnan, 'The divine consciousness and will must become our consciousness and will. This means that our actual self must cease to be a private self; we must give up our particular will, die to our ego, by surrendering its whole nature, its consciousness and character to the

---

[1] *Theologia Germanica*, ch. 10, trans. Susanna Winkworth, London: Macmillan 1937, p. 32.

Divine'.[2] And in Buddhist terms, to quote a leading contemporary exponent of Buddhism to the West, Masao Abe, 'Buddhist salvation is . . . nothing other than an awakening to reality through the death of the ego',[3] an awakening which expresses itself in compassion for all sentient life.

Without going further, it is I think clear that the great postaxial traditions, including Christianity, are directed towards a transformation of human existence from self-centredness to a re-centring in what in our inadequate human terms we speak of as God, or as Ultimate Reality, or the Transcendent, or the Real. Among these options I propose to use the term 'the Real', not because it is adequate— there is no adequate term—but because it is customary in Christian language to think of God as that which is alone finally real, and the term also corresponds to the Sanscrit *sat* and the Arabic *al-Haqq*, and has parallels in yet other languages. And what is variously called salvation or liberation or enlightenment or awakening consists in this transformation from self-centredness to Reality-centredness. For brevity's sake, I'll use the hybrid term 'salvation/liberation'. I suggest that this is the central concern of all the great world religions. They are not primarily philosophies or theologies but primarily ways of salvation/liberation. And it is clear that salvation, to this sense of an actual change in human beings from natural self-centredness towards a re-centering in the Divine, the Ultimate, the Real, is a long process—though there are often peak moments within it—and that this process is taking place not only within Christianity but also, and so far as we can tell to a more or less equal extent, within the other great traditions.

I can now introduce the familiar three-fold distinction within Christian theologies of religion as exclusivist, inclusivist, and pluralist.[4] There are of course many variations within each of these, but the threefold classification itself, when applied to both truth-claims and salvation-claims, seems to cover the range of options. I sometimes hear people say that they do not fit into any of these three categories. I then ask them what their own theology of religions is, and invariably it turns out either that they don't have one, so that naturally it does not exemplify any of the three types, or else they *do* have one and it is manifestly a variation of one or other of the three! You can of course double the number of options by adding the qualifier 'possibly' to each, as Schubert Ogden has done in the case of pluralism: he argues that as well as pluralism there is the view that pluralism is, from the Christian point of view, a theological possibility, a possibility which one may affirm without having to affirm

2 S. Radhakrishnan, *The Principal Upanishads*, London: Allen & Unwin and New York: Humanities Press 1969, p. 105. Sir Sarvepalli Radhakrishnan was Professor of Eastern Religions and Ethics at Oxford University, and subsequently President of India, and was the author of a number of books on Eastern philosophy and religion.

3 *The Buddha Eye*, ed. Frederick Franck, New York: Crossroad 1982, p. 153.

4 This widely used typology first appeared in print in Alan Race's *Christians and Religious Pluralism* (London: SCM Press and Maryknoll, New York, 1983, 2nd ed. 1994). It has recently been criticized by Ian Markham in 'Creating Options: Shattering the "Exclusivist, Inclusivist, and Pluralist" Paradigm', and defended by Gavin D'Costa in 'Creating Confusion: A Response to Markham' both in *New Blackfriars* (January 1993).

that it is in fact realized.[5] This seems clearly right. But I don't think that it affects the basic threefold distinction, and I shall accordingly continue to employ this widely used typology.

So let us speak first in terms of salvation claims. Here, exclusivism asserts that salvation is confined to Christians, or even more narrowly, in the traditional Catholic dogma, that *extra ecclesiam nulla salus*, outside the church there is no salvation. This exclusivist position was however implicitly repudiated by Vatican II, and again by the present Pope in his first encyclical, *Redemptor Hominis*, 1979, in which he said that 'man—every man without any exception whatever has been redeemed by Christ, and . . . every man—with each man without any exception whatever—Christ is in a way united, even when man is unaware of it' (para. 14). The only salvation-exclusivists left are the few Catholic ultra-conservative followers of the late Archbishop Lefebvre, who was excommunicated in 1988, and a much more numerous, vociferous and influential body of Protestant fundamentalists. Their position is a consistent and coherent one for those who can believe that God condemns the majority of the human race, who have never encountered or who have not accepted the Christian gospel, to eternal damnation. Personally, I would view such a God as the Devil! But, more fundamentally, if we mean by salvation an actual salvific change in women and men, then it is, as I have been reminding us, an observable fact that this is not restricted either to any section of Christianity or to Christianity as a whole. Given this very concrete conception of salvation/liberation, then, Christian exclusivism is not a live option, and I shall not now spend any more time on it.

The position taken by Vatican II, and by the Pope in the encyclical from which I just quoted, and also by the majority of both Catholic and Protestant theologians today other than many fundamentalists, is aptly called inclusivism. This acknowledges that the salvific process is taking place throughout the world, within each of the great world faiths and also outside them, but insists that wherever it occurs it is the work of Christ. Salvation, on this view, depends upon Jesus' atoning death on Calvary, though the benefits of that death are not confined to Christians but are available, in principle, to all human beings. Thus people of the other world faiths can be included within the sphere of Christian salvation. In Karl Rahner's famous phrase, they can be 'anonymous Christians'. Many inclusivists feel, understandably, uncomfortable with that imperialistic-sounding phrase; but their position is nevertheless essentially Rahner's—namely that salvation, whenever and wherever it occurs, is exclusively Christian salvation, so that Jews, Muslims, Hindus, Buddhists, and so on, who are saved are saved, and can only be saved, by Christ whether or not they know the source of their salvation.

This Christian inclusivism takes two forms. One defines salvation in traditional terms, holding that in order to be saved one must personally accept Jesus as one's lord and saviour, but adds that those who do not encounter him in this

[5] Schubert Ogden, *Is There Only One True Religion or Are There Many?*, Dallas: Southern Methodist University Press 1992.

life may do so after death. This is an increasingly favoured option among conservative Christians who nevertheless cannot accept that God has ordained the eternal loss of the majority of humankind through no fault of their own. A recent Protestant example is Richard Swinburne in his *Responsibility and Atonement*,[6] and a recent Catholic example is Father J. A. DiNoia's 'Christian theology of religions in a prospective vein' in his *The Diversity of Religion*[7]—meaning by 'prospective' that non-Christians may receive salvation in or beyond death. My only comment upon this appeal to the life to come is that a theologian who insists upon the unique superiority of Christianity but who cannot accept the exclusion of non-Christians as such from salvation, has no option but to take this step, even though it involves abandoning the traditional teaching that God's grace in Christ must be accepted in this present life and that death forecloses the options.[8] There should therefore be no concealment of the fact that one part of the dogmatic structure is being modified in order to retain the acceptability of another part and that this is being done, under the pressure of our modern sensibility, in order to make room for the salvation of the non-Christian majority of humankind. For those who define salvation in exclusively Christian terms some such doctrinal modification is today unavoidable. But it can also be dangerous to the long-term health of the dogma that is being saved. The new extension is analogous to the epicycles that were added to preserve the old Ptolemaic astronomy for a little longer before it finally collapsed. We should be warned that such theological epicycles tend to appear in the last days of a dying dogma!

The other form of inclusivism is compatible with the wider understanding of salvation as salvation/liberation, the actual transformation of men and women, and ultimately through them of societies, and can gladly acknowledge that this is happening—and happening in varying degrees now, in this life—outside Christianity as well as within it. It insists, however, that the salvific influences of the Torah in the lives of Jews, of Islam in the lives of Muslims, of Hindu spiritual practices in the lives of Hindus, of the Buddhadharma in the lives of Buddhists, and so on, are all ultimately due to the salvific work of Christ, who is secretly at work within all these traditions. This is the idea of the unknown Christ of Hinduism—unknown, that is, to Hindus,—and likewise the unknown Christ of

---

[6] Oxford: Clarendon Press 1992, p. 173.

[7] Washington: Catholic University of America Press 1992, ch. 3.

[8] Thus St. Augustine, affirming that unbaptized infants go to hell, says, 'If, therefore [after a string of biblical quotations], as so many and such divine witnesses agree, neither salvation nor eternal life can be hoped for by any man without baptism and the Lord's body and blood, it is vain to promise these blessings to infants without them', *On Forgiveness of Sins, and Baptism*, Book I, ch. 34. (The Nicene and Post-Nicene Fathers, First Series, Vol. 5, ed. Philip Schaff, Grand Rapids, Michigan: Eerdmans 1956, p. 28.) The Council of Florence (1438–45) declared that everyone outside the church will go to hell 'unless before the end of life they are joined to the church' (*Denzinger*, 714). John Calvin wrote that 'the strange notion of those who think that unbelievers as to the coming of Christ, were after his death freed from their sin, needs no longer refutation; for it is an indubitable doctrine of Scripture, that we obtain not salvation in Christ except by faith; then there is no hope left for those who continue to death unbelieving' (*Commentary on the Catholic Epistles*, trans. John Owen, Edinburgh: Calvin Society 1856, p. 113).

Buddhism, and so on. Here Christ has to mean, not the historical Jesus of Nazareth, but the resurrected Jesus in his divine glory, now thought of as the heavenly Christ. As a very general idea this sounds promising. However, the problem is to spell it out more precisely. It needs to be shown by what kind of invisible causality the saving death of Jesus around 30 CE has operated to make the other great religious traditions effective contexts of salvation/liberation, apparently to much the same extent as Christianity. It will not suffice to speak of the work of the resurrected Christ, since this presumably began with Jesus' resurrection around 30 CE—unless one is prepared to defend the idea of a causality operating backwards through time to account for the spiritually liberating power of the Buddha's teachings some five hundred years earlier, and indeed, to cover the beginnings of Hinduism and Judaism, operating backwards through time for more than a thousand years. This would, surely, be a philosophical quagmire that few would wish to get into.

In order to make sense of the idea of Christ at work within the world religions, including those that precede Christianity, it will be necessary to leave aside the historical figure of Jesus of Nazareth, and his death on the cross, and to speak instead of a non-historical, or supra-historical, Christ-figure or Logos (i.e. the second person of the Trinity) who secretly inspired the Buddha, and the writers of the Upanishads, and Moses and the great Hebrew prophets, and Confucius and Lao-Tze and Zoroaster before the common era, as well as Muhammad, Guru Nanak, Ramakrishna and many others since. But this Christ figure, or Logos, operating before and thus independently of the historical life and death of Jesus of Nazareth, then becomes in effect a name for the world-wide and history-long presence and impact upon human life of the Divine, the Transcendent, the Ultimate, the Real. In other words, in order to make sense of the idea that the great world religions are all inspired and made salvific by the same transcendent influence we have to go beyond the historical figure of Jesus to a universal source of all salvific transformation. Christians may call this the cosmic Christ or the eternal Logos; Hindus and Buddhists may call it the Dharma; Muslims may call it Allah; Taoists may call it the Tao; and so on. But what we then have is no longer (to put it paradoxically) an exclusively Christian inclusivism, but a plurality of mutually inclusive inclusivisms which is close to the kind of pluralism that I want to recommend. I am suggesting in effect that religious inclusivism is a vague conception which, when pressed to become clear, moves towards pluralism. I will try presently to indicate what such a pluralism involves.

TRUTH-CLAIMS

But first let's return to something I pointed out earlier, namely that the three-fold exclusivism, inclusivism, pluralism scheme can be applied both to salvation-claims and also to truth-claims. Thus far we've been looking at it in terms of salvation-claims. But what about truth-claims? For it's undoubtedly the case that the great world faiths have developed very different belief-systems. According to some, the ultimate is personal, according to others non-personal. Among those which speak of a personal God, Christianity teaches that the one and only God is triune and that Jesus of Nazareth was the second person of this Trinity living a human life; whilst Judaism teaches that the one and only God is not triune but strictly unitary, and has selected the Jewish race as God's chosen people and frequently intervened in their history in Palestine, Egypt, and Babylonia; whilst Islam teaches that the one and only God is unitary but is directly self-revealed in the Qur'an, and has intervened in the life of the Muslim community in Mecca and Medina. Again, Vaishnavite Hinduism believes in the personal Vishnu, who has become incarnate in Krishna and in a number of other earthly figures; and Saivite Hinduism believes in the divine lord Shiva, whose cosmic dance is the life of the universe. And so on. Again, among the non-theistic traditions, advaitic Hinduism speaks of the universal consciousness of Brahman, which in the depths of our being we all are; whilst different strands of Buddhism speak of the universal Buddha nature, or of the Dharmakaya, or Nirvana, or Sunyata; and Taoism of the eternal Tao whose nature cannot be spoken in human terms. There are thus many different conceptions of the Ultimate, the Real, related to correspondingly different forms of religious experience and, arising from these, correspondingly different belief-systems. But if any one of these belief-systems is true, in the sense of reflecting reality, must not all the others be false, at least in so far as they differ from it? As Bertrand Russell wrote, 'it is evident as a matter of logic that, since [the great world religions] disagree, not more than one of them can be true'.[9] And yet I now want to question this basic assumption that there can be at most one true religion, in the sense of a religion teaching saving truth about the Ultimate and our relationship to the Ultimate. I want to suggest a different approach altogether, and shall do so by means of a series of three analogies.

Consider, first, the psychologist Jastrow's famous ambiguous duck-rabbit picture which Wittgenstein used in his discussion of seeing-as in the Philosophical Investigations.

Suppose there is a culture in which ducks are a familiar sight but rabbits are completely unknown and have never even been heard of; and another culture in which rabbits are familiar but ducks completely unknown. So when people in the

9 Bertrand Russell, *Why I am Not a Christian*, London: Allen & Unwin 1957, p. xi.

duck-knowing culture see the ambiguous figure they naturally report that it's the picture of a duck. Indeed they may well claim to know that this is what it is; for lacking the concept of rabbit they are not aware that the picture is ambiguous. And of course the other way round with the rabbit-knowing culture. Here it's manifestly a rabbit and there is again no ambiguity about it. The people of these two cultures are fully entitled to affirm with full conviction that this is the picture of a duck, or of a rabbit, as the case may be. And each group, when told of another group who claim that the figure is something entirely different and alien to them, will maintain that that group are confused or mistaken in some perhaps inexplicable way.

But Wittgenstein would be able to offer an account of the situation according to which each group is right in what it affirms but wrong in its inference that the other group is mistaken. They are both, he could point out, right in virtue of the fact that what is actually there is capable of being equally correctly seen in two quite different ways, as a duck or as a rabbit.

The analogy that I am suggesting here is with the religious experience component of religion. And the possibility that I want to point to is that the ultimate ineffable Reality is capable of being authentically experienced in terms of different sets of human concepts, *as* Jahweh, *as* the Holy Trinity, *as* Allah, *as* Shiva, *as* Vishnu, and again *as* Brahman, *as* the Dharmakaya, *as* the Tao, and so on, these different personae and impersonae occurring at the interface between the Real and our differing religious mentalities and cultures.

A second analogy may help to suggest how this may be possible. This is the wave-particle complementarity in physics. It seems that if in an experimental situation you act upon light in one way, it is observed to have wave-like properties, and if in another way, to have particle-like properties. The properties it is observed to have depend upon how the observer acts in relation to it. As Ian Barbour writes, in describing Niels Bohr's complementarity principle, 'No sharp line can be drawn between the process of observation and what is observed';[10] and he quotes Henry Folse's interpretation of Bohr as implying an ontology which 'characterizes physical objects through their powers to appear in different phenomenal manifestations rather than through determinate properties corresponding to those of phenomenal objects as was held in the classical framework'.[11] The analogy that I have in mind here is with spiritual practices—prayer, forms of meditation, sacraments, common worship. In these practices we act in relation to the Real. The suggestion here is that if in the activity of I—Thou prayer we approach the Real as personal then we shall experience the Real as a personal deity. What we are then likely to be aware of will be a specific divine personality, involved in a particular strand of human history, the one who has chosen

[10] Ian Barbour, *Religion in an Age of Science*, Vol. I, London: SCM Press and New York: Harper & Row 1990, p. 98.

[11] Henry Folse, *The Philosophy of Niels Bohr: The Framework of Complementarity*, New York: North Holland 1985, p. 237, quoted by Barbour, op. cit., p. 99.

the Jewish people; or the heavenly Father of Jesus' teaching; or the divine being who spoke to the Arab peoples in the Qur'an, and so on. Or if our religious culture leads us to open ourselves to the Real in various forms of meditation, as the infinite non-personal being-consciousness-bliss of Brahman, or as the eternal Dharmakaya ever expressing itself in the limitless compassion of the Buddhas, then this is likely to be the way in which we shall experience the Real. Putting it in familar Christian language, revelation is a relational matter, taking different forms in relation to people whose religious receptivity has been formed by different traditions, with their different sets of concepts and their different kinds of spiritual practice.

A third analogy comes from cartography. Because the earth is a three-dimensional globe, any map of it on a two-dimensional surface must inevitably distort it, and there are different ways of systematically distorting it for different purposes, including for example the familiar cylindrical projection invented by Mercator which is used in constructing many of our maps of the world. But it does not follow that if one type of map is accurate the others must be inaccurate. If they are properly made, they are all accurate—and yet in another sense they are all inaccurate, in that they all inevitably distort. However, one may be more useful for one purpose, another for another—for great circle navigating, for shorter journeys, for travel in the tropics, for travel nearer to the Poles, and so on. The analogy here is with theologies, both the different theologies of the same religion and the even more different theologies and philosophies of different religions. It could be that representations of the infinite divine reality in our finite human terms must be much *more* radically inadequate than a two-dimensional representation of the three-dimensional earth. And it could be that the conceptual maps drawn by the great traditions, although finite picturings of the Infinite, are all more or less equally reliable within their different projections, and more or less equally useful for guiding us on our journey through life. For our pilgrim's progress is our life-response to the Real. The great world faiths orient us in this journey, and in so far as they are, as we may say, in soteriological alignment with the Real, to follow their path will relate us rightly to the Real, opening us to what, in different conceptualites, we will call divine grace or supernatural enlightenment that will in turn bear visible fruit in our lives.

Discussion Questions

1. Hick says that religious inclusivism, "when pressed to become clear, moves towards pluralism." Explain how he thinks this happens.

2. Speaking from within the Christian tradition, Hick appeals to the notions of the divine logos and the *cosmic Christ*. How do these concepts help him develop his notion of religious pluralism?

3. How might God be understood in a way that responds to the varieties of human experience of the ineffable? Give some specifics.

4. Discuss the three analogies Hick uses to buttress his claim that various cultures can conceptualize their experience of the divine in ways that are different but not exclusive. Do some of these analogies seem to you to work better than others?

5. Given Hick's analysis, how would you describe your own attitudes both toward your own religion and other world religions?

RETROSPECTIVE

Philosophy and Religion

The theme of this chapter follows the title of the influential book *The Varieties of Religious Experience* by William James. It is therefore entirely fitting to begin with a chapter from that book dealing with mysticism, the most intense and private form of religious experience. James points out that mysticism can take many forms, from the ecstatic experience of union with the ineffable to the sense of the presence of God within. It knows no boundaries of religious tradition or cultural background. The empirical fact that many persons have had a mystical experience of one kind or another points to the significance of the nonrational side of our natures and also signals that any account of religion, whether Eastern or Western, must come to terms with mysticism.

Rudolf Otto also finds that religion makes its entry through the nonrational side of our nature in the experience of the numinous. He describes how the numinous can press upon us in many and varied ways: It may be a gentle feeling of overpowering presence, or the emotion of awe aroused by feelings of an ultimate reality that we can only characterize as the Wholly Other. According to Otto, whatever differences various religions may possess, the experience of the numinous is basic to them all.

With Martin Buber we come to the interpersonal and intersubjective aspects of religious experience. The experiences he describes are difficult to put in words, so he creates new ones: *I-Thou* and *I-It*. These word-pairs name the two ways of relating and show that a true relation to God, in contrast to an idolatrous one, is precisely the difference between I-Thou and I-It. In every genuine I-Thou relationship with other persons we catch a glimpse of the Eternal Thou and wish for a fuller relationship with that ultimate person, The Eternal Thou.

The final selection by John Hick confronts head-on the sheer variety of religions themselves. The issue Hick explores is how to hold one's own religious experience as authoritative and true without de-legitimizing the traditions and experience of other faiths. It is a difficult issue and not without its hazards, one of which would be to relativize all religious experience as equally spurious. Hick avoids this relativizing turn by suggesting the complementarity of religions and offers three analogies as ways to this about his claim.

We begin the book with an analysis of the varieties of religious experience, but we quickly will move on to other existential themes: the relation of religion to life and its implications for death and human destiny. A philosophical study of religion cannot remain at the level of experience forever, since philosophy must also confront thorny conceptual problems, such as the existence and nature of God, the problem of evil, the relations between faith and reason, and the nature of religious language. Our exploration of philosophical themes in religion has just begun.

ADDITIONAL READINGS

Anyone interested in knowing more about mysticism should consult Evelyn Underhill, *Mysticism* (New York: Dutton, 1915, reprinted 1961), which is a classic on the subject. For an excellent survey of the various kinds of mysticism, see the article by Ronald Hepburn, "Mysticism, Nature and Assessment of," in *The Encyclopedia of Philosophy* (1967), 5, 429–34. Helpful both for understanding mysticism and as background for his own views is the book by Rudolf Otto, *Mysticism, East and West* (New York: Macmillan, 1932). Additional insight into the philosophy of Buber is found in the book by Maurice Friedman, *Martin Buber: The Life of Dialogue*, 3d ed. (Chicago: University of Chicago Press, 1976). For an overall study of religious experience, the classic source is William James, *Varieties of Religious Experience* (New York: Longmans, Green and Co., 1902; reprinted ed. New York: New American Library, 1974), which is available in numerous editions. An examination of the grounds for belief based on religious experience is given by William P. Alston, *Perceiving God: The Epistemology of Religious Experience* (Ithaca, NY: Cornell University Press, 1991). An examination of the various aspects of the phenomenon of religion is found in Ninian Smart, *Dimensions of the Sacred: An Anatomy of the World's Beliefs* (Berkeley: University of California Press, 1996).

CHAPTER TWO

RELIGION AND LIFE

INTRODUCTION

Religion and Life

The relation of religion to life is a topic that could be explored in many different ways, but this chapter will confine itself to two: The first centers on the relation of religion to conduct, that is, to ethics; the second on the question of the meaning of life.

If asked to describe why they believe in God, most followers of a theistic religion could say that their religion offers salvation, or makes them a better person, or adds meaning to their life that they would not have without it. All these answers center on the claim that belief in God or some transcendent reality adds a sense of meaning and purpose to life that otherwise would not be present. Without such meaning, life would appear to be aimless and without any goal or significance. Paul Tillich's definition of faith as our ultimate concern is another way of saying much the same thing; our faith commitment, whatever it may be, is the centering act that gives unity and focus to our personality.

Those who argue that one need not focus one's life on a transcendent reality to have a meaningful life point out the numerous thought systems of antiquity that provided a coherent framework for living, yet were devoid of any transcendent allegiances. Whether it be the generation of a code of ethical conduct or an explanation of the human place in the overall scheme of things, such systems did not appeal to a transcendent reality to deal with these issues. Stoicism, the ethics of Epicureanism, and, closer to our time, utilitarianism were all developed independently of a religious framework.

RELIGION AND MORALITY

Those who argue that religious faith provides the *only* legitimate meaning for life would also be sympathetic to the view that religion gives guidance for the living of life. In short, for these persons, there is an intimate connection between religion and ethics. The most extreme way of putting this point would be to say that there can be no ethical thinking separate from and independent of religion. This claim can be shown to be false on both historical and philosophical grounds. As has already been noted, the history of philosophy presents us with numerous ethical systems that are not tied to any religious tradition. The *Nicomachean Ethics* of Aristotle, for example, espouses many principles of conduct that most Jewish and Christian moralists would find generally acceptable, yet it is an ethical system completely divorced from religion in the conventional sense. Indeed, Aristotle's metaphysical views include no personal God in either a Christian or a Jewish sense, yet many of Aristotle's ethical principles are compatible with both of these religions. As a philosophical inquiry, ethics must be autonomous from religion, else it ceases to be a philosophical inquiry and becomes theology instead. Of course, one might choose to argue that no genuine ethical insight can be gained apart from religion, but this would be to take a philosophical position that would require some kind of supporting argument, and if it could be established, it would entail the reduction of ethics to religion. That many ethical systems claim autonomy from religion shows that this claim is at least subject to dispute.

Whereas the first erroneous claim is that there can be no morality without religion, the second erroneous claim is that there can be no religion without morality, since religion necessarily has moral content. Again, there is solid historical evidence against this view. Many primitive religions had no moral concern at all; the term *primitive* here is not intended to be pejorative, but simply to indicate a less developed religion. Many of the ancient Greek religions, for example, were concerned only with placating the gods and thereby avoiding divine wrath. Professor Nowell-Smith puts it well when he says, "In none of the earliest cultures were the gods endowed with high moral attributes; nor were they thought to concern themselves much with the behavior of human beings as long as the latter performed their religious duties punctiliously. Religion seems to have been concerned with averting of disasters and with salvation in the life after death, and both were to be achieved by means of ritual."[1]

Although religion and ethics can be separate areas of concern, one reason we tend to see them as interrelated is because of their close connection in both Judaism and Christianity. In both traditions moral demands for upright living are at the heart of religious obligation. The Hebrew prophets of the eighth century B.C.E. emphasized, in a highly developed way, the moral implications of faith in the living God: "And what does the Lord require of you but to do justice, and to

[1] Patrick H. Nowell-Smith, "Religion and Morality," *The Encyclopedia of Philosophy* (1967), 7, p. 155.

love kindness, and to walk humbly with your God?" (Micah 6:8). The New Testament also echoes this: "We love, because he first loved us. If any one says, 'I love God,' and hates his brother, he is a liar; for he who does not love his brother whom he has seen, cannot love God whom he has not seen" (1 John 4:19, 20). Even religions with no personal God, such as Buddhism and Confucianism, place a priority on ethics, so much so that Confucianism is virtually an ethical system. But not all religions can claim the higher degree of ethical content that these religions have.

THE AUTONOMY OF ETHICS

There seem, then, to be grounds for believing in the independence of morality from religion. Although the preponderance of the philosophical tradition is on the side of the autonomy of ethics, there has been wide disagreement as to the source of our knowledge of ethics. Some philosophical traditions argue for the existence of a special moral sense; others find the source of ethics to be in the power of reason. Philosophers also disagree whether the rightness of an action is a function of the motives of the agent or of the consequences of the action. It is an intriguing characteristic of these philosophical debates that although philosophers of different schools have often agreed on *what* is right, they do not always agree on *why* it is right.

One ancient ethical system that had a profound effect on Christian moral philosophy was that of the Stoics. Believing that rational beings can discover the principles of right action through the power of reason, they claimed that correct conduct is that which conforms to the *lex naturale*, or natural law. The view that there is a natural law independent of individual whim and fancy had a profound effect on the development of Roman civil law, which directly influenced the formation of the Western legal system. Natural law also provided a metaphysical foundation for ethics through much of the Middle Ages. Christian philosophers of the Middle Ages viewed the natural law doctrine as also being the law of God. That we are aware of the natural law provided medieval Christian philosophers with evidence for the existence of God. But when they explored further the question of the status of the natural law, they confronted a dilemma. Is the natural law our duty merely because God says it is, or does God give us rational insight into the natural law because it is good in itself? If we say that something is our duty merely because God commanded it, and God could have commanded the exact opposite, which would likewise have been good, this makes morality conventional and arbitrary. But if we say that goodness is independent of God, this would seem to make God subservient to an independent morality, which would be in conflict with the divine attributes of omniscience and omnipotence. The solution to this dilemma was to suggest a third alternative: It is God's nature to be good; therefore God wills only the good for us, since God cannot act contrary to God's nature. This view of God as ultimate in reality, in truth, and in goodness established an unbreakable connection between religion and morality in the minds of the philosophers of the Middle Ages.

By the eighteenth century, however, there was a different mood in ethics. Too many wars had been fought in the name of God (invoked by persons on both sides) for philosophers to be content to allow morality to be defined by religious zealots. So attempts were made to determine a rational basis for morality independent of any religious context. No philosopher better represented this spirit of the Enlightenment, as the age was called, than Immanuel Kant. Kant argued for the view that an action was morally significant only if it was done for the sake of duty. Compulsion, fear of punishment, the command of an authority, even concern for desirable consequences would diminish the moral significance of an act. The only reason for ascribing moral worth to an action is that it is done by a person of goodwill out of a sense of duty. At one level, we would probably want to agree with Kant. If someone refuses to tell a lie because of the fear of punishment, that person is acting not out of a sense of duty to tell the truth, but from fear of consequences. In contrast, if someone tells the truth, even though the consequences might be unpleasant, there is more moral significance to this action than there would be if the person were telling the truth only out of a fear of punishment.

Not only did Kant think that ethics was autonomous, but he went further, suggesting that religion is subordinate to ethics. True religion, according to Kant, is the recognition of all duties as divine commands.[2] The implication of Kant's view is that we should judge the claims of religion by the principles of morality and be willing to analyze ethical problems independently of religious presuppositions and commitments.

We will explore several reactions to these issues in the readings in this chapter. In the first, William Paley, a voice from the eighteenth century, gives expression to a point of view that continues to have a following: Human duty is to do God's will, and we know God's will both through the revelations of that will in scripture and also through the power of human reason. Next, we will look at Friedrich Nietzsche's claim that when belief in God disappears, we must become our own source of meaning and value, and on these terms the goal of life is to achieve greatness. The third reading is from the great Russian novelist and philosopher Count Leo Tolstoy, who presents the view that life has absolutely no meaning apart from God. Finally, a recent philosopher, Konstantin Kolenda, argues that life can experience a religious dimension even without belief in a traditional God.

---

[2] Immanuel Kant, *Critique of Practical Reason*, trans. Lewis White Beck, 3d ed. (Upper Saddle River, NJ, 1993), p. 136.

Life's Goal
Is to Obey God's Will

Paley's answer to the question of life's goal is simple and direct: Obey God's will. The reason for obeying God's will is hope for a future life, and Paley is skeptical of all other motivations for moral behavior. We know of God's will through two sources: God's "express declarations" in scripture and "the light of nature," or what philosophers have called natural theology. In determining the content of natural theology as it relates to human conduct, Paley appeals to something akin to the later view known as utilitarianism: Those things that tend to increase human happiness are consistent with the will of God, since God "wills and wishes the happiness of his creatures."

Paley was an eighteenth-century cleric known principally for two works: *Principles of Moral and Political Philosophy* and *Natural Theology*. As mentioned in Chapter 4, dealing with the cosmological argument, Paley's exposition of the design argument from his *Natural Theology* was a widely circulated statement of the argument for the existence of God based on evidence of design in nature. In *Principles of Moral and Political Philosophy*, Paley argues for the view that God's will for humans is that they be happy, so a morality based on following God's will can be expected to result in human happiness in this life and everlasting happiness in the life to come.

Paley's view is certainly one that finds support in any religion for which scripture is the source of knowledge about God and God's will, but like all scripture-based religions, how we interpret scripture to understand God's will is what gives rise to disagreements and controversies. Nonetheless, looking to divine revelation as the source of principles to guide human conduct is a point of view that finds widespread support even today—if not always in Christianity, certainly in Islam.

An Islamic philosopher of the eleventh century, Abu Hamid Muhammad Al-Ghazzali, would have been quite comfortable with Paley's view. Consider this statement of his:

> This world is a stage or market-place passed by pilgrims on their way to the next. It is here that they are to provide themselves with provisions for the way; or, to put it plainly, man acquires here, by the use of his bodily senses, some knowledge of the works of God, and, through them, of God Himself, the sight of whom will constitute his future beatitude. It is for the acquirement of his knowledge that the spirit of man has descended into this world of water and clay. As long as his senses remain with him he is said to be "in this world"; when they depart, and only his essential attributes remain, he is said to have gone to "the next world."[1]

The implication of such a view is that nothing in human experience has any prior claim on human action. Government, education, social policy—all are subordinated to following the will of God. Who is properly to interpret the will of God? This, after all, is the nub of the issue. In Paley's work, it is clear that there are two paths to divine knowledge: revelation and the conclusions that reason, unaided by revelation, can reach concerning the divine nature. In his book, *Natural Theology*, Paley says, "It is one of the advantages of the revelations which we acknowledge, that . . . they introduce the Deity to human apprehension under an idea more personal, more determinate, more within its compass, than the theology of nature can do."[2] But it is clear for Paley that the results of both natural theology (that is, the insights about God gained through the use of reason) and revealed theology (what can be known of God's will through scripture) are the same:

> Nevertheless, if we be careful to imitate the documents of our religion, by confining our explanations to what concerns ourselves, and do not affect more precision in our ideas than the subject allows of, the several terms which are employed to denote the attributes of the Deity, may be made, even in natural religion, to bear a sense consistent with truth and reason, and not surpassing our comprehension.[3]

Such sentiments are also consistent with Al-Ghazzali's view. In a passage that Paley would have found in agreement with his own arguments, Al-Ghazzali points out the marvels of the teeth for chewing food, of the tongue and salivary glands for digesting the food, and of the fingers and hand for grasping and carrying, and adds, "When a man further considers how his various wants of food, lodging, etc., are amply supplied from the storehouse of creation, he becomes aware that God's mercy is as great as His power and wisdom." The conclusion Al-Ghazzali reaches is "Thus from his own creation man comes to know God's existence, from the wonders of his bodily frame God's power and wisdom, and from the ample provision made for his various needs God's love."[4]

---

[1] Al-Ghazzali, *The Alchemy of Happiness*, trans. Claud Field (London: The Octagon Press, 1980), p. 42.

[2] William Paley, *Natural Theology*, American edition (Boston: Gould and Lincoln, 1864), p. 246.

[3] *Ibid.*, p. 247.

[4] Al-Ghazzali, *The Alchemy of Happiness*, pp. 31–32.

Views such as Paley's and Al-Ghazzali's raise the question of the extent to which divine law will take precedence over secular law. In the West the tradition of basing political decisions on principles that have autonomy from religion is the guiding approach, though there are always those who urge a return to moral values based on religious convictions. In some Moslem countries the same debate occurs, with Islamic fundamentalists calling for a total subordination of politics to religion. Other voices within other Moslem societies urge accommodation with secular traditions and values. It is a debate that will likely continue for some time, both in Eastern and Western nations. At the heart of the debate is the question to what extent ethics can be separate from religion and what sense can be made of the claim that there can be meaningful life apart from religious commitment.

Moral Obligation

∞

WILLIAM PALEY

Let it be remembered, that to be *obliged*, is "to be urged by a violent motive, resulting from the command of another."

And then let it be asked, "Why am I obliged to keep my word?" and the answer will be, Because I am "urged to do so by a violent motive," (namely, the expectation of being after this life rewarded, if I do, or punished for it, if I do not), "resulting from the command of another," (namely, of God).

This solution goes to the bottom of the subject, as no further question can reasonably be asked.

Therefore, private happiness is our motive, and the will of God our rule.

When I first turned my thoughts to moral speculations, an air of mystery seemed to hang over the whole subject; which arose, I believe, from hence—that I supposed, with many authors whom I had read, that to be *obliged* to do a thing, was very different from being *induced* only to do it; and that the obligation to practise virtue, to do what is right, just, etc. was quite another thing, and of another kind, than the obligation which a soldier is under to obey his officer, a servant his master; or any of the civil and ordinary obligations of human life. Whereas, from what has been said, it appears, that moral obligation is like all

Source: William Paley, *Works*, vol. 4. Edinburgh, 1823.

other obligations; and that *obligation* is nothing more than an *inducement* of sufficient strength, and resulting, in some way, from the command of another.

There is always understood to be a difference between an act of *prudence*, and
an act of *duty*. Thus, if I distrusted a man who owed me a sum of money, I should
reckon it an act of prudence to get another person bound with him; but I should
hardly call it an act of duty. On the other hand, it would be thought a very unusual and loose kind of language, to say, that, as I had made such a promise, it
was *prudent* to perform it; or that, as my friend, when he went abroad, placed a
box of jewels in my hands, it would be *prudent* in me to preserve it for him till
he returned.

Now, in what, you will ask, does the difference consist? inasmuch as, according to our account of the matter, both in the one case and the other, in acts of
duty as well as acts of prudence, we consider solely what we ourselves shall gain
or lose by the act.

The difference, and the only difference, is this; that, in the one case, we consider what we shall gain or lose in the present world; in the other case, we consider also what we shall gain or lose in the world to come.

They who would establish a system of morality, independent of a future state,
must look out for some different idea of moral obligation; unless they can show
that virtue conducts the possessor to certain happiness in this life, or to a much
greater share of it than he would attain by a different behaviour.

To us there are two great questions:

 I. Will there be after this life any distribution of rewards and punishments at all?
 II. If there be, what actions will be rewarded, and what will be punished?

The first question comprises the credibility of the Christian Religion, together with the presumptive proofs of a future retribution from the light of nature. The second question comprises the province of morality. . . .

As the will of God is our rule; to inquire what is our duty, or what we are
obliged to do, in any instance, is, in effect, to inquire what is the will of God in
that instance? which consequently becomes the whole business of morality.

Now there are two methods of coming at the will of God on any point:

 I. By his express declarations, when they are to be had, and which must be
    sought for in Scripture.
 II. By what we can discover of his designs and disposition from his works; or, as
    we usually call it, the light of nature.

And here we may observe the absurdity of separating natural and revealed religion from each other. The object of both is the same—to discover the will of God;—
and, provided we do but discover it, it matters nothing by what means. . . .

The method of coming at the will of God, concerning any action, by the light
of nature, is to inquire into "the tendency of the action to promote or diminish the

general happiness." This rule proceeds upon the presumption, that God Almighty wills and wishes the happiness of his creatures; and consequently, that those actions which promote that will and wish, must be agreeable to him; and the contrary. . . .

When God created the human species, either he wished their happiness, or he wished their misery, or he was indifferent and unconcerned about both.

If he had wished our misery, he might have made sure of his purpose, by forming our senses to be so many sores and pains to us, as they are now instruments of gratification and enjoyment; or by placing us amidst objects so ill-suited to our perceptions, as to have continually offended us, instead of ministering to our refreshment and delight. He might have made, for example, every thing we tasted, bitter; every thing we saw, loathsome; every thing we touched, a sting; every smell a stench; and every sound a discord.

If he had been indifferent about our happiness or misery, we must impute to our good fortune (as all design by this supposition is excluded) both the capacity of our senses to receive pleasure, and the supply of external objects fitted to produce it. But either of these (and still more both of them) being too much to be attributed to accident, nothing remains but the first supposition, that God, when he created the human species, wished their happiness; and made for them the provision which he has made, with that view, and for that purpose. . . .

We conclude, therefore, that God wills and wishes the happiness of his creatures. And this conclusion being once established, we are at liberty to go on with the rule built upon it, namely, "that the method of coming at the will of God concerning any action, by the light of nature, is to inquire into the tendency of that action to promote or diminish the general happiness."

Discussion Questions

1. To what would you attribute the appeal for many people today of the scriptural-literalist approach to understanding God's will?

2. Does Paley's view offer any guidance for separating divine law from secular law? What would be your response to those who say that there should be no separation?

3. Do you agree that the expectation of a future reward, or the fear of future punishment, is an adequate basis for promoting ethical behavior? Give reasons for your answer.

4. Paley was confident that there are two sources for knowledge of God: natural and revealed religion. Do you agree? If so, on what basis? If not, why not?

5. Overall, do you find the view expressed by Paley convincing? Why or why not?

Life's Goal
Is to Achieve Greatness

Nietzsche can be read on many levels. On one level, he is diagnosing a major metaphysical problem that he thinks Western religion and culture have yet to recognize. On another level, he is a social philosopher identifying those forces that create great civilizations. On still a third level, he is an antagonistic critic of organized religion, which he sees as contributing to a decline in the aristocratic values he so much admires.

Which of these is the correct Nietzsche? The answer: all of them. And in the brief selection from his works that follows, we will see all three themes articulated.

Consider the first level of reading—Nietzsche as diagnostician of a crisis at the heart of Western religion. Nietzsche sees himself as the prophet of the end of an era. Whereas for centuries belief in God provided the foundation for Western morality and culture, Nietzsche argues that this is no longer the case. The striking phrase "God is dead" communicates with greater rhetorical force than the statement that there is no God. To announce that *God is dead* implies that at one time God was alive, at least in the sense that God and the resulting theistic values provided cohesion for society and meaning for individual lives. Nietzsche claims that even though people no longer generally believe in God in the sense of a deep religious commitment, they nonetheless continue to follow a value system for which God is the metaphysical prop.

When a society finally recognizes that the metaphysical basis for its value system is gone, what is it to do? Nietzsche's answer is that we must become God; that is, we ourselves will be the source of meaning and value. Life will have no other meaning than that which we give to it. Not everyone is capable of carrying such a burden. In fact, only a noble few will have the courage to face up to the new realities and be willing to provide a new standard for behavior.

The two parables in the selection that follows emphasize the crisis of the age that Nietzsche sees himself as announcing. The first shows that without the security offered by belief in God, we are like a ship that has left the safety of the land and are embarked on a wild and terrifying sea: "Times will come when thou wilt feel that it is infinite, and that there is nothing more frightful than infinite." The second parable of the madman in the marketplace makes the same point. The madman, with a lighted lamp, rushes into the marketplace at midday to announce the death of God. The announcement is met with bemused responses from the crowd. So the madman concludes, "I come too early . . . this prodigious event is still on its way." Though the madman's hearers do not really believe in God, they have not yet realized the full magnitude of the implication of their unbelief. The meaning of this was yet to be understood. "How shall we console ourselves?" the madman asks. "Shall we not ourselves have to become Gods, merely to seem worthy of it?"

Nietzsche sees the problem in this way: When the full implications of the death of God are realized, the loss of the existing morality will lead to an era of nihilism—the absence of any values at all. This brings us to the second Nietzsche, the social philosopher. The escape from nihilism can be achieved only by the development of a new morality under the leadership of the aristocratic elite. Being a philosopher of culture, Nietzsche was convinced that such a cycle had occurred before. Whenever there is an absence of value, the resulting chaos is overcome only when great individuals emerge as the creators of meaning and value. These noble persons determine what is good and what is bad on the basis of their own values, and if they are truly noble, they are also persons of courage and creativity. They do not view suffering and hardship as bad, for suffering may be good if it leads to great accomplishments. Courage is a virtue when it results in the overcoming of obstacles and the generation of noble standards of conduct. A society is great only when it gives rise to great individuals—creative artists, powerful warriors, great writers, and creative geniuses in all areas of endeavor. This is the expression of what Nietzsche calls master morality, with its emphasis on creativity, respect among those who are equals, and strength of will as a supreme virtue. In short, the goal of life is to create greatness in all human endeavors.

Within every society, however, there are numerous persons not capable of greatness, whom Nietzsche describes as "the cowardly, the timid, the insignificant, and those thinking merely of narrow utility." For such persons, the master morality is impossible; so in their weakness they console themselves with a slave morality that resents those who are creative and powerful. Slave morality exalts as virtuous all those dispositions that make existence for the unfit a bit more endurable: "It is here that sympathy, the kind, helping hand, the warm heart, patience, diligence, humility, and friendliness attain to honour." There is thus a great reversal of values between the master morality and the slave morality. What the master morality considers evil, the slave morality exalts as virtue. And what slave morality considers despicable, master morality honors as good. These two moralities cannot coexist; slave morality, when it becomes ascendent, drags down the nobility and results in a general stagnation in society.

Enter Nietzsche the critic of religion. The ethical standards of Judaism and Christianity represent for Nietzsche the slave morality par excellence. Even when God was still alive as the foundation of these values, the resulting morality was hostile to creating greatness in a society. Nietzsche looks for the standards of value not to the Hebrew prophets or the teachings of Jesus, but to the Greek sense of aristocracy and to the heroes of German and Scandinavian legends. Nietzsche is convinced that, since the God of the Judaeo-Christian religious tradition is dead in the hearts and minds of people, the only alternative to the coming chaos is the emergence of a new aristocracy with its master morality.

Nietzsche died in the first year of the twentieth century and did not live to see the two world wars that broke out in Europe in the first half of the century. Whereas the dominant mood of nineteenth-century philosophy was a commitment to progress with its promise of inevitable achievements, Nietzsche stood somewhat alone as the prophet of an impending crisis. In one sense, Nietzsche was right: All was not well with European culture, and it is significant that the two world wars, with the greatest devastation ever witnessed in human history, began in the most civilized and technologically advanced nations of the world.

It may be significant that the central figure in the parable of the person announcing the death of God is a madman—not a scholar, not a philosopher, not a theologian, but an insane person. Was Nietzsche saying that European society contained within itself the seeds of its own destruction and that the Western world was on the brink of going through a period of madness? Perhaps. Did he also mean to imply that experiencing the death of God and attempting to become God will drive us to insanity? Again perhaps. Nietzsche's writing is enigmatic and often gives rise to multiple interpretations.

The Joyful Wisdom

FRIEDRICH NIETZSCHE

In the Horizon of the Infinite.—We have left the land and have gone aboard ship! We have broken down the bridge behind us—nay, more, the land behind us! Well, little ship! look out! Beside thee is the ocean; it is true it does not always roar, and sometimes it spreads out like silk and gold and a gentle reverie. But times will come when thou wilt feel that it is infinite, and that there is nothing

Source: Friedrich Nietzsche, *The Joyful Wisdom*, in *The Complete Works of Nietzsche*, (Edinburgh: T.N. Foulis, 1910).

more frightful than infinite. Oh, the poor bird that felt itself free, and now strikes against the walls of this cage! Alas, if homesickness for the land should attack thee, as if there had been more *freedom* there—and there is no "land" any longer!

The Madman.—Have you ever heard of the madman who on a bright morning lighted a lantern and ran to the market-place calling out unceasingly: "I seek God! I seek God!"—As there were many people standing about who did not believe in God, he caused a great deal of amusement. Why! Is he lost? said one. Has he strayed away like a child? said another. Or does he keep himself hidden? Is he afraid of us? Has he taken a sea-voyage? Has he emigrated?—the people cried out laughingly, all in a hubbub. The insane man jumped into their midst and transfixed them with his glances. "Where is God gone?" he called out. "I mean to tell you! *We have killed him*—you and I! We are all his murderers! But how have we done it? How were we able to drink up the sea? Who gave us the sponge to wipe away the whole horizon? What did we do when we loosened this earth from its sun? Whither does it now move? Whither do we move? Away from all suns? Do we not dash on unceasingly? Backwards, sideways, forwards, in all directions? Is there still an above and below? Do we not stray, as through infinite nothingness? Does not empty space breathe upon us? Has it not become colder? Does not night come on continually, darker and darker? Shall we not have to light lanterns in the morning? Do we not hear the noise of the grave-diggers who are burying God? Do we not smell the divine putrefaction?—for even Gods putrefy! God is dead! God remains dead! And we have killed him! How shall we console ourselves, the most murderous of all murderers? The holiest and the mightiest that the world has hitherto possessed has bled to death under our knife—who will wipe the blood from us? With what water could we cleanse ourselves? What lustrums, what sacred games shall we have to devise? Is not the magnitude of this deed too great for us? Shall we not ourselves have to become Gods, merely to seem worthy of it? There never was a greater event— and on account of it, all who are born after us belong to a higher history than any history hitherto!"—Here the madman was silent and looked again at his hearers; they also were silent and looked at him in surprise. At last he threw his lantern on the ground, so that it broke in pieces and was extinguished. "I come too early," he then said, "I am not yet at the right time. This prodigious event is still on its way, and is travelling—it has not yet reached men's ears. Lightning and thunder need time, the light of the stars needs time, deeds need time, even after they are done, to be seen and heard. This deed is as yet further from them than the furthest star—*and yet they have done it!*"—It is further stated that the madman made his way into different churches on the same day, and there intoned his *Requiem aeternam deo*. When led out and called to account, he always gave the reply: "What are these churches now, if they are not the tombs and monuments of God?"— . . .

In a tour through the many finer and coarser moralities which have hitherto prevailed or still prevail on the earth, I found certain traits recurring regularly together and connected with one another, until finally two primary types revealed themselves to me, and a radical distinction was brought to light. There is *master-*

morality and *slave-morality*;—I would at once add, however, that in all higher and mixed civilisations, there are also attempts at the reconciliation of the two moralities; but one finds still oftener the confusion and mutual misunderstanding of them, indeed, sometimes their close juxtapositions—even in the same man, within one soul. The distinctions of moral values have either originated in a ruling caste, pleasantly conscious of being different from the ruled—or among the ruled class, the slaves and dependents of all sorts. In the first case, when it is the rulers who determined the conception "good," it is the exalted, proud disposition which is regarded as the distinguishing feature, and that which determines the order of rank. The noble type of man separates from himself the beings in whom the opposite of this exalted, proud disposition displays itself; he despises them. Let it at once be noted that in this first kind of morality the antithesis "good" and "bad" means practically the same as "noble" and despicable";—the antithesis "good" and "*evil*" is of a different origin. The cowardly, the timid, the insignificant, and those thinking merely of narrow utility are despised; moreover, also, the distrustful, with their constrained glances, the self-abasing, the dog-like kind of men who let themselves be abused, the mendicant flatterers, and above all the liars:—it is a fundamental belief of all aristocrats that the common people are untruthful. . . .

A morality of the ruling class, however, is more especially foreign and irritating to present-day taste in the sternness of its principle that one has duties only to one's equals; that one may act towards beings of a lower rank, towards all that is foreign, just as seems good to one, or "as the heart desires," and in any case "beyond good and evil": it is here that sympathy and similar sentiments can have a place. The ability and obligation to exercise prolonged gratitude and prolonged revenge—both only within the circle of equals—artfulness in retaliation, *raffinement* of the idea in friendship, a certain necessity to have enemies (as outlets for the emotions of envy, quarrelsomeness, arrogance—in fact, in order to be a good *friend*): all these are typical characteristics of the noble morality, which, as has been pointed out, is not the morality of "modern ideas," and is therefore at present difficult to realise, and also to unearth and disclose—It is otherwise with the second type of morality, *slave-morality*. Supposing that the abused, the oppressed, the suffering, and unemancipated, the weary, and those uncertain of themselves, should moralise, what will be the common element in their moral estimates? Probably a pessimistic suspicion with regard to the entire situation of man will find expression, perhaps a condemnation of man, together with his situation. The slave has an unfavourable eye for the virtues of the powerful; he has a scepticism and distrust, a *refinement* of distrust of everything "good" that is there honoured—he would fain persuade himself that the very happiness there is not genuine. On the other hand, *those* qualities which serve to alleviate the existence of sufferers are brought into prominence and flooded with light; it is here that sympathy, the kind, helping hand, the warm heart, patience, diligence, humility, and friendliness attain to honour; for here these are the most useful qualities, and almost the only means of supporting the burden of existence. Slave-morality is essentially the morality of utility. . . .

A last fundamental difference: the desire for *freedom*, instinct for happiness and the refinements of the feeling of liberty belong as necessarily to slave-morals and morality, as artifice and enthusiasm in reverence and devotion are the regular symptoms of an aristocratic mode of thinking and estimating—Hence we can understand without further detail why love *as a passion*—it is our European specialty—must absolutely be of noble origin; as is well known, its invention is due to the Provençal poet-cavaliers, those brilliant ingenious men of the *"gai saber,"* to whom Europe owes so much, and almost owes itself.

Discussion Questions

1. Do you think Nietzsche is correct in his claim that Western civilization no longer accepts a religious basis for ethics but nonetheless persists in advocating the values that were derived from the Judaeo-Christian tradition? What reasons can you advance to support your answer?

2. Why does Nietzsche equate slave morality with a morality derived from religious principles? Do you think this is a legitimate analysis?

3. Explain what Nietzsche means when he suggests a morality that is "beyond good and evil."

4. Evaluate Nietzsche's claim that democracy is an instance of slave morality and is derived from Judaeo-Christian values.

5. What aspects of Nietzsche's point of view do you find most convincing? Least convincing? Why?

To Know God Is to Live

Leo Tolstoy (1828–1910) is one of the most puzzling intellectuals of the nineteenth century. Born into the Russian aristocracy, in his later years he found common cause with the peasants and renounced his title, no longer to be addressed as Count Tolstoy. Though he inherited great wealth, he tried to give it all away and aspired to a life of poverty as the Christian ideal. He was a highly successful novelist who produced two of the most complex novels of all time, *War and Peace* and *Anna Karenina*, and was at the height of his powers when he had the spiritual crisis that led to his attempts to change his life. Although he wrote his major works in the nineteenth century, the themes he explored have more in common with the existential philosophers of the twentieth century than with the didactic novelists of the nineteenth. He advocated emotion as a guide to understanding great art, especially emotion resulting in lofty religious feelings of brotherhood, yet he thought Beethoven's Ninth Symphony was not great art.

Tolstoy confronts the question of what life can mean when death is the only certainty. Unlike others, Tolstoy finds none of the humanly constructed answers adequate. Art and poetry are in the end not satisfying. Neither can science explain ultimate meanings. Ignoring the problem through the pursuit of sensuous enjoyment, what Tolstoy refers to as epicureanism, is likewise an unsatisfactory response. And finally, destroying one's life is the response of strength, a response he would not accept.

God is the cure for the sickness of soul that pained Tolstoy. But he knows that there are no philosophical arguments sufficient to prove that God exists. Yet there is a reason beyond reason, a call of the self to a higher purpose for life that is found only in God. "'He exists,' said I to myself. And I had only for an instant to admit that, and at once life rose within me, and I felt the possibility and joy of being." All this is reminiscent of the distinction between rational and nonrational approaches to the question that we encountered in Chapter 1. If the former fails to give us the purpose for living we seek, Tolstoy finds that the latter is the only way of proceeding. "To know God and to live is one and the same thing. God is life."

The following selection dates from his later years after his crisis of faith. In it, Tolstoy does not advance philosophical arguments or proofs for the conclusions he reaches. Rather, he shares his own existential anguish and the only solution to the problem he finds acceptable—a solution we could describe as the leap of faith, to use Kierkegaard's salient phrase. Tolstoy's writing, though free from academic complexity, conveys a power and simplicity that survives translation into another language and needs nothing further in the way of analysis and exposition. Better at this point to let him speak for himself.

A Confession

LEO TOLSTOY

There is an Eastern fable, told long ago, of a traveller overtaken on a plain by an enraged beast. Escaping from the beast he gets into a dry well, but sees at the bottom of the well a dragon that has opened its jaws to swallow him. And the unfortunate man, not daring to climb out lest he should be destroyed by the enraged beast, and not daring to leap to the bottom of the well lest he should be eaten by the dragon, seizes a twig growing in a crack in the well and clings to it. His hands are growing weaker and he feels he will soon have to resign himself to the destruction that awaits him above or below, but still he clings on. Then he sees that two mice, a black and a white one, go regularly round and round the stem of the twig to which he is clinging and gnaw at it. And soon the twig itself will snap and he will fall into the dragon's jaws. The traveller sees this and knows that he will inevitably perish; but while still hanging he looks around, sees some drops of honey on the leaves of the twig, reaches them with his tongue and licks them. So I too clung to the twig of life, knowing that the dragon of death was inevitably awaiting me, ready to tear me to pieces; and I could not understand why I had fallen into such torment. I tried to lick the honey which formerly con-soled me, but the honey no longer gave me pleasure, and the white and black mice of day and night gnawed at the branch by which I hung. I saw the dragon clearly and the honey no longer tasted sweet. I only saw the unescapable dragon and the mice, and I could not tear my gaze from them. And this is not a fable but the real unanswerable truth intelligible to all.

Source: Abridged from Leo Tolstoy, *A Confession and the Gospel in Brief*, trans. by Aylmer Maude (1921). Reprinted by permission of Oxford University Press.

The deception of the joys of life which formerly allayed my terror of the dragon now no longer deceived me. No matter how often I may be told, 'You cannot understand the meaning of life so do not think about it, but live,' I can no longer do it; I have already done it too long. I cannot now help seeing day and night going round and bringing me to death. That is all I see, for that alone is truth. All else is false.

The two drops of honey which diverted my eyes from the cruel truth longer than the rest: my love of family, and of writing—art as I called it—were no longer sweet to me.

'Family' . . . said I to myself. But my family—wife and children—are also human. They are placed just as I am: they must either live in a lie or see the terrible truth. Why should they live? Why should I love them, guard them, bring them up, or watch them? That they may come to the despair that I feel, or else be stupid? Loving them, I cannot hide the truth from them: each step in knowledge leads them to the truth. And the truth is death.

'Art, poetry?' . . . Under the influence of success and the praise of men, I had long assured myself that this was a thing one could do though death was drawing near—death which destroys all things, including my work and its remembrance; but soon I saw that that too was a fraud. It was plain to me that art is an adornment of life, an allurement to life. But life had lost its attraction for me, so how could I attract others? As long as I was not living my own life but was borne on the waves of some other life—as long as I believed that life had a meaning, though one I could not express—the reflection of life in poetry and art of all kinds afforded me pleasure: it was pleasant to look at life in the mirror of art. But when I began to seek the meaning of life and felt the necessity of living my own life, that mirror became for me unnecessary, superfluous, ridiculous, or painful. I could no longer soothe myself with what I now saw in the mirror, namely, that my position was stupid and desperate. It was all very well to enjoy the sight when in the depth of my soul I believed that my life had a meaning. Then the play of lights—comic, tragic, touching, beautiful, and terrible—in life amused me. But when I knew life to be meaningless and terrible, the play in the mirror could no longer amuse me. No sweetness of honey could be sweet to me when I saw the dragon and saw the mice gnawing away my support.

Nor was that all. Had I simply understood that life had no meaning I could have borne it quietly, knowing that that was my lot. But I could not satisfy myself with that. Had I been like a man living in a wood from which he knows there is no exit, I could have lived; but I was like one lost in a wood who, horrified at having lost his way, rushes about wishing to find the road. He knows that each step he takes confuses him more and more, but still he cannot help rushing about.

It was indeed terrible. And to rid myself of the terror I wished to kill myself. I experienced terror at what awaited me—knew that that terror was even worse than the position I was in, but still I could not patiently await the end. However convincing the argument might be that in any case some vessel in my heart would give way, or something would burst and all would be over, I could not patiently await that end. The horror of darkness was too great, and I wished to free myself from it as quickly as possible by noose or bullet. That was the feeling which drew me most strongly toward suicide.

Not finding an explanation in science I began to seek for it in life, hoping to find it among the people around me. And I began to observe how the people around me—people like myself—lived, and what their attitude was to this question which had brought me to despair.

And this is what I found among people who were in the same position as myself as regards education and manner of life.

I found that for people of my circle there were four ways out of the terrible position in which we are all placed.

The first was that of ignorance. It consists in not knowing, not understanding, that life is an evil and an absurdity. People of this sort—chiefly women, or very young or very dull people—have not yet understood that question of life which presented itself to Schopenhauer, Solomon, and Buddha. They see neither the dragon that awaits them nor the mice gnawing the shrub by which they are hanging, and they lick the drops of honey. But they lick those drops of honey only for a while: something will turn their attention to the dragon and the mice, and there will be an end to their licking. From them I had nothing to learn—one cannot cease to know what one does know.

The second way out is epicureanism. It consists, while knowing the hopelessness of life, in making use meanwhile of the advantages one has, disregarding the dragon and the mice, and licking the honey in the best way, especially if there is much of it within reach. Solomon expresses this way out thus: 'Then I commended mirth, because a man hath no better thing under the sun, than to eat, and to drink, and to be merry: and that this should accompany him in his labour the days of his life, which God giveth him under the sun.

'Therefore eat thy bread with joy and drink thy wine with a merry heart. . . . Live joyfully with the wife whom thou lovest all the days of the life of thy vanity . . . for this is thy portion in life and in thy labours which thou takest under the sun. . . . Whatsoever thy hand findeth to do, do it with thy might, for there is no work, nor device, nor knowledge, nor wisdom, in the grave, whither thou goest.'

That is the way in which the majority of people of our circle make life possible for themselves. Their circumstances furnish them with more of welfare than of hardship, and their moral dullness makes it possible for them to forget that the advantage of their position is accidental, and that not everyone can have a thousand wives and palaces like Solomon, that for everyone who has a thousand wives there are a thousand without a wife, and that for each palace there are a thousand people who have to build it in the sweat of their brows; and that the accident that has today made me a Solomon may tomorrow make me a Solomon's slave. The dullness of these people's imagination enables them to forget the things that gave Buddha no peace—the inevitability of sickness, old age, and death, which today or tomorrow will destroy all these pleasures.

So think and feel the majority of people of our day and our manner of life. The fact that some of these people declare the dullness of their thoughts and imaginations to be a philosophy, which they call Positive, does not remove them, in my opinion, from the ranks of those who, to avoid seeing the question, lick the honey. I could not imitate these people; not having their dullness of imagination I could not artificially produce it in myself. I could not tear my eyes from the mice and the dragon, as no vital man can after he has once seen them.

The third escape is that of strength and energy. It consists in destroying life, when one has understood that it is an evil and an absurdity. A few ex-ceptionally strong and consistent people act so. Having understood the stupid-ity of the joke that has been played on them, and having understood that it is better to be dead than to be alive, and that it is best of all not to exist, they act accordingly and promptly end this stupid joke, since there are means: a rope round one's neck, water, a knife to stick into one's heart, or the trains on the railways; and the number of those of our circle who act in this way becomes greater and greater, and for the most part they act so at the best time of their life, when the strength of their mind is in full bloom and few habits degrading to the mind have as yet been acquired.

I saw that this was the worthiest way of escape and I wished to adopt it.

The fourth way out is that of weakness. It consists of seeing the truth of the situation and yet clinging to life, knowing in advance that nothing can come of it. People of this kind know that death is better than life, but not having the strength to act rationally—to end the deception quickly and kill themselves— they seem to wait for something. This is the escape of weakness, for if I know what is best and it is within my power; why not yield to what is best? . . . I found myself in that category.

During that time this is what happened to me. During that whole year, when I was asking myself almost every moment whether I should not end matters with a noose or a bullet—all that time, together with the course of thought and ob-servation about which I have spoken, my heart was oppressed with a painful feel-ing, which I can only describe as a search for God.

I say that that search for God was not reasoning, but a feeling, because that search proceeded not from the course of my thoughts—it was even directly con-trary to them—but proceeded from the heart. It was a feeling of fear, orphanage, isolation in a strange land, and a hope of help from someone.

Though I was quite convinced of the impossibility of proving the existence of a Deity (Kant had shown, and I quite understood him, that it could not be proved), I yet sought for God, hoped that I should find Him, and from old habit addressed prayers to that which I sought but had not found. I went over in my mind the arguments of Kant and Schopenhauer showing the impossibility of prov-ing the existence of a God, and I began to verify those arguments and to refute them. Cause, said I to myself, is not a category of thought such as are Time and Space. If I exist, there must be some cause for it, and a cause of causes. And that first cause of all is what men have called 'God.' And I paused on that thought, and tried with all my being to recognize the presence of that cause. And as soon as I acknowledged that there is a force in whose power I am, I at once felt that I could live. But I asked myself: What is that cause, that force? How am I to think of it? What are my relations to that which I call 'God'? And only the familiar replies occurred to me: 'He is the Creator and Preserver.' This reply did not satisfy me, and I felt I was losing within me what I needed for my life. I became terrified and began to pray to Him whom I sought, that He should help me. But the more I prayed the more apparent it became to me that He did not hear me, and that there was no one to whom to address myself. And with despair in my heart that there is no God at all, I said: 'Lord, have mercy, save me! Lord, teach me!' But no one had mercy on me, and I felt that my life was coming to a standstill.

But again and again, from various sides, I returned to the same conclusion that I could not have come into the world without any cause or reason or meaning; I could not be such a fledgling fallen from its nest as I felt myself to be. Or, granting that I be such, lying on my back crying in the high grass, even then I cry because I know that a mother has borne me within her, has hatched me, warmed me, fed me, loved me. Where is she—that mother? If I have been deserted, who has deserted me? I cannot hide from myself that someone bore me, loving me. Who was that someone? Again 'God'? He knows and sees my searching, my despair, and my struggle.

'He exists,' said I to myself. And I had only for an instant to admit that, and at once life rose within me, and I felt the possibility and joy of being. But again, from the admission of the existence of a God I went on to seek my relation with Him; and again I imagined *that* God—our Creator in Three Persons who sent His Son, the Saviour—and again *that* God, detached from the world and from me, melted like a block of ice, melted before my eyes, and again nothing remained, and again the spring of life dried up within me, and I despaired and felt that I had nothing to do but to kill myself. And the worst of all was, that I felt I could not do it.

Not twice or three times, but tens and hundreds of times, I reached those conditions, first of joy and animation, and then of despair and consciousness of the impossibility of living.

I remember that it was in early spring: I was alone in the wood listening to its sounds. I listened and thought ever of the same thing, as I had constantly done during those last three years. I was again seeking God.

'Very well, there is no God,' said I to myself; 'there is no one who is not my imagination but a reality like my whole life. He does not exist, and no miracles can prove His existence, because the miracles would be my imagination, besides being irrational.

'But my *perception* of God, of Him whom I seek,' I asked myself, 'where has that perception come from?' And again at this thought the glad waves of life rose within me. All that was around me came to life and received a meaning. But my joy did not last long. My mind continued its work.

'The conception of God is not God,' said I to myself. 'The conception is what takes place within me. The conception of God is something I can evoke or can refrain from evoking in myself. That is not what I seek. I seek that without which there can be no life.' And again all around me and within me began to die, and again I wished to kill myself.

But then I turned my gaze upon myself, on what went on within me, and I remembered all those cessations of life and reanimations that recurred within me hundreds of times. I remembered that I only lived at those times when I believed in God. As it was before, so it was now; I need only be aware of God to live; I need only to forget Him, or disbelieve Him, and I died.

What is this animation and dying? I do not live when I lose belief in the existence of God. I should long ago have killed myself had I not had a dim hope of finding Him. I live, really live, only when I feel Him and seek Him. 'What more do you seek?' exclaimed a voice within me. 'This is He. He is that without which one cannot live. To know God and to live is one and the same thing. God is life.'

'Live seeking God, and then you will not live without God.' And more than ever before, all within me and around me lit up, and the light did not again abandon me.

And I was saved from suicide. When and how this change occurred I could not say. As imperceptibly and gradually the force of life in me had been destroyed and I had reached the impossibility of living, a cessation of life and the necessity of suicide, so imperceptibly and gradually did that force of life return to me. And strange to say the strength of life which returned to me was not new, but quite old—the same that had borne me along in my earliest days.

I quite returned to what belonged to my earliest childhood and youth. I returned to the belief in that Will which produced me and desires something of me. I returned to the belief that the chief and only aim of my life is to be better, i.e., to live in accord with that Will. And I returned to the belief that I can find the expression of that Will in what humanity, in the distant past hidden from me, has produced for its guidance: that is to say, I returned to a belief in God, in moral perfection, and in a tradition transmitting the meaning of life. There was only this difference, that then all this was accepted unconsciously, while now I knew that without it I could not live.

Discussion Questions

1. Tolstoy lists four escapes from the despair he faces and obviously thinks this is an exhaustive list. Do you agree, or are there other responses one might pursue?

2. Camus wrote, "There is only one truly philosophical question, and that is suicide." Would Tolstoy agree? Give reasons for your answer.

3. Tolstoy seeks for the meaning of life in a turn toward a simple Christian lifestyle. Could one find the same religious answer without adopting the simplicity of life that Tolstoy favored?

4. If Tolstoy had an opportunity to discuss the issue of life's meaning with Nietzsche, what do you think he would tell him?

5. Tolstoy seems to dwell on a personal search for meaning. Is his approach very useful in dealing with social institutions and organizations? Discuss.

A World Without God

In the introduction to this chapter, we mentioned that religions such as Buddhism and Confucianism offer a view of life that does not include belief in a personal God. By a personal God, we mean something like the transcendent God of Judaism and Christianity, that is, a God beyond time and space yet aware of human concerns and activities. A personal God is one with whom we can establish a relationship, an Eternal Thou who hears and answers prayers. For those who believe in such a deity, God is a reality, known by human beings both through the power of reason and through the evidences in nature of God's creative activity visible in the world around us. But what are the alternatives to the traditional Jewish and Christian views of God? And can one find meaning and purpose in life through such alternatives? These are the issues raised by Konstantin Kolenda in his book, *Religion Without God*.

The religious impulse, Kolenda argues, arises from our awareness of human finitude; another way of saying this is that religion grows out of our awareness that we all die. Because religions—at least some of them—give us a hope for continued existence after death, they attempt to provide what Kolenda calls *compensation* for human finitude. Compensation is a key notion for Kolenda's analysis, and he uses the term in a way that might be compared to the experience of a blind person whose loss of sight leads to a compensating increase in other faculties—hearing, touch, smell. As Kolenda states, "These instances of compensation show how a limitation in one respect can lead a person to rechannel his attention and effort in another direction in order to make up for the loss or absence of ability caused by his limitation."[1]

Does this metaphor work? After all, a blind person has lost only one sense, that of sight; a dead person's loss is total. How can we possibly use compensation as a way of explaining the religious impulse? While this is a strong objection, it is not fatal to Kolenda's position: Compensation, as he uses the term, means the desire of human beings to strive for perfection, to make life better through the

---

[1] Konstantin Kolenda, *Religion Without God* (Buffalo: Prometheus Books, 1976), p. 67.

creation of ideals that direct one's achievement in this life. As Kolenda puts it, "In other words, I may compensate in thought, in imagination, for what I find myself to be. I may complete the actual with the ideal. I can try to fill out my destiny by eliminating from it—in thought and desire—all imperfections, whether they are imperfections in knowledge or in moral status or in aesthetic vision."[2] The idea of God then becomes a name for these ideals.

In the selection that follows, Kolenda says, "The idea of God is man's recognition of his own longing to take his highest ideals seriously. The very presence of this longing testifies to the reality of religiousness, of the religious impulse." We can imagine someone objecting to this as using the traditional term God, and all the accompanying religious vocabulary, to name something decidedly untraditional and bearing so little resemblance to the original meanings of these terms as to distort them beyond all recognition. To this sort of objection Kolenda might reply that the traditional vocabulary of religion is itself based on misconceptions and distortions of religious feeling. At their best, human beings have a longing to be freed from the vices and limitations of human experience. These essentially religious feelings emerge at their strongest in moments of great despondency or great joy. At either extreme such feelings give rise to a vocabulary of expression that, at times, "may crystallize into a full-fledged theology," including "the exertion of questionable metaphysical pictures and the exertion of social and political control, establishing special castes of priests, of religious orders, and of church power, that affects all spheres of life," or even become a suppression of human creativity, an "opiate of the people." Kolenda proposes as an alternative to search for concepts that "would capture the phenomenon of religiousness without leading us in that direction." He suggests something akin to reading a folktale and getting from it a moral without believing in a world inhabited by witches, trolls, goblins, or fairy godmothers.

The test of the religious impulse, as Kolenda describes it, is not intellectual, but moral: Does religion make the life of a believer better, more complete, richer? Kolenda picks up on a word used by St. Thomas Aquinas, *radiance*, to describe the experiences that lie at the root of the religious dimension of life. "A rich, well-rounded life," Kolenda says, "is still our ideal, and a life wasted on trivialities fills us with regret."

As you read through the selection that follows, you will see clearly described a way of understanding the traditional vocabulary of religion in a new and enlightening way.

[2] Kolenda, *Religion Without God*, p. 69.

Reality and God

KONSTANTIN KOLENDA

Critics of religion claim that, contrary to the Christian belief, man was not made in God's image, but that instead God was made in man's image; the concept of God is a projection of man's ideals. The upshot of this claim is not obvious. It may be a way of deflating religion by treating the concept of God as a figment of man's imagination or as a wish fulfillment. But this is not the only alternative. The search for God indicates that the religious impulse is an important aspect of being human. That impulse testifies to the peculiar status of ideals. Although not actualities, they nevertheless betray an ineradicable impetus to endow the universe with a meaning that transcends individual destinies. Dostoyevsky realized this in his rather startling observation that the very idea of God does great credit to man. What is astonishing, said Dostoyevsky, is not that God should exist, but rather that such a noble idea should enter the head of such a despicable creature as man.

This observation mitigates the initial negative verdict about man's nature. Indeed, it does more than that—it almost reverses that verdict. Alongside of Sodom and Gomorrah there is a vision of the Madonna in the heart of man, an intense if often unacknowledged and unrealized desire to shed one's evil for the sake of good. When Satan says, "Evil, be my good," he must somehow rationalize that evil is the preferable or better alternative. Explanations for such a perverse inversion of values are not hard to come by; they usually involve a combination of ignorance, desperation, and self-deception.

The notion of God, it seems to me, is the limiting target of compensation. It encapsulates the desire to escape finitude, the search for realization of highest potentialities, the urge to translate ideals into actuality. God is the embodiment of perfection, but if compensation as the tendency toward perfection is logically prior to perfection, then the notion of compensation is a more primitive, more fundamental religious concept.

The traditional name for the unification of all the attributes of perfection is God: all-wise, all-good, all-powerful. One should not fail to recognize a purely intellectual, philosophical element in this ideal, even though other elements may tend to overshadow it. The concept of God answers the highest intellectual

Source: Konstantin Kolenda, *Religion Without God* (Buffalo: Prometheus Books, 1976). Copyright 1976 by Prometheus Books. Selections are taken from Chapter 3, "Compensation." Used by permission of Prof. Pauline Kolenda.

demands because He contains in Himself all knowledge and all truth. It is not surprising, therefore, that many philosophers were inclined to say that the quest for knowledge ends in Godlike knowledge. The notion of all-inclusiveness, of the absence of limitations, similarly satisfies the demand of the intellect not to leave anything outside of the mind's ken. God's mind is contrasted with man's precisely for that reason.

No matter how partial, each person uses this ideal vision to escape fragmentation and achieve some sort of integration. But the notion of integration is characteristically normative and open-ended. Just how much experience and what kind of experience would make my life really satisfying? This is an inescapable question for every one of us, no matter how halfhearted and backsliding our attempt to answer it is. A Faustian man may be single-minded and heroic in setting his sights as high as possible and, as a result, suffer titanic anguish. I am proffering a more modest and realistic notion of compensation. In each destiny there is a desire to secure as much of life's possibilities as it is in our power to attain. Since every human being seeks such compensation, such rounding out of the actual with the ideal, according to his or her talents, insights, and abilities, it follows that in one important sense, every human being cannot help loving God if God is conceived of as the integration of highest ideals. This integration is not only theoretical or philosophical, but also involves the employment of poetic imagination, or moral vision and aspiration.

The idea of God is man's recognition of his own longing to take his highest ideals seriously. The very presence of this longing testifies to the reality of religiousness, of the religious impulse. Here we have, it appears, an analogue to what in theology is known as the ontological proof of God's existence. The argument runs roughly as follows. If we but recognize clearly what the concept of God signifies, we are bound to recognize that his nonexistence is inconceivable; God's essence implies his existence. Our argument here is similar, although it is moving in a wider conceptual territory. If the notion of compensation is essentially religious and if its presence is discoverable in all human lives, then the essence of religiousness implies its existence. The conception coincides with its own object.

There is one important difference between this proof, let us call it "superontological," and the orthodox ontological proof of the theologians. There is no need to assert the transcendence of God because we are led to postulate the existence of God as a transcendent being only when we inaccurately describe the religious impulse. Conceived in a certain way, religiousness invites a transcendent object when we interpret religiousness as a sense of distance between what we are and what we wish to be, or between the world as it is and as it could be, or as a vision of fully realized ideal possibilities. Because it seems natural to speak here of a *vision*, one is inevitably tempted to postulate an independent *object* of that vision, to separate that object from the vision itself and to see it as transcendent. When the Christian says that man was made in God's image or that man is God's creature, a carrier of the divine spark, he has already made such a separation. The same happens when another picture is invoked, namely, the picture of divine grace—that grace is available and within reach if only a man would reach out toward it.

Granted that in such theological pictures the transcendental leap has been already made, we must inquire into the ground from which it is made. The transcendental leap seems to be based on natural experience, namely, the experience of spiritual longing toward perfection, *away* from vices, from suffering, from confining and frustrating limitations. When that longing is strong enough—and it is very strong in moments of despondency or deep despair and, equally, in times of ecstasy or great joy—the moral and practical imagination of some gifted men reaches the superlatives of affirmation, thus giving rise to transcendent language. In time this language may crystallize into a full-fledged theology, brought about by a sustained effort to formulate and to formalize the highest reaches of human aspiration. While this phenomenon testifies to the persistence, ubiquity, near universality of religious feeling, it runs the danger of distorting the original feeling, of imposing on it a misleading conceptual garb. It may also be bent to nonreligious uses, such as the creation of questionable metaphysical pictures and the exertion of social and political control, establishing special castes of priests, of religious orders, and of church power, that affect all spheres of life. Under some circumstances religiousness may undergo transformations that make it into an opiate of the people.

However, to attack or reject religiousness on these grounds is to identify it with its distortions. The original phenomena of religiousness can be described in some other terms that do not require an object. If that is true, then doctrinal formulations may not necessarily lead in the direction of transcendental theology. We should ask ourselves what pictures or models or concepts would capture the phenomenon of religiousness without leading us in that direction.

We have one negative clue. The model of vision will not do—it is too closely tied to the notion of a transcendent object. Would some other perceptual model be more felicitous? Not likely. All sense perception presupposes an object perceived. We must look in another direction. Perhaps we should think of religiousness as *being in a certain state:* amazement, astonishment, wonder, well-being, fulfillment, satisfaction, assurance, security, safety, ecstasy, joy, and more. In sum, the manifestations of finding the world *good*, as God found it to be when he beheld it following the act of creation, are the symptoms of religiousness. Although triggered by specific events or encounters, the target of such states of mind is not particular events or encounters but the whole scheme of things that made these occurrences possible. Shakespeare's exclamation, "O brave new world that has such people in it!" need not be seen in Huxley's ironic sense. It may be generalized to call attention to the possibility and actuality of genuinely valuable experiences in the world. Rilke's speculations on the meaning of life come to mind:

Are we, perhaps, here just for saying: House, Bridge, Fountain, Gate, Jug, Olive tree, Window,—possibly: Pillar, Tower? . . . but for saying, remember, oh, for such saying as never the things themselves hoped so intensely to be.

Duino Elegies

As we have seen, the universe experiences itself through individual destinies. It celebrates itself in their intellectual, moral, and artistic achievements. Religiousness also lives in centers of consciousness, in individual destinies. A religious feeling may occur in an instant of participation, when we are struck or astonished by the beauty of nature or by the spectacular achievements of other persons. It also may well up from the inner resources in our own attentive and creative moments. In either case, we find ourselves in a heightened state of awareness and appreciation, and we declare the world—and our destiny in it—good.

Celebration, of course, has its counterpart: mourning. But mourning and its various concomitants—suffering, despondency, gloom—are states of a soul capable of appreciating the *loss* of what is being mourned. The depths of spiritual agony are proportionate to the heights of frustrated hopes. Even the devil, we are told, is a fallen angel. The claims made in the name of religion often emphasize its regenerative, redemptive power, but salvation, we should remember, is salvation from hell. The light shineth in the darkness, and the darkness overcometh it not.

Defining religiousness as states of affirmation, whether resulting from either superlative encounters or the conquest of our darkest moments, sidesteps the insuperable problem of transcendence brought on by the unhappy model of vision. At the same time it illustrates our "superontological" proof, namely, that the essence of religiousness implies its existence. This proof turns out to be a truism. Nonetheless, like other truisms defended in this essay, it is a revealing truism, leading us to see more clearly a centrally important dimension of our experience.

Religious belief is more than just an intellectual attitude. It does not seem sufficient to believe *that there* is an object corresponding to that belief. A religious believer is also expected to be related to that object in a certain way. The *belief that* must be supplemented by the *belief in*. Christians are asked to believe *in* God. That relationship is likened to an attitude of trust, reliance, and confidence— analogous to that expressed in the statement, "I believe in John," which really means, "I am convinced of John's integrity, honesty, and goodwill toward me." To believe in God is to trust him, to rely on his power, justice, goodness, and mercy. The linking of the two kinds of belief, namely, believing that God exists and believing in Him, is a function of the Christian conception of God as personal.

But if the target of religiousness is not an independent being, the belief *in* that being, conceived along the lines of believing in a person, is not possible. Is the element of belief altogether irrelevant to religiousness? Not necessarily.

The feeling of religiousness reflects a conviction that the scheme of things makes sense, is meaningful, and provides an indefinite range of positive phenomena that justify it. But the conviction that the world makes sense is a belief based on evidence. This evidence is provided by the very occurrence of phenomena found intrinsically satisfying. Thus it is not merely a matter of faith; it is a matter of knowledge. Our utterly satisfying high-level or peak experiences confirm the knowledge that the world provides suitable material for religious feeling. In other words, the essence of religiousness implies its own existence.

The natural religiousness of man is open to two dangers. It may be usurped by a theoretical tendency to transport the object of religious attitude away from real existence into a mysterious, supernatural, otherworldly, transcendent realm. Alternatively, it may be reduced to something less than it is; religion may be seen as a modest effort of the lonely individual to embellish his life by pursuing moral or aesthetic ideals, by lending his energies to the task of improving mankind, or by discerning in nature some beauty and design. These latter objectives are usually associated with narrower forms of humanism or with the liberal watering down of traditional religious faiths in which the believer ceases really to believe and views all religious pronouncements as only symbolic or metaphorical renderings of the more tender longings of the human heart. . . .

One of the stumbling blocks of religion is the hard and fast dichotomy between the profane and the sacred. "Sunday religion" is one of the effects of such dichotomizing. Actual daily life is much more generous with opportunities for the encounter with values that point in the direction of religious experience. The very notion of value carries with it a claim on our attention. To say that something has value or is valuable is to invite participation in it. There is a difference between declaring that I like something and saying that it is good. The latter is an objective claim. I may like something without claiming that it is good. Indeed, I may confess to liking something knowing full well that it is not worth much. The situation is different when we are inclined to call something good or valuable. When we do so, we are saying that others are likely to find in it something good as well, that its value is objective.

We can enrich our vocabulary while dealing with this point. The term I wish to introduce is the one St. Thomas Aquinas used to characterize beautiful objects. He spoke of them as having *radiance*. Radiance is the capacity of something—object, event, act, or process—to attract attention to itself. Radiance accompanies participation. We are attracted to some features of both nature and man. Paying attention to them, and sometimes being absorbed in them, makes our lives deeper, wiser, better, more thrilling, and more satisfying. All sorts of phenomena, on an indefinite scale of value and attractiveness, can manifest radiance.

Examples of radiance are all around us. When we are moved by music, by a spoken word, by a display of intellectual power, by an admirable deed, a skillful performance, an ingenious invention, by a winning smile, or a generous impulse, we are exposed to their radiance. Their very character is such that it is a loss for us to miss them. If we fail to respond to them, we impoverish our destiny, especially when we waste our attention on something less interesting or less worthy or, even worse, when we dissipate it altogether. . . .

The phenomena we are discussing are not supernatural or otherworldly; they happen in time and in particular human careers. Yet they are the materials for a religious attitude toward one's destiny and toward the destiny of mankind. Things that constitute the flesh and blood of religion are the phenomena of love, aspiration, the urge toward perfection—moral and artistic and scientific. Thus the lives of saints, moral heroes, artistic geniuses, intellectual discoverers, benefactors of mankind (statesmen, scientists, engineers, inventors, ecologists) are the proper subjects for the investigation of the possibilities for participation, radiance, and religion.

The secrets of the universe are stored in the ongoing experience of mankind, in the careers of all human destinies. Rather than seeking the key to these secrets in such shortcuts as empty mystical visions or occult manifestations, we should look for it in the longings and achievements of actual persons, living or dead—in all dimensions of the human spirit. But we need not neglect or ignore the spiritual nourishment available in daily experience, in the arena of our familiar pursuits. My life, my destiny, is where I am, and I should seize the opportunity to respond to radiance around me and to "brighten the corner" where I am. I rob myself when I fail to respond to the beauty around me, whether it is in nature or in the man-made world. I rob others when I fail to use talents that could provide satisfying experiences for them. In either way, my destiny is impoverished—and so is the universe. A religious attitude will not be indifferent to this loss.

Discussion Questions

1. Kolenda says that his view is an alternative one to the view that the concept of God is "a figment of man's imagination" or mere "wish fulfillment." Detail ways in which this is so. If you do not agree that Kolenda has succeeded, give your reasons.

2. Kolenda states that "perhaps we should think of religiousness as being in a certain state: amazement, astonishment, wonder, well-being, fulfillment, satisfaction, assurance, security, safety, ecstasy, joy, and more." Do you agree? Why or why not?

3. It is a mistake, Kolenda says, to reduce human religiousness to merely "a modest effort of the lonely individual to embellish his life by pursuing moral or aesthetic ideals," and he denies that his view amounts to this. Explain in what ways you find his view different from this.

4. Kolenda offers what he calls a superontological proof. Explain.

5. A key notion for understanding the religiousness Kolenda describes is *radiance*. Can you think of other ways of describing the same experience?

Religion and Life

The relationship of religion to life can be discussed on many levels, and we have examined only two of them. The first is the proper goal of life and how we are to know it, and we saw two very different answers. Paley's answer is simple and direct: Life's goal is to obey God's will. A contrasting answer given by Nietzsche for those living in the age of the "death of God" is that life's goal is to create our own values and meaning. A second question is whether life can be meaningful without belief in a transcendent God. Leo Tolstoy and Konstantin Kolenda provide us with opposite answers to this question. Tolstoy argues that only belief in a transcendent God can rescue human beings from despair over life's meaning. Kolenda argues that belief in the traditional God of Jewish and Christian theism is not necessary to support the view that "the scheme of things makes sense" and is meaningful.

The German theologian Rudolf Bultmann argued that modern, secular humans could no longer believe in the worldview of the New Testament and that the message of the gospel should be demythologized, that is, stripped of its outdated prescientific trappings. Without this, so Bultmann thought, the essential message of the gospel, which is one of self-renewal and the discovery of authenticity, would not occur.

We see much that contradicts Bultmann's claim. Contemporary scientifically trained persons seem perfectly able to believe both in the durability of scientific methods of inquiry and in a transcendent being and the world presented by such belief. Even those who are not attracted to the traditional canons of religious belief seem to be searching for something more than a spiritless universe that operates according to the impersonal laws of cause and effect. Books touting belief in angels are a modern growth industry, and various forms of spirituality abound. There will always be those who believe that we can, and will, find meaning in life without appealing to a transcendent reality. And there will always be those who argue that without such belief, there is no lasting meaning for life. It is a debate that is likely to continue.

ADDITIONAL READINGS

Two excellent collections of essays on the relation between religion and ethics are Gene Outka and John P. Reeder, Jr., eds., *Religion and Morality* (Garden City, NY: Doubleday-Anchor, 1973), and Ian Ramsey, ed., *Christian Ethics and Contemporary Philosophy* (London: SCM Press, 1966). Another fine source for a summary and bibliography is Patrick H. Nowell-Smith, "Religion and Morality," in

The Encyclopedia of Philosophy (1967), 7, 150–58. An interesting discussion of issues related to the themes of this chapter is Paul Edwards, "Life, Meaning and Value of," in *The Encyclopedia of Philosophy* (1967), 4, 467–77. A good collection of essays on the connections between religion and life is the book edited by Joseph Runzo, *Ethics, Religion, and the Good Society* (Louisville: Westminster/John Knox Press, 1992). Reflections for how religious belief brings value to life is the theme of Howard Lesnick, *Listening for God: Religion and Moral Discernment* (New York: Fordham University Press, 1998).

CHAPTER 3

RELIGION AND HUMAN DESTINY

INTRODUCTION

Religion and Death

That everybody dies is a fact confirmed by experience. But is death the end of everything for an individual? At death the body decays and returns to dust, but what of the *soul*, the *ego*, the *self*? Does the consciousness of the individual survive the dissolution of the body? If so, how?

This constellation of questions represents an ancient human concern. The earliest Greek philosophers dealt with death and the proper human attitude toward this inevitable fact. Human beings seem to be unique among the earth's creatures in that we not only die but are also fully aware of the inevitability of death; coupled with this awareness seems to be a refusal to believe that death is the end. Among peoples both ancient and modern can be found the stubborn conviction that there is some kind of future existence in store for us, and this is a belief that seems to span all cultures and all periods. The belief in some kind of future life seems to have been present even in the Neanderthal age. Archaeologists have discovered that prehistoric graves were filled with food and implements, presumably intended to be used by the deceased in a future life—a testimony to the belief in some kind of afterlife among our earliest ancestors.

Attitudes toward death are conditioned by other viewpoints, particularly our attitude toward the nature of human reality. If we think that human beings are something special and unique in nature, this would seem to reinforce the conviction that human beings are in some sense immune to the inevitable destruction and decay that are an intrinsic part of nature. If, on the other hand, we accept the naturalistic view that human beings are just another part of nature, a chance byproduct of an impersonal cosmos, then human destiny would appear to be to live for a few years and then cease to exist totally and completely. Both of these viewpoints have appeared whenever human beings began to reflect on death, and neither of them can be characterized as a particularly modern view.

The startling thing about us is that we try to avoid thinking about death at all. We are perhaps more removed from death than any previous people. Unlike former peoples who confronted death almost constantly, many of us have never seen a person die. We segregate our dying and place them in sterile surroundings to pass away out of the sight of friends and loved ones. We treat death as a kind of obscenity not to be mentioned in polite company, and all the skills of the contemporary funeral industry are calculated to shield us from the brutal fact of death. We do not even refer to the dead directly, but instead speak of the "deceased," the "departed," or the "loved one." All the skills of the cosmetic arts are employed to make a corpse appear "natural" as it lies in an expensive hardwood casket, cushioned in layers of velvet and satin. If some future archaeologists were to attempt to reconstruct our attitudes toward death from our burial practices, they would probably conclude that our primary interest was in disguising death.

THREE ATTITUDES TOWARD DEATH

The fact of death presents philosophy with a strange paradox. On the one hand, empirical evidence tells us that everyone dies. But we know so little of death, that it is at once the most obvious and the least well-known fact of human existence. For a philosophy wedded to stubborn empirical facts, death is a closed topic; yet the anticipation of death and even the fear of death are also empirical facts that must be taken into account in any serious philosophical reflection on the nature of human existence. Although variations exist in these views, there are basically three attitudes toward death and human destiny that have appeared in the history of philosophy and are also represented in various religious traditions.

The first view is that the soul is immortal by nature and will survive the dissolution of the body. This is Plato's view, and it is based on a distinction between the body and the soul that inhabits the body. At death the body decays, but the soul escapes the imprisonment of the body, to live on. This view of the soul's natural immortality was incorporated into both Christian and Jewish thought in the Middle Ages.

The second view, in some sense the opposite of the first, is that there is no separate soul substance, but that the soul or "life" of the body is merely a function of the material nature of the body. When the body dies, the activity we refer to as life, or consciousness, ceases, and there is no continued consciousness after death. This view was held by ancient Greek philosophers who accepted a materialistic view of reality and is represented in this chapter by the selection from Epicurus.

A third view is that the soul or life of the individual is not immortal by nature but one can hope, through the power of God, for a re-creation in a new embodied existence. This is the view of Christianity.

Still another view is the Buddhist rejection of any idea of an individual, permanent soul or self. According to Buddhists this is an imaginary and false belief that creates harmful thoughts of attachment, craving, and selfishness. The Buddhist no-soul doctrine offers an alternative and is coupled with the view that release from cravings for an enduring ego leads to enlightenment. Since there is no separate or permanent human soul, there is nothing to survive death.

SOME CENTRAL QUESTIONS

The philosophical literature dealing with death and human destiny focuses on three principal concerns:

1. What evidence supports the belief that death is not the end of consciousness?
2. What is the proper attitude toward death—fear or calm acceptance?
3. Is life more, or less, meaningful if death is the end of all consciousness?

The first question is directly confronted in the selection from Plato and in the passage from the New Testament, though the two answers are not the same. The second question is central to all the readings in this chapter, but especially to that from Epicurus. Finally, the third question is essential to the views of Buddhism as articulated by Walpola Rahula.

The third question will call for your own philosophical analysis. Do you find life more meaningful on the supposition of continued existence after death, or does the possibility of death as the end of all consciousness make this present life more meaningful? We will return to this question in the retrospective to the chapter.

The Immortality of the Soul

The idea that death is not the end of consciousness is an ancient belief. It seems to be as old as early humanoid activity. The noted philosopher John Hick, who has written extensively on this topic, gives the following summary:

> Neanderthal man, living on earth from about 100,000 to about 25,000 years ago, placed food and flint implements in the graves which he dug. Old Stone Age men, the Cro-Magnons, who roamed through southern Europe and Africa from about 25,000 to about 10,000 years ago, hunting bison, horses, and other large beasts, likewise buried weapons, ornaments and food with their dead and daubed red ochre (the colour of blood) on corpses or in graves. In the New Stone Age, from about 10,000 to about 5,000 years ago, neolithic men adopted even more complex funeral practices. . . . All this shows that our prehistoric ancestors assumed that in some sense and in some form humans continue to exist after their deaths, so as to have a use for the precious objects which were buried with them.[1]

When the idea of an existence after death arose among the ancient Greeks, it was not necessarily a hopeful doctrine. According to views that can be traced back to Homer, the dead inhabit a realm known as Hades (which means "the realm of the unseen"), where even the shades of people dwell in a shadowy existence that could not even be called consciousness. The authority on ancient Greek philosophy, John Burnet, suggests that "the traditional Athenian beliefs about the soul were cheerless enough, and we cannot wonder at the popularity of the Eleusinian Mysteries, which promised a better lot of some sort to the initiated after death."[2] The Eleusinian Mysteries Burnet refers to was one of a number of secret societies that promised their members a better lot in the next world. These mystery religions were so successful in keeping their rites secret that not much is known about them, except that they were extremely popular.

---

[1] John Hick, *Death and Eternal Life* (New York: Harper & Row, 1976), p. 55.
[2] John Burnet, "The Socratic Doctrine of the Soul," *Proceedings of the British Academy*, 1915–16 (London: Published for the British Academy by Humphrey Milford, Oxford University Press, 1916), p. 248.

Not all Greek thinkers shared this belief in an afterlife, as the next selection from Epicurus will show. However, belief in the soul's immortality was a common doctrine in Greek antiquity, and in the fourth century B.C.E. the Greek philosopher Plato attempted to give philosophical support to this view. When Plato speaks of the soul's immortality, though, he means not only that the soul survives the death of the body but that the soul also existed before its birth into a body. By suggesting a radical distinction between the soul and body, Plato emphasizes the importance of purifying the soul through the pursuit of wisdom and virtue. The body (*soma*) is the prison of the soul (*psyche*), and the goal of life is to be freed from the entrapment of the body, which belongs to the sensible world and shares its corruptible nature. The soul is related to the unchanging and imperishable realm of eternal reality, wisdom is the pursuit of the eternal, and in this quest the body is only a hindrance to the soul. In Plato's view the entire life of a philosopher should be a turning away from the body toward the soul and the eternal. This is the pursuit of wisdom, and philosophy is the love of wisdom.

According to Plato's views, the soul of a philosopher at death is freed from the cycle of death and rebirth and will not have to be reborn into another body. But a soul that has not been purified by the pursuit of wisdom will be reborn into another body and can achieve release from the cycle of death and rebirth only if it devotes itself to the search for wisdom in some subsequent incarnation. For Plato, philosophy is a way to salvation. There are echoes here of themes from Hindu thought with its doctrines of karma and reincarnation.

In the selection that follows from Plato's work known as *Phaedo*, he advances arguments for the soul's immortality and attempts to demonstrate that the pursuit of virtue and the purification of the soul is life's most important task. Plato puts these words into the mouth of his teacher Socrates, and the occasion for this discussion is the impending death by poison that Socrates faces as the sentence of an Athens court. The reasons for this sentence are detailed in others of Plato's works, but in *Phaedo* we see why Socrates is willing to submit to the sentence even if it is unjust. One interpretation of these events is that the Athenian court did not really expect the sentence to be carried out, assuming that the friends and followers of Socrates would help him escape from imprisonment. That, however, Socrates refuses to do on the grounds that, were he to do so, he would be guilty of flaunting the laws of Athens, and that would be an unjust act deserving punishment. Besides, he argues, death is not the greatest of evils, and in the ensuing discussion with two of his followers—Simmias and Cebes—Socrates examines various arguments for the view that death is not the end of consciousness.

Though Socrates finds some of the arguments weaker than others, the conclusion of the discussion is inescapable to him: "The soul is immortal and imperishable, and our souls will indeed exist in the other world." As you read through this dialogue, ask yourself which of the arguments you find most convincing and if you have encountered them in other forms.

Phaedo

PLATO

Good, said Simmias; I will tell you my difficulty, and Cebes will tell you why he is dissatisfied with your statement. I think, Socrates, and I daresay you think so too, that it is very difficult, and perhaps impossible, to obtain clear knowledge about these matters in this life. Yet I should hold him to be a very poor creature who did not test what is said about them in every way, and persevere until he had examined the question from every side, and could do no more. It is our duty to do one of two things. We must learn, or we must discover for ourselves, the truth of these matters; or, if that be impossible, we must take the best and most irrefragable of human doctrines and, embarking on that, as on a raft, risk the voyage of life, unless a stronger vessel, some divine word, could be found, on which we might take our journey more safely and more securely. And now, after what you have said, I shall not be ashamed to put a question to you; and then I shall not have to blame myself hereafter for not having said now what I think. Cebes and I have been considering your argument, and we think that it is hardly sufficient.

I daresay you are right, my friend, said Socrates. But tell me, where is it insufficient?

To me it is insufficient, he replied, because the very same argument might be used of a harmony, and a lyre, and its strings. It might be said that the harmony in a tuned lyre is something unseen, and incorporeal, and perfectly beautiful, and divine, while the lyre and its strings are corporeal, and with the nature of bodies, and compounded, and earthly, and akin to the mortal. Now suppose that, when the lyre is broken and the strings are cut or snapped, a man were to press the same argument that you have used, and were to say that the harmony cannot have perished and that it must still exist, for it cannot possibly be that the lyre and the strings, with their mortal nature, continue to exist, though those strings have been broken, while the harmony, which is of the same nature as the divine and the immortal, and akin to them, has perished, and perished before the mortal lyre. He would say that the harmony itself must still exist somewhere, and that the wood and the strings will rot away before anything happens to it. And I think, Socrates, that you too must be aware that many of us believe the soul to be most probably a mixture and harmony of the elements by which our body is, as it were, strung and held together, such as heat and cold,

Source: Plato, *Phaedo,* trans. F. J. Church. © 1951. Reprinted by permission of Prentice Hall, Upper Saddle River, NJ. (Footnotes deleted.)

and dry and wet, and the like, when they are mixed together well and in due proportion, or overstrung by disease or other evils, the soul, though most divine, must perish at once, like other harmonies of sound and of all works of art, while what remains of each body must remain for a long time, until it be burned or rotted away. What then shall we say to a man who asserts that the soul, being a mixture of the elements of the body, perishes first at what is called death? . . .

And, consider the question in another way, Simmias, said Socrates. Do you think that a harmony or any other composition can exist in a state other than the state of the elements of which it is composed?

Certainly not.

Nor, I suppose, can it do or suffer anything beyond what they do and suffer?

He assented.

A harmony therefore cannot lead the elements of which it is composed; it must follow them?

He agreed.

And much less can it be moved, or make a sound, or do anything else in opposition to its parts.

Much less, indeed, he replied.

Well, is not every harmony by nature a harmony according as it is adjusted?

I don't understand you, he replied.

If it is tuned more, and to a greater extent, he said, supposing that to be possible, will it not be more a harmony, and to a greater extent, while if it is tuned less, and to a smaller extent, will it not be less a harmony, and to a smaller extent?

Certainly.

Well, is this true of the soul? Can one soul be more a soul, and to a greater extent, or less a soul, and to a smaller extent, than another, even in the smallest degree?

Certainly not, he replied.

Well then, he replied, please tell me this; is not one soul said to have intelligence and virtue and to be good, while another is said to have folly and vice and to be bad? And is it not true?

Yes, certainly.

What then will those who assert that the soul is a harmony say that the virtue and the vice which are in our souls are? Another harmony and another discord? Will they say that the good soul is in tune, and that, herself a harmony, she has within herself another harmony, and that the bad soul is out of tune herself, and has no other harmony within her?

I, said Simmias, cannot tell. But it is clear that they would have to say something of the kind.

But it has been conceded, he said, that one soul is never more or less a soul than another. In other words, we have agreed that one harmony is never more, or to a greater extent, or less, or to a smaller extent a harmony than another. Is it not so?

Yes, certainly.

And the harmony which is neither more nor less a harmony, is not more or less tuned. Is that so?

Yes.

And has that which is neither more nor less tuned a greater, or a less, or an equal share of harmony?

An equal share.

Then, since one soul is never more nor less a soul than another, it has not been more or less tuned either?

True.

Therefore it can have no greater share of harmony or of discord?

Certainly not.

And, therefore, can one soul contain more vice or virtue than another, if vice be discord and virtue harmony?

By no means.

Or rather, Simmias, to speak quite accurately, I suppose that there will be no vice in any soul if the soul is a harmony. I take it there can never be any discord in a harmony which is a perfect harmony.

Certainly not.

Neither can a soul, if it be a perfect soul, have any vice in it?

No; that follows necessarily from what has been said.

Then the result of this reasoning is that all the souls of all living creatures will be equally good if the nature of all souls is to be equally souls.

Yes, I think so, Socrates, he said.

And do you think that this is true, he asked, and that this would have been the fate of our argument, if the hypothesis that the soul is a harmony had been correct?

No, certainly not, he replied.

Well, said he, of all the parts of a man, should you not say that it was the soul, and particularly the wise soul, which rules?

I should.

Does she yield to the passions of the body or does she oppose them? I mean this. When the body is hot and thirsty, does not the soul drag it away and prevent it from drinking, and when it is hungry does she not prevent it from eating? And do we not see her opposing the passions of the body in a thousand other ways?

Yes, certainly.

But we have also agreed that, if she is a harmony, she can never give a sound contrary to the tensions, and relaxations, and vibrations, and other changes of the elements of which she is composed; that she must follow them, and can never lead them?

Yes, he replied, we certainly have.

Well, now, do we not find the soul acting in just the opposite way, and leading all the elements of which she is said to consist, and opposing them in almost everything all through life; and lording it over them in every way, and chastising them, sometimes severely, and with a painful discipline, such as gymnastic and medicine, and sometimes lightly; sometimes threatening and sometimes admonishing the desires and passions and fears, as though she were speaking to something other than herself, as Homer makes Odysseus do in the *Odyssey*, where he says that

> He smote upon his breast, and chid his heart:
> "Endure, my heart, e'en worse hast thou endured."

Do you think that when Homer wrote that, he supposed the soul to be a harmony and capable of being led by the passions of the body, and not of a nature to lead them and be their lord, being herself far too divine a thing to be like a harmony?

Certainly, Socrates, I think not.

Then, my excellent friend, it is quite wrong to say that the soul is a harmony. For then, you see, we should not be in agreement either with the divine poet Homer or with ourselves.

That is true, he replied. . . .

My good friend, said Socrates, do not be overconfident, or some evil eye will overturn the argument that is to come. However, that we will leave to God; let us, like Homer's heroes, "advancing boldly," see if there is anything in what you say. The sum of what you seek is this. You require me to prove to you that the soul is indestructible and immortal; for if it be not so, you think that the confidence of a philosopher, who is confident in death, and who believes that when he is dead he will fare infinitely better in the other world than if he had lived a different sort of life in this world, is a foolish and idle confidence. You say that to show that the soul is strong and godlike, and that she existed before we were born men, is not enough; for that does not necessarily prove her immortality, but only that she lasts a long time, and has existed an enormous while, and has known and done many things in a previous state. Yet she is not any the more immortal for that; her very entrance into man's body was, like a disease, the beginning of her destruction. And, you say, she passes this life in misery, and at last perishes in what we call death. You think that it makes no difference at all to the fears of each one of us, whether she enters the body once or many times; for everyone but a fool must fear death, if he does not know and cannot prove that she is immortal. That, I think, Cebes, is the substance of your objection. I state it again and again on purpose, that nothing may escape us, and that you may add to it or take away from it anything that you wish.

Cebes replied: No, that is my meaning. I don't want to add or to take away anything at present.

Socrates paused for some time and thought. Then he said, It is not an easy question that you are raising, Cebes. We must examine fully the whole subject of the causes of generation and decay. If you like, I will give you my own experiences, and if you think that you can make use of anything that I say, you may employ it to satisfy your misgivings.

Indeed, said Cebes, I should like to hear your experiences.

Listen, then, and I will tell you, Cebes, he replied. When I was a young man, I had a passionate desire for the wisdom which is called Physical Science. I thought it a splendid thing to know the causes of everything; why a thing comes into being, and why it perishes, and why it exists. I was always worrying myself with such questions as, Do living creatures take a definite form, as some persons say, from the fermentation of heat and cold? Is it the blood, or the air, or fire by which we think? Or is it none of these, but the brain which gives the senses of hearing and sight and smell, and do memory and opinion come from these, and knowledge from memory and opinion when in a state of quiescence? Again, I used to examine the destruction of these things, and the changes of the heaven and the earth, until at last I concluded that I was wholly and absolutely unfitted for these studies. I will prove that to you conclusively. I was so completely blinded by these studies that I forgot what I had formerly seemed to myself and to others to know quite well; I unlearned all that I had been used to think that I understood; even the cause of man's growth. Formerly I had thought it evident on the face of it that the cause of growth was eating and drinking, and that, when from food flesh is added to flesh, and bone to bone, and in the same way to the other parts of the body their proper elements, then by degrees the small bulk grows to be large, and so the boy becomes a man. Don't you think that my belief was reasonable?

I do, said Cebes.

Then here is another experience for you. I used to feel no doubt, when I saw a tall man standing by a short one, that the tall man was, it might be, a head the taller, or, in the same way, that one horse was bigger than another. I was even clearer that ten was more than eight by the addition of two, and that a thing two cubits long was longer by half its length than a thing one cubit long.

And what do you think now? asked Cebes.

I think that I am very far from believing that I know the cause of any of these things. Why, when you add one to one, I am not sure either that the one to which one is added has become two, or that the one added and the one to which it is added become, by the addition, two. I cannot understand how, when they are brought together, this union, or placing of one by the other, should be the cause of their becoming two, whereas, when they were separated, each of them was one, and they were not two. Nor, again, if you divide one into two, can I convince myself that this division is the cause of one becoming two; for then a thing becomes two from exactly the opposite cause. In the former case it was because two units were brought together, and the one was added to the other; while now it is because they are separated, and the one divided from the other. Nor, again, can I persuade myself that I know how one is generated; in short, this method does not show me the cause of the generation or destruction or existence of anything. I have in my own mind a confused idea of another method, but I cannot admit this one for a moment.

But one day I listened to a man who said that he was reading from a book of Anaxagoras, which affirmed that it is Mind which orders and is the cause of all things. I was delighted with this theory; it seemed to me to be right that Mind should be the cause of all things, and I thought to myself, If this is so, then Mind will order and arrange each thing in the best possible way. So if we wish to discover the cause of the generation or destruction or existence of a thing, we must discover how it is best for that thing to exist, or to act, or to be acted on. Man therefore has only to consider what is best and fittest for himself, or for other things, and then it follows necessarily that he will know what is bad; for both are included in the same science. These reflections made me very happy: I thought that I had found in Anaxagoras a teacher of the cause of existence after my own heart, and I expected that he would tell me first whether the earth is flat or round, and that he would then go on to explain to me the cause and the necessity, and tell me what is best, and that it is best for the earth to be of that shape. If he said that the earth was in the center of the universe, I thought that he would explain that it was best for it to be there; and I was prepared not to require any other kind of cause, if he made this clear to me. In the same way I was prepared to ask questions about the sun, and the moon, and the stars, about their relative speeds, and revolutions, and changes; and to hear why it is best for each of them to act and be acted on as they are acted on. I never thought that, when he said that things are ordered by Mind, he would introduce any reason for their being as they are, except that they are best so. I thought that he would assign a cause to each thing, and a cause to the universe, and then would go on to explain to me what was best for each thing, and what was the common good of all. I would not have sold my hopes for a great deal: I seized the books very eagerly, and read them as fast as I could, in order that I might know what is best and what is worse.

All my splendid hopes were dashed to the ground, my friend, for as I went on reading I found that the writer made no use of Mind at all, and that he assigned no causes for the order of things. His causes were air, and ether, and water, and many other strange things. I thought that he was exactly like a man who should begin by saying that Socrates does all that he does by Mind, and who, when he tried to give a reason for each of my actions, should say, first, that I am sitting here now, because my body is composed of bones and muscles, and that the bones are hard and separated by joints, while the muscles can be tightened and loosened, and, together with the flesh and the skin which holds them together, cover the bones; and that therefore, when the bones are raised in their sockets, the relaxation and contraction of the muscles make it possible for me now to bend my limbs, and that that is the cause of my sitting here with my legs bent. And in the same way he would go on to explain why I am talking to you: he would assign voice, and air, and hearing, and a thousand other things as causes; but he would quite forget to mention the real cause, which is that since the Athenians thought it right to condemn me, I have thought it right and just to sit here and to submit to whatever sentence they may think fit to impose. . . .

I follow you and entirely agree with you, he said.

Now begin again, and answer me, he said. And imitate me; do not answer me in the terms of my question: I mean, do not give the old safe answer which I have already spoken of, for I see another way of safety, which is the result of what we have been saying. If you ask me, what is that which must be in the body to make it hot, I shall not give our old safe and stupid answer, and say that it is heat; I shall make a more refined answer, drawn from what we have been saying, and reply, fire. If you ask me, what is that which must be in the body to make it sick, I shall not say sickness, but fever; and again to the question what is that which must be in number to make it odd, I shall not reply oddness, but unity, and so on. Do you understand my meaning clearly yet?

Yes, quite, he said.

Then, he went on, tell me, what is that which must be in a body to make it alive?

A soul, he replied.

And is this always so?

Of course, he said.

Then the soul always brings life to whatever contains her?

No doubt, he answered.

And is there an opposite to life, or not?

Yes. What is it?

Death.

And we have already agreed that the soul cannot ever receive the opposite of what she brings?

Yes, certainly we have, said Cebes.

Well; what name did we give to that which does not admit the idea of the even?

The uneven, he replied. And what do we call that which does not admit justice or music?

The unjust, and the unmusical.

Good; and what do we call that which does not admit death?

The immortal, he said.

And the soul does not admit death? No. Then the soul is immortal?

It is.

Good, he said. Shall we say that this is proved? What do you think?

Yes, Socrates, and very sufficiently.

Well, Cebes, he said, if the odd had been necessarily imperishable, must not three have been imperishable?

Of course.

And if cold had been necessarily imperishable, snow would have retired safe and unmelted, whenever warmth was applied to it. It would not have perished, and it would not have stayed and admitted the heat.

True, he said.

In the same way, I suppose, if warmth were imperishable, whenever cold attacked fire, the fire would never have been extinguished or have perished. It would have gone away in safety.

Necessarily, he replied.

And must we not say the same of the immortal? he asked. If the immortal is imperishable, the soul cannot perish when death comes upon her. It follows from what we have said that she will not ever admit death, or be in a state of death, any more than three, or the odd itself, wilt ever be even, or fire, or the heat itself which is in fire, cold. But, it may be said, Granted that the odd does not become even at the approach of the even; why, when the odd has perished, may not the even come into its place? We could not contend in reply that it does not perish, for the uneven is not imperishable; if we had agreed that the uneven was imperishable, we could have easily contended that the odd and three go away at the approach of the even; and we could have urged the same contention about fire and heat and the rest, could we not?

Yes, certainly.

And now, if we are agreed that the immortal is imperishable, then the soul will be not immortal only, but also imperishable; otherwise we shall require another argument.

Nay, he said, there is no need of that, as far as this point goes; for if the immortal, which is eternal, will admit of destruction, what will not?

And all men would admit, said Socrates that God, and the essential form of life, and all else that is immortal, never perishes.

All men, indeed, he said; and, what is more, I think, all gods would admit that.

Then if the immortal is indestructible, must not the soul, if it be immortal, be imperishable?

Certainly, it must.

Then, it seems, when death attacks a man, his mortal part dies, but his immortal part retreats before death, and goes away safe and indestructible.

It seems so.

Then, Cebes, said he, beyond all question the soul is immortal and imperishable, and our souls wilt indeed exist in the other world.

Discussion Questions

1. Which of the arguments advanced in the dialogue do you find to be most compelling? The least?

2. Plato here defends the view that immortality means life *before* birth as well as *after* death. What arguments does the dialogue advance to support such a view?

3. There is a dualism of mind/body assumed in the discussion. What reasons are advanced to support the superiority of the mental over the physical?

4. Plato's theory of knowledge is used implicitly to support belief in the soul's immortality. Explain.

5. In the examination of the issues, Socrates gives reasons for repudiating a materialistic view of reality. What are they? Is a materialistic view incompatible with belief in the soul's immortality?

The Finality of Death

Not all ancient Greeks accepted the attitude toward death expressed by Plato. For most the prospect of death created a sense of terror, and this partially explains the popularity of the mystery religions with their offer of safe passage through the underworld and the hope of a brighter future in the life to come.

An alternative view of reality found expression in the works of two Greek philosophers of the fifth century B.C.E.—Democritus and his contemporary Leucippus. These two thinkers are credited with developing the view known as atomism, a form of materialism that left no place for any doctrine of personal immortality. According to the atomist view of reality, all things are composed of atoms—small, indivisible bits of matter—that differ from each other only in size and shape. The atoms are the irreducible building blocks of reality and cannot be further divided; the very term "atom" itself means "uncuttable," that is, something that cannot be divided into additional component parts. In the generation of new things, atoms are arranged into ever-increasing levels of complexity until animal life emerges, human beings appear, and thought processes develop. In the process of decay and corruption atoms find new arrangements and new combinations; they are used over and over again, but objects composed of them are only temporary and transitory. When a human being dies, the atoms that composed the person's body will be reused in some other reality. The human soul, according to the atomists, being composed of extremely small atoms, simply dissipates into the upper atmosphere. How do the atoms become organized and arranged into complex entities such as worlds and their contents? It is purely by chance, the atomists argued. The motion of the atoms sometimes produces order and sometimes it produces chaos. There is no overarching mind directing the process. There are no ultimate purposes. Everything is temporary and fleeting.

The atomistic theory of Democritus and Leucippus provided an explanation for the view that it is folly to think of human beings as immortal. Only the gods are immortal. Did the Greeks really believe all the stories about the gods contained in the popular stories and fables? Maybe, maybe not. Regardless of whether they really believed the myths behind the popular ceremonies, they did make a decisive distinction between the mortality of humans and the immortality of divine beings.

In this context, the doctrine of a future life was at best speculative. It was only later that belief in the doctrine of the human soul's immortality became widespread. When Plato argued for the soul's immortality it was perceived by some of his contemporaries as a new and startling doctrine, as evidenced by Glaucon's incredulous response to it in the tenth book of Plato's *Republic* (608D). Regardless of which view of reality they held, most people still looked upon death with fear and dread. It was this attitude that the atomists sought to dispel.

The atomistic theory is strikingly modern in some respects. The attempt to explain reality in terms of matter in motion seems to predate some of the views of contemporary scientific thought. Though today atoms are not considered to be little bits of stuff floating through space, the basic view that the complex objects we observe can be explained in terms of more fundamental building blocks that we cannot observe is compatible with the way science looks at the world.

The materialistic metaphysics of Democritus and Leucippus provided the framework for the ethical writings of the Greek philosopher Epicurus, and it is in his work that we see the logical implications of atomism. It is the *fear* of death, not death itself, that is the enemy. If death means the complete cessation of consciousness, as the atomists taught, then death becomes a nonissue. Epicurus was simple and direct on this point: "Death . . . is therefore of no concern to us; for while we exist death is not present, and when death is present we no longer exist." And with a sentiment that Buddhist thinkers would find appealing, Epicurus says that the desire for immortality of one's soul or self is what brings unhappiness. Take away that desire and you take away the unhappiness associated with it.

But what about life lived on these terms? Does the loss of hope for a future life render the present one less meaningful? Epicurus gives answers that are straightforward and clear. Pleasure is the goal of life, but the wise person brings reason to bear on this pursuit. After laying out his agreement with the views of Leucippus, whom he cites in the following extract, Epicurus proceeds to explain how the prudent and thoughtful person will live given the transitory nature of human existence. In his ethical writings Epicurus counsels moderation, for both privation and excess bring pain. The good and happy life is one lived without dependence on expensive and fleeting pleasures, costly food and drink, or a life of debauchery. It is better to eat plain food, enjoy simple pleasures, and take delight in the life of the mind. It is ironic that the name *epicure* now refers to the person who seeks rarefied and costly food and drink. Though the term comes from his name, Epicurus would not have been pleased with this application. The life Epicurus recommended would strike most of us as entirely the opposite of that sought by the epicure.

Epicurus offers an interesting contrast to Plato. Whenever human beings have reflected on questions of human destiny, both views have cropped up: the view that we survive death, and the opposing view that death is the end of all consciousness. It is an old debate, and one that is likely to continue.

Letter to Menoeceus

EPICURUS

I. INTRODUCTION

Epicurus to Menoeceus, greeting.

Let no young man delay the study of philosophy, and let no old man become weary of it; for it is never too early nor too late to care for the well-being of the soul. The man who says that the season for this study has not yet come or is already past is like the man who says it is too early or too late for happiness. Therefore, both the young and the old should study philosophy, the former so that as he grows old he may still retain the happiness of youth in his pleasant memories of the past, the latter so that although he is old he may at the same time be young by virtue of his fearlessness of the future. We must therefore study the means of securing happiness, since if we have it we have everything, but if we lack it we do everything in order to gain it.

II. BASIC TEACHINGS

A. The Gods

The gods exist; but it is impious to accept the common beliefs about them. They have no concern with men.[1]

Practice and study without ceasing that which I was always teaching you, being assured that these are the first principles of the good life. After accepting god as the immortal and blessed being depicted by popular opinion, do not ascribe to him anything in addition that is alien to immortality or foreign to blessedness, but rather believe about him whatever can uphold his blessed immortality. The gods do indeed exist, for our perception of them is clear; but they are not such as the crowd imagines them to be, for most men do not retain the picture of the gods that they first receive. It is not the man who destroys the gods of popular belief who is impious, but he who describes the gods in the terms accepted by the many. For the opinions of the many about the gods are not perceptions but false

Source: Letters, Principal Doctrines, and Vatican Sayings by Epicurus, trans. R. Geer. © 1964. Reprinted by permission of Prentice Hall, Upper Saddle River, NJ.

[1] See Lucretius, I. 62–135, *et passim*.

suppositions. According to these popular suppositions, the gods send great evils to the wicked, great blessings (to the righteous), for they, being always well disposed to their own virtues, approve those who are like themselves, regarding as foreign all that is different.

B. Death

> *Philosophy showing that death is the end of all consciousness relieves us of all fear of death. A life that is happy is better than one that is merely long.*[2]

Accustom yourself to the belief that death is of no concern to us, since all good and evil lie in sensation and sensation ends with death. Therefore the true belief that death is nothing to us makes a mortal life happy, not by adding to it an infinite time, but by taking away the desire for immortality. For there is no reason why the man who is thoroughly assured that there is nothing to fear in death should find anything to fear in life. So, too, he is foolish who says that he fears death, not because it will be painful when it comes, but because the anticipation of it is painful; for that which is no burden when it is present gives pain to no purpose when it is anticipated. Death, the most dreaded of evils, is therefore of no concern to us; for while we exist death is not present, and when death is present we no longer exist. It is therefore nothing either to the living or to the dead since it is not present to the living, and the dead no longer are.

But men in general sometimes flee death as the greatest of evils, sometimes (long for it) as a relief from (the evils) of life. (The wise man neither renounces life) nor fears its end; for living does not offend him, nor does he suppose that not to live is in any way an evil. As he does not choose the food that is most in quantity but that which is most pleasant, so he does not seek the enjoyment of the longest life but of the happiest.

He who advises the young man to live well, the old man to die well, is foolish, not only because life is desirable, but also because the art of living well and the art of dying well are one. Yet much worse is he who says that it is well not to have been born, but

> *once born, be swift to pass through Hades' gates.*[3]

If a man says this and really believes it, why does he not depart from life? Certainly the means are at hand for doing so if this really be his firm conviction. If he says it in mockery, he is regarded as a fool among those who do not accept his teaching.

---

[2] See Lucretius, III. 830–1094.
[3] Theognis, vss. 425, 427.

Remember that the future is neither ours nor wholly not ours, so that we may neither count on it as sure to come nor abandon hope of it as certain not to be. . . .

Discussion Questions

1. Epicurus said that his view is not pessimistic. Do you agree? Why or why not?

2. One of the claims Epicurus made was that it is the quality of life, not its quantity, that is important. What argument does he offer for this claim?

3. Does atomism logically entail that death is the end of human consciousness, or can one accept the metaphysics of atomism and still believe in life after death?

4. What aspects of Epicurus's views do you find appealing? What aspects do you find unappealing?

5. Epicurus argued for moderation in all things. Assuming the same view of ultimate reality as he held, could one argue the opposite and still be consistent? Explain.

The Hope for Resurrection

Contemporary attitudes toward death and human destiny have deep roots. The view that one's death is the end of one's consciousness finds its antecedents in the Greek atomists and their materialistic metaphysics. Those believing in the possibility of pastlife regressions and those whose near-death experiences convince them that death is not final continue the ancient belief that the soul lives on after death. A third view that is as old as Christianity is the hope for resurrection from the dead. This doctrine is embedded in the earliest Christian creeds and, according to the New Testament, is central to the Christian faith.

With its roots in Judaism, Christianity shared the same view of human nature as did the religion of Israel—that is, to be human is to be in a body. For most of its pre-Christian period, Judaism did not possess any view of an afterlife. It focused instead on the ethical obligations of living in covenant relationship with God. Like the Greeks, the ancient Hebrews had a vague notion that the soul (*nephesh*) of a person went at death into the shadowy world of *Sheol*, a place comparable to the Greek *Hades*. *Sheol* was a land of forgetfulness where nothing was totally real. Occasionally, but very rarely, do Jewish Scriptures suggest that a shade from *Sheol* can be called back to earth—as the shade of the prophet Samuel was called back to speak to King Saul at the request of the witch of Endor.[1] But this occurrence is rare in Jewish thought, and had no enduring religious significance.

It was only in the late books of the Old Testament—Job, Daniel and the latter parts of Isaiah—that a different possibility for human destiny was recognized. This was not conceived, in the Greek fashion, as the immortality of the soul; the Jews had a much too unitary view of the human personality to conceive of a disembodied soul existing apart from a body. What developed, rather, was the view that at the Day of the Lord (a phrase used to refer to a time of both blessing and judgment), some of the righteous dead would come back to earth in bodily form and as real persons. In Job we find this raised only as a

---

[1] 1 Samuel 28:8–20.

tentative possibility: "If a man die, shall he live again?"[2] In Daniel, however, the possibility is more vivid: "And many of those who sleep in the dust of the earth shall awake, some to everlasting life, and some to shame and everlasting contempt."[3] The doctrine of the resurrection of the dead was still highly controversial in Judaism during the emergence of Christianity. We can see this reflected in the New Testament Gospels as one of the ongoing quarrels between the Pharisees and Sadducees. The Pharisees supported the doctrine of resurrection, whereas the Sadducees, defenders of the "old-time religion," rejected it as a modernistic innovation.

The differences between the Greek and Hebrew views of human destiny are significant. For Plato, human beings are incarnated souls. In Jewish thought, human beings are animated bodies. It is not surprising that the Christian view of human destiny reflects more the Jewish idea of resurrection than the Greek view of the soul's natural immortality. The following selection from 1 Corinthians and written by Paul of Tarsus is thought by many scholars to be the earliest literary reference to the resurrection of Jesus. What is significant in this statement is that Paul does not propose any philosophical arguments to support a doctrine of the immortality of the soul. Indeed, the trouble with such doctrines is that they assume the soul is by nature immortal. For Paul, in contrast, the Christian hope for resurrection is not based on some inherent quality of the human soul but centers wholly in the power of God to bring new life to our mortal bodies.

Though the New Testament was written in Greek, and Paul was doubtless familiar with Greek attitudes toward the doctrine of the immortality of the soul (he quotes the Greek playwright Menander: "Let us eat and drink . . . "), he follows a different course in the following selection. The Christian hope is for resurrection of the body, and the support he gives for this is not a set of philosophical arguments but the claim that Jesus was risen from the dead. The resurrection of Jesus is not only the basis for the Christian hope for individual resurrection; it also formed the heart of early Christian preaching. The evidence cited in support of the resurrection of Jesus is the many persons who saw Jesus after his resurrection, and the list given includes the "more than five hundred of his followers" mentioned in verse 6. In the Gospels reference is made to the empty tomb of Jesus as evidence for his resurrection, but Paul does not include that here, focusing instead on the eyewitness accounts.

A great deal hinges on the resurrection of Jesus. For Paul, this validated all the struggles that he and others were enduring, including his controversy with his opponents at Ephesus, referred to here as "wild beasts." Conversely, "if

[2] Job 14:14.
[3] Daniel 12:2.

Christ has not been raised from death, then we have nothing to preach and you have nothing to believe" (verse 14). What was ironic about the attitude of the Corinthian Christians to whom Paul was writing is that they apparently did not believe in the resurrection of the dead but nevertheless continued to practice baptism, including being baptized for departed friends—an act that seems to have been unique to Corinth, and did not reflect universal Christian practice. Since baptism, in Paul's view, is symbolic of the death and resurrection of Christ,[4] it would make no sense to practice it if one denies that the resurrection of the dead is assured by Christ's resurrection.

Paul does not stop with the proclamation of the Christian hope of resurrection; he also offers an analogy for conceiving of what this means. Reflecting the Jewish view that to exist is to have a body, Paul suggests that the resurrected state will be a bodily state. He gives the analogy of a seed that, when planted, dies in order to give rise to a full-grown plant. This metaphor taken from the processes of nature points to the resurrection body being as different from our present body as the plant is from the seed. But despite all its differences, the resurrection body will be a body; a "spiritual body," as Paul puts it, not a disembodied spirit, as was conceived in Greek thought. The transformation from the earthly to the spiritual body would occur through the power of God, and even those who are alive when Jesus returns again would experience such a transformation. Paul's comments toward the end of the selection indicate that he shares a view widely held by early Christians that the return of Jesus would occur during their lifetime. Even though they were wrong about this, it does not affect Paul's doctrine of resurrection, for the doctrine did not hinge upon the mistaken belief in the imminent return of Jesus.

Whereas the distinction between the Greek view of the soul's natural immortality and the Christian doctrine of bodily resurrection is very clear in the following passage, the difference between the two views was successively blurred over time. By the time of Thomas Aquinas in the thirteenth century, the two doctrines had merged, and arguments in the Greek fashion were used by Christian writers. But for Paul, the evidence supporting the Christian hope for resurrection from the dead is not philosophical argument but the resurrection of Christ, which was attested to by hundreds of eyewitnesses. Take away this, says Paul, and there is little left.

4 Romans 6:3–5.

The Resurrection of the Body

1 CORINTHIANS 15

THE RESURRECTION OF CHRIST

And now I want to remind you, my friends, of the Good News which I preached to you, which you received, and on which your faith stands firm. That is the gospel, the message that I preached to you. You are saved by the gospel if you hold firmly to it—unless it was for nothing that you believed.

I passed on to you what I received, which is of the greatest importance: that Christ died for our sins, as written in the Scriptures; that he was buried and that he was raised to life three days later, as written in the Scriptures; that he appeared to Peter and then to all twelve apostles. Then he appeared to more than five hundred of his followers at once, most of whom are still alive, although some have died. Then he appeared to James, and afterward to all the apostles.

Last of all he appeared also to me—even though I am like someone whose birth was abnormal.[1] For I am the least of all the apostles—I do not even deserve to be called an apostle, because I persecuted God's church. But by God's grace I am what I am, and the grace that he gave me was not without effect. On the contrary, I have worked harder than any of the other apostles, although it was not really my own doing, but God's grace working with me. So then, whether it came from me or from them, this is what we all preach, and this is what you believe.

OUR RESURRECTION

Now, since our message is that Christ has been raised from death, how can some of you say that the dead will not be raised to life? If that is true, it means that Christ was not raised; and if Christ has not been raised from death, then we have nothing to preach and you have nothing to believe. More than that, we are shown to be lying about God, because we said that he raised Christ from death—but if it is true that the dead are not raised to life, then he did not raise Christ. For if the dead are not raised, neither has Christ been raised. And if Christ has not been raised, then your faith is a delusion and you are still lost in your sins. It would also mean that the believers in Christ who have died are

---

1 Whose birth was abnormal, *or* who was born at the wrong time.

lost. If our hope in Christ is good for this life only and no more,[2] then we deserve more pity than anyone else in all the world.

But the truth is that Christ has been raised from death, as the guarantee that those who sleep in death will also be raised. For just as death came by means of a man, in the same way the rising from death comes by means of a man. For just as all people die because of their union with Adam, in the same way all will be raised to life because of their union with Christ. But each one will be raised in his proper order: Christ, first of all; then, at the time of his coming, those who belong to him. Then the end will come; Christ will overcome all spiritual rulers, authorities, and powers, and will hand over the Kingdom to God the Father. For Christ must rule until God defeats all enemies and puts them under his feet. The last enemy to be defeated will be death. For the scripture says, "God put *all* things under his feet." It is clear, of course, that the words "all things" do not include God himself, who puts all things under Christ. But when all things have been placed under Christ's rule, then he himself, the Son, will place himself under God, who placed all things under him; and God will rule completely over all.

Now, what about those people who are baptized for the dead? What do they hope to accomplish? If it is true, as some claim, that the dead are not raised to life, why are those people being baptized for the dead? And as for us—why would we run the risk of danger every hour? My brothers, I face death every day! The pride I have in you, in our life in union with Christ Jesus our Lord, makes me declare this. If I have, as it were, fought "wild beasts" here in Ephesus simply from human motives, what have I gained? But if the dead are not raised to life, then, as the saying goes, "Let us eat and drink, for tomorrow we will die."

Do not be fooled. "Bad companions ruin good character." Come back to your right senses and stop your sinful ways. I declare to your shame that some of you do not know God.

THE RESURRECTION BODY

Someone will ask, "How can the dead be raised to life? What kind of body will they have?" You fool! When you plant a seed in the ground, it does not sprout to life unless it dies. And what you plant is a bare seed, perhaps a grain of wheat or some other grain, not the full-bodied plant that will later grow up. God provides that seed with the body he wishes; he gives each seed its own proper body.

And the flesh of living beings is not all the same kind of flesh; human beings have one kind of flesh animals another, birds another, and fish another.

And there are heavenly bodies and earthly bodies; the beauty that belongs to heavenly bodies is different from the beauty that belongs to earthly bodies. The sun has its own beauty, the moon another beauty, and the stars a different beauty; and even among stars there are different kinds of beauty.

---

[2] If our hope in Christ is good for this life only and no more; *or* If all we have in this life is our hope in Christ.

This is how it will be when the dead are raised to life. When the body is buried, it is mortal; when raised, it will be immortal. When buried, it is ugly and weak; when raised, it will be beautiful and strong. When buried, it is a physical body; when raised, it will be a spiritual body. There is, of course, a physical body, so there has to be a spiritual body. For the scripture says, "The first man, Adam, was created a living being"; but the last Adam is the life-giving Spirit. It is not the spiritual that comes first, but the physical, and then the spiritual. The first Adam, made of earth, came from the earth; the second Adam came from heaven. Those who belong to the earth are like the one who was made of earth; those who are of heaven are like the one who came from heaven. Just as we wear the likeness of the man made of earth, so we will wear[3] the likeness of the man from heaven.

What I mean, brothers, is that what is made of flesh and blood cannot share in God's Kingdom, and what is mortal cannot possess immortality.

Listen to this secret truth: we shall not all die, but when the last trumpet sounds, we shall all be changed in an instant, as quickly as the blinking of an eye. For when the trumpet sounds, the dead will be raised, never to die again, and we shall all be changed. For what is mortal must be changed into what is immortal; what will die must be changed into what cannot die. So when this takes place, and the mortal has been changed into the immortal, then the scripture will come true: "Death is destroyed; victory is complete!"

> *"Where, Death, is your victory?*
> *Where, Death, is your power to hurt?"*

Death gets its power to hurt from sin, and sin gets its power from the Law. But thanks be to God who gives us the victory through our Lord Jesus Christ!

So then, my dear brothers, stand firm and steady. Keep busy always in your work for the Lord, since You know that nothing you do in the Lord's service is ever useless.

Discussion Questions

1. Are the doctrines of bodily resurrection and immortality of the soul mutually exclusive? Give reasons for your answer.

2. Of the evidence cited by Paul in support of the resurrection of the body, which do you find most convincing?

3. Explain the differences between the Greek and Hebrew views of human destiny.

4. Examine the metaphors Paul used to describe the resurrection body. Discuss the significance of these metaphors.

5. How is the significance of the resurrection of Jesus reflected in early Christian attitudes toward baptism?

---

3 We will wear; *some manuscripts have* let us wear.

Death in Buddhism

One of the dangers of juxtaposing Western and Eastern discussions of a philosophical issue is reading the Eastern response as merely a variation of the Western view. This would be a mistake for at least two reasons: First, it assumes that the point of reference is Western and that the Eastern view should be discussed in terms of how it differs from the Western view; and second, such an approach would gloss over the fact that fundamental terms have entirely different histories in the two traditions and that the issue itself may be discussed from the vantage point of varying assumptions.

For example, consider the notion of the soul, the self, or the ego. For the moment, let's assume that these are roughly synonymous. Recall that in Western thought as far back as Plato, the guiding assumption of much of Western philosophy is that there is a self, and philosophical discussion centered around such questions as its nature, its future, the grounds for believing that there are other selves, and how I know of the "I" that I identify as myself. For the philosophy of René Descartes, the existence of a self was so important that the formula *cogito ergo sum*—I think, therefore I am—becomes the indubitable starting point for his arguments for the reliability of empirical knowledge. If we change from this set of fundamental issues and assumptions, the discussion of human destiny will proceed differently. A point of departure that totally rejects the notion of individual souls or selves will deal with a different collection of issues than does traditional Western analysis of the topic. This is precisely what we encounter in Buddhism. In the book from which the following reading is taken, Walpola Rahula says, "Buddhism does not recognize a spirit opposed to matter, as is accepted by most other systems of philosophies and religions. Mind is only a faculty or organ (*indriya*) like the eye or the ear." Just as each sense organ has its proper role—smells for the nose, colors for the eyes, sounds for the ears—so ideas are for the mind.

Several terminological distinctions are important for understanding Rahula. He says of the definition of an individual person, "What we call a 'being', or an 'individual', or 'I' . . . is only a combination of ever-changing physical and mental forces or energies, which may be divided into five groups or aggregates." These he lists as matter, sensations, perceptions, mental formations, and consciousness.

The five aggregates are like blocks in a structure that can be disassembled and reassembled again and again to create new entities. The aggregates combine to provide for *dukkha*, which in Buddhism is synonymous with life itself. Literally meaning "suffering," *dukkha* is the human condition. One of the four Noble Truths annunciated by Buddha is that "all life is *dukkha*." This means not that every moment is filled with suffering, but that throughout human existence we are never very far from the possibility of suffering or from the underlying anxiety that characterizes human life.

The temptation here is to see Buddhism as only a collection of negativities, but this would be to commit the mistake warned against earlier: Letting the Western definition of an issue define the boundaries of that issue. In the reading that follows, we can see that the point of view of Buddhism is freed from many of the constants of the Western view. There is no beginning of the world process, no God, no soul (*atman*), and no independent existence of an individual after death. The life process itself is in constant flux but continues nonetheless. The metaphor that best describes this process for Buddhist thought is that of the candle flame. The flame passes from one candle to another, in constant flux, but in continuity through various entities.

Rahula explains why belief in the self is considered troublesome: "it produces harmful thoughts of 'me' and 'mine', selfish desire, craving, attachment, hatred, illwill, conceit, pride, egoism, and other defilements, impurities and problems." Nonetheless, such beliefs are entrenched in our thinking, and rooting them out is difficult, yet in purging ourselves of such selfish views lies the path of liberation. When Rahula cites statements from Buddha, the citation frequently begins with "O bhikkhus. . . ." The term *bhikkhu* refers to a mendicant monk, those disciples of Buddha seeking the path to enlightenment and liberation.

Given these premises about the human condition, Buddhism does not have a doctrine of a permanent future life. Since there is nothing permanent even in this life, there is nothing permanent to pass from one life to another life. As Rahula explains, "from the Buddhist point of view, the question of life after death is not a great mystery, and a Buddhist is never worried about this problem."

Buddhism is an ancient religion. Since its beginnings in India in the fifth century B.C.E., it has spread throughout Asia and, indeed, to the rest of the world as well. In its expansion, Buddhism developed many variations and added new doctrines. One of the branches of Buddhism in Japan—perhaps even the largest Buddhist sect in that country, but also with followers in China—is known as Pure Land Buddhism. Pure Land Buddhists seek a rebirth in paradise—the Pure Land—which will offer pleasures and enjoyments to those who are reborn there. Though still a minority position in Buddhism, Pure Land Buddhism gives eloquent testimony to the power of the hope for rebirth in another life. Such a hope, however, is not part of the majority report of Buddhism, and as you will see in the reading that follows, the question of human destiny is posed in entirely different terms. As Rahula explicates Buddhist doctrine, the very longing for another life is itself a form of attachment that we must avoid. "As long as there is this 'thirst' to be and to become," Rahula says, "the cycle of continuity (*samsāra*) goes on. It can stop only when its driving force, this 'thirst', is cut off through wisdom which sees Reality, Truth, Nirvāna."

The Doctrine of No-Soul: Anatta

WALPOLA RAHULA

These five Aggregates together, which we popularly call a 'being', are *dukkha* itself (*saṅkhāra-dukkha*). There is no other 'being' or 'I', standing behind these five aggregates, who experiences *dukkha*. As Buddhaghosa says:

'Mere suffering exists, but no sufferer is found;

The deeds are, but no doer is found.'

There is no unmoving mover behind the movement. It is only movement. It is not correct to say that life is moving, but life is movement itself. Life and movement are not two different things. In other words, there is no thinker behind the thought. Thought itself is the thinker. If you remove the thought, there is no thinker to be found. Here we cannot fail to notice how this Buddhist view is diametrically opposed to the Cartesian *cogito ergo sum*: 'I think, therefore I am.'

According to the Buddha's teaching the beginning of the life-stream of living beings is unthinkable. The believer in the creation of life by God may be astonished at this reply. But if you were to ask him, 'What is the beginning of God?' he would answer without hesitation 'God has no beginning', and he is not astonished at his own reply. The Buddha says: 'O bhikkhus, this cycle of continuity (*saṃsāra*) is without a visible end, and the first beginning of beings wandering and running round, enveloped in ignorance (*avijjā*) and bound down by the fetters of thirst (desire, *taṇhā*) is not to be perceived.' And further, referring to ignorance which is the main cause of the continuity of life the Buddha states: 'The first beginning of ignorance (*avijjā*) is not to be perceived in such a way as to postulate that there was no ignorance beyond a certain point.' Thus it is not possible to say that there was no life beyond a certain definite point. . . .

We have seen earlier that a being is nothing but a combination of physical and mental forces or energies. What we call death is the total non-functioning of the physical body. Do all these forces and energies stop altogether with the non-functioning of the body? Buddhism says 'no'. Will, volition, desire, thirst to exist, to continue, to become more and more, is a tremendous force that moves whole lives, whole existences, that even moves the whole world. This is the greatest force, the greatest energy in the world. According to Buddhism, this

Source: Walpola Rahula, *What the Buddha Taught.* Copyright © 1974 by W. Rahula. Used by permission of Grove/Atlantic, Inc.

force does not stop with the non-functioning of the body, which is death; but it continues manifesting itself in another form, producing re-existence which is called rebirth.

Now, another question arises: If there is no permanent, unchanging entity or substance like Self or Soul (*ātman*), what is it that can re-exist or be reborn after death? Before we go on to life after death, let us consider what this life is, and how it continues now. What we call life, as we have so often repeated, is the combination of the Five Aggregates, a combination of physical and mental energies. These are constantly changing; they do not remain the same for two consecutive moments. Every moment they are born and they die. 'When the Aggregates arise, decay and die, O Bhikkhu, every moment you are born, decay and die.' Thus, even now during this life time, every moment we are born and die, but we continue. If we can understand that in this life we can continue without a permanent, unchanging substance like Self or Soul, why can't we understand that those forces themselves can continue without a Self or a Soul behind them after the non-functioning of the body?

When this physical body is no more capable of functioning, energies do not die with it, but continue to take some other shape or form, which we call another life. In a child all the physical, mental and intellectual faculties are tender and weak, but they have within them the potentiality of producing a full grown man. Physical and mental energies which constitute the so-called being have within themselves the power to take a new form, and grow gradually and gather force to the full.

As there is no permanent, unchanging substance, nothing passes from one moment to the next. So quite obviously, nothing permanent or changing can pass or transmigrate from one life to the next. It is a series that continues unbroken, but changes every moment. The series is, really speaking, nothing but movement. It is like a flame that burns through the night: it is not the same flame nor is it another. A child grows up to be a man of sixty. Certainly the man of sixty is not the same as the child of sixty years ago, nor is he another person. Similarly, a person who dies here and is reborn elsewhere is neither the same person, nor another (*na ca so na ca añño*). It is the continuity of the same series. The difference between death and birth is only a thought-moment: the last thought-moment in this life conditions the first thought-moment in the so-called next life, which, in fact, is the continuity of the same series. During this life itself, too, one thought-moment conditions the next thought-moment. So from the Buddhist point of view, the question of life after death is not a great mystery, and a Buddhist is never worried about this problem. . . .

What in general is suggested by Soul, Self, Ego, or to use the Sanskrit expression *Ātman*, is that in man there is a permanent, everlasting and absolute entity, which is the unchanging substance behind the changing phenomenal world. According to some religions, each individual has such a separate soul which is created by God, and which, finally after death, lives eternally either in hell or heaven, its destiny depending on the judgment of its creator. According to others, it goes through many lives till it is completely purified and becomes finally united with God or Brahman, Universal Soul or Ātman. According to the teaching of the Buddha, the idea of self is an imaginary, false belief which has no corresponding reality, and it produces harmful thoughts of 'me' and 'mine', selfish desire, craving, attachment, hatred, ill-will, conceit, pride, egoism, and other defilements, impurities and problems. It is the source of all the troubles in the world from personal conflicts to wars between nations. In short, to this false view can be traced all the evil in the world.

Two ideas are psychologically deep-rooted in man: self-protection and self-preservation. For self-protection man has created God, on whom he depends for his own protection, safety and security, just as a child depends on its parent. For self-preservation man has conceived the idea of an immortal Soul or Ātman, which will live eternally. In his ignorance, weakness, fear, and desire, man needs these two things to console himself. Hence he clings to them deeply and fanatically.

The Buddha's teaching does not support this ignorance, weakness, fear, and desire, but aims at making man enlightened by removing and destroying them, striking at their very root. According to Buddhism, our ideas of God and Soul are false and empty. Though highly developed as theories, they are all the same extremely subtle mental projections, garbed in an intricate metaphysical and philosophical phraseology. These ideas are so deep-rooted in man, and so near and dear to him, that he does not wish to hear, nor does he want to understand, any teaching against them. . . .

The question of Free Will has occupied an important place in Western thought and philosophy. But according to Conditioned Genesis, this question does not and cannot arise in Buddhist philosophy. If the whole of existence is relative, conditioned and interdependent, how can will alone be free? Will, like any other thought, is conditioned. So-called 'freedom' itself is conditioned and relative. Such a conditioned and relative 'Free Will' is not denied. There can be nothing absolutely free, physical or mental, as everything is interdependent and relative. If Free Will implies a will independent of conditions, independent of cause and effect, such a thing does not exist. How can a will, or anything for that matter, arise without conditions, away from cause and effect, when the whole of existence is conditioned and relative, and is within the law of cause and effect? Here again, the idea of Free Will is basically connected with the ideas of God, Soul, justice, reward and punishment. Not only is so-called free will not free, but even the very idea of Free Will is not free from conditions.

According to the doctrine of Conditioned Genesis, as well as according to the analysis of being into Five Aggregates, the idea of an abiding, immortal substance in man or outside, whether it is called Ātman, 'I', Soul, Self, or Ego, is considered only a false belief, a mental projection. This is the Buddhist doctrine of *Anatta*, No-Soul or No-Self.

Discussion Questions

1. Rahula claims that the concept of an ego, self, or soul is the source of a great deal of what is harmful in human life. Which of the reasons he gives do you find most convincing?

2. Is the idea that life is a continuum, but that there is no hope for a permanent future life for an individual, a doctrine that can find a reception in the West? Why or why not? What cultural forces in Western thought work for (or against) this notion?

3. Discuss the Five Aggregates. What is the closest Western correlate?

4. Compare Rahula's discussion of death with that offered by Epicurus. Are there points of agreement? Points of contrast?

5. Rahula says that there is no free will independent of conditions. Discuss specifically what this means.

RETROSPECTIVE

Religion and Death

Like other issues in the philosophy of religion, the question of death and human destiny does not lend itself to precise conclusions. The evidence is ambiguous, but this ambiguity leaves the question of life after death an open one for religion.

Running like counterpoint throughout all the readings in this section is the question of the proper attitude toward death: Is life made more meaningful by the view that death is the cessation of consciousness, or is it made less meaningful by that belief? Whatever your answer, there is little doubt that attitudes toward death have profound implications for attitudes toward life. In Buddhism, for example, concern about death is just another of the attachments that one must separate from in order to live a full and meaningful life. But others have argued that life becomes more meaningful if we see it as preparation for an afterlife. The recent French philosopher Gabriel Marcel, for example, argues that life is debased by the view that death ends all.

> Here we must stress a paradox to which we cannot, I think, direct our attention too closely; theoretically one might have imagined—and this indeed was what many people did in the nineteenth century—that as soon as the majority of men in a given society ceased to believe in an afterlife, life in this world would be more and more lovingly taken care of and would become the object of an increased regard. *What has happened is something quite different, the very opposite in fact: this cannot, I think, be overemphasized.* Life in this world has become more and more widely looked upon as a sort of worthless phenomenon, devoid of any intrinsic justification, and as thereby subject to countless interferences which in a different metaphysical context would have been considered sacrilegious.[1]

[1] Gabriel Marcel, *The Mystery of Being* (Chicago: Henry Regnery Company, Gateway Edition, 1960), vol. 2, pp. 165–66.

However you decide this issue, there is one final point that the readings force upon us: A completely impregnable argument for life after death is not available. Even Paul acknowledges that there are persons who in his own time refuse to believe in the resurrection and found eyewitness testimony to the resurrection of Jesus inconclusive. But at the same time, there is likewise no unassailable proof of the impossibility of another life. Here again we encounter uncertainty, which leaves room for a faith commitment. Seen from the viewpoint of faith, death need not be viewed as the final chapter in the story of human destiny. This point is well made by the distinguished American philosopher Geddes MacGregor.

> If I can see this life as the gift of God I shall be so thankful for each moment of it that to complain of death would be as churlish as to call a benefactor parsimonious who for fifty years had inexplicably given me an annuity and then as inexplicably let the flow of the cornucopia stop. In the face of such a record of generosity, moreover, I should be inclined to interpret the cessation as, rather, auguring a new and even larger beneficence.[2]

ADDITIONAL READINGS

A good bibliography and historical survey of attitudes toward death is Robert G. Olson, "Death," *The Encyclopedia of Philosophy* (1967), 2, 307–309. John Hick provides a thorough and readable analysis of the various dimensions of the topic in his massive *Death and Eternal Life* (New York: Harper & Row, 1976). A debate of sorts on the topic of death is constituted by the two articles on "Death" by D. M. Mackinnon and Antony Flew in *New Essays in Philosophical Theology*, ed. Antony Flew and Alasdair MacIntyre (London: SCM Press, 1955). A popularization of scientific views as they bear on the issues of soul, self, and God can be found in the book by Angela Tilby, *Soul: God, Self and the New Cosmology* (New York: Doubleday, 1992). The author was involved in the production of the BBC series entitled "Soul," and the book is, in some sense, a companion volume. A valuable survey of past and present beliefs about life after death is David L. Edwards, *After Death: Past Beliefs and Real Possibilities* (London: Cassell, 1999).

---

[2] Geddes MacGregor, *Philosophical Issues in Religious Thought* (Boston: Houghton Mifflin Company, 1973), p. 296.

CHAPTER FOUR

ARGUMENTS
FOR GOD'S EXISTENCE

INTRODUCTION

The Existence of God

Probably no single issue in religion has received more philosophical attention than the question of God's existence. For both Judaism and Christianity, the existence of God is the fundamental fact of life, and the reality of the living God is the basic presupposition of these religions. Yet, surprising as it is to those who have never encountered it, neither the Old Testament nor the New Testament contains any arguments for God's existence. Arguing for God's existence would be as foreign to biblical writers as arguing for the air we breathe would be to us. The writer of Psalm 19 could say, "The heavens are telling the glory of God; and the firmament proclaims his handiwork," but this is not an *argument*; it is less concerned with proclaiming God's existence than with describing how the created order reflects God's glory and majesty. The closest references to the religious problem of atheism are found in the Hebrew psalms, notably in Psalm 14:1 (also Psalms 10:4 and 51:13), which says, "The fool says in his heart, 'There is no God.'" But the concern here is with *practical* atheism: the person who lives without taking God into account. What we might call intellectual atheism, a denial that there is a reality called God, was hardly considered a possibility, even for the "fool."

There are several reasons for the absence of arguments for God's existence in the Bible. One of the most obvious is that the religious problem facing ancient Israel was not atheism but polytheism. The first of the Ten Commandments consequently forbids polytheism: "You shall have no other gods before me" (Exodus 20:3). And the Hebrew confession of faith, the Shema, affirms: "Hear, O Israel, the Lord our God, the Lord is one" (Deuteronomy 6:4). For the New Testament

117

writers, who were steeped in the faith of Israel, there was likewise no question that God exists; they saw their task not as arguing for the existence of God, but as proclaiming a unique activity of God in human history in the person of Jesus of Nazareth.

A second reason for the absence of arguments for God's existence in the Bible is that its authors were not attracted to argumentative modes of thought. We owe our dependence upon logic, reason, dialectical disputation, and the power of argument to the Greeks, and even in Greece the importance of logic was not appreciated until around the fourth century B.C.E. Although Christianity has its roots in the soil of Judaism, it was nurtured in a world in which the Greek language and Greek culture prevailed. (The New Testament, for example, was written in Greek.) It was only a matter of time until Christian writers, armed with the deductive powers of Greek philosophy, would attempt to express Christian doctrines in Greek philosophical categories and to argue for the basic doctrines of the Christian faith. Origen, Augustine, Anselm, and Thomas Aquinas were but a few of the more notable Christian writers whose approach to Christian doctrine shows the influence of Greek philosophical thought.

A third reason for the lack of argument in the Old Testament is that Judaism was not an especially evangelical religion; Jews were not concerned with convincing non-Jews of the truth of their faith and therefore developed no apologetic approach (that is, a defense of the truth of their religious convictions). But Christianity *was* evangelistic, and as it engaged in its ever-expanding missionary enterprise, it found it necessary to be able to present arguments for its beliefs and reasons for its claims, especially when confronted with the task of convincing someone completely unacquainted with the Christian Scriptures of the truth of the Christian faith. Much of the impetus behind the systematic exposition of the Christian faith by Thomas Aquinas was to provide a point of approach to those who would accept the dictates of reason, but not the writings of the prophets and apostles.

NATURAL AND REVEALED THEOLOGY

Before going any further, we must clarify some terminology. Within the Christian tradition, there have existed two views of how we acquire knowledge of God. The one view insists that we can know about God only through his own self-disclosure, that is, through *revelation*. The second view is that an alternative route to knowledge of God is provided by what has come to be called *natural theology*, a claim that reason, unaided by divine revelation, can discover truths about God.

Revelation is just what the name implies—a divine self-disclosure through such means as visions, dreams, oracles, or, as was the case with the faith of Israel, through God's mighty actions within human history. Claims to mystical experience could also be considered revelation, but since they are usually intensely private and, in the view of mystics, beyond articulation, mystical experiences cannot provide a basis for doctrines about the nature of God in the same way as, say, the prophetic tradition of ancient Israel. For the Hebrews, God's self-revelation was principally in terms of the significant events in the life of Israel—the call of Abraham, the Exodus, the giving of the Law on Mt. Sinai. Christians likewise interpreted revelation principally in terms of God's self-disclosure in Jesus of Nazareth. The Scriptures are records of this divine self-disclosure and, in a secondary sense, are referred to as revelation themselves. To be strictly accurate, one should follow the distinctions made by the twentieth-century theologian Karl Barth and say that the Scriptures contain the revelation of God, that is, they bear witness to God's redemptive actions on humankind's behalf. There is, of course, a significant difference between bearing witness to God's actions and arguing for God's existence. An argument for the existence of God does not presuppose the claims of Scripture, but attempts to discover truths about God solely through the use of reason apart from any divine self-disclosure.

Natural theology, however, is "natural" in two senses. In the first sense, the claim is made that nature itself gives evidence not only of God's existence, but of God's nature as well. In a second sense, such an approach to theology is natural in that human reason, unaided by revelation, is able to achieve knowledge of God, since it is within the nature of reason itself to aspire to such knowledge. Perhaps the most forceful advocate of the power of natural theology was the thirteenth-century thinker Thomas Aquinas, who had great confidence in the power of human reason to ascend to knowledge of God. Thomas argued that there can be no conflict between natural and revealed theology, since both aim at knowledge and knowledge gained in one way cannot disagree with knowledge gained in another way. This twofold path, as he referred to it, was necessary because some people do not accept Scripture, and for them, rational arguments are necessary. We will say more about this in the discussion of faith and reason.

There is a further distinction to be made within natural theology itself, for arguments have taken one of two forms. Arguments *a priori* are attempts to determine knowledge of God solely by means of intellectual insight, independently of the senses. *A posteriori* arguments are based on observations about the world that lead to a claim that God is the logical result of reasoning about these facts. We will return later to a more detailed examination of a priori and a posteriori arguments, but perhaps brief examples may clarify the differences between the two approaches. The classic a priori argument for God's existence was formulated by Anselm, who attempts to prove that God exists on the basis of nothing other than the idea of God itself. More precisely, Anselm argues on the basis of the concept of God's *being*; hence the argument is called the ontological argument (from the Greek *ontos*, which means "being"). Here no appeal is made to facts derived from human experience; the argument centers solely on an analysis of the concept of God. The a posteriori approach begins with knowledge derived from sense experiences and argues on this basis to the claim that God is the only adequate explanation for these experiences. One such argument is based on the perception of order in the world. According to this argument, only a supreme intelligence could be capable of instilling order and purpose in the universe; therefore, God must exist. The Greeks referred to the universe as a *cosmos*, an ordered system, and such arguments are called cosmological. Teleological arguments (from the Greek *telos*, "purpose") are a form of cosmological argument emphasizing one type of order, namely, the purposive quality that the cosmos seems to exhibit. Similar arguments have been based on the human experience of moral obligation. All a posteriori arguments begin with some fact of human experience and attempt to argue on the basis of this experience to God as its source.

The philosopher's task is to evaluate the strength of such arguments and to attempt to spot their weaknesses and their strengths. It is for this reason that natural theology is sometimes referred to as philosophical theology. Philosophers have directed attention to the idea of revelation or to some specific claim of revelation, but here their concern is with the concept of revelation itself and the problems it poses, such as the difficulty of validating the genuineness of an alleged revelation and verifying its truth claims. The specific content of a revelation, whatever it may happen to be, is probably not in itself of philosophical concern; the study of the content of revelation takes one into the realm of what has usually been referred to as dogmatic or systematic theology.

Since our attention will primarily be directed to natural theology, the following diagram may prove helpful in sorting out the distinctions just made:

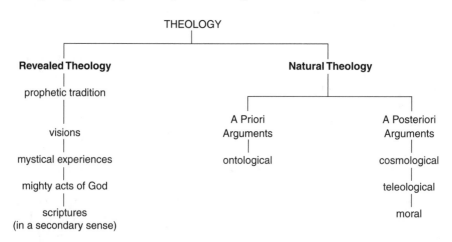

We will begin with what is perhaps the most difficult of all arguments for the existence of God: the ontological argument. Reading the ontological argument is much like looking at an optical illusion that seems to show a flight of stairs running upward that soon appear to change their direction and run downward. At times the ontological argument seems to make perfectly good sense (although even then it may be unconvincing), but at other times the very form of the argument itself seems totally elusive. Perhaps this is one of the reasons the ontological argument has attracted so much philosophical attention. Even those who are convinced that the argument is invalid may not be able to agree on the reasons for its invalidity, and there are also defenders of the argument who think that it offers a significant way of thinking about God. With these considerations in mind, we will look at the form of the argument proposed by the seventeenth-century philosopher René Descartes.

The Ontological Argument

As was mentioned in the introduction to this chapter, the name for the ontological argument is derived from the Greek word for "being" (*ontos*); the argument takes as its point of departure only the concept of the being of God. Its classic formulation was by Anselm of Canterbury, though the argument has since been restated by other philosophers.

There are several reasons for the emergence of an argument based solely on the idea of God's being, but two predominated in the thinking of the eleventh century. The first was that Plato's philosophical view provided a virtually unchallenged metaphysical framework for Christian thought in Anselm's time. At the heart of Plato's metaphysics is the notion of a great chain of being, in terms of which one can rank objects according to their degree of reality. Images and reflections are at the lowest end of the chain, and above these (that is, having more reality) are physical objects, then mathematical objects, and finally pure Forms that are eternal and unchanging. Topping off this hierarchy is the idea of the Good, which was itself the Form of all Forms. Drawing on this metaphysical system, the medievals developed the view that God was to be conceived of as highest in the order of Being as well as first in the order of Truth and Goodness. To refer to God as the Supreme Being—that is, the greatest reality—was very much in line with this medieval metaphysics, and consequently an argument based only on an analysis of the idea of God's being would suggest itself.

A second reason for the importance of the ontological argument in medieval thought was a passage of Scripture, Exodus 3:13. This text is part of the story of Moses and the burning bush. According to the story, Moses witnessed a *theophany*, a manifestation of God, in the bush that burned but was not consumed. A voice spoke to Moses out of the bush and commissioned him to be the deliverer of Israel from Egyptian slavery. It is interesting to note that Moses' reaction was typical of the response to the numinous that Rudolf Otto describes, but more surprising was Moses' reluctance. He made excuses—he was a nobody, he could not speak well—and finally he asked the voice from the bush to identify itself. In effect, he said, "If I go to the people of Israel, they will ask me the name of the God who sends me. What shall I say to them?" The voice replied that Moses should tell the people that I AM sent him. This term in Hebrew is a tenseless form of the verb *to be* that could be translated either I AM WHAT I AM or I WILL BE WHAT I WILL BE. In point of fact, subsequent Jewish interpreters took I AM to be the name of God, and they treated it with reverence, refusing even to pronounce it. I AM is written with four Hebrew consonants (Hebrew has no vowels) and is transliterated into English as YHWH. Called the *tetragrammaton*, the word was probably pronounced as *Yahweh*. Most English translations of the Old Testament substitute the term *The Lord* for the tetragrammaton, which follows the ancient Hebrew practice of substituting *adonai* (The Lord) for the sacred name of God in public reading. Medieval scholars interpreted Exodus 3:13 to mean that God revealed to Moses that God's name was *being*. Consequently, an analysis of the concept of God's being would fit in well both with Platonic metaphysics and with the view that *being* was God's name.

We can, however, consider the ontological argument quite apart from this historical background that forms the cultural context in which the argument was first formulated. The argument begins with the idea of the being of God, and Anselm defines the term *God* as "a being than which nothing greater can be conceived." There is really nothing surreptitious about this definition of the term *God*, for it is what Judaism and Christianity have always meant by the term. Given this definition of the name of God, the argument is based on the claim that it is greater for something to exist in reality than it is for something to exist only in human understanding. Anselm gives as an example the painter who has an idea or concept of a possible painting. At this stage the idea of the painting is not as great as it could be, for when the painter has committed the idea to canvas, the completed painting is greater than the mere idea of it, since it exists both in the painter's understanding *and* in reality.

In a similar way, Anselm argues that when a person claims to understand what the term *God* means, but also says that God does not exist, such a person cannot really be thinking of that "being than which nothing greater can be conceived." For a being that existed in reality as well as in a person's understanding would be greater than a being that existed only as an idea in someone's mind. In short, that being than which nothing greater can be conceived could not exist in the understanding alone but would have to exist in reality as well, for it is greater to exist both in the understanding *and* in reality than it is to exist in the understanding alone.

One of the difficulties in Anselm's ontological argument is what he means by *greater*. He says that a being that exists in reality *and* in the understanding is greater than a being that exists only in the understanding. This use of *greater* is usually taken to mean "more perfect": That which exists in reality is more perfect than that which is merely an idea in the understanding. Anselm's example is that the idea of a painting in the painter's mind is not as perfect (since it does not exist in reality) as the actually existing reality of the painting after it has been committed to canvas.

The reformulation of the ontological argument by the seventeenth-century French philosopher René Descartes faces this issue squarely. Although there is no evidence that Descartes was familiar with Anselm's argument, he offers a version of the argument that is similar to Anselm's, with the exception that Descartes explicitly states that existence is a perfection. In his development of the argument, Descartes writes with all the precision of a mathematician, which he was. That Descartes was a mathematician is important for two reasons: He was struck by the clarity and precision of mathematical reasoning and was impressed with the certainty that mathematical reasoning could attain. When one develops geometrical proofs, they are both precise and certain. Other mathematicians will agree with them if they do not contain errors, and if they are erroneous, the source of the difficulty can be discovered. Descartes hoped to bring the same kind of precision and certainty to philosophy that he had achieved in mathematics. In fact, Descartes was obsessed with a desire for certainty in everything, and he argues that natural science must be based on certainty rather than on the mere calculation of probabilities, which was the prevailing view of his contemporaries.

Without going into detail concerning Descartes's system, a few comments in summary will help to situate his version of the ontological argument in his philosophy. Descartes devotes considerable attention to an attempt to arrive at something absolutely certain upon which philosophy could be based, and in previous sections of the work from which the selection is taken, he advanced arguments to prove that we can be certain of our own existence. His famous statement, *cogito ergo sum*, "I think, therefore I am," was taken by him to be irrefutable. But if we can be certain of our own existence as a thinking being, what else can we be certain of? We cannot trust our senses totally, for they frequently deceive us, but we can trust the mathematical constructions of our reason. Geometry, in fact, is a science of mathematical relations, and the interesting thing about geometry is that the mathematician is not concerned with the actual existence of the objects of mathematics. A geometrician can prove the nature of a triangle, for example, without ever seeing a real triangle, and the statements that geometry can prove about a triangle are true and certain regardless of whether there are or are not actually existing triangles. We can prove that the interior angles of a triangle equal two right angles, that the square of the hypotenuse of a right triangle is equal to the sum of the squares of the other two sides (the Pythagorean theorem), and so forth, without ever observing or measuring an existing triangle. When we are dealing with triangles, however, the issue is somewhat clouded, since we *have* in fact seen triangles and can draw them at will on a chalkboard. But geometry can also deal with figures that we have not seen—a hundred-sided figure, for example, or a figure with a thousand sides—with the same precision and clarity brought to bear on the geometry of triangles.

All this was extremely impressive to Descartes, and he begins his ontological argument with the observation that the idea of geometry forms a model for his subsequent argument. Geometry shows that "from my mere ability to elicit the idea of some objects from my consciousness, that all the properties that I clearly and distinctly perceive the object to have do really belong to it. . . ." When

Descartes uses the word *perceive* here, he means, not sense perception, but a kind of purely mental insight. Quite apart from whether or not the objects of geometry exist, we can discover certain things about them purely by the use of reason unaided by the senses. In other words, Descartes is making the claim that geometry is an a priori science.

Can the same approach be used in developing a proof of God's existence? A troubling problem emerges at this point: It is quite clear that geometry can devise concepts of many figures that in fact have no real existence outside the mind of the person who conceives them. Descartes underscores this point by distinguishing between *essence* and *existence*. Geometry is concerned with the essence, the "whatness" of the objects with which it deals; it is unconcerned with the existence of the objects and in fact cannot prove (or disprove) their existence from a mere consideration of their essence. To be sure, we can form the idea of a figure with a thousand sides, but this does not prove that a thousand-sided figure anywhere exists. In the same way, if I form the idea of God in my mind, this does not prove that God exists in reality.

Descartes, however, sees a way around this problem. When we form in our minds the idea of God, it is an idea of a most perfect being, a being who is all-wise, all-knowing, all-powerful, completely good—in short, a being perfect in every respect. But if God is truly perfect in every respect, then existence must be a part of God's essence, that is, one of the perfections God enjoys. Perhaps this point can be made clearer by going back to the distinction between existence and essence. Whenever we investigate the essence of something, we list all the qualities without which the thing would not be what it is. For example, we can describe the essence of a triangle in the following way:

Triangle
three sides
three angles
the three angles equal two right angles
etc.

We do not have to list *existence* as part of the essence of *triangle*, since we have already admitted that mathematical objects do not have to exist in order to be the concern of geometry. Now, let us try the same thing with the idea of God's essence. As we do this, remember that we are going to list all the qualities that form a part of our idea of God's being.

God
All-wise
All-knowing
All-powerful
All-good
Existence

Descartes argues that in the case of God, existence is one of the qualities that necessarily forms part of the idea of God (unlike a triangle, which cannot claim existence as a part of its essence).

This point is so important for Descartes's argument that he repeats it in several ways. We certainly can form ideas of nonexisting things—winged horses, centaurs, golden mountains, and the like—and our ability to form ideas in no way proves the existence of the objects of which we are thinking. But some qualities are so necessarily a part of the idea of a thing that we cannot think of that thing without including these qualities. Descartes gives the example of the ideas of mountain and valley. These two ideas are inseparable. One cannot think of a mountain that has no valley or a valley not formed by a mountain. The mere thought of the idea *mountain/valley* does not, of course, prove that there are mountains and valleys, but only that if we think of *mountain*, we must also think of *valley* as part of the idea. Similarly, to have an idea of Pegasus does not prove that Pegasus exists, but if we think of Pegasus, we must think of a winged horse. And the idea of a triangle does not prove that triangles exist, but only that when we think of a triangle, we are thinking of a three-sided figure. It is not necessary that we ever think about triangles, mountains and valleys, or any other thing, but when we do think of them, we must include in our idea the qualities that form the essence of the thing. Neither is there any necessity for us to think about God, but when we do think of God, if we are truly thinking of the Supreme Being, then we must think of God as possessing all perfections. Descartes then claims, "This necessity clearly ensures that, when later on I observe that existence is a perfection, I am justified in concluding that the First and Supreme Being exists." Nonexistence attributed to our idea of God would be just as absurd as four-sidedness as a part of our idea of a triangle. The concept of a nonexisting Supreme Being would be as self-contradictory as the idea of a square circle.

Descartes, like other defenders of the ontological argument, insists that the argument works only in the case of God, for God alone is that being in whom existence and essence are conjoined. Descartes argues that it is necessary to include existence as part of the essence of God, for existence is a perfection without which God would not be the most perfect Being. We can summarize Descartes's argument in the following way:

Existence is a perfection
God is the most perfect being (that is, God shares in all perfections)
Therefore, God exists (since existence is a perfection)

Descartes also claims that he cannot conceive of two or more such Gods, and that God must have existed from all eternity and will exist to all eternity. Descartes does not give arguments for these views, but they were well known to philosophers in his day, and he perhaps assumed that his readers were familiar with them. There cannot be two Gods, since they would mutually limit each other. If God is truly supreme in power, God cannot be limited by any other being; therefore, there cannot be two beings completely unlimited in power. Similar arguments can be used to prove the eternality of God: God cannot have been brought into being, for a greater being would be required to bring God into being (a greater being cannot proceed from a lesser being). Similarly, God cannot cease to exist, for this would require a being greater in power to destroy God, but this is impossible, since God is the greatest being. Hence, God is eternal. This is only a sketch of the type of arguments Descartes undoubtedly had in mind, but since they are not essential to a consideration of Descartes's ontological argument, it would carry us too far afield to consider them in more detail here.

The Most Perfect Being

∞

RENÉ DESCARTES

The most important point, I think, is that I find within myself innumerable ideas of a kind of objects that, even if perhaps they have no existence anywhere outside me, cannot be called nonentities; my thinking of them (*a me cogitentur*) is in a way arbitrary, but they are no figments of mine; they have their own genuine and unchangeable natures. For example, when I imagine a triangle, it may be that no such figure exists anywhere outside my consciousness (*cogitationem*), or never has existed; but there certainly exists its determinate nature (its essence, its form), which is unchangeable and eternal. This is no figment of mine, and does not depend on my mind, as is clear from the following: various properties can be proved of this triangle, e.g., that its three angles are together equal to two right angles, that its greatest side subtends its greatest angle, and so on; willy-nilly, I now clearly see them, even if I have not thought of them (*cogitaverim*) in any way when I have previously imagined a triangle; they cannot, then, be figments of mine.

It would be irrelevant for me to say that perhaps this idea of a triangle came to me from external objects by way of the sense-organs (since I have sometimes seen bodies of triangular shape); for I can mentally form countless other figures, as to which there can be no suspicion that they ever came my way through the senses, and yet I can prove various properties of them, just as I can of the triangle. All

Source: Elizabeth Anscombe et al., *Philosophical Writings: Descartes.* © 1971. Reprinted by permission of Prentice Hall, Upper Saddle River, NJ.

these properties are true, since I perceive them clearly; and so they are something, not mere nothingness; for it is obvious that whatever is true is something; and I have already proved abundantly that whatever I clearly perceive is true. Even apart from that proof, my mind is assuredly so constituted that I cannot but assent to them, at least at the time of clearly perceiving them; moreover, I remember that even previously at a time when I was utterly immersed in the objects of sensation, I regarded this kind of truths as the most certain of all—namely, those that I recognized as evident in regard to figures, and numbers, and other matters of arithmetic, or of geometry, or in general of pure abstract mathematics.

Now if it follows, from my mere ability to elicit the idea of some object from my consciousness (*cogitatione*), that all the properties that I clearly and distinctly perceive the object to have do really belong to it; could not this give rise to an argument by which the existence of God might be proved? I assuredly find in myself the idea of God—of a supremely perfect being—no less than the idea of a figure or a number; and I clearly and distinctly understand that everlasting existence belongs to his nature, no less than I can see that what I prove of some figure, or number, belongs to the nature of that figure, or number. So, even if my meditations on previous days were not entirely true, yet I ought to hold the existence of God with at least the same degree of certainty as I have so far held mathematical truths.

At first sight, indeed, this is not quite clear; it bears a certain appearance of being a fallacy. For, since I am accustomed to the distinction of existence and essence in all other objects, I am readily convinced that existence can be disjoined even from the divine essence, and that thus God can be conceived (*cogitari*) as nonexistent. But on more careful consideration it becomes obvious that existence can no more be taken away from the divine essence than the magnitude of its three angles together (that is, their being equal to two right angles) can be taken away from the essence of a triangle; or than the idea of a valley can be taken away from the idea of a hill. So it is not less[1] absurd to think of God (that is, a supremely perfect being) lacking existence (that is, lacking a certain perfection), than to think of a hill without a valley.

"Perhaps I cannot think of (*cogitare*) God except as existing, just as I cannot think of a hill without a valley. But from my thinking of a hill with a valley, it does not follow that there is any hill in the world; similarly, it appears not to follow, from my thinking of God as existent, that God does exist. For my thought (*cogitatio*) imposes no necessity on things; and just as I can imagine a winged horse, although no horse has wings, so, it may be, I can feign the conjunction of God and existence even though no God should exist."

There is a lurking fallacy here. What follows from my inability to think of a mountain apart from a valley is not that a mountain and a valley exist somewhere,

---

[1] The Latin word is *magis*, but the sense seems to require *minus*. So the French version: [*moins de répugnance.*—TR.]

but only that mountain and valley, whether they exist or not, are mutually inseparable. But from my inability to think of God as nonexistent, it follows that existence is inseparable from God and thus that he really does exist. It is not that my thought makes this so, or imposes any necessity on anything; on the contrary, the necessity of the fact itself, that is, of God's existence, is what determines me to think this way. I am not free to think of God apart from existence (that is, of a supremely perfect being apart from the supreme perfection) in the way that I can freely imagine a horse either with or without wings.

Moreover, I must not say at this point: "After supposing God to have all perfections, I must certainly suppose him to be existent, since existence is one among perfections; but the initial supposition was not necessary. In the same way, there is no necessity for me to think all quadrilaterals can be inscribed in a circle; but given that I do think so, I shall necessarily have to admit that a rhombus can be inscribed in a circle; this, however, is obviously false." For there is indeed no necessity for me ever to happen upon any thought of (*cogitationem de*) God; but whenever I choose to think of (*cogitare de*) the First and Supreme Being, and as it were bring out the idea of him from the treasury of my mind, I must necessarily ascribe to him all perfections, even if I do not at the moment enumerate them all, or attend to each. This necessity clearly ensures that, when later on I observe that existence is a perfection, I am justified in concluding that the First and Supreme Being exists. In the same way, it is not necessary that I should ever imagine any triangle; but whenever I choose to consider a rectilinear figure that has just three angles, I must ascribe to it properties from which it is rightly inferred that its three angles are not greater than two right angles; even if I do not notice this at the time. When, on the other hand, I examine what figures can be inscribed in circles, it is in no way necessary for me to think all quadrilaterals belong to this class; indeed, I cannot even imagine this, so long as I will admit only what I clearly and distinctly understand. Thus there is a great difference between such false suppositions and my genuine innate ideas, among which the first and chief is my idea of God. In many ways, I can see that this idea is no fiction depending on my way of thinking (*cogitatione*), but an image of a real and immutable nature. First, I can frame no other concept of anything to whose essence existence belongs, except God alone; again, I cannot conceive of two or more such Gods; and given that one God exists, I clearly see that necessarily he has existed from all eternity, and will exist to all eternity; and I perceive many other Divine attributes, which I can in no wise diminish or alter.

Whatever method of proof I use, it always comes back to this: I am not utterly convinced of anything but what I clearly and distinctly perceive. Of the things I thus perceive, some are obvious to anybody; others are discovered only by those who undertake closer inspection and more careful investigation, but, when once discovered, are regarded as no less certain than the others. It is not so readily apparent that the square on the base of a right-angled triangle is equal to the squares of the sides, as it is that the base subtends the greatest angle; but once it has been seen to be so, it is just as much believed. Now as regards God, assuredly there would be nothing that I perceived earlier or more readily, if it were not that I am overwhelmed by prejudices, and my consciousness (*cogitationem*) beset in every direction by images of sensible objects. For what is intrinsically more obvious than that the Supreme Being is; that God, to whose essence alone existence belongs, exists? And though it took careful consideration for me to see this, yet now I am as certain of it as I am of anything else that appears most certain; not only that, but I can further see that the certainty of everything else depends on this, so that apart from this no perfect knowledge is ever possible. . . .

Discussion Questions

1. What aspects of the Judaeo-Christian religious tradition make the ontological argument an especially significant way of thinking about God?

2. Explain what it means to say that the ontological argument is purely a priori, hence deductive.

3. Do you think the ontological argument would convince a nonbeliever? Why or why not? What does your answer to this question tell you about the nature of faith?

4. A common response to the ontological argument is to say that just because we can think of something does not prove that it exists. Is this an adequate refutation of the argument? What might Descartes have said to this objection?

5. Most defenders of the ontological argument claim that it works only in the case of God. Explain the basis for this claim.

The Cosmological Arguments

The ontological argument is an attempt to argue for God's existence on purely a priori grounds, and what is distinctive about the argument is that it makes no appeal to sense experience or to alleged facts about the world. Since it begins with the definition of God and seeks to infer from this the necessity of God's existence, the a priori form of argument can be called *deductive*. The ontological argument attempts to deduce the existence of God solely from an examination of the concept of God's being.

If you were to stop the average person on the street and ask for an argument for God's existence, you would probably not get an answer in any way resembling the ontological argument. What you would probably get by way of response is something like the following: "Well, something had to create the world. It did not just happen, and I suppose that there must be a God in order to account for the order and beauty of the world." Whether or not our streetside observer would recognize it as such, this is a cosmological type of argument. The term *cosmological* has already been introduced, but a little refinement of it is in order at this point.

The ancient Greeks were the first to refer to the world as a *cosmos*, an ordered system in contrast with a disordered, random *chaos*. The insight that the world is orderly, that it functions according to rational principles, was a brilliant leap forward in the history of thought, an advance absolutely essential to the development of modern physical science. We take the regularity and uniformity of nature so much for granted that we cease to be startled by the insight that nature is orderly, but it was this view, perhaps more than any other, that gave rise to the creative impulses of ancient Greek philosophical and scientific thought. The Greeks also questioned how the universe came to be orderly. One prevailing view, advanced by atomists, was that through endless eons of random motion, a world just happened to form and that what is operative in the world is simply random order due to the chance motions of atoms. The alternative view, held by other Greek thinkers, was that the regularity and uniformity of nature are due to the activity of something more like a mind than anything else we can imagine. Behind the visible world is an Intelligence or Reason that imposes the order and structure upon nature that we can observe in the processes of the world. With various refinements, these two opposed views continue to be the two poles in ongoing debate about the nature of nature.

It is not surprising that believers would identify God with the world of Reason or Intelligence that the Greeks first glimpsed as standing behind the world process. All similar arguments that move from the existence of the world, or certain facts about the world, to God as the best explanation for these facts are called *cosmological arguments*. Whatever their differences may be, all cosmological arguments start from the basic premise that there are certain facts about the world that we must explain. From this point of departure, the arguments proceed to propose God, or at least an absolute mind, as the best explanation of these facts about nature. Any argument that argues inductively from the world to God is cosmological. Such arguments presume that the universe is a cosmos, not a chaos, and seek to understand the principle by which the order of the universe can be explained. (As an interesting aside, the Greek word *cosmos* has another English derivative—*cosmetics*, which provide a way of bringing order out of what would otherwise perhaps be a chaotic situation.) Because they begin with alleged facts about the world known through sense experience, all arguments of the cosmological type are arguments a posteriori.

We will consider three principal a posteriori arguments, since most of the variations that cosmological arguments have undergone through the years can be reduced to one of these three types. The first argument is the *argument from contingency*, and its most frequent formulation is in terms of an argument from causation. The second type is the *design argument*, which takes as its point of departure the order and apparent purposiveness in the world. Sometimes this argument is referred to as the teleological proof (from the Greek *telos*, meaning purpose or end). The third type is the moral argument, which proceeds from the claim that human beings have an awareness of moral obligation, and this can be adequately accounted for only by the existence of a supreme mind. Sometimes writers reserve the term *cosomological* for only the first type—arguments from contingency or causation. And, as has already been mentioned, since cosmological arguments begin with observed facts and argue from them to God as the most plausible explanation for these facts, all cosmological arguments are inductive in their form of reasoning.

The classic formulation of cosmological arguments was by Thomas Aquinas, a thirteenth-century Dominican monk who without question was one of the greatest intellectuals of the Middle Ages. Thomas offered five proofs, the first three of which can be reduced to the argument from contingency. The fifth argument was essentially a design argument. The fourth argument presupposes a Platonic metaphysics that assumes that there are degrees of reality—a view briefly discussed in the introduction. Because of the Platonic view it presupposes, the fourth argument is not generally discussed as a convincing argument in contemporary circles. Thomas claims no originality for his proofs, deriving their general outline from similar proofs worked out by the Greek philosopher

Aristotle. Because Thomas's treatment of the arguments is brief and presumes a familiarity with Aristotelian terminology, we will mainly concentrate on the more recent formulations of the arguments, an approach that has the added benefit of demonstrating that cosmological arguments are still taken seriously by philosophers. As background material, however, we will look at relevant features of the Thomistic arguments when discussing the cosmological proofs in their contemporary forms.

Basic to the cosmological type of argument is the notion of *contingency*, which is closely connected with the idea of dependence. Something that is contingent can be dependent upon something else in many senses, and in his first two arguments Thomas Aquinas pinpoints two indications of dependency: the fact that every change in the world is the result of some source of change, and the plausible view that every effect results from a prior cause. There is really nothing mystifying about this; they are facts about the world that seem to be confirmed by all our experience. Everything that changes presupposes some previous source of the change. Things change not simply by themselves, but as a result of something acting upon them. Change here can include the almost bewildering variety of processes in nature. Trees grow and die; human beings are born, mature, and grow old; mountains erode away; rivers alter their courses. So widespread is the fact of change in nature that it would appear that change is a fundamental fact of the world. But how are we to account for this universal flux of things if nothing changes by itself? The obvious answer is that something else acts upon an object to cause change. In other words, to change is to be changed. But the cause of a given change is itself the result of some previous source of change, and so on. Following out this line of argument, Thomas concludes that we are led ultimately to a source of change that is itself unchanged, and this is what we mean by God.

Generalizing somewhat from this line of reasoning, Thomas suggests in his second argument that causation is also a fact about the world. Everything that happens has a cause. That cause itself is the effect of some prior cause, and so forth, until we ultimately reach an uncaused cause, which is God. Perhaps a crude metaphor will help. Imagine a train proceeding down a railroad track. If someone asked you what makes the last car in the train move, you could reply that the car in front of it imparts motion to the car. If your questioner then asked what makes that car move, you could also reply that its motion is imparted by the car in front of it, and so on. If your questioner had a particularly stubborn sort of mind, these questions would continue until at last you reached the engine, which you would describe as the source of motion for the entire train, the engine being the source of motion that is itself unmoved by any other car on the train.

There is, however, one major flaw with this metaphor. It is easy to imagine the train itself as analogous to a series of causes in time. This would make the cosmological argument say, in effect, that what happens at the present moment is dependent on what happened in the moment prior to it; that in turn is the result of some past cause, until we finally reach God, who at some distant moment in time created the world and set the world process in motion. Most modern inter-preters of the cosmological argument reject this interpretation, although it was popular in the eighteenth century. They rather see the cosmological argument as saying that at any point in time there is a series of relationships of dependence that lead to God as the source of all change and all causation. In other words, at this present moment God is the source of all change in an ultimate sense and the cause of there being something rather than nothing.

Perhaps this last point will be clarified by a further examination of the no-tion of contingency. In fact, Thomas's third argument is based squarely on the no-tion of the contingency of the world, since, to a great extent, the arguments from change and causation presuppose it. To say that something is contingent means, among other things, that a contingent thing is merely possible; that is, it does not have to exist. In the world, everything appears to be contingent, or merely possi-ble. But if *all* physical things were merely possible, then at some time they would not have existed, since among the possibilities of a contingent being is the possi-bility of nonexistence. But should nothing exist, there would not be anything in existence now (since things do not come into being out of nothing). This, how-ever, is absurd because there are existing things now. This leads to the conclusion that there is a Being that is not merely contingent but necessary, a Being that does not depend upon anything else for its existence. All other, merely contin-gent things depend upon it. And this necessary Being is what we mean by God.

In this form, which is essentially the way Thomas Aquinas presents it, the argument from contingency is implied but is not as forcibly presented as in the following selection from the contemporary philosopher, Richard Taylor. Taylor is a clear and straightforward writer, and not much in the way of exposition and commentary is required. But it is important to underscore the importance of the *principle of sufficient reason*. This principle flows directly out of the analysis of the notion of contingency and claims that it is a basic pattern of thought to ex-pect that there is a reason for everything that exists. Things do not happen without a cause or without some reason sufficient to explain their happening. We might not know what this reason is, but basic to our human modes of thought is the conviction that things do not happen for no reason at all. This consideration points up the fact that Thomas Aquinas's arguments from change and causation are merely variants of the principle of sufficient reason.

There is a world. That much is obvious to us. But how can we explain its ex-istence? The principle of sufficient reason demands that there be an explanation, for it would be rationally intolerable to say that there is no sufficient reason for the world's existence. Taylor devotes considerable attention to arguing that we de-mand a similar explanation for the existence of anything. Where can we find a sufficient reason for the world's existence? We can scarcely find this reason within the world itself, for everything in the world is contingent. We must, therefore, seek the sufficient reason for the existence of the world in a Being that is purely necessary, and this Being is God.

Two important admissions need to be made here. The first is that we cannot prove that the principle of sufficient reason is true; yet without assuming this principle, we could prove nothing else. A scientist attempting to find a cure for cancer does not know what the cause of cancer is, but nonetheless believes that there is a cause, for this is the basic presupposition of all scientific research. Or go back to the metaphor of the train. Your inquirer would find you exceedingly tiresome were you to keep answering the question about the motion of the train's cars by attributing the motion of each car to that of the car in front. At some point your friend would say, "But what makes the whole train move?" You could then logically, but perhaps not very plausibly, reply that the explanation you are giving is perfectly correct. The motion of any given car is provided by the car in front of it, since there is no self-moving engine, but rather an infinity of railroad cars. We would reject such a response as absurd, since it amounts in effect to saying that there is no sufficient reason for the motion of the train. In short, to say that there is no sufficient reason is to say that there is no explanation at all, and this we would find implausible because it violates an assumption underlying all rational thought. We could reply that the world is just what it is and there is no logical necessity for an unmoved mover or uncaused cause of the world; everything in the world is caused by some prior cause in an infinity of causes. While perhaps not illogical, such an explanation, at least in Taylor's view, is implausible.

The second admission is that there is nothing in the argument from contingency to prove that the world had a beginning in time. In fact, Thomas Aquinas thought there was no argument to prove that the world had a beginning and that this was an item to be accepted by faith. Taylor subjects the argument from contingency to considerable scrutiny and shows, however, that there is no contradiction in maintaining that the world is both contingent and without beginning in time. Strange as it may at first appear, the argument from contingency is not the least damaged by the view that the world is eternal, for it can be eternal—that is, have had no beginning in time—and yet still be dependent upon God.

A final thrust of Taylor's analysis is to scrutinize the notion of God as self-caused. An obvious question, which frequently occurs even to children, is "Who caused God?" Obviously, nothing could have caused God, for that would make of this cause a being greater than God, which is contradictory. The only logical response to the question is that God is God's own principle of sufficient reason; that is, God is self-caused. God is not dependent upon anything. God had no beginning and will have no end. This characteristic is referred to as *aseity*, which is the idea of a being without beginning or end and without dependence upon anything else for its existence. To speak of God as first cause is therefore to speak of a Being that is its own sufficient reason, a Being that is necessary and eternal. Although the ontological argument and the cosmological arguments begin with different premises, they conclude at the same point by affirming the existence of a necessary Being who is the cause (in the sense of sufficient reason) of everything else.

The Argument from Contingency

RICHARD TAYLOR

THE PRINCIPLE OF SUFFICIENT REASON

Suppose you were strolling in the woods, and, in addition to the sticks, stones, and other accustomed litter of the forest floor, you one day came upon some quite unaccustomed object, something not quite like what you had ever seen before and would never expect to find in such a place. Suppose, for example, that it is a large ball, about your own height, perfectly smooth and translucent. You would deem this puzzling and mysterious, certainly, but if one considers the matter, it is no more inherently mysterious that such a thing should exist than that anything else should exist. If you were quite accustomed to finding such objects of various sizes around you most of the time, but had never seen an ordinary rock, then upon finding a large rock in the woods one day you would be just as puzzled and mystified. This illustrates the fact that something that is mysterious ceases to seem so simply by its accustomed presence. It is strange indeed, for example, that a world such as ours should exist; yet few men are very often struck by this strangeness, but simply take it for granted.

Suppose, then, that you have found this translucent ball and are mystified by it. Now whatever else you might wonder about it, there is one thing you would hardly question; namely, that it did not appear there all by itself, that it owes its existence to something. You might not have the remotest idea whence and how it came to be there, but you would hardly doubt that there was an explanation. The idea that it might have come from nothing at all, that it might exist without there being any explanation of its existence, is one that few people would consider worthy of entertaining.

This illustrates a metaphysical belief that seems to be almost a part of reason itself, even though few men ever think upon it; the belief, namely, that there is some explanation for the existence of anything whatever, some reason why it should exist rather than not. The sheer nonexistence of anything, which is not to be confused with the passing out of existence of something, never requires a reason; but

Source: Richard Taylor, *Metaphysics,* 4th ed. © 1974. Reprinted by permission of Prentice Hall, Upper Saddle River, N.J.

existence does. That there should never have been any such ball in the forest does not require any explanation or reason, but that there should ever be such a ball does. If one were to look upon a barren plain and ask why there is not and never has been any large translucent ball there, the natural response would be to ask why there should be; but if one finds such a ball, and wonders why it is there, it is not quite so natural to ask why it should *not* be, as though existence should simply be taken for granted. That anything should not exist, then, and that, for instance, no such ball should exist in the forest, or that there should be no forest for it to occupy, or no continent containing a forest, or no earth, nor any world at all, do not seem to be things for which there needs to be any explanation or reason; but that such things should be, does seem to require a reason.

The principle involved here has been called the principle of sufficient reason. Actually, it is a very general principle, and is best expressed by saying that, in the case of any positive truth, there is some sufficient reason for it, something which, in this sense, makes it true—in short, that there is some sort of explanation, known or unknown, for everything.

Now some truths depend on something else, and are accordingly called *contingent*, while others depend only upon themselves, that is, are true by their very natures and are accordingly called *necessary*. There is, for example, a reason why the stone on my window sill is warm; namely, that the sun is shining upon it. This happens to be true, but not by its very nature. Hence, it is contingent, and depends upon something other than itself. It is also true that all the points of a circle are equidistant from the center, but this truth depends upon nothing but itself. No matter what happens, nothing can make it false. Similarly, it is a truth, and a necessary one, that if the stone on my window sill is a body, as it is, then it has a form, because this fact depends upon nothing but itself for confirmation. Untruths are also, of course, either contingent or necessary, it being contingently false, for example, that the stone on my window sill is cold, and necessarily false that it is both a body and formless, because this is by its very nature impossible.

The principle of sufficient reason can be illustrated in various ways, as we have done, and if one thinks about it, he is apt to find that he presupposes it in his thinking about reality, but it cannot be proved. It does not appear to be itself a necessary truth, and at the same time it would be most odd to say it is contingent. If one were to try proving it, he would sooner or later have to appeal to considerations that are less plausible than the principle itself. Indeed, it is hard to see how one could even make an argument for it, without already assuming it. For this reason it might properly be called a presupposition of reason itself. One can deny that it is true, without embarrassment or fear of refutation, but one is then apt to find that what he is denying is not really what the principle asserts. We shall, then, treat it here as a datum—not something that is provably true, but as something which all men, whether they ever reflect upon it or not, seem more or less to presuppose.

THE EXISTENCE OF A WORLD

It happens to be true that something exists, that there is, for example, a world, and although no one ever seriously supposes that this might not be so, that there might exist nothing at all, there still seems to be nothing the least necessary in this, considering it just by itself. That no world should ever exist at all is perfectly comprehensible and seems to express not the slightest absurdity. Considering any particular item in the world it seems not at all necessary in itself that it should ever have existed, nor does it appear any more necessary that the totality of these things, or any totality of things, should ever exist.

From the principle of sufficient reason it follows, of course, that there must be a reason, not only for the existence of everything in the world but for the world itself, meaning by "the world" simply everything that ever does exist, except God, in case there is a god. This principle does not imply that there must be some purpose or goal for everything, or for the totality of all things; for explanations need not, and in fact seldom are, teleological or purposeful. All the principle requires is that there be some sort of reason for everything. And it would certainly be odd to maintain that everything in the world owes its existence to something, that nothing in the world is either purely accidental, or such that it just bestows its own being upon itself, and then to deny this of the world itself. One can indeed *say* that the world is in some sense a pure accident, that there simply is no reason at all why this or any world should exist, and one can equally say that the world exists by its very nature, or is an inherently necessary being. But it is at least very odd and arbitrary to deny of this existing world the need for any sufficient reason, whether independent of itself or not, while presupposing that there is a reason for every other thing that ever exists.

Consider again the strange ball that we imagine has been found in the forest. Now we can hardly doubt that there must be an explanation for the existence of such a thing, though we may have no notion what that explanation is. It is not, moreover, the fact of its having been found in the forest rather than elsewhere that renders an explanation necessary. It matters not in the least where it happens to be, for our question is not how it happens to be *there* but how it happens to exist at all. If we in our imagination annihilate the forest, leaving only this ball in an open field, our conviction that it is a contingent thing and owes its existence to something other than itself is not reduced in the least. If we now imagine the field to be annihilated, and in fact everything else as well to vanish into nothingness, leaving only this ball to constitute the entire physical universe, then we cannot for a moment suppose that its existence has thereby been explained, or the need of any explanation eliminated, or that its existence is suddenly rendered self-explanatory. If we now carry this thought one step further and suppose that no other reality ever has existed or ever will exist, that this ball forever constitutes the entire physical universe, then we must still insist on there being some reason independent of itself why it should exist rather than not. If there must be a reason for the existence of any particular thing, then the necessity of such a reason is not eliminated by the mere supposition that certain other things do *not* exist. And again, it matters not at all what the thing in question is, whether it be large and complex, such as the world we actually find ourselves in, or whether it be something small, simple and insignificant, such as a ball, a bacterium, or the merest grain of sand. We do not avoid the necessity of a reason for the existence of something merely by describing it in this way or that. And it would, in any event, seem quite plainly absurd to say that if the world were comprised entirely of a single ball about six feet in diameter, or of a single grain of sand, then it would be contingent and there would have to be some explanation other than itself why such a thing exists, but that, since the actual world is vastly more complex than this, there is no need for an explanation of its existence, independent of itself.

BEGINNINGLESS EXISTENCE

It should now be noted that it is no answer to the question, why a thing exists, to state *how long* it has existed. A geologist does not suppose that he has explained why there should be rivers and mountains merely by pointing out that they are old. Similarly, if one were to ask, concerning the ball of which we have spoken, for some sufficient reason for its being, he would not receive any answer upon being told that it had been there since yesterday. Nor would it be any better answer to say that it had existed since before anyone could remember, or even that it had existed; for the question was not one concerning its age but its existence. If, to be sure, one were to ask where a given thing came from, or how it came into being, then upon learning that it had always existed he would learn that it never really *came* into being at all; but he could still reasonably wonder why it should exist at all. If, accordingly, the world—that is, the totality of all things excepting God, in case there is a god—had really no beginning at all, but has always existed in some form or other, then there is clearly no answer to the question, where it came from and when; it did not, on this supposition, *come* from anything at all, at any time. But still, it can be asked why there is a world, why indeed there is a beginningless world, why there should have perhaps always been something rather than nothing. And, if the principle of sufficient reason is a good principle, there must be an answer to that question, an answer that is by no means supplied by giving the world an age, or even an infinite age.

CREATION

This brings out an important point with respect to the concept of creation that is often misunderstood, particularly by those whose thinking has been influenced by Christian ideas. People tend to think that creation—for example, the creation of the world by God—*means* creation *in time*, from which it of course logically follows that if the world had no beginning in time, then it cannot be the creation of God. This, however, is erroneous, for creation means essentially *dependence*, even in Christian theology. If one thing is the creation of another, then it depends for its existence on that other, and this is perfectly consistent with saying that both are eternal, that neither ever came into being, and hence, that neither was ever created at any point of time. Perhaps an analogy will help convey this point. Consider, then, a flame that is casting beams of light. Now there seems to be a clear sense in which the beams of light are dependent for their existence upon the flame, which is their source, while the flame, on the other hand, is not similarly dependent for its existence upon them. The beams of light arise from the flame, but the flame does not arise from them. In this sense, they are the creation of the flame; they derive their existence from it. And none of this has any reference to time; the relationship of dependence in such a case would not be altered in the slightest if we supposed that the flame, and with it the beams of light, had always existed, that neither had ever *come* into being.

Now if the world is the creation of God, its relationship to God should be thought of in this fashion; namely, that the world depends for its existence upon God, and could not exist independently of God. If God is eternal, as those who believe in God generally assume, then the world may (though it need not) be eternal too, without that altering in the least its dependence upon God for its existence, and hence without altering its being the creation of God. The supposition of God's eternality, on the other hand, does not by itself imply that the world is eternal too; for there is not the least reason why something of finite duration might not depend for its existence upon something of infinite duration—though the reverse is, of course, impossible.

GOD

If we think of God as "the creator of heaven and earth," and if we consider heaven and earth to include everything that exists except God, then we appear to have, in the foregoing considerations, fairly strong reasons for asserting that God, as so conceived, exists. Now of course most people have much more in mind than this when they think of God, for religions have ascribed to God ever so many attributes that are not at all implied by describing him merely as the creator of the world; but that is not relevant here. Most religious persons do, in any case, think of God as being at least the creator, as that being upon which everything ultimately depends, no matter what else they may say about him in addition. It is, in fact, the first item in the creeds of Christianity that God is the "creator of heaven and earth." And, it seems, there are good metaphysical reasons, as distinguished from the persuasions of faith, for thinking that such a creative being exists.

If, as seems clearly implied by the principle of sufficient reason, there must be a reason for the existence of heaven and earth—i.e., for the world—then that reason must be found either in the world itself, or outside it, in something that is literally supranatural, or outside heaven and earth. Now if we suppose that the world—i.e., the totality of all things except God—contains within itself the reason for its existence, we are supposing that it exists by its very nature, that is, that it is a necessary being. In that case there would, of course, be no reason for saying that it must depend upon God or anything else for its existence; for if it exists by its very nature, then it depends upon nothing but itself, much as the sun depends upon nothing but itself for its heat. This, however, is implausible, for we find nothing about the world or anything in it to suggest that it exists by its own nature, and we do find, on the contrary, ever so many things to suggest that it does not. For in the first place, anything that exists by its very nature must necessarily be eternal and indestructible. It would be a self-contradiction to say of anything that it exists by its own nature, or is a necessarily existing thing, and at the same time to say that it comes into being or passes away, or that it ever could come into being or pass away. Nothing about the world seems at all like this, for concerning anything in the world, we can perfectly easily think of it as being annihilated, or as never having existed in the first place, without there being the slightest hint of any absurdity in such a supposition. Some of the things in the universe are, to be sure, very old; the moon, for example, or the stars and the planets. It is even possible to imagine that they have always existed. Yet it seems quite impossible to suppose that they owe their existence to nothing but themselves, that they bestow existence upon themselves by their very natures, or that they are in themselves things of such nature that it would be impossible for them not to exist. Even if we suppose that something, such as the sun, for instance, has existed forever, and will never cease, still we cannot conclude just from this that it exists by its own nature. If, as is of course very doubtful, the sun has existed forever and will never cease, then it is possible that its heat and light have also existed forever and will never cease; but that would not show that the heat and light of the sun exist by their own natures. They are obviously contingent and depend on the sun for their existence, whether they are beginningless and everlasting or not.

There seems to be nothing in the world, then, concerning which it is at all plausible to suppose that it exists by its own nature, or contains within itself the reason for its existence. In fact, everything in the world appears to be quite plainly the opposite, namely, something that not only need not exist, but at some time or other, past or future or both, does not in fact exist. Everything in the world seems to have a finite duration, whether long or short. Most things, such as ourselves, exist only for a short while; they come into being, then soon cease. Other things, like the heavenly bodies, last longer, but they are still corruptible, and from all that we can gather about them, they too seem destined eventually to perish. We arrive at the conclusion, then, that although the world may contain some things that have always existed and are destined never to perish, it is nevertheless doubtful that it contains any such thing and, in any case, everything in the world is capable of perishing, and nothing in it, however long it may already have existed and however long it may yet remain, exists by its own nature, but depends instead upon something else.

Although this might be true of everything in the world, is it necessarily true of the world itself? That is, if we grant, as we seem forced to, that nothing in the world exists by its own nature, that everything in the world is contingent and perishable, must we also say that the world itself, or the totality of all these perishable things, is also contingent and perishable? Logically, we are not forced to, for it is logically possible that the totality of all perishable things might itself be imperishable, and hence, that the world might exist by its own nature, even though it is comprised exclusively of things that are contingent. It is not logically necessary that a totality should share the defects of its members. For example, even though every man is mortal, it does not follow from this that the human race, or the totality of all men, is also mortal; for it is possible that there will always be human beings, even though there are no human beings who will always exist. Similarly, it is possible that the world is in itself a necessary thing, even though it is comprised entirely of things that are contingent.

This is logically possible, but it is not plausible. For we find nothing whatever about the world, any more than in its parts, to suggest that it exists by its own nature. Concerning anything in the world, we have not the slightest difficulty in supposing that it should perish, or even that it should never have existed in the first place. We have almost as little difficulty in supposing this of the world itself. It might be somewhat hard to think of everything as utterly perishing and leaving no trace whatever of its ever having been, but there seems to be not the slightest difficulty in imagining that the world should never have existed in the first place. We can, for instance, perfectly easily suppose that nothing in the world had ever existed except, let us suppose, a single grain of sand, and we can thus suppose that this grain of sand has forever constituted the whole universe. Now if we consider just this grain of sand, it is quite impossible for us to suppose that it exists by its very nature, and could never have failed to exist. It clearly depends for its existence upon something other than itself, if it depends on anything at all. The same will be true if we consider the world to consist, not of one grain of sand, but of two, or of a million, or as we in fact find, of a vast number of stars and planets and all their minuter parts.

It would seem, then, that the world, in case it happens to exist at all—and this is quite beyond doubt—is contingent and thus dependent upon something other than itself for its existence, if it depends upon anything at all. And it must depend upon something, for otherwise there could be no reason why it exists in the first place. Now that upon which the world depends must be something that either exists by its own nature or does not. If it does not exist by its own nature, then it, in turn, depends for its existence upon something else, and so on. Now then, we can say either of two things; namely (1) that the world depends for its existence upon something else, which in turn depends on still another thing, this depending upon still another, *ad infinitum*; or (2) that the world derives its existence from something that exists by its own nature and that is accordingly eternal and imperishable, and is the creator of heaven and earth. The first of these alternatives, however, is impossible, for it does not render a sufficient reason why anything should exist in the first place. Instead of supplying a reason why any world should exist, it repeatedly begs off giving a reason. It explains what is dependent and perishable in terms of what is itself dependent and perishable, leaving us still without a reason why perishable things should exist at all, which is what we are seeking. Ultimately, then, it would seem that the world, or the totality of contingent or perishable things, in case it exists at all, must depend upon something that is necessary and imperishable, and that accordingly exists, not in dependence upon something else, but by its own nature.

"SELF-CAUSED"

What has been said thus far gives some intimation of what meaning should be attached to the concept of a self-caused being, a concept that is quite generally misunderstood, sometimes even by scholars. To say that something—God, for example—is self-caused, or is the cause of its own existence, does not mean that this being brings itself into existence, which is a perfectly absurd idea. Nothing can *bring* itself into existence. To say that something is self-caused (*causa sui*) means only that it exists, not contingently or in dependence upon something else, but by its own nature, which is only to say that it is a being which is such that it can neither come into being nor perish. Now whether such a being in fact exists or not, there is in any case no absurdity in the idea. We have found, in fact, that the principle of sufficient reason seems to point to the existence of such a being, as that upon which the world, with everything in it, must ultimately depend for its existence.

"NECESSARY BEING"

A being that depends for its existence upon nothing but itself, and is in this sense self-caused, can equally be described as a necessary being; that is to say, a being that is not contingent, and hence not perishable. For in the case of anything that exists by its own nature and is dependent upon nothing else, it is impossible that it should not exist, which is equivalent to saying that it is necessary. Many persons have professed to find the gravest difficulties in this concept, too, but that is partly because it has been confused with other notions. If it makes sense to speak of anything as an *impossible* being, or something that by its very nature does not exist, then it is hard to see why the idea of a necessary being, or something that in its very nature exists, should not be just as comprehensible. And of course, we have not the slightest difficulty in speaking of something, such as a square circle or a formless body, as an impossible being. And if it makes sense to speak of something as being perishable, contingent, and dependent upon something other than itself for its existence, as it surely does, then there seems to be no difficulty in thinking of something as imperishable and dependent upon nothing other than itself for its existence.

"FIRST CAUSE"

From these considerations we can see also what is properly meant by a first cause, an appellative that has often been applied to God by theologians, and that many persons have deemed an absurdity. It is a common criticism of this notion to say that there need not be any first cause, because the series of causes and effects that constitute the history of the universe might be infinite or beginningless and must, in fact, be infinite in case the universe itself had no beginning in time.

This criticism, however, reflects a total misconception of what is meant by a first cause. *First* here does not mean first in time, and when God is spoken of as a first cause, he is not being described as a being which, at some time in the remote past, *started* everything. To describe God as a first cause is only to say that he is literally a *primary* rather than a secondary cause, an *ultimate* rather than a derived cause, or a being upon which all other things, heaven and earth, ultimately depend for their existence. It is, in short, only to say that God is the creator, in the sense of creation explained above. Now this, of course, is perfectly consistent with saying that the world is eternal or beginningless. As we have seen, one gives no reason for the existence of a world merely by giving it an age, even if it is supposed to have an infinite age. To use a helpful analogy, we can say that the sun is the first cause of daylight and, for that matter, of the moonlight of the night as well, which means only that daylight and moonlight ultimately depend upon the sun for their existence. The moon, on the other hand, is only a secondary or derivative cause of its light. This light would be no less dependent upon the sun if we affirmed that it had no beginning, for an ageless and beginningless light requires a source no less than an ephemeral one. If we supposed that the sun has always existed, and with it its light, then we would have to say that the sun has always been the first—i.e., the primary or ultimate—cause of its light. Such is precisely the manner in which God should be thought of, and is by theologians often thought of, as the first cause of heaven and earth.

Discussion Questions

1. Show how the notion of the contingency of the world is a basic presupposition of the cosmological argument.

2. Taylor admits that the principle of sufficient reason is not a necessary truth and that it cannot be proved; yet he insists that it is a basic presupposition of thinking. Do you agree? Why or why not?

3. Some thinkers have argued that the notion of a noncontingent being, that is, a necessary being, is a meaningless juxtaposition of words. What would be your response to this?

4. Do you agree with Taylor that it is not contradictory to hold that the world has always existed yet is contingent? Give reasons for your answer.

5. What would be your answer to the question "Who caused God?"

6. In what sense does the cosmological argument point to God as "first cause"? In what sense does it *not* point to God as "first cause"?

The Design Argument

The argument from design, or teleological argument, begins with the alleged fact that the world exhibits order and regularity. Indeed, one may even go so far as to claim that the natural order appears to exhibit purpose in that all aspects of nature are intricately interdependent in such a way as to produce intelligent life. The design argument was extremely popular in the eighteenth century, and as was mentioned previously, a form of it appeared in the thirteenth century as Thomas Aquinas's fifth argument. Its classic formulation is by William Paley, whose book *Natural Theology*, written in 1802, lays out in great detail the considerations for the teleological argument and also answers many possible objections to it.

Paley begins with a parable. Suppose that you are walking along a meadow and there discover a watch lying on the ground. Paley suggests that your attitude toward the watch would be vastly different from your attitude toward a nearby stone. You would immediately conclude that the watch, unlike the stone, was not placed there by the forces of wind and weather but was the product of an intelligent designer. This supposition would hold even if you did not know what the contrivance was or had never seen a watch before or knew nothing about how watches were made. The very intricacy and detail of the mechanism would alone be sufficient to establish that it was the product of a conscious intelligence, that is, a watchmaker. Even if the watch did not keep perfect time, or if parts of it were badly made, you would still conclude that the mechanism did not come into existence accidentally or by chance, but was the deliberate result of the work of a watchmaker.

Paley explicitly admits that the argument is based on analogy. Anyone who has taken a College Board exam knows about analogies, where one is asked: A is to B as C is to what? In this case, the analogy is: Watch is to watchmaker as world is to God. Paley is much impressed by the intricacy of human and animal bodies and finds the human eye to be a particularly notable example of an intricate and marvelous machine. By so squarely posing his argument as one of analogy, Paley opens himself up to the counterattacks leveled at the argument by David Hume in his *Dialogues Concerning Natural Religion*. Hume's basic attack is on the analogy itself. We have no right, Hume insists, to claim that the analogy of the world as a machine is a proper one. Other analogies might work equally well—for example, the world as a kind of animal or vegetable; why all this preoccupation with mechanical contrivances? Hume also accuses Paley of assuming too much. After all, we do not know what kinds of forces are necessary to bring a world into being; besides, we have no basis for assuming that in the business of world-making anything like human intelligence is the operative principle. Because of our innate egotism, we assume that human intelligence is the highest principle in nature, but according to Hume, this is an unproven assumption.

An additional shortcoming of Paley's presentation of the design argument is that it was formulated before the publication of Darwin's *Origin of Species*, so we do not know how Paley would fit evolution into his argument. In Paley's day, the only counterresponse to a design argument was that the universe came into being purely by chance through the random forces of nature over an incredibly lengthy period of time, and all the diversity in nature and the intricacy of animal forms was due purely to chance. Today, the theory of evolution is generally taken to provide an explanation for the biological diversity in nature, and since Paley's examples of design were virtually all biological in nature, this has seriously weakened the impact of his argument.

However, an evolutionary view as an explanation for biological diversity does not, by itself, undercut the design argument. Contemporary defenders of the argument cite evolution as just another evidence of design and as further proof of divine creation.

There have been other objections raised against the cosmological type of argument. Kant rejects all arguments of the cosmological type because they assume that we can apply the notion of cause and effect to the world as a totality. Kant holds that causality is a perfectly valid principle—indeed, one that is essential to rational thought. But he insists that we can legitimately apply it only to things that can be experienced by the senses. Obviously, no one has an experience of the world as a whole, so we therefore have no grounds for assuming that the principle of causality has any validity as an explanatory principle outside the realm of experience. David Hume goes even further and questions the defensibility of the principle of causality itself. We do, to be sure, attribute cause and effect to the events we experience, but Hume argues that this is only a convenient fiction, a customary way of thinking, that we impose on experience. The principle of cause and effect, he argues, has no experiential validation, for we never experience a necessary connection between events, but only events following one another in time. Given the repeated succession of events, we think of them as causally connected, but this is something we can never prove.

Obviously, such an attack on the principle of causality, if accepted, undermines the force of the cosmological form of argument. Even for Kant, who argues that causality is a legitimate principle of human reason, the principle has no application beyond the realm of empirical experience and therefore cannot be used to prove that there is a cause of the world. Allied with this is a second Kantian objection to the cosmological argument. To prove the God of traditional Jewish and Christian belief, the cosmological argument must point to the existence of a necessary being. But Kant does not think that such a notion is acceptable. Of all the arguments for God's existence covered thus far, Kant thinks the design argument the best, but he points out that the most it can do is point to the possible existence of a mighty being who created the world out of existing materials. This being would be a kind of artificer who imposed a certain degree of order on the world (though not perfect order), but such a being is hardly the God of traditional theistic belief.

Like the argument based on the principle of sufficient reason considered previously, the design argument cannot claim to offer logical proof of God's existence. It is rather an appeal to the plausibility that the order of the world is due to intelligent design, not randomness and chance, that it is more plausible to attribute the world to a conscious designer than to accident and caprice. There is, to be sure, much disorder in the world, and the existence of evil is itself a challenge to the design argument; the world does not exhibit perfect order, and it could be better. Any argument for God's existence, however, must come to terms with the problem of evil, so the problem of evil does not strike at the design argument alone. Paley notes that the existence of some disorder in the world does not negate the degree of order that the world does exhibit, and he further suggests that even though the world may not be perfect, it does exhibit some degree of order, and it is to the explanation of this empirical fact that the design argument addresses itself.

Natural Theology

WILLIAM PALEY

CHAPTER I. STATE OF THE ARGUMENT

In crossing a heath, suppose I pitched my foot against a *stone*, and were asked how the stone came to be there; I might possibly answer that, for anything I knew to the contrary, it had lain there forever: nor would it perhaps be very easy to show

Source: William Paley, *Natural Theology.* First published in 1802. This extract is from an 1864 American edition of the work.

the absurdity of this answer. But suppose I had found a *watch* upon the ground, and it should be inquired how the watch happened to be in that place; I should hardly think of the answer which I had given, that, for anything I knew, the watch might have always been there. Yet why should not this answer serve for the watch as well as for the stone? Why is it not admissible in the second case, as in the first? For this reason, and for no other, viz. that, when we come to inspect the watch, we perceive (what we could not discover in the stone) that its several parts are framed and put together for a purpose, e.g. that they are so formed and adjusted as to produce motion, and that motion so regulated as to point out the hour of the day; that if the different parts had been differently shaped from what they are, of a different size from what they are, or placed after any other manner, or in any other order, than that in which they are placed, either no motion at all would have been carried on in the machine, or none which would have answered the use that is now served by it. To reckon up a few of the plainest of these parts, and of their offices, all tending to one result: We see a cylindrical box containing a coiled elastic spring, which, by its endeavor to relax itself, turns round the box. We next observe a flexible chain (artificially wrought for the sake of flexure) communicating the action of the spring from the box to the fusee. We then find a series of wheels, the teeth of which catch in, and apply to each other, conducting the motion from the fusee to the balance, and from the balance to the pointer; and at the same time, by the size and shape of those wheels, so regulating that motion, as to terminate in causing an index, by an equable and measured progression, to pass over a given space in a given time. We take notice that the wheels are made of brass in order to keep them from rust; the springs of steel, no other metal being so elastic; that over the face of the watch there is placed a glass, a material employed in no other part of the work; but in the room of which, if there has been any other than a transparent substance, the hour could not be seen without opening the case. This mechanism being observed (it requires indeed an examination of the instrument, and perhaps some previous knowledge of the subject, to perceive and understand it; but being once, as we have said, observed and understood,) the inference, we think, is inevitable; that the watch must have had a maker; that there must have existed, at sometime, and at some place or other, an artificer or artificers, who formed it for the purpose which we find it actually to answer; who comprehended its construction, and designed its use.

I. Nor would it, I apprehend, weaken the conclusion, that we had never seen a watch made: that we had never known an artist capable of making one; that we were altogether incapable of executing such a piece workmanship ourselves, or of understanding in what manner it was performed; all this being no more than what is true of some exquisite remains of ancient art, of some lost arts, and, to the generality of mankind, of the more curious productions of modern manufacture. Does one man in a million know how oval frames are turned? Ignorance of this kind exalts our opinion of the unseen and unknown artist's skill, if he be unseen and unknown, but raises no doubt in our minds of the existence and agency of such an artist, at some former time, and in some place or other. Nor can I perceive that it varies at all the inference, whether the question arise concerning human agent, or concerning an agent of a different species, or an agent possessing, in some respects, a different nature.

II. Neither, secondly, would it invalidate our conclusion, that the watch sometimes went wrong, or that it seldom went exactly right. The purpose of the machinery, the design and the designer, might be evident, and in the case supposed would be evident, in whatever way we accounted for the irregularity of the movement, or whether we could account for it or not. It is not necessary that a machine be perfect, in order to show with what design it was made: still less necessary, where the only question is, whether it were made with any design at all.

III. Nor, thirdly, would it bring any uncertainty into the argument, if there were a few parts of the watch, concerning which we could not discover, or had not yet discovered, in what manner they conduced to the general effect; or even some parts, concerning which we could not ascertain whether they conduced to that effect in any manner whatever. For, as to the first branch of the case; if by the loss, or disorder, or decay of the parts in question, the movement of the watch were found in fact to be stopped, or disturbed, or retarded, no doubt would remain in our minds as to the utility or intention of these parts, although we should be unable to investigate the manner according to which, or the connexion by which, the ultimate effect depended upon their action or assistance; and the more complex is the machine, the more likely is this obscurity to arise. Then, as to the second thing supposed, namely that there were parts which might be spared, without prejudice to the movement of the watch, and that we had proved this by experiment—these superfluous parts, even if we were completely assured that they were such, would not vacate the reasoning which we had instituted concerning other parts. The indication of contrivance remained, with respect to them, nearly as it was before.

IV. Nor, fourthly, would any man in his senses think the existence of the watch, with its various machinery, accounted for, by being told that it was one out of possible combinations of material forms; that whatever he had found in the place where he found the watch, must have contained some internal configuration or other; and that this configuration might be the structure now exhibited, viz. of the works of a watch, as well as a different structure.

V. Nor, fifthly, would it yield his inquiry more satisfaction to be answered, that there existed in things a principle of order, which had disposed the parts of the watch into their present form and situation. He never knew a watch made by the principle of order; nor can he even form to himself an idea of what is meant by a principle of order distinct from the intelligence of the watchmaker.

VI. Sixthly, he would be surprised to hear that the mechanism of the watch was no proof of contrivance, only a motive to induce the mind to think so.

VII. And not less surprised to be informed, that the watch in his hand was nothing more than the result of the laws of *metallic* nature. It is a perversion of language to assign any law as the efficient, operative cause of anything. A law presupposes an agent; for it is only the mode according to which an agent proceeds:

it implies a power; for it is the order, according to which that power acts. Without this agent, without this power, which are both distinct from itself, the *law* does nothing; is nothing. The expression, "the law of metallic nature," may sound strange and harsh to a philosophic ear; but it seems quite as justifiable as some others which are more familiar to him, such as "the law of vegetable nature," "the law of animal nature," or indeed as "the law of nature" in general, when assigned as the case of phenomena, in exclusion of agency and power; or when it is substituted into the place of these.

VIII. Neither, lastly, would our observer be driven out of his conclusion, or from his confidence in its truth, by being told that he knew nothing at all about the matter. He knows enough for his argument. He knows the utility of the end: he knows the subserviency and adaptation of the means to the end. These points being known, his ignorance of other points, his doubts concerning other points, affect not the certainty of his reasoning. The consciousness of knowing little need not beget a distrust of that which he does know.

CHAPTER II. STATE OF THE ARGUMENT CONTINUED

Suppose, in the next place, that the person who found the watch, should, after sometime, discover that, in addition to all the properties which he had hitherto observed in it, it possessed the unexpected property of producing, in the course of its movement, another watch like itself, (the thing is conceivable;) that it contained within it a mechanism, a system of parts, a mould for instance, or a complex adjustment of lathes, files, and other tools, evidently and separately calculated for this purpose; let us inquire, what effect ought such a discovery to have upon his former conclusion.

I. The first effect would be to increase his admiration of the contrivance, and his conviction of the consummate skill of the contriver. Whether he regarded the object of the contrivance, the distinct apparatus, the intricate, yet in many parts intelligible mechanism, by which it was carried on, he would perceive, in this new observation, nothing but an additional reason for doing what he had already done,—for referring the construction of the watch to design, and to supreme art. If that construction *without* this property, or, which is the same thing, before this property had been noticed, proved intention and art to have been employed about it, still more strong would the proof appear, when he came to the knowledge of this farther property, the crown and perfection of all the rest.

II. He would reflect, that though the watch before him were, *in some sense*, the maker of the watch which was fabricated in the course of its movements, yet it was in a very different sense from that in which a carpenter, for instance, is the maker of a chair; the author of its contrivance, the cause of the relation of its parts to their use. With respect to these, the first watch was no cause at all to the second: in no such sense as this was it the author of the constitution and order, either of the parts which the new watch contained, or of the parts by the aid and instrumentality of which it was produced. We might possibly say, but with great latitude of expression, that a stream of water ground corn; but no latitude of expression would allow us to say, no stretch of conjecture could lead us to think, that the stream of water built the mill, though it were too ancient for us, to know who the builder was. What the stream of water does in the affair, is neither more nor less than this; by the application of an unintelligent impulse to a mechanism previously arranged, arranged independently of it, and arranged by intelligence, an effect is produced, viz. the corn is ground. But the effect results from the arrangement. The force of the stream cannot be said to be the cause or author of the effect, still less of the arrangement. Understanding and plan in the formation of the mill were not the less necessary, for any share which the water has in grinding the corn; yet is this share the same as that which the watch would have contributed to the production of the new watch, upon the supposition assumed in the last section. Therefore,

III. Though it be now no longer probable, that the individual watch which our observer had found was made immediately by the hand of an artificer, yet doth not this alteration in any-wise affect the inference, that an artificer had been originally employed and concerned in the production. The argument from design remains as it was. Marks of design and contrivance are no more accounted for now than they were before. In the same thing, we may ask for the cause of different properties. We may ask for the cause of the color of a body, of its hardness, of its heat; and these causes may be all different. We are now asking for the cause of that subserviency to a use, that relation to an end, which we have remarked in the watch before us. No answer is given to this question by telling us that a preceding watch produced it. There cannot be design without a designer; contrivance, without a contriver; order, without choice; arrangement, without anything capable of arranging; subserviency and relation to a purpose, without that which could intend a purpose; means suitable to an end, and executing their office in accomplishing that end, without the end ever having been contemplated, or the means accommodated to it. Arrangement, disposition of parts, subserviency of means to an end, relation of instruments to a use, imply the presence of intelligence and mind. No one, therefore, can rationally believe, that the insensible, inanimate watch, from which the watch before us issued, was the proper cause of the mechanism we so much admire in it;—could be truly said to have constructed the instrument, disposed its parts, assigned their office, determined their order, action, and mutual dependency, combined their several motions into one result, and that also a result connected with the utilities of other beings. All these properties, therefore, are as much unaccounted for as they were before.

IV. Nor is anything gained by running the difficulty farther back, *i.e.* by supposing the watch before us to have been produced from another watch, that from a former, and so on indefinitely. Our going back ever so far brings us no nearer to the least degree of satisfaction upon the subject. Contrivance is still unaccounted for. We still want a contriver. A designing mind is neither supplied by this supposition, nor dispensed with. If the difficulty were diminished the farther we went back, by going back indefinitely we might exhaust it. And this is the only case to which this sort of reasoning applies. Where there is a tendency, or, as we increase the number of terms, a continual approach towards a limit, *there*, by supposing the number of terms to be what is called infinite, we may conceive the limit to be attained; but where there is no such tendency, or approach, nothing is effected by lengthening the series. There is no difference, as to the point in question, (whatever there may be as to many points,) between one series and another; between a series which is finite, and a series which is infinite. A chain, composed of an infinite number of links, can no more support itself, than a chain composed of a finite number of links. And of this we are assured, (though we never *can* have tried the experiment,) because, by increasing the number of links, from ten, for instance, to a hundred, from a hundred to a thousand, &c. we make not the smallest approach, we observe not the smallest tendency, towards self-support. There is no difference in this respect (yet there may be a great difference in several respects) between a chain of a greater or less length, between one chain and another, between one that is finite and one that is infinite. This very much resembles the case before us. The machine which we are inspecting demonstrates, by its construction, contrivance and design. Contrivance must have had a contriver; design, a designer; whether the machine immediately proceeded from another machine or not. That circumstance alters not the case. That other machine may, in like manner, have proceeded from a former machine: nor does that alter the case; contrivance must have had a contriver. That former one from one preceding it: no alteration still; a contriver is still necessary. No tendency is perceived, no approach towards a diminution of this necessity. It is the same with any and every succession of these machines; a succession of ten, of a hundred, of a thousand; with one series as with another; a series which is finite, as with a series which is infinite. In whatever other respects they may differ, in this they do not. In all, equally, contrivance and design are unaccounted for.

The question is not simply, How came the first watch into existence? which question, it may be pretended, is done away by supposing the series of watches thus produced from one another to have been infinite, and consequently to have had no such *first* for which it was necessary to provide a cause. This, perhaps, would have been nearly the state of the question, if nothing had been before us but an unorganized, unmechanized substance, without mark or indication of contrivance. It might be difficult to show that such substance could not have existed from eternity, either in succession (if it were possible, which I think it is not, for unorganized bodies to spring from one another), or by individual perpetuity. But that is not the question now. To suppose it to be so, is to suppose that it made no difference whether we had found a watch or a stone. As it is, the metaphysics of that question have no place; for, in the watch which we are examining, are seen contrivance, design; an end, a purpose; means for the end, adaptation to the purpose. And the question which irresistibly presses upon our thoughts, is, whence this contrivance and design? The thing required is the intending mind, the adapting hand, the intelligence by which that hand was directed. This question, this demand, is not shaken off, by increasing the number or succession of substances, destitute of these properties; nor the more, by increasing that number to infinity.

If it be said, that, upon the supposition of one watch being produced from another in the course of that other's movements, and by means of the mechanism within it, we have a cause for the watch in my hand, viz. the watch from which it proceeded: I deny, that for the design, the contrivance, the suitableness of means to an end, the adaptation of instruments to a use, (all which we discover in a watch,) we have any cause whatever. It is in vain, therefore to assign a series of such causes, or to allege that a series may be carried back to infinity; for I do not admit that we have yet any cause at all of the phenomena, still less any series of causes either finite or infinite. Here is contrivance, but no contriver: proofs of design, but no designer.

V. Our observer would farther also reflect, that the maker of the watch before him, was, in truth and reality, the maker of every watch produced from it; there being no difference (except that the latter manifests a more exquisite skill) between the making of another watch with his own hands, by the mediation of files, lathes, chisels, &c. and the disposing, fixing, and inserting of these instruments, or of others equivalent to them, in the body of the watch already made, in such a manner as to form a new watch in the course of the movements which he had given to the old one. It is only working by one set of tools instead of another.

The conclusion which the *first* examination of the watch, of its works, construction, and movement, suggested, was, that it must have had, for the cause and author of that construction, an artificer, who understood its mechanism, and designed its use. This conclusion is invincible. A *second* examination presents us with a new discovery. The watch is found, in the course of its movement, to produce another watch, similar to itself: and not only so, but we perceive in it a system or organization, separately calculated for that purpose. What effect would this discovery have or ought it to have, upon our former inference? What, as hath already been said, but to increase, beyond measure, our admiration of the skill which had been employed in the formation of such a machine! Or shall it, instead of this, all at once turn us round to an opposite conclusion, viz. that no art or skill whatever has been concerned in the business, although all other evidences of art and skill remain as they were, and this last and supreme piece of art be now added to the rest? Can this be maintained without absurdity? Yet this is atheism.

Discussion Questions

1. Does the argument from design lead to the same conception of God as does the ontological argument? Give reasons for your answer.

2. One of the facts about the world that counts again the design argument is the disorder found in the world. Paley responds to this objection in his formulation of the argument, but do you find his response adequate?

3. What is your analysis of the effect of evolution on the argument?

4. Can the attacks on the argument based on a criticism of the notion of causality be adequately answered? If so, how?

5. What is your own assessment of the force of this argument?

The Moral Argument

The arguments based on design and on the principle of sufficient reason both proceed from observed characteristics about physical nature to God as the best explanation for them. The moral argument uses at its point of departure a feature about human nature: the capacity to make moral judgments. God, so the argument goes, is the best explanation for human moral capability.

The moral argument can take several different forms. In its oldest form it presumes an objective morality that is independent of particular eras and specific cultures. Defenders of this view of morality point to the consistency among religions and ethical systems regarding basic ethical values: honesty, faithfulness in keeping one's word, refraining from murder, honoring one's parents, and so on. This view of morality finds its basis in the doctrine of *lex naturalis*, the natural law, a set of principles that can be known by all reasonable people at all times. Whether it be the Tao of Lao Tsu, the Ten Commandments, the Hindu Code of Manu, the Analects of Confucius, or other ancient thought systems, all of these embody a common understanding of right and wrong that can best be explained as implanted in human beings by God.

Another form of the argument simply points to the human moral awareness itself, not to any specific content, as evidence of the imprint of the divine nature. Whether we call it a moral sense or conscience, this capacity to recognize moral obligations sets us apart from the natural order of things and signals that humans bear within their nature a capability that can best be explained as coming from God. This moral sense does not always function well, and it is darkened by sin and evil; but it is there nonetheless as evidence that we are not just products of nature but bear within ourselves evidence of divine creativity.

Both of these versions of the moral argument have to explain the variety of beliefs and practices among human cultures as well as the fact that human beings are capable of great evil. If there is within us a recognition of moral law, why do we not agree more on what that law is? And why do we not follow it more consistently? There are answers to these objections: To know the good does not force us to do the good. And underlying the wide variety of cultural practices one can still see a common understanding of right and wrong. Defenders of natural law explain many cultural differences as examples of *positive law*, the specific rules and regulations that societies adopt to regulate their communal life. For example, natural law demands the impartial administration of justice but leaves open how this is to be accomplished: trial by jury (a particular Anglo-Saxon provision), hearing by a panel of judges, adjudication by a single judge, or varieties of mediation and conciliation. These arrangements are all matters of positive law and can reflect a great deal of variety and still be true to the demands of the natural law.

The discussion of these two versions of the moral argument are given in a brief form here for the reason that neither of them is Immanuel Kant's argument. He does not accept the notion of a moral sense, believing instead that human beings use the same faculty to make moral judgments as they do to gain knowledge of the world. That faculty is *reason*. Kant also does not argue for a universal morality or anything like natural law. Instead he proposes to explain in purely formal terms what makes an action moral and articulates a formula that can be applied anywhere by anyone to determine what the moral action is. This formula he calls the *categorical imperative*. That it is categorical means it is not conditional on any particular end to be achieved. To say that it is imperative means it is a *command*, but a command that we give to ourselves. Here is Kant's best-known formulation of the categorical imperative: *Act on the principle that you can will to be a universal law of nature.* Some people think this sounds like the Golden Rule: Do unto others as you would have them do unto you. Kant says that the categorical imperative is different. To capture that difference would be to state it in the following way: Do unto others what you are willing for everybody to do.

When Kant says that the categorical imperative is a formal principle, he means that it functions in some ways like a formula in logic. Because the principle has no specific content, it can be applied universally. Here is how it works: You are thinking about doing something. Ask yourself what the principle is that you would be applying in your proposed action. Then ask whether everybody could follow that same principle. If the answer is no, then your contemplated action is not a moral one. The categorical imperative is an important contribution to moral thinking and has generated a huge amount of commentary and analysis, but further discussion of it here would take us away from the consideration of Kant's moral argument. However, the categorical imperative remains in the background of Kant's discussion of moral grounds for belief in God even though the argument does not depend on it.

The basic premise of Kant's argument is that we, as rational beings, have a recognition of the *summum bonum*, the *highest good*. Without giving away all the details of Kant's argument, he says that the highest good is when virtue and happiness come together. As rational beings, we believe that moral goodness ought to lead to happiness: The virtuous should prosper, the wicked should be miserable. But, alas, the world is not like this. Crime pays, often very well. The evildoers enjoy their ill-gotten gain. The righteous are not always happy, and in some cases doing good leads to misery, not happiness. As rational beings we find this state of affairs intolerable and an affront to reason. Kant chooses his words carefully: It is a *demand* of reason that this dismal state of affairs not be the final word, and this implies that there must be a future life in which virtue will be rewarded and vice punished. To bring this about we have to postulate the existence of a "wise creator" who can assure that the demands of moral reasoning not be frustrated but ultimately vindicated. This is Kant's argument in a nutshell. As he develops it he comments on the relation between morality and religion and offers additional insight into the basis for his postulation of God. As you work through this selection, note that when Kant uses the term *practical* reason he means the use of reason in making moral judgments.

In one of his other works, *Critique of Pure Reason*, Kant argues against the traditional proofs for God's existence, though he finds the design argument the most compelling. In his moral philosophy Kant reinstates God as a requirement for making sense of moral duty. However, Kant never calls his analysis a *proof* of God's existence and is careful to call God a *postulate*. This is consistent with the conclusion of *Critique of Pure Reason* where he holds fast to his refutation of the traditional proofs for God's existence but says this is not the end of the matter. "For although we have to surrender the language of knowledge, we still have sufficient ground to employ, in the presence of the most exacting reason, the quite legitimate language of a firm faith."[1]

God as a Postulate
of Practical Reason

IMMANUEL KANT

The moral law led, in the foregoing analysis, to a practical problem which is assigned solely by pure reason and without any concurrence of sensuous incentives. It is the problem of the completeness of the first and principal part of the highest good, viz., morality; since this problem can be solved only in eternity, it led to the postulate of immortality. The same law must also lead us to affirm

Source: Immanuel Kant, *Critique of Practical Reason*, trans. White Beck. © 1993. Reprinted by permission of Prentice Hall, Upper Saddle River, NJ. (Some footnotes deleted.)

[1] Immanuel Kant, *Critique of Pure Reason*, A745, B773.

the possibility of the second element of the highest good, i.e., happiness proportional to that morality; it must do so just as disinterestedly as heretofore, by a purely impartial reason. This it can do on the supposition of the existence of a cause adequate to this effect, i.e., it must postulate the existence of God as necessarily belonging to the possibility of the highest good (the object of our will which is necessarily connected with the moral legislation of pure reason). We proceed to exhibit this connection in a convincing manner.

Happiness is the condition of a rational being in the world, in whose whole existence everything goes according to wish and will. It thus rests on the harmony of nature with his entire end and with the essential determining ground of his will. But the moral law commands as a law of freedom through motives wholly independent of nature and of its harmony with our faculty of desire (as incentives). Still, the acting rational being in the world is not at the same time the cause of the world and of nature itself. Hence there is not the slightest ground in the moral law for a necessary connection between the morality and proportionate happiness of a being which belongs to the world as one of its parts and as thus dependent on it. Not being nature's cause, his will cannot by its own strength bring nature, as it touches on his happiness, into complete harmony with his practical principles. Nevertheless, in the practical task of pure reason, i.e., in the necessary endeavor after the highest good, such a connection is postulated as necessary: we *should* seek to further the highest good (which therefore must be at least possible). Therefore also the existence is postulated of a cause of the whole of nature, itself distinct from nature, which contains the ground of the exact coincidence of happiness with morality. This supreme cause, however, must contain the ground of the agreement of nature not merely with a law of the will of rational beings but with the idea of this law so far as they make it the supreme ground of determination of the will. Thus it contains the ground of the agreement of nature not merely with actions moral in their form but also with their morality as the motives to such actions, i.e., with their moral intention. Therefore, the highest good is possible in the world only on the supposition of a supreme cause of nature which has a causality corresponding to the moral intention. Now a being which is capable of actions by the idea of laws is an intelligence (a rational being), and the causality of such a being according to this idea of laws is his will. Therefore, the supreme cause of nature, in so far as it must be presupposed for the highest good, is a being which is the cause (and consequently the author) of nature through understanding and will, i.e., God. As a consequence, the postulate of the possibility of a highest derived good (the best world) is at the same time the postulate of the reality of a highest original good, namely, the existence of God. Now it was our duty to promote the highest good; and it is not merely our privilege but a necessity connected with duty as a requisite to presuppose the possibility of this highest good. This presupposition is made only under the condition of the existence of God, and this condition inseparably connects this supposition with duty. Therefore, it is morally necessary to assume the existence of God.

It is well to notice here that this moral necessity is subjective, i.e., a need, and not objective, i.e., duty itself. For there cannot be any duty to assume the existence of a thing, because such a supposition concerns only the theoretical use of reason. It is also not to be understood that the assumption of the existence of God is necessary as a ground of all obligation in general (for this rests, as has been fully shown, solely on the autonomy of reason itself). All that here belongs to duty is the endeavor to produce and to further the highest good in the world, the existence of which may thus be postulated though our reason cannot conceive it except by presupposing a highest intelligence. To assume its existence is thus connected with the consciousness of our duty, though this assumption itself belongs to the realm of theoretical reason. Considered only in reference to the latter, it is a hypothesis, i.e., a ground of explanation. But in reference to the comprehensibility of an object (the highest good) placed before us by the moral law, and thus as a practical need, it can be called faith and even pure rational faith, because pure reason alone (by its theoretical as well as practical employment) is the source from which it springs.

From this deduction it now becomes clear why the Greek schools could never succeed in solving their problem of the practical possibility of the highest good. It was because they made the rule of the use which the human will makes of its freedom the sole and self-sufficient ground of its possibility, thinking that they had no need of the existence of God for this purpose. They were certainly correct in establishing the principle of morals by itself, independently of this postulate and merely from the relation of reason to the will, thus making the principle of morality the *supreme* practical condition of the highest good; but this principle was not the *entire* condition of its possibility. The Epicureans had indeed raised a wholly false principle of morality, i.e., that of happiness, into the supreme one, and for law had substituted a maxim of arbitrary choice of each according to his inclination. But they proceeded consistently enough, in that they degraded their highest good in proportion to the baseness of their principle and expected no greater happiness than that which could be attained through human prudence (wherein both temperance and the moderation of inclinations belong), though everyone knows prudence to be scarce enough and to produce diverse results according to circumstances, not to mention the exceptions which their maxims continually had to admit and which made them worthless as laws. The Stoics, on the other hand, had chosen their supreme practical principle, virtue, quite correctly as the condition of the highest good. But as they imagined the degree of virtue which is required for its pure law as completely attainable in this life, they not only exaggerated the moral capacity of man, under the name of "sage," beyond all the limits of his nature, making it into something which is contradicted by all our knowledge of men; they also refused to accept the second component of the highest good, i.e., happiness, as a special object of human desire. Rather, they made their sage, like a god in the consciousness of the excellence of his person, wholly independent of nature (as regards his own contentment), exposing him to the evils of life but not subjecting him to them. (They also represented him as free from everything morally evil.) Thus they really left out of the highest good the second element (personal happiness), since they placed the highest good only in acting and in contentment with one's own personal worth, including it in the consciousness of moral character. But the voice of their own nature could have sufficiently refuted this.

The doctrine of Christianity[1], even when not regarded as a religious doctrine, gives at this point a concept of the highest good (the Kingdom of God) which is alone sufficient to the strictest demand of practical reason. The moral law is holy (unyielding) and demands holiness of morals, although all moral perfection to which man can attain is only virtue, i.e., a law-abiding disposition resulting from respect for the law and thus implying consciousness of a continuous propensity to transgress it or at least to a defilement, i.e., to an admixture of many spurious (not moral) motives to obedience to the law; consequently, man can achieve only a self-esteem combined with humility. And thus with respect to the holiness required by the Christian law, nothing remains to the creature but endless progress, though for the same reason hope of endless duration is justified. The worth of a character completely accordant with the moral law is infinite, because all possible happiness in the judgment of a wise and omnipotent dispenser of happiness has no other limitation than the lack of fitness of rational beings to their duty. But the moral law does not of itself promise happiness, for the latter is not, according to concepts of any order of nature, necessarily connected with obedience to the law. Christian ethics supplies this defect of the second indispensable component of the highest good by presenting a word wherein reasonable beings single-mindedly devote themselves to the moral law; this is the Kingdom of God, in which nature and morality come into a harmony, which is foreign to each as such, through a holy Author of the world, who makes possible the derived highest good.

---

1 The view is commonly held that the Christian precept of morals has no advantage over the moral concept of the Stoics in respect to its purity; but the difference between them is nevertheless obvious. The Stoic system makes the consciousness of strength of mind the pivot around which all moral intentions should turn; and, if the followers of this system spoke of duties and even defined them accurately, they nevertheless placed the incentives and the real determining ground of the will in an elevation of character above the base incentives of the senses which have their power only through weakness of the mind. Virtue was, therefore, for them a certain heroism of the sage who, raising himself above the animal nature of man, was sufficient to himself, subject to no temptation to transgress the moral law, and elevated above duties though he propounded duties to others. But all this they could not have done had they conceived this law in the same purity and rigor as does the precept of the Gospel. If I understand by "idea" a perfection to which the senses can give nothing adequate, the moral ideas are not transcendent, i.e., of such a kind that we cannot even sufficiently define the concept or of which we are uncertain whether there is a corresponding object (as are the ideas of speculative reason); rather, they serve as models of practical perfection, as an indispensable rule of moral conduct, and as a standard for comparison. If I now regard Christian morals from their philosophical side, it appears in comparison with the ideas of the Greek schools as follows: the ideas of the Cynics, Epicureans, Stoics, and Christians are, respectively, the simplicity of nature, prudence, wisdom, and holiness. In respect to the way they achieve them, the Greek schools differ in that the Cynics found common sense sufficient, while the others found it in the path of science, and thus all held it to lie in the mere use of man's natural powers. Christian ethics, because it formulated its precept as pure and uncompromising (as befits a moral precept), destroyed man's confidence of being wholly adequate to it, at least in this life; but it re-established it by enabling us to hope that, if we act as well as lies in our power, what is not in our power will come to our aid from another source, whether we know in what way or not. Aristotle and Plato differed only as to the origin of our moral concepts.

The holiness of morals is prescribed to them even in this life as a guide to conduct, but the well-being proportionate to this, which is bliss, is thought of as attainable only in eternity. This is due to the fact that the former must always be
the pattern of their conduct in every state, and progressing toward it is even in
this life possible and necessary, whereas the latter, under the name of happiness,
cannot (as far as our own capacity is concerned) be reached in this life and therefore is made only an object of hope. Nevertheless, the Christian principle of
morality is not theological and thus heteronomous, being rather the autonomy of
pure practical reason itself, because it does not make the knowledge of God and
His will the basis of these laws but makes such knowledge the basis only of succeeding to the highest good on condition of obedience to these laws; it places the
real incentive for obedience to the law not in the desired consequences of obedience but in the conception of duty alone, in true observance of which the worthiness to attain the latter alone consists.

In this manner, through the concept of the highest good as the object and
final end of pure practical reason, the moral law leads to religion. Religion is the
recognition of all duties as divine commands, not as sanctions, i.e., arbitrary and
contingent ordinances of a foreign will, but as essential laws of any free will as
such. Even as such, they must be regarded as commands of the Supreme Being because we can hope for the highest good (to strive for which is our duty under the
moral law) only from a morally perfect (holy and beneficent) and omnipotent
will; and, therefore, we can hope to attain it only through harmony with this will.
But here again everything remains disinterested and based only on duty, without
being based on fear or hope as incentives, which, if they became principles, would
destroy the entire moral worth of the actions. The moral law commands us to
make the highest possible good in a world the final object of all our conduct. This
I cannot hope to effect except through the agreement of my will with that of a
holy and beneficent Author of the world. And although my own happiness is included in the concept of the highest good as a whole wherein the greatest happiness is thought of as connected in exact proportion to the greatest degree of
moral perfection possible to creatures, still it is not happiness but the moral law
(which, in fact, sternly places restricting conditions upon my boundless longing
for happiness) which is proved to be the ground determining the will to further
the highest good.

Therefore, morals is not really the doctrine of how to make ourselves happy
but of how we are to be *worthy* of happiness. Only if religion is added to it can
the hope arise of someday participating in happiness in proportion as we endeav-
ored not to be unworthy of it.

One is worthy of possessing a thing or a state when his possession is har-
monious with the highest good. We can easily see now that all worthiness is a
matter of moral conduct, because this constitutes the condition of everything
else (which belongs to one's state) in the concept of the highest good, i.e., participation in happiness. From this there follows that one must never consider
morals itself as a doctrine of happiness, i.e., as an instruction in how to acquire

happiness. For morals has to do only with the rational condition (*conditio sine qua non*) of happiness and not with means of achieving it. But when morals (which imposes only duties instead of providing rules for selfish wishes) is completely expounded, and a moral wish has been awakened to promote the highest good (to bring the Kingdom of God to us), which is a wish based on law and one to which no selfish mind could have aspired, and when for the sake of this wish the step to religion has been taken—then only can ethics be called a doctrine of happiness, because the *hope* for it first arises with religion.

From this it can also be seen that, if we inquire into God's final end in creating the world, we must name not the happiness of rational beings in the world but the highest good, which adds a further condition to the wish of rational beings to be happy, viz., the condition of being worthy of happiness, which is the morality of these beings, for this alone contains the standard by which they can hope to participate in happiness at the hand of a *wise* creator. . . .

Discussion Questions

1. What do you take to be the force of the term "postulate" in Kant's argument. Does this weaken the argument's force?

2. Kant says, "through the concept of the highest good as the object and final end of pure practical reason, the moral law leads to religion." Explain what you take this to mean.

3. Kant's argument turns on the notion of the highest good. Do you agree with his premise that rational beings demand that virtue and happiness go together? Give reasons for your answer.

4. Kant faults the Epicureans for making happiness the supreme moral principle. What are his objections to this?

5. What does Kant mean by the statement, "religion is the recognition of all duties as divine commands"? Do you agree?

RETROSPECTIVE

The Existence of God

What is the final force of the arguments for God's existence? For each argument there seems to be a counterargument, and we have to admit that all the arguments for God's existence—ontological, cosmological, and moral—fail to provide a logically irrefutable proof. The debate among philosophers over the relative merits and demerits of these arguments has been going on for a long time and will likely continue, at least as long as there are philosophers around to continue them.

There are, however, several positive outcomes of the debate about the existence of God despite its seeming inconclusiveness. First, a review of the material just covered shows that serious philosophical issues divide people of goodwill on both sides of the controversy. A second positive effect of the dialogue generated by a discussion of the arguments is that it does clarify some of the options: Either there is an ultimate Principle behind the visible universe—call it God—or else the universe is just a brute fact for which no explanation is possible. The arguments also focus our attention upon aspects of the world that evoke a sense of wonder and mystery, and that cannot fully be accounted for except on the theistic hypothesis. The order and regularity of the world, as well as human moral awareness, point to God as a possible explanation. But the arguments—all of them—only point; they do not coerce.

The theistic arguments are nonetheless significant. The ontological argument, in particular, is useful because it clarifies some of the logical implications of the concept of God. God is not just the greatest being of which human thinking has formed the idea. God is a being than which nothing greater *can* be conceived. God is a being eternal and necessary, omnipotent and unlimited.

But would any of the arguments we have just investigated convince an atheist that God exists? Probably not. Even if a person agreed that the reasoning of one of the arguments is sound, the argument alone would probably not lead an unbeliever to embrace belief in God. As the discussion of religious experience showed, there is more to religion than rational argument, and the dynamics of faith certainly involve more than logical debate. This points to one of the most important contributions of the existence-of-God debate: If someone were to construct an absolutely undeniable proof of the existence of God, a proof so strong that it could not be refuted, or a proof against which there are no cogent counterarguments, this might not be a good thing for religion, at least for the Judaeo-Christian tradition. For basic to this tradition is the view that religion is a matter of faith, not of demonstrable proof. "We walk by faith and not by sight," a New Testament writer states. What this means is that faith is possible only where there is also room for doubt. That the arguments for the existence of God, and the counterarguments against them, remain inconclusive leaves open the possibility of faith. However, there is still another barrier to faith: The problem of evil. And that is the topic of the next chapter.

ADDITIONAL READINGS

A great deal has been written about the ontological argument. Two excellent collections of representative essays dealing with the topic are Alvin Plantinga, *The Ontological Argument* (Garden City, NY: Doubleday-Anchor, 1965), and John Hick and Arthur C. McGill, eds., *The Many-Faced Argument* (New York: Macmillan, 1967). *The Encyclopedia of Philosophy* has articles on each of the arguments discussed in this section, and other arguments are discussed in the article by G. C. Nerlick, "Popular Arguments for the Existence of God," *The Encyclopedia of Philosophy* (1967), 6, 407–11. All the articles in this valuable encyclopedia also contain helpful bibliographies. An overall discussion and analysis of theistic arguments is found in John Hick, *Arguments for the Existence of God* (London: Macmillan, 1970). Another treatment of the issues by a noted Catholic theologian is Hans Küng, *Does God Exist? An Answer for Today* (Garden City, NY: Doubleday, 1980). Richard M. Gale gives an analysis of the work of analytic philosophers supporting theism in *On the Nature and Existence of God* (Cambridge: Cambridge University Press, 1991). The question of how evolution can be approached theologically is explored by John F. Haught, *God After Darwin: A Theology of Evolution* (Boulder, CO: Westview Press, 2000). *Belief in God in an Age of Science* (New Haven, CT: Yale University Press, 1998) offers reflections on theism by an internationally known physicist who is also a theologian.

CHAPTER FIVE

THE PROBLEM OF EVIL

INTRODUCTION

God and Evil

God either cannot or will not prevent evil. If God cannot prevent evil, then God is limited in power. If God will not prevent evil, then God is limited in benevolence. But if God is not limited in either power or benevolence, why is there evil in the world?

This paraphrase of the statement of the problem of evil made by the Greek philosopher Epicurus three centuries before the Christian era shows that the problem of evil not only is a concern for the Christian religion, but has arisen whenever human beings have attempted to reconcile the existence of evil with belief in a divine being of infinite power and goodness. We should neither underestimate the difficulty of the problem of evil nor think that there are easy solutions to it. The problem of evil is perhaps the most powerful objection ever raised against belief in God, and it cannot be dismissed lightly. For those who reject belief in an omnipotent and all-good God, it is probably the appalling depth and extent of human suffering and misery more than anything else that makes the assertion of a benevolent God seem so implausible.

An attempt to justify the goodness of God in spite of the presence of evil in the world is called a *theodicy*, from two Greek words meaning *god* and *justice*. Generating a theodicy is particularly difficult for the Judaeo-Christian tradition, because it has maintained three affirmations about God:

1. Evil exists
2. God is all powerful
3. God is completely benevolent.

Since the problem of evil arises as a theological issue only when we insist on maintaining all three of these affirmations, we could obviously resolve the problem of evil by denying any one of them. Theodicies have been developed that address the problem of evil in this way, but since they would require giving up one of the three principal affirmations, they have not found much acceptance within the Judaeo-Christian tradition.

That there is evil in the world is too obvious to be questioned. What may not be so obvious at first is that there is evil in the world because there are human beings in the world, for it would be fair to say that if there were no sentient creatures like us—beings capable of feeling pain, mental anguish, and the destruction of our fondest aspirations—then there would be no evil. Human beings are therefore the place where evil makes its appearance in the world. In an allied sense, evil arises because certain aspects of our worldly situation give rise to human suffering. The list of the sources of suffering is enormous and includes disease, war, famine, human cruelty to other human beings, psychological distress, and disappointment, to name only some. In attempting to sort out the various faces of evil, philosophers distinguish between natural evil and moral evil. *Natural evil* refers to those aspects of nature itself that produce pain and injury to human beings, such as natural disasters, disease, and death. *Moral evil* is suffering that is due to human perversity, and human beings are capable of causing great physical and psychological pain to their fellows with an ingenuity that is ample evidence of the enormity of the problem posed by moral evil.

These two kinds of evil raise different, though related, questions for theism. Natural evil raises questions about the order of nature. Moral evil raises questions about human nature. In both cases, the question for the theist is why God allows a world such as ours to exist. Why does the natural order produce human suffering? Could God have created the world in such a way that it would not produce events that caused human suffering? If so, why did God not do so? The question posed by moral evil is why God allows us to inflict misery and suffering on others. Could God have created free beings who nonetheless would not produce misery and suffering for their fellow human beings? These are some of the issues that will be addressed by the theodicies we will examine.

As a preliminary to further consideration of the problem of evil, ask yourself what amount of evil is attributable to natural causes and what amount is attributable to human perversity. Would you say that the two kinds of evil are roughly equivalent? Or would you claim that 60 percent of the evil in the world could be classed as moral evil, with only 40 percent attributable to natural evil? Or is the imbalance even higher—90 percent moral evil and only 10 percent natural? As you ponder this, consider that much of what we refer to as natural evil has indirect human causes. We could eliminate much of the starvation in the world if the world's resources were allocated differently. Many persons in the world still suffer from diseases for which there are known cures. And steps could be taken to alleviate many natural disasters, while for those that are unavoidable, human resources could be used to reduce much of the suffering caused by them. Considerations such as these have led thinkers to concentrate mainly on the problem of moral evil in their theodicies, since moral evil seems to constitute the major part of the problem of evil in general.

THEMES IN THEODICIES

Before turning to a brief survey of themes that are found in various theodicies, one more point needs to be made. The problem of evil emerges only for those who believe in an all-powerful and all-good God. For the atheist, the presence of evil in the world does not pose an intellectual difficulty; evil is just another fact of life—although a monstrous one. It is simply the case that there are features of the world that we find repugnant, and while this may give rise to the conclusion that the world is absurd, the atheist does not feel obliged to explain why there is evil in the world; that is just the way the world is. The existence of evil becomes a problem only for the theist who believes not only in God, but also in a certain kind of God, a God who is both all-powerful and completely benevolent. Even when the problem of evil does not arise as a theological difficulty, the enormous problem of suffering can still be felt. Buddhism, which has no doctrine of a personal god, nevertheless considers salvation from suffering to be a central concern, and Buddhism has developed strategies for dealing with this feature of human experience. Still, even though Buddhism offers a profound sensitivity to the problem of suffering, it does not encounter the theological difficulties inherent in the Judaeo-Christian view.

Now refer back to the three affirmations of the Judaeo-Christian tradition that give rise to the problem of evil. Since the problem of evil emerges when all three of these affirmations are held, several theodicies could result simply by denying one or more of these statements. But theodicies that would result from this tactic would sacrifice the traditional Judaeo-Christian beliefs about God and the world, and as a result, such theodicies are not at the heart of Jewish or Christian attempts to defend the goodness of God in spite of the presence of evil in the world. The following themes indicate various approaches to explaining the presence of evil. Most theodicies will contain several of these themes, since no really satisfactory theodicy could be built on any one of them alone.

The Unreality of Evil

One approach to a theodicy results from denying the first of the three affirmations and claiming that evil is unreal. The most extreme form of this kind of theodicy claims that evil is an illusion; a less extreme form admits the reality of evil but denies that evil has any substantial reality.

Evil Is an Illusion.   Certain forms of Hinduism hold the view that evil, along with the whole of the visible world, is an illusion, or *maya*. Not only the experience of evil, but all sense experiences, are thus illusory. The view that evil is an illusion has never formed a part of the traditional view of either Judaism or Christianity, although something akin to this was suggested by Mary Baker Eddy as one of the doctrines of Christian Science. The Judaeo-Christian doctrine of Creation affirms not only that the world is real, but that Creation is basically good. It therefore finds unacceptable any view that suggests the unreality of the world.

Evil Has No Substantial Reality.   Given the belief that the created order is good and that God is the source of creation, St. Augustine espouses a theodicy which holds that evil has no independent, substantial reality. He rejects, as does orthodox Christianity, any theodicy which claims that evil is due to the material aspects of the world. Matter is good; God created it as good, and everything that is created by God is good in its own proper way; things give rise to evil when that which is basically good has been perverted and corrupted. Augustine does not deny that evil is present in the world, but his concern is to explain the metaphysical status of evil, and he concludes that evil is a privation of that which is essentially good.

In other words, Augustine argues that evil is not a substance, a thing in the world, that has independent reality, but appears only as a defect or privation in what is a basically good created order. Disease has no independent reality, for example, but appears as an absence of health. Sin occurs only in a will capable of choosing to do good that chooses evil instead. In short, evil is a kind of parasite on the good, a disorder in what would otherwise be a good creation. Augustine also accepts the Genesis story of the fall of Adam and Eve as an explanation for the origin of defective human nature. Whereas the Hindu doctrine of *maya* is a denial of the reality of evil, Augustine's view is not that evil is an illusion, but only that it has no independent or substantial reality. This fundamental difference between the Augustinian notion of evil as privation of good and the Hindu doctrine of *maya* may call into question their being included in the same category. What they have in common, however, is their focus on the first of the three affirmations that give rise to the theological problem of evil. Augustine attempts to show that natural evil can be accounted for as a defect in what was designed by God as a good created order. Whereas this tactic sheds some light on the question of natural evil, it does not directly address the problem of moral evil. Therefore, Augustine has to include elements of the free-will defense in his theodicy in order to address this latter concern.

A Limited God

Just as the view that evil is an illusion is a denial of the first of the affirmations that give rise to the problem of evil, the view that evil is due to God's limitation is a denial of the second affirmation. This denial has taken two forms: the view that God is limited by an equally powerful evil deity and the view that God is limited by the material of which the world is made, or that God is limited in ability.

Dualistic Theories. The view that there are two opposed but equally powerful deities, the one being the source of good, the other the source of evil, is a dualistic theodicy. Ancient Zoroastrian religion held this view, with *Ahura Mazdah* and *Angra Mainyu* being the opposed good and evil spirits. The good deity is simply incapable of preventing the other from producing evil in the world, and human beings are called upon to choose one of the sides of the struggle, with the outcome of the opposition between good and evil being very much undecided.

Properly speaking, a dualism arises only when an explanation is offered in terms of two equal but opposed ultimate principles or realities, and neither Christianity nor Judaism finds a dualistic explanation acceptable. The devil cannot be interpreted as a being equal to but opposed to God, for the devil is a personification of an evil temporarily tolerated that will ultimately be destroyed.

A Finite God. The theodicy offered by process thought, represented in this chapter by the selection from David Ray Griffin, eliminates the notion of God's omnipotence. God's power is limited through the identification of God with the creation of values, not with the traditional role of being the Supreme Being. More details about this view will emerge in the reading itself, but it is important to note that, while perhaps resolving the problem of evil, a view that rejects God's omnipotence would amount to a major alteration in the traditional Judaeo-Christian beliefs about God.

Denial of God's Benevolence

A denial of the third affirmation, of the complete benevolence of God, will likewise dispel the problem of evil, but at the expense of our traditional concept of God. Though both Christianity and Judaism avow the goodness of God, not all religions have done so. Many of the ancient religions, such as those of Greece, had a polytheistic view in which some gods were good and others were not. Since they were not committed to defending the total goodness of their deities, the Greeks did not face the theological difficulty of the problem of evil. They merely accepted that some gods were benevolent and some were malevolent. The nineteenth-century philosopher John Stuart Mill suggests that perhaps God is not completely benevolent, as traditional theism has held. Mill argues that we simply have no basis in natural theology for assuming that God is completely just or that God wishes the happiness of creatures. The acceptance of either of these suggestions, of course, would result in a major change in the traditional views of the nature of God.

Karma Theories

The principle of *karma* is found in Indian religions, including both Buddhism and Hinduism, and is the view that the evils one suffers in this life, as well as the happiness that one enjoys, are the effects of deeds done in a previous life. The law of *karma* includes a principle of cause and effect, since what happens to us is what we deserve because of deeds done in a previous incarnation. Christian theodicies do not appeal to the principle of *karma*, since it is dependent on the doctrine of reincarnation, which has not been a part of traditional Jewish or Christian beliefs. The doctrine of *karma* can elicit a socially conservative response to suffering, since the belief that people suffer because they deserve to suffer removes some of the impetus toward the alleviation of suffering.

Even though Christianity and Judaism have no doctrine of reincarnation or of *karma*, many persons have assumed that when they suffer, it is because of something they have done. To be sure, evil deeds do often cause suffering and distress for the person who commits them, but as a general explanation for evil, this is unacceptable in the Judaeo-Christian view. In the Old Testament, the book of Job stands as a refutation of the view that persons suffer only in proportion to their misdeeds. Job's friends advised him to admit that he had done evil and to pray for forgiveness so that he might be freed from his suffering. Job stubbornly insisted on his innocence and so represents the refusal of Hebrew religion to attempt to account for evil entirely as punishment for sins. The New Testament likewise rejects the view that people suffer in direct proportion to their misdeeds. In fact, the Christian affirmation is that people sometimes suffer precisely because they are innocent, and the centrality of the cross of Christ in Christian thought also is a repudiation of the view that suffering comes in proportion to what one might deserve.

Harmony Theories

Other theodicies have included the theme of universal harmony, a harmony that either is believed to exist now, but is unknown to us because of our limited viewpoint, or one that will come into being sometime in the future. The Stoic poet Cleanthes gave expression to this viewpoint, even though he did not believe in God in the Jewish or Christian sense. He did believe that reality was ruled by a principle of reason and that everything that happened was part of the universal order of things. Because we are finite creatures, we cannot see the total harmony of the universe and therefore believe certain things to be evil. In the total view of things, however, evil as well as good is necessary to the total harmony. Another way of expressing this view is in terms of an analogy. In a painting, there are dark areas as well as brighter hues. If we looked only at the dark areas, we might think they were ugly, but seen in the context of the painting as a whole, the dark areas contribute to the harmony and perfection of the entire painting and are therefore as essential to the overall beauty of the painting as are the more vibrant colors.

A variation of the harmony theodicy would be to admit that there is no universal harmony at present, but to maintain that there will be one sometime in the future, and the present distress is necessary in order to bring about this future harmony. Some Christian writers have argued for a theodicy with this feature in it, but basic to the Christian view of history is the affirmation that God at some future point will bring about a reordering of things so that the present evils of the world will be eliminated. A recurring objection to all harmony theories, whether they claim that there is presently a harmony or that there will be a future harmony, is the question of the morality of the intensity of our present suffering for the sake of some future harmony. Can we really believe that cancer is necessary to this harmony? Torture? Murder? Ivan Karamazov gives a powerful expression of this objection in *The Brothers Karamazov* when he insists that if the suffering of innocent children is necessary for the eternal harmony, he wants nothing to do with it and will gladly return his ticket to this adventure we call life. Others have objected to the harmony theodicy because it seems to call into question either the goodness or the power of God, or both. Could God not have brought about eternal harmony without our having to pay so high a price? If God could not, then why call God omnipotent? If God could have done this but chose not to, this would seem to call God's goodness into question. So we are back to where we started with the initial statement of the problem of evil.

Free-Will Theories

The most prevalent theme in theodicies is the emphasis on human free will. God chose to create beings having free will. We could not be truly free unless we were free to do evil; therefore, the possibility of evil is inherent in our free will. We may not be able to explain why God created us with free will, or why God created anything, for that matter. But if we believe that there is some ultimate value to be gained by our having the power of free choice, then we have one explanation for our capacity to do evil.

The free-will defense forms a part of the theodicy offered in this chapter by John Hick, though it cannot be classified solely as a free-will type of theodicy. Even if one accepts the free-will theodicy, there is still the fact of natural evil to be explained. St. Augustine held the view that the sin of the first man and woman resulted in a fall not only of humanity, but of nature as well, so that after the original sin the order of nature itself was greatly changed. Hick does not appeal to the Adam-and-Eve story as an explanation for natural evil, yet he offers intriguing suggestions on how the problems of natural evil and moral evil are related.

The foregoing classification of themes in theodicies is not exhaustive, nor is this the only way to organize even the ones referred to. These are, however, the principal themes that have been used in theodicies by both Christian and non-Christian writers, and the enumeration of them here will serve to show some of the kinds of questions that will be raised in our readings.

The "Vale of Soul-Making" Theodicy

God created human beings in a state of perfection. God also placed the first parents of the race, Adam and Eve, in an idyllic situation in which every need was met, but the first human pair willfully rebelled against God and fell from their state of pristine purity. By this fall, the course of human history was changed; the human race is still tainted by the original sin of Adam and Eve, and the entire natural order also reflects the fallenness of humankind.

This interpretation of the story found in the book of Genesis occupies a central place in the historical development of Christian theodicies and is represented by what John Hick calls the "majority report" of St. Augustine, the fifth-century Christian theologian and bishop. Two assumptions are implicit in Augustine's theodicy:

1. Human free will plays a major role in accounting for the presence of evil in the world, and evil results from the willful rebellion of humanity against God.
2. The original situation of humanity was a state of perfection from which our first parents departed, with dire consequences for the entire human race.

In the following selection from the contemporary philosopher John Hick, the first of these assumptions is accepted, but the second one is rejected in favor of what Hick refers to as the "minority" report represented by St. Irenaeus, a Christian writer of the second century.

Before turning to the details of Hick's theodicy, a word is in order about the Adam-and-Eve story. Such stories are referred to by contemporary scholars as myths, the function of a myth being to provide in narrative form a comprehensive view of mankind and the world in terms of which human beings can understand the human situation. Myths are stories involving symbolic elements and accounting for deeds done "in those times" or "once upon a time," that is, at a nondefinable time and place. The term *myth* connotes to many persons the sense of that which is false in contrast to that which is true, but this is not what the term means when applied to religious stories. The truth of a story such as this is found not in its literal meaning but in what it says about the human situation. Like all significant religious stories, the Adam-and-Eve narrative offers a profound insight into the human condition; it loses most of its religious significance, however, if we try to take it as literal or historical fact. Note also the presence in the story of vivid symbols: the serpent in the garden, the forbidden fruit, the tree of knowledge, the tree of life, and the angel with the flaming sword. It is also important to know that the Hebrew term *Adam* means simply *mankind*, so the story can be understood to refer not just to a first human being, but to Everyman, to each of us. If the Adam-and-Eve story is taken in its symbolic elements as pointing to a level of experience of reality that it opens up to us, the story means that we must recognize that we are in rebellion against God and that our actions have profound consequences.

There are several philosophical considerations that prevent an adequate theodicy from being based on the Augustinian interpretation of the Adam-and-Eve story. First is the difficulty of making sense of the claim that a perfect being could willfully sin. If human beings were completely perfect in their original state, then how could they possess the imperfection indicated by willfully choosing to do evil? Second, there is the moral difficulty of explaining how God could hold all human beings responsible for what was done in antiquity by the first man and woman. Third, the nature of the punishment seems out of proportion to the original sin. The entire catalog of human suffering seems to be a morally intolerable penalty for the error of two people who merely wanted to have forbidden knowledge. How can we morally defend a God who punishes us so severely for something over which we had no control?

As with all religious stories, what we make of the Adam-and-Eve narrative depends on which elements of the story we emphasize. If we take the story of Adam and Eve's fall as decisive for the rest of humanity, we confront the sort of problems just mentioned. But if we interpret the story as expressing the fact that each of us fails to live up to our noblest possibilities, then it says something profound about the human situation.[1] It says, among other things, that we are not in the perfected state God intends for us but are in the process of being "formed into the finite likeness of God." A view similar to this is suggested by the theologian Teilhard de Chardin, who views the evolutionary process as having reached the stage wherein we share in our spiritual evolution by developing moral qualities that reflect the nature of God.

Central to Hick's theodicy is the view that God's purpose is to lead us from mere biological life, which he refers to using the Greek term *bios*, to a qualitatively improved spiritual life, to which he gives another Greek term for life, *zoe*. Life as mere *bios* is our natural existence formed through the eons of evolution and culminating in the emergence of the species *Homo sapiens*. At this point we

---

[1] For an insightful interpretation of the Adam-and-Eve story, see Paul Ricoeur, *The Symbolism of Evil*, trans. Emerson Buchanan (Boston: Beacon Press, 1969).

enter into the creative process as sort of co-creators with God. Life should therefore be viewed as an arena for the development of spiritual life and as the final stage in the evolutionary process, for the directions of which we bear responsibility. The evil in the world is not to be seen as God's punishment for the sins of the first human beings, but as a necessary condition for the achievement of *zoe*, spiritual life that reflects the moral attributes of God. The world in which we find ourselves is the "vale of soul-making," to use a phrase of the poet John Keats. Such a world is not a perfect situation, and Hick charges that it is erroneous for antitheists to object to the nature of the world as not being an idyllic paradise. To expect this present world to be a hedonistic paradise in which every desire is gratified would be to think of human beings as pet animals. But clearly, this is not what God intends for us. In the reading that follows, Hick says: "Men are not to be thought of on the analogy of animal pets, whose life is to be made as agreeable as possible, but rather on the analogy of human children, who are to grow to adulthood in an environment whose primary and overriding purpose is not immediate pleasure but the realizing of the most valuable potentialities of human personality."

For us to develop the fullness of our potential requires that we have freedom of choice. Freedom is real only when we are free to do good as well as to do evil, and the natural world provides an environment in which our choices have real consequences, for either good or ill. The human situation is one of struggle to achieve the highest potentialities of the human personality. Like Adam, we find our situation to be one of defection from these possibilities, but the process of soul-making must continue in spite of our frequent and recurring failures. The natural order, with the natural evil that is part of its possibility, thus forms the backdrop for this transition from *bios* to *zoe*. Part of the attractiveness of Hick's theodicy is that it shows that the problems of moral evil and natural evil are interrelated concerns. By rejecting the second major assumption of the Augustinian theodicy, Hick affirms the view that human beings have not been victimized by a primeval fall of the race, but that the Genesis story speaks to a view of humankind in the process of achieving the purposes that God wills for us.

Hick labels his view as both teleological and eschatological. It is teleological in the sense that human existence is seen to be purposive, to be directed toward the achievement of a goal. *Eschatology* refers to the doctrine of the events of the end-time or last days and, in this context, refers to the biblical view that there will be a future perfected state in which all those who have become "children of God" will share. Hick cites numerous biblical passages that support this interpretation of the Christian view of human history, such as the text that speaks of a "new heaven and a new earth." The perfected situation for human beings is thus not to be thought of as having existed in the distant past, but as something that will exist in a glorious future. It is toward this goal that all the drama of human existence is directed, and Hick insists that "our theodicy must find the meaning of evil in the part it is made to play in the eventual outworking of that purpose."

The following selection offers only the general outline of Hick's theodicy, which he works out in more detail in subsequent sections of the book from which the reading is taken. By tying it firmly to early Christian thought, and by fortifying it with numerous biblical references, Hick shows that his "vale of soul-making" theodicy is compatible with traditional Christian affirmations. An adequate theodicy, however, must do more than this. It must also show that the goodness of God is not compromised by the presence of evil in the world. Hick addresses this issue by supporting the view that our present situation, with all the suffering this entails, is necessary to achieve the perfected existence that is God's ultimate goal for humanity. It is the good of this ultimate goal that eventually will justify the present experiences of suffering and evil that are required to reach the goal. Referring to the themes mentioned in the introduction, we can therefore classify Hick's theodicy as involving elements of both the harmony type of theodicy and the free-will theodicy.

Evil and the God of Love

JOHN HICK

Fortunately there is another and better way. As well as the "majority report" of the Augustinian tradition, which has dominated Western Christendom, both Catholic and Protestant, since the time of Augustine himself, there is the "minority report" of the Irenaean tradition. This latter is both older and newer than the other, for it goes back to St. Irenaeus and others of the early Hellenistic Fathers of the Church in the two centuries prior to St. Augustine, and it has flourished again in more developed forms during the last hundred years.

Instead of regarding man as having been created by God in a finished state, as a finitely perfect being fulfilling the divine intention for our human level of existence, and then falling disastrously away from this, the minority report sees man as still in process of creation. Irenaeus himself expressed the point in terms of the (exegetically dubious) distinction between the "image" and the "likeness" of God referred to in Genesis i.26: "Then God said, Let us make man in our

Source: John Hick, *Evil and the God of Love,* rev. ed., pp. 253–261. Copyright © 1966, 1977 by John Hick. Copyright renewed 1994 by John Hick. Reprinted by permission of John Hick.

image, after our likeness."[1] His view was that man as a personal and moral being already exists in the image, but has not yet been formed into the finite likeness of God. By this "likeness" Irenaeus means something more than personal existence as such; he means a certain valuable quality of personal life which reflects finitely the divine life. This represents the perfecting of man, the fulfilment of God's purpose for humanity, the "bringing of many sons to glory,"[2] the creating of "children of God" who are "fellow heirs with Christ" of his glory.[3]

And so man, created as a personal being in the image of God, is only the raw material for a further and more difficult stage of God's creative work. This is the leading of men as relatively free and autonomous persons, through their own dealings with life in the world in which He has placed them, toward that quality of personal existence that is the finite likeness of God. The features of this likeness are revealed in the person of Christ, and the process of man's creation into it is the work of the Holy Spirit. In St. Paul's words, "And we all, with unveiled faces, beholding the glory of the Lord, are being changed into his likeness (εἰκών) from one degree of glory to another; for this comes from the Lord who is the Spirit"[4]; or again, "For God knew his own before ever they were, and also ordained that they should be shaped to the likeness (εἰκών) of his Son."[5] In Johannine terms, the movement from the image to the likeness is a transition from one level of existence, that of animal life (*Bios*), to another and higher level, that of eternal life (*Zoe*), which includes but transcends the first. And the fall of man was seen by Irenaeus as a failure within the second phase of this creative process, a failure that has multiplied the perils and complicated the route of the journey in which God is seeking to lead mankind.

In the light of modern anthropological knowledge some form of two-stage conception of the creation of man has become an almost unavoidable Christian tenet. At the very least we must acknowledge as two distinguishable stages the fashioning of *Homo sapiens* as a product of the long evolutionary process, and his sudden or gradual spiritualization as a child of God. But we may well extend the first stage to include the development of man as a rational and responsible person capable of personal relationship with the personal Infinite who has created him. This first stage of the creative process was, to our anthropomorphic imaginations, easy for divine omnipotence. By an exercise of creative power God caused the physical universe to exist, and in the course of countless ages to bring forth within it organic life, and finally to produce out of organic life personal life; and when man had thus emerged out of the evolution of the forms of organic life, a creature had been made who has the possibility of existing in conscious fellowship

[1] *A. H.* v. vi. 1. Cf. pp. 217ff. above.

[2] Hebrews ii. 10.

[3] Romans viii. 17.

[4] II Corinthians iii. 18.

[5] Romans viii. 29. Other New Testament passages expressing a view of man as undergoing a process of spiritual growth within God's purpose are: Ephesians ii. 21; iii. 16; Colossians ii. 19; I John iii. 2; II Corinthians iv. 16.

with God. But the second stage of the creative process is of a different kind altogether. It cannot be performed by omnipotent power as such. For personal life is essentially free and self-directing. It cannot be perfected by divine fiat, but only through the uncompelled responses and willing cooperation of human individuals in their actions and reactions in the world in which God has placed them. Men may eventually become the perfected persons whom the New Testament calls "children of God," but they cannot be created ready-made as this.

The value-judgment that is implicitly being invoked here is that one who has attained to goodness by meeting and eventually mastering temptations, and thus by rightly making responsible choices in concrete situations, is good in a richer and more valuable sense than would be one created *ab initio* in a state either of innocence or of virtue. In the former case, which is that of the actual moral achievements of mankind, the individual's goodness has within it the strength of temptations overcome, a stability based upon an accumulation of right choices, and a positive and responsible character that comes from the investment of costly personal effort. I suggest, then, that it is an ethically reasonable judgment, even though in the nature of the case not one that is capable of demonstrative proof, that human goodness slowly built up through personal histories of moral effort has a value in the eyes of the Creator which justifies even the long travail of the soul-making process.

The picture with which we are working is thus developmental and teleological. Man is in process of becoming the perfected being whom God is seeking to create. However, this is not taking place—it is important to add—by a natural and inevitable evolution, but through a hazardous adventure in individual freedom. Because this is a pilgrimage within the life of each individual, rather than a racial evolution, the progressive fulfilment of God's purpose does not entail any corresponding progressive improvement in the moral state of the world. There is no doubt a development in man's ethical situation from generation to generation through the building of individual choices into public institutions, but this involves an accumulation of evil as well as of good.[6] It is thus probable that human life was lived on much the same moral plane two thousand years ago or four thousand years ago as it is today. But nevertheless during this period uncounted millions of souls have been through the experience of earthly life, and God's purpose has gradually moved towards its fulfilment within each one of them, rather than within a human aggregate composed of different units in different generations.

If, then, God's aim in making the world is "the bringing of many sons to glory,"[7] that aim will naturally determine the kind of world that He has created. Antitheistic writers almost invariably assume a conception of the divine purpose which is contrary to the Christian conception. They assume that the purpose of a loving God must be to create a hedonistic paradise; and therefore to the extent

---

[6] This fact is symbolized in early Christian literature both by the figure of the Antichrist, who continually opposes God's purposes in history, and by the expectation of cataclysmic calamity and strife in the last days before the end of the present world order.

[7] Hebrews ii. 10.

that the world is other than this, it proves to them that God is either not loving enough or not powerful enough to create such a world. They think of God's relation to the earth on the model of a human being building a cage for a pet animal to dwell in. If he is humane he will naturally make his pet's quarters as pleasant and healthful as he can. Any respect in which the cage falls short of the veterinarian's ideal, and contains possibilities of accident or disease, is evidence of either limited benevolence or limited means, or both. Those who use the problem of evil as an argument against belief in God almost invariably think of the world in this kind of way. David Hume, for example, speaks of an architect who is trying to plan a house that is to be as comfortable and convenient as possible. If we find that "the windows, doors, fires, passages, stairs, and the whole economy of the building were the source of noise, confusion, fatigue, darkness, and the extremes of heat and cold" we should have no hesitation in blaming the architect. It would be in vain for him to prove that if this or that defect were corrected greater ills would result: "still you would assert in general, that, if the architect had had skill and good intentions, he might have formed such a plan of the whole, and might have adjusted the parts in such a manner, as would have remedied all or most of these inconveniences."[8]

But if we are right in supposing that God's purpose for man is to lead him from human *Bios*, or the biological life of man, to that quality of *Zoe*, or the personal life of eternal worth, which we see in Christ, then the question that we have to ask is not, Is this the kind of world that an all-powerful and infinitely loving being would create as an environment for his human pets? or, Is the architecture of the world the most pleasant and convenient possible? The question that we have to ask is rather, Is this the kind of world that God might make as an environment in which moral beings may be fashioned, through their own free insights and responses, into "children of God"?

Such critics as Hume are confusing what heaven ought to be, as an environment for perfected finite beings, with what this world ought to be, as an environment for beings who are in process of becoming perfected. For if our general conception of God's purpose is correct the world is not intended to be a paradise, but rather the scene of a history in which human personality may be formed towards the pattern of Christ. Men are not to be thought of on the analogy of animal pets, whose life is to be made as agreeable as possible, but rather on the analogy of human children, who are to grow to adulthood in an environment whose primary and overriding purpose is not immediate pleasure but the realizing of the most valuable potentialities of human personality.

Needless to say, this characterization of God as the heavenly Father is not a merely random illustration but an analogy that lies at the heart of the Christian faith. Jesus treated the likeness between the attitude of God to man, and the attitude of human parents at their best towards their children, as providing the most adequate way for us to think about God. And so it is altogether relevant to a

8 *Dialogues Concerning Natural Religion*, pt. xi. Kemp-Smith's ed. (Oxford: Clarendon Press, 1935), p. 251.

Christian understanding of this world to ask, How does the best parental love express itself in its influence upon the environment in which children are to grow
up? I think it is clear that a parent who loves his children, and wants them to become the best human beings that they are capable of becoming, does not treat
pleasure as the sole and supreme value. Certainly we seek pleasure for our children, and take great delight in obtaining it for them; but we do not desire for
them unalloyed pleasure at the expense of their growth in such even greater values as moral integrity, unselfishness, compassion, courage, humour, reverence for
the truth, and perhaps above all the capacity for love. We do not act on the
premise that pleasure is the supreme end of life; and if the development of these
other values sometimes clashes with the provision of pleasure, then we are willing to have our children miss a certain amount of this, rather than fail to come
to possess and to be possessed by the finer and more precious qualities that are
possible to the human personality. A child brought up on the principle that the
only or the supreme value is pleasure would not be likely to become an ethically
mature adult or an attractive or happy personality. And to most parents it seems
more important to try to foster quality and strength of character in their children
than to fill their lives at all times with the utmost possible degree of pleasure. If,
then, there is any true analogy between God's purpose for his human creatures,
and the purpose of loving and wise parents for their children, we have to recognize that the presence of pleasure and the absence of pain cannot be the supreme
and overriding end for which the world exists. Rather, this world must be a place
of soul-making. And its value is to be judged, not primarily by the quantity of
pleasure and pain occurring in it at any particular moment, but by its fitness for
its primary purpose, the purpose of soul-making.[9]

In all this we have been speaking about the nature of the world considered simply as the God-given environment of man's life. For it is mainly in
this connection that the world has been regarded in Irenaean and in Protestant
thought.[10] But such a way of thinking involves a danger of anthropocentrism from
which the Augustinian and Catholic tradition has generally been protected by its
sense of the relative insignificance of man within the totality of the created universe. Man was dwarfed within the medieval world-view by the innumerable hosts
of angels and archangels above him—unfallen rational natures which rejoice in
the immediate presence of God, reflecting His glory in the untarnished mirror of

[9] The phrase "the vale of Soul-making" was coined by the poet John Keats in a letter written to
his brother and sister in April 1819. He says, "The common cognomen of this world among the misguided and superstitious is 'a vale of tears' from which we are to be redeemed by a certain arbitrary
interposition of God and taken to Heaven—What a little circumscribed straightened notion! Call the
world if you Please 'The vale of Soul-making.'" In this letter he sketches a teleological theodicy. "Do
you not see," he asks, "how necessary World of Pains and troubles is to school an Intelligence and
make it a Soul?" (*The Letters of John Keats*, ed. by M. B. Forman. London: Oxford University Press,
4th ed., 1952, pp. 334–5).

[10] Thus Irenaeus said that "the creation is suited to [the wants of] man; for man was not made
for its sake, but creation for the sake of man" (*A. H.* v. xxix. 1), and Calvin said that "because we
know that the universe was established especially for the sake of mankind, we ought to look for this
purpose in his governance also" (*Inst.* 1. xvi. 6.).

their worship. However, this higher creation has in our modern world lost its hold upon the imagination. Its place has been taken, as the minimizer of men, by the immensities of outer space and by the material universe's unlimited complexity transcending our present knowledge. As the spiritual environment envisaged by Western man has shrunk, his physical horizons have correspondingly expanded. Where the human creature was formerly seen as an insignificant appendage to the angelic world, he is now seen as an equally insignificant organic excrescence, enjoying a fleeting moment of consciousness on the surface of one of the planets of a minor star. Thus the truth that was symbolized for former ages by the existence of the angelic hosts is today impressed upon us by the vastness of the physical universe, countering the egoism of our species by making us feel that this immense prodigality of existence can hardly all exist for the sake of man—though, on the other hand, the very realization that it is not all for the sake of man may itself be salutary and beneficial to man!

However, instead of opposing man and nature as rival objects of God's interest, we should perhaps rather stress man's solidarity as an embodied being with the whole natural order in which he is embedded. For man is organic to the world; all his acts and thoughts and imaginations are conditioned by space and time; and in abstraction from nature he would cease to be human. We may, then, say that the beauties and sublimities and powers, the microscopic intricacies and macroscopic vastnesses, the wonders and the terrors of the natural world and of the life that pulses through it, are willed and valued by their Maker in a creative act that embraces man together with nature. By means of matter and living flesh God both builds a path and weaves a veil between Himself and the creature made in His image. Nature thus has permanent significance; for God has set man in a creaturely environment, and the final fulfilment of our nature in relation to God will accordingly take the form of an embodied life within "a new heaven and a new earth."[11] And as in the present age man moves slowly toward that fulfilment through the pilgrimage of his earthly life, so also "the whole creation" is "groaning in travail," waiting for the time when it will be "set free from its bondage to decay."[12]

And yet however fully we thus acknowledge the permanent significance and value of the natural order, we must still insist upon man's special character as a personal creature made in the image of God; and our theodicy must still centre upon the soul-making process that we believe to be taking place within human life.

This, then, is the starting-point from which we propose to try to relate the realities of sin and suffering to the perfect love of an omnipotent Creator. And as will become increasingly apparent, a theodicy that starts in this way must be

[11] Revelation xxi. 1.
[12] Romans viii. 21-22.

eschatological in its ultimate bearings. That is to say, instead of looking to the past for its clue to the mystery of evil, it looks to the future, and indeed to that ultimate future to which only faith can look. Given the conception of a divine intention working in and through human time toward a fulfilment that lies in its completeness beyond human time, our theodicy must find the meaning of evil in the part that it is made to play in the eventual outworking of that purpose; and must find the justification of the whole process in the magnitude of the good to which it leads. The good that outshines all ill is not a paradise long since lost but a kingdom which is yet to come in its full glory and permanence.

Discussion Questions

1. Do you find the Augustinian or the Irenaean approach to a theodicy more adequate? Why?

2. Does the distinction between *bios* and *zoe* seem to you to capture a relevant distinction? What are the reasons for your answer?

3. Hick's theodicy may provide an answer to the problem of moral evil, but does it deal adequately with the problem of natural evil? Does Hick attempt to link these two kinds of evil?

4. Is the Adam-and-Eve narrative inimical to the type of theodicy suggested by Hick? If so, why? If not, why not?

5. Do you consider Hick's "vale of soul-making" approach an adequate theodicy? If so, what are your reasons? If not, why not?

6. How many of the themes of theodicies mentioned in the introduction are appealed to in Hick's approach?

Theodicy in Process Thought

The theodicy that the next reading presents totally rejects a metaphysical view (that is, a view about the nature of reality) based on two sorts of entities: minds and material objects. This view, known as *metaphysical dualism*, has often been challenged in philosophy. On the one hand, idealist philosophers deny that there are things other than minds and ideas (hence, this view is called *idealism*), and such views are represented eloquently in the philosophical writings of Bishop Berkeley. Idealism was also a dominant philosophical view in the nineteenth century and is represented in such philosophers as Hegel, Bradley, and Bosanquet. Metaphysical dualism is also challenged by *materialism*, which explains all reality in terms of material substances and reduces all mental phenomena to nonmental ones. The functions of mind are the result of physical activity, and there is no place for a soul or God in a radical materialistic view.

An alternative metaphysics is to be found in the writing of Alfred North Whitehead, who, with Bertrand Russell, wrote the three-volume *Principia Mathematica*, a seminal work of the early twentieth century that was important in the development of mathematical logic. Whitehead objects to both idealism and materialism, which he finds inadequate because they are not compatible with the understanding of the new physics of quantum mechanics. Materialistic metaphysics understands the world to be composed of discrete, individual things that are independent of other things and simply located in space. Whitehead argues that what is needed is a new vocabulary in which to discuss the nature of ultimate reality, a vocabulary that reflects the dynamic, ever changing nature of reality as quantum physics understands it.

Whitehead rejects the notion that the world consists of static, independent entities called material objects. Instead, reality should be understood as a network of interdependent, dynamic realities, which he calls *actual entities*. Tables, trees, stones, and golf balls are actual entities. We now know, thanks to quantum physics, that these realities (we shouldn't call them "substances," since that smacks of the static, independent realities of the older physics) are not inert, but dynamic collections of events. The world, therefore, should be understood as a dynamic world in process; hence, Whitehead's view is often called *process thought*, and the major work in which he articulates his metaphysical view is entitled *Process and Reality*. Until we were able to get beyond the limitations of our physical senses (which present the view that the components of experienced reality are immobile and independent), we could not fathom the dynamic processes that are at the base of everything that is real. But thanks to physics, we now understand that the tree is composed of cells, the cells are composed of atoms, and the atoms are composed of particles, all of which are in motion and in dynamic tension with everything else. Such is the view of reality suggested by Whitehead.

In addition to actual entities, there is *creativity*, whereby the world advances toward new possibilities. There are also *eternal objects*, which are the patterns and structures that permeate all reality. (Previous philosophers called these *universals*.) And most importantly, there is God, whom Whitehead labels the *everlasting* actual entity. Whitehead's metaphysics today remains on the margins of philosophical interest, but it has attracted a following among some theologians, due principally to the work of Charles Hartshorne, a philosopher whose teaching career first at the University of Chicago and later at Emory University places him among the first ranks of American philosophers. While a student at Harvard University, Hartshorne was an assistant to Whitehead, and it is fair to say that he has become Whitehead's foremost interpreter. Hartshorne adopts Whitehead's metaphysics and, from this vantage point, addresses some of the perennial issues in philosophy of religion, especially proofs for the existence of God and the problem of evil. The ongoing interest in Whitehead's metaphysical foundations as a basis for treating traditional problems in the philosophy of religion therefore remains an important strand in American theology and philosophy of religion. The selection that follows is an explication of Hartshorne's application of Whitehead's metaphysics that is used to address the problem of evil and is written by a noted interpreter of process thought, David Ray Griffin.

Since the vocabulary and conceptual framework of process thought are different from those usually brought to a discussion of these issues, a few terminological distinctions are in order. The view that God is wholly transcendent and completely separate from the world is the usual assumption of traditional theism. The opposite view, which identifies God with the world, is called *pantheism*, that is, "God" is simply the name given to the totality of reality. Many interpreters of Hartshorne see him espousing a view midway between these two, a view known as *panentheism*—the view that God is not to be identified totally with the world, nor is God completely separate from the world. In the panenthetistic view, God is not to be identified with the world, but everything in the world is *in* God in some sense, and as Griffin elaborates his position, it is clear that the events of the world process do affect God and that God affects the world.

Process thought, in rejecting metaphysical dualism, argues that actual entities differ only in degree, not in kind. That is, there is a connectedness among all things. Further, those actual entities that we call objects and those actual entities we call mind differ only in degree of complexity and organization. Griffin acknowledges that such a view might be called *panpsychism* (the view that all reality is mental in construct), but he prefers the term *panexperientialism*, which implies that all actual entities are events that are influenced by previous events, though not completely determined by them.

God, according to process thought, relates to the world through interdependence. That is, the world affects God, and God affects the world. Whitehead describes two aspects of God's nature, which he calls the *primordial* and the *consequent* natures. In God's primordial nature are the sources of creativity in the world; in God's consequent nature is the unfolding of the processes of the world itself. Here is how one interpreter of Whitehead, using Whitehead's own words, puts it:

> God can be termed the creator of each temporal actual entity. But the phrase is apt to be misleading by its suggestion that the ultimate creativity of the universe is to be ascribed to God's volition. The true metaphysical position is that God is the aboriginal instance of this creativity, and is therefore the aboriginal condition which qualifies its action. Viewed as primordial, he is the unlimited conceptual realization of the absolute wealth of potentiality. In this aspect, he is not *before* all creation, but *with* all creation. It is the function of actuality to characterize the creativity, and God is the eternal primordial character. But of course, there is no meaning to 'creativity' apart from its 'creatures,' and no meaning to 'God' apart from the creativity and the 'temporal creatures,' and no meaning to the temporal creatures apart from 'creativity' and 'God.'"[1]

In Whitehead, we find elements of both Plato's and Aristotle's philosophy. Without doing too much violence to Whitehead's intent, we could say that God, in God's primordial nature, is Aristotle's Prime Mover. Eternal objects are Platonic forms, which find their expression in physical objects. God is therefore the source of creativity in the world, but within the world there is genuine freedom and novelty. This is the reason Whitehead—and Hartshorne—reject the omnipotence of God, for such a view of God would destroy genuine human freedom. The conclusion they reach is that the possibility of evil is necessary in the world, though no specific evils are necessary. God is identified with value and feels our pain. The appeal of process thought is a call to cooperate with God in creating good and overcoming evil, joining "God's side," as it were, in the ongoing struggle to maximize the potentials for good.

---

[1] Donald W. Wherburne, *A Key to Whitehead's Process and Reality* (Baltimore, MD: Johns Hopkins University Press, 1975, pp. 31–32).

God in Process

DAVID RAY GRIFFIN

In contrast with modern philosophy, which assumed the basic units of nature to be enduring substances devoid of both experience and self-movement, Whitehead and Hartshorne begin with the hypothesis that nature is comprised of creative, experiential events. The term 'events' indicates that the basic units of reality are not enduring things, or substances, but momentary events. Each enduring thing, such as an electron, an atom, a cell, or a psyche, is a temporal *society*, comprised of a series of momentary events, each of which incorporates the previous events of that enduring individual.

The term 'experiential' indicates that the basic unit-events of the world are not "vacuous actualities," devoid of experience. Whitehead called them "occasions of experience." This doctrine does not mean that all events have conscious thoughts and sensory perceptions. It means only that they have something analogous to what we call feeling, memory, desire, and purpose in ourselves. To call this position "anthropomorphism," Hartshorne points out, is to presuppose that these experiential qualities belong uniquely to us. An animal caught in a trap does not have to become a human being in order to suffer.[1] One of the central features of Hartshorne's philosophy is the idea that the basic psychic qualities—such as feeling, memory, desire, and purpose—are "cosmic variables," capable of *infinite* scope, both above and below their human forms. Memory, for example, could include the whole past, or it might extend back only a millionth of a second.[2] Desire and purpose might be equally variable in relation to the future. To say that all events are experiences is therefore not to say that they are very similar to human experiences; it is only to say that they are not absolutely different in kind.

The term 'creative' gives special emphasis to one of these experiential variables. It says that, although all events are influenced by previous events, no event is fully determined by the past. Every event exercises at least some iota of self-determination or self-creation, and then some power to exert creative influence on the future.

Although this position could be called "panpsychism," I prefer the term 'panexperientialism.'[3] The term also suggests that the basic units are enduring things. . . .

Source: Reprinted from *Hartshorne: Process Philosophy and Theology*, Robert Kane and Stephen H. Phillips, eds., by permission of the State University of New York Press. © 1989, State University of New York. All rights reserved.

One advantage of panexperientialism, he says, is that it gives us some idea of what matter is in itself. Modern philosophy has left the nature of matter wholly mysterious,[4] saying that we cannot know what it is in itself, only how it appears to us. But, Hartshorne says, we should take advantage of the fact that in ourselves we have an individual piece of nature that we know from within as well as without.[5] If we are naturalists, and hence regard our own experience as fully natural, not as a supernatural something added to nature, should we not assume that all natural unities have two sides? The fact that it is only ourselves whose inside we know directly does not prevent us from assuming that other people have insides, that is, experiences. And most of us assume that other animals have experience of some sort. Why should we not assume that all natural entities, all the way down to subatomic events, have inside experience as well as outer behavior? We realize that a purely behavioristic approach is inadequate for human beings and other higher animals. By generalizing this insight to all levels of nature, we can have some slight intuition into what things are in themselves.[6] What we call matter is then the outer appearance of something that is, from within, analogous to our own experience.

Probably the most obvious advantage of panexperientialism is that it allows us to solve the notorious mind-body problem. By rejecting the dualistic assumption that lower individuals such as cells and molecules are absolutely different in kind, rather than merely different in degree, from our conscious experience, the problem is dissolved. In Hartshorne's words: "cells can influence our human experiences because they have feelings that we can feel. To deal with the influences of human experiences upon cells, one turns this around. We have feelings that *cells* can feel.[7]

By allowing us to understand our common-sense assumption that our experience is actual, that our bodies are actual, and that the two interact, panexperientialism proves itself superior to its alternatives. Materialism, by reducing mind to matter, forces us to deny that our own experience—the thing we know best in the universe—is really real and efficacious. Berkeleyan idealism, by reducing matter to mind, denies that our body is actual and efficacious. Dualism says that mind and body are both actual but leaves us in the dark about how they interact, or at least seem to interact. Panexperientialism, which is nondualistic without being reductionistic, is the only doctrine that accounts for all the things we presuppose in practice: that our bodies are real and influence our experience; that our experience is partly self-determining and influences our bodies in return.

A third advantage of panexperientialism is that it is, unlike materialism, truly nondualistic. This point, Hartshorne believes, will eventually lead science and science-oriented philosophy to embrace panexperientialism. The scientific mind, because of its drive to find universal explanatory principles, has a natural aversion to dualism.[8] The scientific community thus far, in overcoming the dualism with which modern thought began, has increasingly gravitated toward materialism. But this form of nondualism will not provide the conceptual unity science seeks, Hartshorne says, because it is really dualism in disguise. Because materialists cannot fail to believe that experiencing things exist, their assertion that nonexperiencing individuals exist means that the universe contains two fundamentally different types of individuals: experiencing and nonexperiencing.[9] This dualism is a "temporalized dualism"; in its evolutionary account, it says that mere matter without a trace of experience first existed, and that then experience or mind "emerged."[10] Like other forms of dualism, this temporalized dualism has an unanswerable question. Its form of this question is: "How could mere matter produce life and minds?"[11] Panexperientialist nondualism allows us to avoid this unanswerable question by speaking of "the emergence of species of mind, not of mind as such."[12]

If the case for panexperientialism is so strong—and there are still more advantages to come—why has it not been the most popular theory? The main reason, Hartshorne believes, is that much of the world as we perceive it does not give any evidence of animation, of having experiences and exercising self-determination. Rocks just stay where they are, unless moved by an external force. They show no sign of having feelings, desires, purposes, and the power for self-motion.[13] The difference between ourselves and a rock appears to be absolute, not merely a difference in degree. Hartshorne has a fourfold reply to this objection. Beyond the prior distinction between knowing something from within or only from without, this answer involves the indistinctness of sensory perception, the difference between aggregates and compound individuals, and the difference between high-grade and low-grade individuals. These four factors account for our idea of "matter" as inert, unfeeling stuff. But, Hartshorne adds, thanks to modern science we should now realize that matter in this sense is an illusion.

Ordinary sensory perception, we now know, is indistinct.[14] Even the most precise of our senses, vision, does not give us the true individuals of which the world is comprised. We see a rock, not the billions of molecules of which it is comprised, let alone its atoms and subatomic particles; we see a plant, not the billions of cells of which it is comprised. If we could see individual cells, molecules, atoms, and electrons, we would not think of any of them as inert. The increased distinctness of perception made possible by modern science has in fact shown the inertness of the microscopic world to be an illusion.[15] Scientific experience has hence confirmed what Leibniz suspected, that the unities of sensory perception, such as rocks, plants, and stars, are *pseudo*-unities, produced by blurred perception. By penetrating these pseudo-unities, modern science has undercut the main basis for dualism and materialism.[16] We can think of all the true individuals of nature by analogy with ourselves. . . .

In summary: Hartshorne argues that the ordinary distinction between mind and matter is based on four differences: (1) We know our own "mind" or experiences from within; what we call "matter" we know from without. (2) While through introspection (or retrospection) we know an individual, our sensory perception of outer objects hides the true individuals from us. (3) What we call our mind is a true individual; what we typically call matter is an aggregate of millions or billions of individuals devoid of any overall experiential unity. (4) Our mind is a series of very high-grade experiences, with consciousness, self-consciousness, and hence very sophisticated purposes. The individuals constituting matter are very low-grade individuals, with feelings but no consciousness, let alone self-consciousness, and hence very short-range purposes. . . .

THEISM, PANEXPERIENTIALISM, AND DEEP EMPIRICISM

Hartshorne is probably best known and most discussed for his ideas about the divine nature and existence. Many of his most important contributions indeed come under this topic. It would be a mistake, however, to assume that his theism is separable from his panexperientialism. He says that most errors about God involve errors about the world, and vice versa.[17] His theism is in fact part and parcel of his panexperientialism, and his panexperientialism is part and parcel of his theism. Each implies the other. . . .

From Hartshorne's point of view, a philosophy cannot be consistent unless it is theistic.[18] Before this fact can be clearly seen, however, two major obstacles must be removed. The first of these obstacles is the fact that most people still equate theism with traditional or classical theism, which cannot be made credible. If one thinks of this traditional position as theism, then Hartshorne is an atheist. He fully agrees with the judgment of most modern philosophers that the arguments against the traditional idea of God are "as conclusive as philosophical arguments could well be."[19]

Hartshorne has in fact been one of the twentieth century's major critics of traditional theism, pointing out many ways in which it makes an intelligible, consistent and credible philosophy impossible. I mention six. (1) By asserting that God determines or at least knows the future, the traditional idea of God conflicts with our presuppositions about human freedom and responsibility. (2) By affirming an omnipotent goodness that can determine all details of the world, it conflicts with our presupposition about evil, that is, that not everything that happens is for the best. (3) By combining this idea of omnipotence with an anthropomorphic dualism, according to which only human beings have intrinsic value, supernaturalists developed a view of divine design that was disproved by the facts of evolution.[20] (4) By buttressing this doctrine of omnipotence with a doctrine of creation *ex nihilo*, supernaturalism affirmed the self-contradictory idea of a beginning of time. (5) Traditional theism attributed immutable consciousness to God, although we can think meaningfully of consciousness only as changing. (6) It spoke of God as an impassible being who could not be enriched or pained by anything happening in the world; it thereby contradicted its own injunction to serve God, and our presupposition that our lives have ultimate meaning. One reason Hartshorne is distressed by this traditional idea of God is that it has led, by reaction, to complete atheism.

Modern philosophy became atheistic, however, not only because of problems inherent in traditional theism but also because the modern world view rules out any significant idea of God. I mention four reasons. (1) A reductionism that would not allow the mind to influence the body would certainly not allow downward causation from God to the world, and would have no analogy for this. (2) The mechanistic view of nature allows for no divine influence in the world, because entities that interact only by mechanical impact make influence by a cosmic mind or soul unintelligible. According to the modern cosmology, it is impact, not love, that makes the world go 'round. (3) This mechanistic view also makes it impossible to understand how the world could be in God. (4) The sensationist theory of perception rules out any divine presence in human experience, and hence any direct awareness of God. Accordingly, portraying theism as a viable philosophy requires overcoming not only traditional theism but also the modern world view. . . .

The presence of evil in our world and in every possible world is thereby explained. Evil results from multiple finite freedom, and any world God could have created would have had multiple finite freedom.[21] The possibility of evil is necessary. No particular evils are necessary, but the possibility that evil can occur is necessary. We cannot accuse God of a deficiency in goodness for not interrupting the normal cause-effect relations to prevent particularly horrendous evils. Because the normal cause-effect relations are natural, necessary, given features of reality, they cannot be interrupted. God does influence every event, but divine influence is always persuasion. It could not be unilateral determination.

This position explains not only the possibility of evil in general, Hartshorne points out, but also the possibility of the extreme horrors that human beings have caused and suffered. Freedom and danger necessarily rise proportionately. Because human beings have more freedom than other creatures, they necessarily are more dangerous and more capable of suffering.[22]

Besides explaining evil, this position makes clear that belief in God in no way denies human freedom and human responsibility for the course of human history. We cannot declare that any *status quo* has been sanctioned by divine arrangement, or that God will step in to save us from our foolish ways, such as from nuclear weapons and other ecological threats.

Besides not determining the future, God does not even know the future, beyond those abstract features of the future that are already determined by the present. God's lack of knowledge of the details of the future betokens no divine imperfection. Because all events exercise some self-determining power, the future is simply not knowable, even by omniscience. The partial openness of the future, and our own partial freedom, which we all presuppose in practice, are hence not compromised by this naturalistic theism.

This position also simultaneously overcomes the charge that the idea of God's creation of the world is self-contradictory, and the conflict between creation and evolution. Because there never was a first moment of finite existence, the creation of our world involved a creation not out of nothing but "out of an earlier world and its potentialities for transformation." Divine creative causation, analogously to ours, always involves a transformation of a previous situation. No self-contradictory idea of a beginning of time is therefore implied.[23] Also, because finite events necessarily have their own creative power, divine creative transformation is always persuasion, never unilateral rearrangement. No feature of our world in its present state of evolution is simply a divine product. Darwinian evidence that every species shows signs of "descent with modification" from earlier species is therefore no evidence against a divine creator. . . .

Besides showing belief in God to be intelligible, panexperientialism shows it to be necessary. The idea that the actual world is comprised exhaustively of partially *free* experiences makes it clear that the order of the world can be made intelligible only through the idea of an all-inclusive soul, whose purposes order the world through becoming internalized by the creatures, somewhat as our purposes order our bodies through becoming internalized by our bodily members.[24] . . .

With regard to belief in God, Hartshorne offers many ways in which conscious belief in the God of his metaphysics can have practical importance for our lives. I will mention four.

First, by explicitly recognizing that God's perfect power does not and cannot eliminate, control, or occasionally override the power of the creatures, we can retain faith in the basic goodness of life in the face of its inevitable tragedies.[25] Second, explicit belief in God will encourage us to imitate God— both God's sympathy for all feelings and desires, and God's creativity, in which the creation of new values is combined with respect for old ones.[26] The vision of God will also lead us to aspire to approximate that unity of love with knowledge and power that God alone embodies.[27] Third, theism "implies that love is the supreme good, not pleasure or knowledge or power, and those who think otherwise will be disappointed."[28] Fourth, explicit belief in God provides an answer to the final question of human life: What is its ultimate meaning, what should be our central aim? "Be the aim Nirvana, the Classless Society, the Welfare State, Self-realization," Hartshorne says, "the query is never silenced, what good is it, from the cosmic and everlasting perspective, that one or the other or all of these aims be attained for a time on this ball of rock?"[29] Belief in God, as the One in whom we all live and who cherishes all good things everlastingly, provides an infinite aim for life—to contribute to the divine life. And this infinite aim strengthens rather than weakens our commitment to finite aims.

NOTES

1. Charles Hartshorne, *Beyond Humanism: Essays in the Philosophy of Nature* (Lincoln: University of Nebraska Press, 1968), p. 120 (henceforth BH).

2. BH 116–17.

3. Hartshorne at one time used the term 'panpsychism,' but later switched to 'psychicalism.' I have explained my reasons for eschewing both of those terms in favor of 'panexperientialism' at greater length in Cobb and Griffin, ed., *Mind in Nature*, 97–98.

4. "Physics and Psychics: The Place of Mind in Nature," John B. Cobb, Jr., and David Ray Griffin, ed., *Mind in Nature: Essays on the Interface of Science and Philosophy* (Washington, D.C.: University Press of America, 1977), 90 (henceforth P&P).

5. P&P 90; *The Logic of Perfection and Other Essays in Neoclassical Metaphysics* (Lasalle, Ill.: Open Court, 1962), 183–84 (henceforth LP).

6. BH 202,266; LP 225; P&P 90.

7. LP 229.

8. P&P 90; *Creative Synthesis and Philosophic Method* (London: SCM Press, 1970; Lanham, Md.: University Press of America, 1983), 9 (henceforth CSPM).

9. CSPM 8, 27.

10. *Omnipotence and other Theological Mistakes* (Albany: State University of New York Press, 1984), 83–84 (henceforth OOTM).

11. P&P 92.

12. LP 125.

13. P&P 91; "Why Psychicalism? Comments on Keeling's and Shepherd's Criticisms," *Process Studies* 6/1 (Spring, 1976) 67–72, esp. 67.

14. BH 199, 304, 314.

15. LP xii; *Reality as Social Process: Studies in Metaphysics and Religion* (Glencoe, Ill.: The Free Press, 1953), 33 (henceforth RSP).

16. BH 199, 314.

17. LP xiii, 138–39, 144.

18. BH 86–87.

19. *Man's Vision of God and the Logic of Theism* (1941: Hamden, Conn.: 1964), 58 (henceforth MVG).

20. LP 205; P&P 94. Given Hartshorne's distinction between metaphysical and empirical (in the narrow sense) issues, which is discussed later, one must be careful in saying that Hartshorne believes the traditional doctrine of God to have been disproved by the "facts" of evil and evolution. Hartshorne insists that contingent facts could not disprove a God-idea that was not already inherently incoherent, even apart from these facts (LP 157; CSPM 19–22, 292). What is inconsistent with traditional theism is not simply the great amount of evil in our world, and some of the details of the evolutionary process, but the very reality of processes not controllable by a supreme agent. The reality of creaturely creativity or freedom is not simply a contingent fact about our particular world but a necessary feature of any world. Particular evils and particular facts about the evolutionary process may be important in focusing our attention on the incompatibility of traditional theism and the nature of the world, but the proper lesson to be drawn, Hartshorne says, is that the traditional idea of God, including God's relation to the world, is an incoherent idea.

21. OOTM 15, 21; LP 209; CSPM 237–38; MVB xvi, 14, 30–31, 36, 89.

22. CSPM 13–14; RSP 107; LP 13–14; *The Divine Relativity: A Social Conception of God* (1948; New Haven: Yale University Press, 1964), 136; *Whitehead's Philosophy: Selected Essays 1935–1970* (Lincoln: University of Nebraska Press, 1972), 93–94; *A Natural Theology for our Time* (Lasalle, Ill.: Open Court, 1967), 81–82.

23. MVG 230, 231, 233.

24. LP 157, 285; CSPM 284–85; BH 285.

25. LP 11–14.

26. BH 316; MVB 116, 229.

27. BH 208–09.

28. BH 256.

29. LP 132.

Discussion Questions

1. A key to understanding Hartshorne's (and Griffin's) view is the notion of *panexperientialism*. Do you agree with Griffin that our knowledge of reality based on contemporary physics supports such a view? Why or why not?

2. It is important in Griffin's view to avoid a dualistic view of reality. What, if anything, commends itself to you from the view of process thought as a way of avoiding dualism?

3. Griffin claims that a notion of "immutable consciousness," when applied to God, is contradictory, since consciousness is always changing. What evidence do you think there is for such a claim?

4. The theodicy offered by process thought could be classified as embodying elements of the free-will defense. Do you think it is successful? Give reasons for your answer.

5. The God of process thought is identified with values, not with being. What are the advantages and disadvantages of such a view?

Karma and Evil

There is a natural human tendency to accept blame for the bad things that happen to us, to blame oneself for the misfortunes one experiences. "What did I do to deserve this?" seems to be a predictable lament whenever something bad enters our lives. In the Hebrew Scriptures, the book of Job issues a denial of such a view. Job is a righteous man who undergoes all kinds of dire trials—the loss of his fortune, his family, and even his health. His friends urge him to admit that his sufferings are the result of his misconduct. One after another, they ply him with the same appeal: Admit your wrongdoing, and maybe God will remove these plagues from you. Job stands steadfast: "As God lives . . . I hold fast my righteousness, and will not let it go; my heart does not reproach me for any of my days" (Job 27, 1,6). The writer of the book of Job agrees with Job that his trials are not the result of his actions.

Both Jewish and Christian Scriptures for the most part reject the notion that one's suffering is in direct proportion to one's guilt. Christian writers adopt the Jewish image of the Suffering Servant of the Lord whose suffering brings redemption, a view reaching its culmination in the death of Jesus, whose suffering and death are understood to bring redemption from sin and death to all. But nonetheless, the view persists that somehow we get what we deserve and that our present woes are due to our misdeeds. The philosopher Immanuel Kant argues that in a perfectly rational world, evildoers would suffer and the righteous would be happy. But the world is not like that, and it is not possible to tell who is righteous by how things are going for the wicked.

Whereas both Judaism and Christianity repudiate the notion that we get what we deserve in this life, other religions are not so sure. Hinduism, Jainism, and, in a modified way, Buddhism all agree that there is a law of cause and effect that explains our present situation. The deeds that bring about that situation are not entirely those done in this life, but also those from a previous life. The doctrine of *reincarnation* is the view that we have successive lives, and the doctrine of *karma* is the principle of moral cause and effect that spans these successive lives, rendering much of the experience of the present life the result of a previous one. Some proponents of this view leave open the possibility that persons who have done particularly evil deeds may not be reborn as a human being at all, but as an animal—even an insect. The doctrine that human souls can migrate from one life-form to another in successive lives, depending on how well they live each of those lives, is the view known as *transmigration*.

The word *karma* is from a Sanskrit word meaning "deed" or "action." Basic to this view is the belief that we are caught in a continuous cycle of birth, death, and rebirth, known as *samsara*, so that the deeds done in our past lives affect our situation in our present one. Even though karma is a principle of cause and effect (that is, the effects seen in this life are caused by those in a previous one), karma does not eliminate our free will. We can do something about our situation: Through the development of spirituality, good works, devotion to a savior, and patient acceptance of our given situation, we can even mitigate the conditions of the present life and certainly improve the possibilities for our next one. The goal of human existence is eventually to get out of the cycle of birth, death, and rebirth, by achieving release, *moksha*.

The question that we have to answer is how effective is karma in a theodicy? And does karma really excuse God from responsibility for evil in the world? In general, is a religion containing doctrines of reincarnation and karma (such as Hinduism) any more effective in resolving the problem of evil than are Christianity and Judaism which have no such doctrines?

The selection that follows, written by a noted American interpreter of Hinduism, addresses these questions in the context of that religious tradition. Wendy Doniger briefly sketches the main points of the doctrine of karma and then raises several important philosophical issues. She is careful to note that there are many strands of Hindu thought, and sometimes "village Hinduism," that is, the religion of the common folk, may not always reflect the religious views of scholars and teachers. It does not, for example, offer much solace to parents grieving over the death of a child to be told that all this was due to bad karma from a previous life.

Doniger's discussion of the issues is clear and approachable, and there is no need here to replicate that discussion. However, one issue that she deals with is the same we encountered in previously examined theodicies: Can we really maintain a doctrine of divine omnipotence and be successful in constructing a theodicy? Even with the doctrine of karma, we come back to the same issue: Is God bound by the law of karma? That is, can God ignore karma and bring about good things for people with bad karma? If so, then the blame for evil again "is cast at his feet." But if God is bound by the law of karma, then in what sense can we speak of God as omnipotent, all powerful? This is not an easy set of questions, especially when some Hindu scholars see God as capable of countering the effect of karma and offering a respite to those who repent from their past and seek righteousness. However we understand karma, it does not remove the need to live one's life as well as one can.

According to Doniger, "Karma is the hand one is dealt; one can play it badly or well."

Karma in Hindu Thought

WENDY DONIGER

The belief that Indians did not recognize the problem of evil is widespread.
"For Hindu thought there is no Problem of Evil," writes Alan Watts,[1] and a
Hindu scholar concurs: "Hinduism is not puzzled by the Problem of Evil."[2] Similarly, it is often said that there is no concept of evil at all in India. Mircea Eliade
remarked that not only was there no conflict between good and evil in India, but
there was in fact a confusion between them. He suggested a reason for this confusion: "Many demons are reputed to have won their demonic prowess by good
actions performed in previous existences. In other words *good* can serve to make
evil. . . . All these examples are only particular and popular illustrations of the
fundamental Indian doctrine, that good and evil have no meaning or function except in a world of appearances."[3] Sir Charles Eliot regarded this tendency to confuse good and evil as an innate characteristic of pantheism, which "finds it hard
to distinguish and condemn evil."[4] Statements of this kind are generally based on
Vedāntic Hinduism and Buddhism, which are concerned more with ignorance
than with sin, valuing virtue only as an adjunct to knowledge, by means of which
the philosophic saint rises above both good and evil; and many varieties of Indian
religion regard suffering rather than sin as the fault in the world.[5] These beliefs
do not, however, apply to most of Purānic Hinduism.

Another source of the statement that Indians do not have a Problem of Evil
is the belief that evil is unreal in Indian thought. "Wrong . . . in India is *māyā*,
[illusion] *asat*, [nonexistent] by definition not real. . . . The problem of evil is
a false one, [and] the brahmin gives it the treatment false problems deserve."[6]
The counterargument is simply that, though many *Vedāntists* did maintain that
evil was logically unreal, suffering was always subjectively accepted as real.[7]
From the "other" Indian point of view—the same affective strain that rejects
the implications of karma—"evil, suffering, waste, terror, and fear are real enough.
. . . Therefore there is a sense in which evil is real, and a sense in which karma

Source: Wendy Doniger O'Flaherty, *The Origins of Evil in Hindu Mythology.* Copyright © 1976 by
the Regents of the University of California. Used with permission of the University of California Press.
  1 Watts (1957), p. 35.
  2 Buch, p. 9.
  3 Eliade (1938), pp. 20ff., and (1965), p. 96.
  4 Eliot, I, ci.
  5 *Ibid.*, I, lxxii and lxxix.
  6 Smith, p. 10.
  7 Herman, pp. 436–438.

and rebirth are real as well. The dogma of unreality is betrayed by the activity and concern of the faithful."[8]

Philosophers and theologians may set up their logical criteria, but a logical answer to an emotional question is difficult both to construct and to accept. The usual example of extraordinary evil given in Indian texts is the death of a young child. If one says to the parents of this child, "You are not real, nor is your son; therefore you cannot really be suffering," one is not likely to be of much comfort. Nor will the pain be dulled by such remarks as "God can't help it" or "God doesn't know about it." It is only the ethical hypothesis that is *emotionally* dispensable: God is not good, or God does not wish man to be without evil (two very different arguments). And this is the line most actively developed by Hindu mythological theodicy. . . .

THE "SOLUTION" OF KARMA

It has been argued that "the most complete formal solution of the problem of theodicy is the special achievement of the Indian doctrine of *karma*, the so-called belief in the transmigration of souls."[9] This doctrine, simply stated, "solves" the problem by blaming evil on itself; one's present experience is the direct result of the action (karma), good and bad, accumulated in past lives and affixed to the transmigrating soul. Karma is a thing that can be transferred to one person from another, whittled away by good deeds performed in the present life, but never entirely destroyed; it is thus justified by evils of the past and will be balanced by rewards in future births; it is not God's fault, nor man's fault, nor a devil's fault; it is part of the eternal cycle, and ultimately all is justified and balanced.

The flaws in this solution are immediately apparent. The hypothesis of karma violates the hypothesis of omnipotence[10] and thus bypasses rather than resolves theodicy. If God is under the sway of karma, he is not omnipotent; if, as some theologians insist, God controls karma, then once again the blame is cast at his feet: "While the problem of extraordinary or gratuitous evil can be explained by a reference to previous Karma, this cannot, the plain man might feel, justify that evil."[11] . . .

Moral guilt does not constitute a special problem in village Hinduism, as it would if karma were strictly interpreted; people do not believe that there is nothing they can do to avoid or remove karma. Hindus often behave as if they did not believe in karma, and some definitely claim that they do not accept karma or believe in a supreme deity.[12] There is a clear gulf between philosophy and cult here, as Devendranath Tagore recognized when he criticized the Upaniṣads: "I became disappointed. . . . These Upanishads could not meet all our needs. Could not fill our hearts."[13] It is the particular talent of mythology to bridge the gap between the affective and cognitive aspects of religion—to fill the heart.

[8] *Ibid.*, p. 439.
[9] Weber (1963), p. 145.
[10] Herman, p. 417.
[11] *Ibid.*, p. 511.
[12] Sharma, p. 350.
[13] Smith, p. 10.

This pattern of differentiation has been observed in another Hindu village as well: the theory of karma generates anxiety and guilt about one's probable (but unknown) past sins, as well as feelings of helplessness, but "the beliefs concerning ways whereby fate can be subverted seem to function to allay such feelings— to give the individual mother some feeling of control over her social environment."[14] Ghosts and evil spirits, as well as semi-gods who have achieved powers from asceticism, are "agents working outside fate": devotion to God can overcome karma.[15] This simple faith has an elaborate, classical foundation in the philosophy of Rāmānuja, who maintained that God could "even override the power of *karma* to draw repentant sinners to him."[16] Thus the doctrine of karma is deeply undermined by other important strains of Indian religion in which the individual is able to swim against the current of time and fate.

Karma as a philosophy merely formalizes an intuition that has depressed most of the pessimists among us at one time or another—the feeling that we cannot escape our past, we cannot start fresh, that, as F. Scott Fitzgerald wrote, "we beat on, boats against the current, borne back ceaselessly into the past." Placing the initial wave of this current in a previous birth, or in a birth at some other point on a circle, simply transfers the blame from the realm of known events to the realm of unknown ones; in this way, the emotional intuition of the force of the past becomes logically airtight. The idea of the Golden Age is also based on a widespread (though by no means universal) intuition—a feeling that the skies were bluer, apples sweeter, when we were young. The myth reintroduces these underlying natural emotions into a philosophical framework which was invented precisely in order to form a rigid superstructure to protect that intuition in the first place.

How did Indians come to accept these alternative, conflicting views of theodicy? Obeyesekere, arguing against Weber's "existential" level of theodicy, attacks this question:

> In what sense could we say that a theodicy existed previous to the development of karma? Certainly not in the classical European sense of theodicy, which is explicitly related to the attributes of a monotheistic deity. . . . In a culture which possesses a theory of suffering like that of karma the problem of explaining unjust suffering simply cannot arise.[17]

But there are problems of the theodicy type in many texts of the Vedas and Brāhmaṇas, though karma does not appear until the later period of the Upaniṣhads.[18] The concept of the sinful deity, which explains the origin of evil as a result of the malevolence of gods toward men, definitely predates the doctrine of karma and continues to prevail despite karma. The wish to escape death (the basis

---

14 Kolenda, p. 78.
15 Ibid., pp. 76–77, and 79.
16 Basham, p. 332.
17 Obeyesekere, pp. 10–11.
18 Keith, p. 570ff.

of the antagonism between gods and men) and the fear of premature death (one of the classical sources of theodicy) are also well attested in Vedic texts. In karma-influenced texts this fear of death is changed into the wish to escape from life, but this line is seldom developed in the mythology, which reverts to Vedic assumptions, allows mortals to challenge death, and describes the resulting wrath of the gods—and our resulting suffering. Thus the patterns of theodicy were established before the doctrine of karma and continued to develop alongside it. . . .

Karma is the hand one is dealt; one can play it badly or well. (Of course, the ability to play is also part of one's karma, and this leads to metaphysical intricacies). This is not the place, nor am I the scholar, for a lengthy exposition of the Indian doctrine of free will. Suffice it to say that Indian ideas on this subject differ radically from Western ones; in particular, we must face the disquieting ability of Indians to believe several seemingly contradictory tenets at once. Thus we find, in varying proportions, the concepts of free will, fate, and God's grace emerging from different texts at different periods. Moreover, there is significant evidence of a difference of opinion on this subject within individual texts. . . . The belief that God intended man to live in a state of perfection, but that man, by the exercise of his free will, destroyed this perfection and thus either brought about the evils of the world or caused God to destroy him, arises very seldom in Sanskrit texts. There the blame is usually cast either upon God (who through his own shortcomings causes man to be born with the imperfections that are inevitably to result in his downfall) or (rarely) upon demons who spoil the world for mankind and cause the gods to destroy it: men are good until evil gods corrupt them. The belief that man himself is the author of his woes is, however, entirely consonant with the early mythology of the degeneration of civilization and the evil nature of man, and it reemerges in certain myths of heresy in which men corrupt one another.

Bibliography

Basham, A. L. *The Wonder That Was India*. London, 1954.

Buch, Maganlal A. *The Principles of Hindu Ethics*. Baroda, 1921.

Eliade, Mircea. "Notes de Démonologie," *Zalmoxis* 1 (1938).

———. *Mephistopheles and the Androgyne*. Trans. J. M. Cohen. New York, 1965.

Eliot, Sir Charles. *Hinduism and Buddhism*. 3 vols. London, 1921.

Herman, Arthur Ludwig. *The Problem of Evil and Indian Thought*. Ph.D. dissertation, University of Minnesota. Published by Motilal Barnarsidass (New Delhi, 1976).

Keith, Arthur Berriedale. *Indian Mythology*. Vol. 6, part 1, of *The Mythology of All Races*, ed. L. H. Grey. Boston, 1917.

Kolenda, Pauline Mahar. "Religious Anxiety and Hindu Fate." *Journal of Asian Studies* 23, no. 2 (1964. Supplement, "Aspects of Religion in South Asia."):71–81.

Obeyesekere, Gananath. "Theodicy, Sin and Salvation in a Sociology of Buddhism." In Leach, Edmund R. (ed.), *Dialectic in Practical Religion*. Cambridge Papers in Social Anthropology, no. 5, pp. 7–40. Cambridge, 1968.

Sharma, Ursula. "Theodicy and the Doctrine of *Karma*." *Man*, n.s.8 (1973):348–364.

Smith, Ronald Morton. "Sin in India." Unpublished paper presented at a conference on Tradition in South Asia, School of Oriental and African Studies, University of London, 15 May, 1970.

Watts, Alan. *The Way of Zen*. New York, 1957.

Weber, Max. *The Sociology of Religion*. Trans. by Ephraim Fischoff, intro. by Talcott Parsons. 4th ed. London, 1963.

Discussion Questions

1. Do you think karma is a pessimistic or an optimistic doctrine? Give reasons for your answer.

2. Some have argued that karma is a socially conservative doctrine in that it provides grounds for explaining social inequities as being deserved by those experiencing them. Others have responded that karma is socially progressive, since doing good deeds in this life will improve the next life. Which side do you think has the stronger case?

3. What is your evaluation of karma as an important component of a theodicy? Does it provide a satisfactory resolution of the *problem* of evil? Why or why not?

4. Doniger says that "the hypothesis of karma . . . bypasses rather than resolves theodicy." Do you agree? Give reasons for your answer.

5. What strands of belief in Jewish and Christian thought rule out the possibilities of belief in karma?

6. Is the theodicy of karma any more or less congenial or credible than other theodicies?

A Limited God

David Ray Griffin's summary of the views of Charles Hartshorne offered an understanding of God who is limited both in power and knowledge. Finding these views framed in the context of a view of reality compatible with quantum physics gives them a modern ring. In the selection that follows from John Stuart Mill, we find an older statement that defends an even greater limitation on God's power and knowledge as well as on God's benevolence.

The view that Mill advances is so different from the traditional God of Jewish and Christian belief that it would seem a small step for him to deny the existence of God altogether. That he does not is due to the force of natural theology in general and the design argument in particular. By denying the omnipotence of God and placing limits on God's benevolence, Mill offers a theodicy at the expense of the traditional view of God. A secondary effect of Mill's analysis is to discover what attributes natural theology can attribute to God, and it turns out that this is a God very different from that of traditional theism.

DIVINE OMNIPOTENCE

The traditional view is that God is all-powerful, but not only does natural theology fail to provide evidence to support divine omnipotence, it even offers positive evidence against it. Mill gives two arguments to support this claim. The first argument is based on the existence in nature of numerous contrivances. By *contrivances* Mill seemed to mean some kind of device or mechanism for achieving a particular end, and Mill probably had in mind such natural processes as evolution. Anytime a person has to resort to a contrivance to accomplish an end, this indicates a lack of power. For example, if you wanted to lift a one-thousand-pound weight, a task clearly beyond the capability of most persons, you would have to rig up a block and tackle, which would be a contrivance to accomplish the task of lifting the weight. Such a contrivance would be an indication of your intelligence, but also an admission of the limits of your strength. The existence of multiple contrivances in nature, therefore, points to limitations on God's power. If

God were truly omnipotent, God would not have had to fill nature with so many contrivances but could have accomplished the divine purpose—whatever that might be—directly and without the use of adaptations. Mill also suggests that perhaps the limitation on God's power was posed by the materials God had to work with in creating the universe, namely matter and energy, or matter and force, as Mill refers to them. There is nothing in the design argument to support the claim that the creator of the cosmos created either matter or energy, and the most that the design argument can do is suggest that God took existing materials and fashioned a world out of them.

A second indication of a limitation on God's power, according to Mill, is our scanty knowledge of God. Natural theology points to the "traces" of God's creative activity in the cosmos, but these traces supply less than complete knowledge of God's purposes. So it could be argued, Mill suggests, that the limited knowledge God gave us of the divine activity is a further indication of God's limitation. A wholly powerful God could have given us more knowledge of the divine purpose. The view of God suggested by natural theology is that of a being with great but perhaps limited power, who could only leave traces of divine creativity in the universe. This would make the God of natural theology more like *Demiurge* (or *Demiourgos*, to use Mill's older spelling) of ancient Greek religion. The term *Demiourgos* was the Greek word for workman, and referred to a kind of tinker or handyman who traveled about making and fixing things for people, using materials supplied by his customers. Plato applied the term *Demiurge* to his notion of a creator-god who fashioned a world out of existing materials; that is, Plato's creator, god merely shaped the world out of what was available. According to Mill, this is the most that natural theology can give us, not the God of traditional Jewish and Christian thought who created the world *ex nihilo*, out of nothing.

DIVINE OMNISCIENCE

That God is omniscient, or all-knowing, forms a part of the traditional view of God in Judaeo-Christian belief. What evidence can natural theology supply to support the existence of this divine attribute? Very little, Mill says. Mill admits that natural theology does not supply evidence that counts as strongly against omniscience as it does against divine omnipotence, but natural theology also offers no proof in support of this attribute. In other words, natural theology does not disprove or prove that God is omniscient. This consideration suggests that in addition to perhaps being limited by the available materials from which to create a world, God may also have been limited in intelligence. There are no grounds, Mill says, for supposing that the contrivances that form the natural order were the best possible or even the best of which divine creativity was possible. Likewise, there is no indication from natural theology that the creator could have foreseen the bad side effects that the created order would produce, side effects that we experience as evil. Even if we accept the view that God fashioned the best world of which the divine intelligence was capable—and there is really no proof for this—there is no evidence that God foresaw the numerous problems that have cropped up in the world. The world may be thought of as a well-contrived machine that contains inherent defects that the designer had not foreseen, defects that became apparent only subsequently. The existence of evil, thought of in this way, may have been simply an unforeseen by-product of the world created by God's limited intelligence.

DIVINE MORAL ATTRIBUTES

At the outset of his discussion of the moral attributes of God, Mill dismisses the problem—to him insuperable—of reconciling infinite power and infinite benevolence with the existence of evil in the world. He sets a more modest task for himself. If we grant that God was perhaps limited in power and in intelligence, then what can we say about God's moral attributes if we confine ourselves to what we can know from natural theology?

Mill answers that we can see some evidence for God's benevolence, but no proof for the view that God is wholly benevolent or completely just. There is certainly design in nature, but the apparent purpose of this design seems to be to provide for continuity of the created order for a certain period of time. Natural theology simply gives no evidence that God cares about us individually or that God has some final purpose to be achieved by creating human beings. It can be argued that God shows some concern for human happiness, but that is apparently not God's primary concern. As for divine justice, there is simply no evidence in nature at all that God's activity can be measured by the standards of human justice. Mill even goes so far as to suggest that justice is a human improvement in nature and that if we had conformed to the standards of the natural order, we would never have achieved civilized society and its resulting justice.

Mill's conclusion is that natural theology gives us no evidence for the traditional God of Judaeo-Christian belief: All natural theology can offer is evidence of "a being of great but limited power . . . who desires, and pays some regard to, the happiness of his creatures, but who seems to have other motives of action which he cares more for, and who can hardly be supposed to have created the universe for that purpose alone." Since Mill does not think that divine justice can be demonstrated through natural theology, the difficulty of reconciling divine justice with the fact of evil in the world likewise disappears. Therefore it would not be completely accurate to call Mill's view a theodicy; instead, it is a reinterpretation of the God of traditional theism, a God that would be compatible with "natural religion."

The Divine Attributes

JOHN STUART MILL

The question of the existence of a Deity, in its purely scientific aspect . . . is next to be considered. Given the indications of a Deity, what sort of a Deity do they point to? What attributes are we warranted, by the evidence which Nature affords of a creative mind, in assigning to that mind?

It needs no showing that the power if not the intelligence must be so far superior to that of Man, as to surpass all human estimate. But from this to Omnipotence and Omniscience there is a wide interval. And the distinction is of immense practical importance.

It is not too much to say that every indication of Design in the Kosmos is so much evidence against the Omnipotence of the Designer. For what is meant by Design? Contrivance: the adaptation of means to an end. But the necessity for contrivance—the need of employing means—is a consequence of the limitation of power. Who would have recourse to means if to attain his end his mere word was sufficient? The very idea of means implies that the means have an efficacy which the direct action of the being who employs them has not. Otherwise they are not means, but an incumbrance. A man does not use machinery to move his arms. If he did, it could only be when paralysis had deprived him of the power of moving them by volition. But if the employment of contrivance is in itself a sign of limited power, how much more so is the careful and skilful choice of contrivances? Can any wisdom be shown in the selection of means, when the means have no efficacy but what is given them by the will of him who employs them, and when his will could have bestowed the same efficacy on any other means? Wisdom and contrivance are shown in overcoming difficulties, and there is no room for them in a Being for whom no difficulties exist. The evidences, therefore, of Natural Theology distinctly imply that the author of the Kosmos worked under limitations; that he was obliged to adapt himself to conditions independent of his will, and to attain his ends by such arrangements as those conditions admitted of.

And this hypothesis agrees with what we have seen to be the tendency of the evidences in another respect. We found that the appearances in Nature point indeed to an origin of the Kosmos, or order in Nature, and indicate that origin to be Design but do not point to any commencement, still less creation, of the two

Source: John Stuart Mill, *Three Essays on Religion* (London: Longmans, Green & Co., 1875), pp. 176–90, 194.

great elements of the Universe, the passive element and the active element, Matter and Force. There is in Nature no reason whatever to suppose that either Matter or Force, or any of their properties, were made by the Being who was the author of the collocations by which the world is adapted to what we consider as its purposes; or that he has power to alter any of those properties. It is only when we consent to entertain this negative supposition that there arises a need for wisdom and contrivance in the order of the universe. The Deity had on this hypothesis to work out his ends by combining materials of a given nature and properties. Out of these materials he had to construct a world in which his designs should be carried into effect through given properties of Matter and Force, working together and fitting into one another. This did require skill and contrivance, and the means by which it is effected are often such as justly excite our wonder and admiration: but exactly because it requires wisdom, it implies limitation of power, or rather the two phrases express different sides of the same fact.

If it be said, that an Omnipotent Creator, though under no necessity of employing contrivances such as man must use, thought fit to do so in order to leave traces by which man might recognize his creative hand, the answer is that this equally supposes a limit to his omnipotence. For if it was his will that men should know that they themselves and the world are his work, he, being omnipotent, had only to will that they should be aware of it. Ingenious men have sought for reasons why God might choose to leave his existence so far a matter of doubt that men should not be under an absolute necessity of knowing it, as they are of knowing that three and two make five. These imagined reasons are very unfortunate specimens of casuistry; but even did we admit their validity, they are of no avail on the supposition of omnipotence, since if it did not please God to implant in man a complete conviction of his existence, nothing hindered him from making the conviction fall short of completeness by any margin he chose to leave. It is usual to dispose of arguments of this description by the easy answer, that we do not know what wise reasons the Omniscient may have had for leaving undone things which he had the power to do. It is not perceived that this plea itself implies a limit to Omnipotence. When a thing is obviously good and obviously in accordance with what all the evidences of creation imply to have been the Creator's design, and we say we do not know what good reason he may have had for not doing it, we mean that we do not know to what other, still better object—to what object still more completely in the line of his purposes, he may have seen fit to postpone it. But the necessity of postponing one thing to another belongs only to limited power. Omnipotence could have made the objects compatible. Omnipotence does not need to weigh one consideration against another. If the Creator, like a human ruler, had to adapt himself to a set of conditions which he did not make, it is as unphilosophical as presumptuous in us to call him to account for any imperfections in his work; to complain that he left anything in it contrary to what, if the indications of design prove anything, he must have intended. He must at least know more than we know, and we cannot judge what greater good would have had to be sacrificed, or what greater evil incurred, if he had decided to remove this particular blot. Not so if he be omnipotent. If he be that, he must himself have willed that the two desirable objects should be incompatible; he must himself have willed that the obstacle to his supposed design should be insuperable. It cannot therefore be his design. It will not do to say that it was, but that he had other designs which interfered with it; for no one purpose imposes necessary limitations on another in the case of a Being not restricted by conditions of possibility.

Omnipotence, therefore, cannot be predicated of the Creator on grounds of natural theology. The fundamental principles of natural religion as deduced from the facts of the universe, negate his omnipotence. They do not, in the same manner, exclude omniscience: if we suppose limitation of power, there is nothing to contradict the supposition of perfect knowledge and absolute wisdom. But neither is there anything to prove it. The knowledge of the powers and properties of things necessary for planning and executing the arrangements of the Kosmos, is no doubt as much in excess of human knowledge as the power implied in creation is in excess of human power. And the skill, the subtlety of contrivance, the ingenuity as it would be called in the case of a human work, is often marvellous. But nothing obliges us to suppose that either the knowledge or the skill is infinite. We are not even compelled to suppose that the contrivances were always the best possible. If we venture to judge them as we judge the works of human artificers, we find abundant defects. The human body, for example, is one of the most striking instances of artful and ingenious contrivance which nature offers, but we may well ask whether so complicated a machine could not have been made to last longer, and not to get so easily and frequently out of order. We may ask why the human race should have been so constituted as to grovel in wretchedness and degradation for countless ages before a small portion of it was enabled to lift itself into the very imperfect state of intelligence, goodness and happiness which we enjoy. The divine power may not have been equal to doing more; the obstacles to a better arrangement of things may have been insuperable. But it is also possible that they were not. The skill of the Demiourgos was sufficient to produce what we see; but we cannot tell that this skill reached the extreme limit of perfection compatible with the material it employed and the forces it had to work with. I know not how we can even satisfy ourselves on grounds of natural theology, that the Creator foresees all the future; that he foreknows all the effects that will issue from his own contrivances. There may be great wisdom without the power of foreseeing and calculating everything: and human workmanship teaches us the possibility that the workman's knowledge of the properties of the things he works on may enable him to make arrangements admirably fitted to produce a given result, while he may have very little power of foreseeing the agencies of another kind which may modify or counteract the operation of the machinery he has made. . . .

We now pass to the moral attributes of the Deity, so far as indicated in the Creation; or (stating the problem in the broadest manner) to the question, what indications Nature gives of the purposes of its author. This question bears a very different aspect to us from what it bears to those teachers of Natural Theology who are incumbered with the necessity of admitting the omnipotence of the Creator. We have not to attempt the impossible problem of reconciling infinite benevolence and justice with infinite power in the Creator of such a world as this. The attempt to do so not only involves absolute contradiction in an intellectual point of view but exhibits to excess the revolting spectacle of a jesuitical defence of moral enormities.

On this topic I need not add to the illustrations given of this portion of the subject in my Essay on Nature. At the stage which our argument has reached there is none of this moral perplexity. Grant that creative power was limited by conditions the nature and extent of which are wholly unknown to us, and the goodness and justice of the Creator may be all that the most pious believe; and all in the work that conflicts with those moral attributes may be the fault of the conditions which left to the Creator only a choice of evils.

It is, however, one question whether any given conclusion is consistent with known facts, and another whether there is evidence to prove it: and if we have no means for judging of the design but from the work actually produced, it is a somewhat hazardous speculation to suppose that the work designed was of a different quality from the result realized. Still, though the ground is unsafe we may, with due caution, journey a certain distance on it. Some parts of the order of nature give much more indication of contrivance than others; many, it is not too much to say, give no sign of it at all. The signs of contrivance are most conspicuous in the structure and processes of vegetable and animal life. But for these, it is probable that the appearances in nature would never have seemed to the thinking part of mankind to afford any proofs of a God. But when a God had been inferred from the organization of living beings, other parts of Nature, such as the structure of the solar system, seemed to afford evidences, more or less strong, in confirmation of the belief: granting, then, a design in Nature, we can best hope to be enlightened as to what that design was, by examining it in the parts of Nature in which its traces are the most conspicuous.

To what purpose, then, do the expedients in the construction of animals and vegetables, which excite the admiration of naturalists, appear to tend? There is no blinking the fact that they tend principally to no more exalted object than to make the structure remain in life and in working order for a certain time: the individual for a few years, the species or race for a longer but still a limited period. And the similar though less conspicuous marks of creation which are recognized in inorganic Nature, are generally of the same character. The adaptations, for instance, which appear in the solar system consist in placing it under conditions which enable the mutual action of its parts to maintain instead of destroying its stability, and even that only for a time, vast indeed if measured against our short span of animated existence, but which can be perceived even by us to be limited: for even the feeble means which we possess of exploring the past, are believed by those who have examined the subject by the most recent lights, to yield evidence that the solar system was once a vast sphere of nebula or vapour, and is going through a process which in the course of ages will reduce it to a single and not very large mass of solid matter frozen up with more than arctic cold. If the machinery of the system is adapted to keep itself at work only for a time, still less perfect is the adaptation of it for the abode of living beings since it is only adapted to them during the relatively short portion of its total duration which intervenes between the time when each planet was too hot and the time when it became or will become too cold to admit of life under the only conditions in which we have experience of its possibility. Or we should perhaps reverse the statement, and say that organization and life are only adapted to the conditions of the solar system during a relatively short portion of the system's existence.

The greater part, therefore, of the design of which there is indication in Nature, however wonderful its mechanism, is no evidence of any moral attributes, because the end to which it is directed, and its adaptation to which end is the evidence of its being directed to an end at all, is not a moral end: it is not the good of any sentient creature, it is but the qualified permanence, for a limited period, of the work itself, whether animate or inanimate. The only inference that can be drawn from most of it, respecting the character of the Creator, is that he does not wish his works to perish as soon as created; he wills them to have a certain duration. From this alone nothing can be justly inferred as to the manner in which he is affected towards his animate or rational creatures.

After deduction of the great number of adaptations which have no apparent object but to keep the machine going, there remain a certain number of provisions for giving pleasure to living beings, and a certain number of provisions for giving them pain. There is no positive certainty that the whole of these ought not to take their place among the contrivances for keeping the creature or its species in existence; for both the pleasures and the pains have a conservative tendency; the pleasures being generally so disposed as to attract to the things which maintain individual or collective existence, the pains so as to deter from such as would destroy it.

When all these things are considered it is evident that a vast deduction must be made from the evidences of a Creator before they can be counted as evidences of a benevolent purpose: so vast indeed that some may doubt whether after such a deduction there remains any balance. Yet endeavouring to look at the question without partiality or prejudice and without allowing wishes to have any influence over judgment, it does appear that granting the existence of design, there is a preponderance of evidence that the Creator desired the pleasure of his creatures. This is indicated by the fact that pleasure of one description or another is afforded by almost everything, the mere play of the faculties, physical and mental, being a never-ending source of pleasure, and even painful things giving pleasure by the satisfaction of curiosity and the agreeable sense of acquiring knowledge; and also that pleasure, when experienced, seems to result from the normal working of the machinery, while pain usually arises from some external interference with it, and resembles in each particular case the result of an accident. Even in cases when pain results, like pleasure, from the machinery itself, the appearances do not indicate that contrivance was brought into play purposely to produce pain: what is indicated is rather a clumsiness in the contrivance employed for some other purpose. The author of the machinery is no doubt accountable for having made it susceptible of pain; but this may have been a necessary condition of its susceptibility to pleasure; a supposition which avails nothing on the theory of an Omnipotent Creator but is an extremely probable one in the case of a contriver working under the limitation of inexorable laws and indestructible properties of matter. The susceptibility being conceded as a thing which did enter into design, the pain itself usually seems like a thing undesigned; a casual result of the collision of the organism with some outward force to which it was not intended to be exposed, and which, in many cases, provision is even made to hinder it from being exposed to. There is, therefore, much appearance that pleasure is agreeable to the Creator, while there is very little if any appearance that pain is so: and there is a certain amount of justification for inferring, on grounds of Natural Theology alone, that benevolence is one of the attributes of the Creator. But to jump from this to the inference that his sole or chief purposes are those of benevolence, and that the single end and aim of Creation was the happiness of his creatures, is not only not justified by any evidence but is a conclusion in opposition to such evidence as we have. If the motive of the Deity for creating sentient beings was the happiness of the beings he created, his purpose, in our corner of the universe at least, must be pronounced, taking past ages and all countries and races into account, to have been thus far an ignominious failure; and if God had no purpose but our happiness and that of other living creatures it is not credible that he would have called them into existence with the prospect of being so completely baffled. If man had not the power by the exercise of his own energies for the improvement both of himself and of his outward circumstances, to do for himself and other creatures vastly more than God had in the first instance, done, the Being who called him into existence would deserve something very different from thanks at his hands. Of course it may be said that this very capacity of improving himself and the world was given to him by God, and that the change which he will be thereby enabled ultimately to effect in human existence will be worth purchasing by the sufferings and wasted lives of entire geological periods. This may be so; but to suppose that God could not have given him these blessings at a less frightful cost, is to make a very strange supposition concerning the Deity. It is to suppose that God could not, in the first instance, create anything better than a Bosjesman or an Andaman islander, or something still lower; and yet was able to endow the Bosjesman or the Andaman islander with the power of raising himself into a Newton or a Fénelon. We certainly do not know the nature of the barriers which limit the divine omnipotence; but it is a very odd notion of them that they enable the Deity to confer on an almost bestial creature the power of producing by a succession of efforts what God himself had no other means of creating.

Such are the indications of Natural Religion in respect to the divine benevolence. If we look for any other of the moral attributes which a certain class of philosophers are accustomed to distinguish from benevolence, as for example Justice, we find a total blank. There is no evidence whatever in Nature for divine justice, whatever standard of justice our ethical opinions may lead us to recognize. There is no shadow of justice in the general arrangements of Nature; and what imperfect realization it obtains in any human society (a most imperfect realization as yet) is the work of man himself, struggling upwards against immense natural difficulties, into civilization, and making to himself a second nature, far better and more unselfish than he was created with. But on this point enough has been said in another Essay, already referred to, on Nature.

These, then, are the net results of Natural Theology on the question of the divine attributes. A Being of great but limited power, how or by what limited we cannot even conjecture; of great, and perhaps unlimited intelligence, but perhaps, also, more narrowly limited than his power: who desires, and pays some regard to, the happiness of his creatures, but who seems to have other motives of action which he cares more for, and who can hardly be supposed to have created the universe for that purpose alone. Such is the Deity whom Natural Religion points to. . . .

Discussion Questions

1. Evaluate Mill's claim that natural theology fails to provide evidence in support of divine omnipotence. Do you agree with Mill? Why or why not?

2. Do you agree that a deity limited either in power or in intelligence is not a proper object of worship? Give reasons for your answer.

3. Would you classify Mill's approach as a theodicy or merely a defense of theism?

4. Would you agree that Mill does not so much provide a response to the problem of evil as show the limits of natural theology? Explain and defend your answer.

5. What advantages, if any, does Mill's view have over an atheistic position?

6. What do you think of Mill's response to the problem of evil? What are your reasons?

RETROSPECTIVE

God and Evil

Throughout the previous discussion of the problem of evil, the traditional affirmations that God is all-powerful (omnipotent), all-knowing (omniscient), and all good have framed part of the discussion. Although John Stuart Mill rejects all three notions as unsupported by natural theology, they nonetheless form a part of the traditional view of God and lead to further problems for the theist. The following offers a brief sketch of these problems and some of the possible responses to them.

OMNIPOTENCE

The omnipotence of God poses the difficulty of absolving God of at least some of the responsibility for evil in the world. John Hick's answer is that the task of soul-making requires a world of real possibilities, some of which produce pain and suffering. If we found ourselves in a situation analogous to pet animals in a cage whose every whim and desire was fulfilled, we would never develop the strength of character appropriate to God's purposes for us. Further, it would be difficult to understand in what sense human beings were free if that freedom didn't include the possibility of acting in ways that produce pain and suffering to others. Learning *not* to do so is part of the task of moving from mere biological life to spiritual life. Of course, there is still the problem of natural evil—those aspects of nature that cause suffering and death, such as floods, hurricanes, earthquakes, famines, and disease. Here Hick's answer can also apply. Whether we respond to natural disasters with compassion and help for others or with indifference and disdain for their suffering is a choice we can make.

An additional problem is the difficulty of even imagining a world in which there is no possibility for pain and suffering. Such a world would not be one in which natural science is possible, for science assumes the predictability and regularity of events. If the world were arranged so that when I picked up a stick to strike someone nature interfered, making this impossible—either by turning the stick to jelly or rendering my muscles inoperable—this would not be a world of science. Not only would my human freedom be eliminated, but a world like this would also present us with a natural order that is constantly adjusting itself to compensate for our changing moods and attitudes. In its most extreme form, the laws of nature would constantly be rearranged to even prevent our having evil thoughts, much less translating those thoughts into actions. In such an environment we would be automatons, not human beings. In short, it is within God's power to create or not create a world, but it is not possible for a world to contain free beings without also exhibiting a relatively stable physical nature.

This point brings us to a final one: Does divine omnipotence mean that God can create a stone too heavy to lift or make a square circle? The answer is that God can do anything that it is possible to do, and a square circle is an impossibility. It is a nonsense phrase, and it makes no sense to speak it about God. Similarly, a stone too heavy for God to lift possesses an aura of nonsense as well, although it implies an important point: God can impose self-limitations, and the creation of a world populated by free beings is precisely that. Giving humans the power to choose between good and evil and the ability to exercise free choice can best be understood as a divine self-limitation, though we cannot understand the reasons for this or be able to analyze the depths of the divine purpose.

OMNISCIENCE

Some of the same questions about human freedom raised by divine omnipotence recur in a consideration of omniscience. If God knows everything, including all future human actions, to what extent are such actions free? This is an ancient question to which the early Christian theologians responded in various ways. Augustine, for example, argued that God's existence is independent of time, and therefore what seems to us as the future is really the eternally present. Thomas, amplifying a point also made by Augustine, distinguished between knowing a state of affairs and being the cause of that state of affairs. Consider human knowledge of the past. Knowing an event in the past does not mean that the event was involuntary. Our knowing the past brings the past into the present; similarly God's knowledge of the future is timeless and eternal.

Both J. S. Mill's limited God and Charles Hartshorne's views of God as the principle of creativity for the future avoid some of the semantic and logical difficulties inherent in omnipotence and omniscience. In terms of God's knowledge, Hartshorne's view is that God can know all that it is possible to know, and until a future event occurs, God cannot know it. The only knowledge that God can have is what is knowable, just as the only things God can do are those that are possible.

DIVINE BENEVOLENCE

The affirmation that God is all-loving is also part of the traditional Judaeo-Christian view of God and perhaps even more than omnipotence and omniscience creates difficulties for any theodicy. How can a truly benevolent God allow the continuation of human suffering? Hick offers one explanation for how a loving God could create—and tolerate—a world in which so much evil is possible with his "Vale of Soul-Making" theodicy. The doctrine of karma also defends God's goodness by attributing much of human misery to human, not divine, choices. But none of the selections in this chapter responds head-on to the belief most difficult to reconcile with divine goodness: the doctrine of hell.

Part of the problem of dealing with the doctrine itself stems from the fierce images in which hell has been portrayed in religious art, especially that of the Middle Ages, in which the torments of the damned are represented by grotesque images of devils and their gruesome inflictions. It is important, however, not to confuse the doctrine itself with the images it has spawned and to understand what the doctrine actually is. Just as human freedom entered into a discussion of divine omnipotence and omniscience, it is also central to an understanding of the doctrine of hell. A recent article in a Jesuit journal that restates a traditional understanding of the doctrine says that "hell is best understood as the condition of total alienation from all that is good, hopeful and loving in the world. What's more, this condition is chosen by the damned themselves, the ultimate exercise of free will, not a punishment engineered by God."[1] This same view was underscored by Pope John Paul II who told a group of pilgrims that "hell is the state of those who freely and definitely separate themselves from God, the source of all life and joy."[2] To be sure, belief in hell has not always been explained this way and has sometimes been used in preaching as a threat and incentive to do good, such as in the famous sermon by Jonathan Edwards, "Sinners in the Hands of an Angry God." However, stripped of its images and its use in hortatory literature, the doctrine is a logical extension of belief in human freedom. If human beings are free to choose good or evil, the choice of evil for all eternity must be a possibility.

The notion of the eternality of hell is part of what makes the doctrine so unpalatable. Is there *no* reprieve or appeal? A full response to this question calls for a great deal of theological analysis, but C. S. Lewis poses an interesting response in his book *The Great Divorce*. In this fable, a bus regularly makes the trip from hell to heaven, and inhabitants of the former are free at any time to make the journey. The story follows the experience of one such group, and when they arrive at heaven, the hell of it is that they find it intolerable and take the return trip back to hell. If the damned refuse to be saved, God will not coerce their freedom; to cite one of the characters in Lewis's book, "Every disease that submits to a cure shall be cured: but we will not call blue yellow to please those who insist on still having jaundice, nor make a midden of the world's garden for the sake of some who cannot abide the smell of roses."[3]

All discussions of the problem of evil at some point seem to return to the difficulties posed by affirming human freedom. If humans are free, then the world must possess certain characteristics, choices must be genuine, consequences inevitable. The process of growth from *Bios* to *Zoe* produces spirituality, though the cost may at times be high. In the final analysis the question that shades off into mystery is why did God create free beings in the first place? To that we do not have an answer. A tantalizing response, however, is that of the contemporary philosopher Paul Ricoeur: "Perhaps we must believe that God, wishing to be known and loved freely, took this risk which is named man."[4]

---

[1] As reported by Gustav Niebuhr, "Hell Is Getting a Makeover From Catholics." *New York Times*, 18 September 1999, A17.

[2] Ibid.

[3] C. S. Lewis, *The Great Divorce* (London: Geoffrey Bles, 1946), p. 112.

[4] Paul Ricoeur, "The Image of God and the Epoch of Man," *History and Truth*, trans. Charles Kelbley (Evanston, IL: Northwestern University Press, 1965), p. 128.

ADDITIONAL READINGS

Various types of theodicies are discussed in highly readable terms in Chapter 9 of Ed. L. Miller, *God and Reason* (New York: The Macmillan Company, 1972). A defense of the theistic position is offered by Alvin Plantinga, *God, Freedom and Evil* (New York: Harper & Row, 1974; paperback edition, Grand Rapids, MI: Eerdmans, 1978), a book that is important, but difficult in places. As always, John Hick is an excellent guide to the many dimensions of the problem in his book *Evil and the God of Love*, rev. ed. (New York: Harper & Row, 1977). Hick also offers an overview of the history of the discussion of the problem and an extensive bibliography in his article "Evil, the Problem of," *The Encyclopedia of Philosophy* (1967), 4, 136-41. A fine discussion of the problem of evil in the context of the theistic arguments is James F. Ross, *Philosophical Theology* (Indianapolis IN: Hackett Publishing Co., 1980). Peter Geach, *Providence and Evil* (Cambridge: Cambridge University Press, 1977), offers an analysis of such concepts as omnipotence and divine foreknowledge as they relate to the problem of evil. Harold Kushner, *When Bad Things Happen to Good People* (New York: Avon, 1981) argues that God does not have the power to stop all evil. An argument offering a morally sufficient reason for the presence of evil is Bruce R. Reichenbach, *Evil and a Good God* (New York: Fordham University Press, 1982).

CHAPTER SIX

FAITH AND REASON

INTRODUCTION

Opinion, Belief, and Knowledge

The relationship between faith and reason has been a background concern in all the readings from the very first. In one sense, it was raised by the questioning of a purely rational approach to religion in the writings of Otto and Buber. If there is a nonrational aspect to religion, as both Otto and Buber insist, then one should not look to rational argument and analysis alone for a thorough understanding of religion. Most philosophers, however, have concluded that there is a place for rational inquiry in religion, and the various arguments for God's existence that we have examined are attempts to provide rational arguments to support belief in God. Even though these arguments do not offer an absolute proof of God's existence, they offer some rational support for belief in God. They do not, however, give conclusive evidence; were the evidence for God's existence conclusive and not subject to doubt, faith would be impossible. Faith is not knowledge, and because we do not have absolutely certain knowledge of God's existence, there is room for faith.

The quest for knowledge and the desire for certainty are two of the concerns most characteristic of Western philosophy. This attitude toward the goal of philosophy is perhaps given its clearest expression by Descartes when he sets forth as one of his five rules for the direction of the mind to refuse to believe anything that is subject to doubt. Descartes thinks that his version of the ontological argument offers proof of God's existence, and he accordingly accepts God as one of the proven principles of philosophy. It is clear to us, though perhaps it was not obvious to Descartes, that all such arguments for God's existence are less than absolutely convincing; at least we have to admit that they are not completely coercive in their effect. If we cannot have rational certainty of the existence of God, are we to conclude that the only philosophically defensible attitude is to doubt that God exists? Some philosophers have argued for this view, based on the principle that we have no right to extend belief beyond the available evidence. Other thinkers have argued that we are justified in believing in God even though we cannot claim absolute certainty for these beliefs.

Two questions emerge in the continuing dialogue between faith and reason: (1) Do we have what can legitimately be called *knowledge* of God based on rational proofs? and (2) Even without such a proof, is it rational to *believe* in God? Since there are two ways of approaching the question of God, either through faith or through reason, and since there are two attitudes toward each of these, we can begin to see the issues in this debate taking shape. Some philosophers have thought that we can relate to God through both faith and reason. Others have denied that we can have rationally justified knowledge of God and have also rejected faith as a defensible attitude. Still others, such as the Danish philosopher Søren Kierkegaard, though agreeing that we cannot have knowledge of God, have pointed to faith as the only way of having access to a relationship with God. Perhaps the following table of possibilities will illustrate the different attitudes possible toward the relation between faith and reason. *Reason* includes what we can claim to *know* with demonstrable certainty or strong evidence; *faith* covers what we believe without proof or strong evidence. In short, can we claim knowledge of God, or can we legitimately defend faith in him, or neither?

FAITH	REASON	
Yes	Yes	Thomas Aquinas
No	No	Antony Flew
Yes	No	Søren Kierkegaard
No	Yes	Voltaire (deism)

The foregoing tabulation is a little too pat in that it ignores the subtleties of the positions of these philosophers, but it does provide a general idea of their respective attitudes toward the relation of faith and reason in the selections included in this chapter.

As we flesh out these viewpoints you will see that there are many other issues raised by the readings, but our attention in this chapter is focused on the relation between faith and reason. The question is basically: Are we justified in claiming to have knowledge of God? If not, is it defensible to have faith in what we cannot prove with complete certainty? Thomas Aquinas is the most optimistic on these questions, claiming both that we can have knowledge of God and that faith is defensible. Antony Flew does not think we can claim to have knowledge of God and, further, thinks that our claims to faith are equally indefensible. If you accept the claim that we are never justified in believing what we are unable to prove with absolute certainty, then ask yourself if you are willing to apply this same criterion to other areas of life. Quite apart from the question of religious faith, are we *ever* justified in accepting something and acting on it, even though we cannot be certain about it? This is the issue raised by the selection from William James, who argues that we can—and must—act on principles for which we do not have empirical evidence and of which we cannot be certain.

Before turning to the readings themselves, we should clarify for ourselves the difference between belief and knowledge. Here Immanuel Kant can be our guide, for one of his ongoing concerns was to discover the basic structures of human knowledge. Kant argues that in every rational judgment there is a subjective factor and an objective factor. We might say that the subjective factor is the degree of certainty we ourselves have about something, whereas the objective factor is the demonstrable evidence we can elicit to support this certainty. Sometimes we are quite convinced of the truth of something even though the evidence is not very strong to support the conviction. At other times, our subjective conviction may not be very strong even though the objective evidence is sufficient. Using these distinctions, Kant defines three modes of awareness: opinion, belief, and knowledge.

The following example illustrates the application of Kant's analysis. Suppose you are having an argument with a friend about the population of the greater Paris area. You are sure that the population is eight million persons. Your friend disagrees and is equally sure that it is at least nine million or more. Here you both are experiencing a high degree of what Kant called subjective sufficiency for your views; that is, you both are persuaded that your judgment about the population of the Paris metropolitan area is correct. Obviously, the only way to resolve the dispute is to consult a current atlas or almanac for a report based on objective data. Let's suppose that the current almanac reports that the population of the greater Paris area is nine and one-quarter million persons. Your friend could reply, "I was certain that I was right, but here is the evidence to support my certainty." Your friend would then have objective sufficiency for his claim for which he previously only had subjective sufficiency. If you are a particularly stubborn sort of person, you could reply, "I don't care what the almanac says, I still am not convinced." Here you cannot claim objective sufficiency for your viewpoint, even though you still experience subjective sufficiency for it.

To summarize, Kant argues that every judgment has both a subjective and an objective pole. Each of these, in turn, can be either sufficient or insufficient. This gives us four possibilities that can be viewed as producing four different levels of awareness:[1]

---

[1] Immanuel Kant, *Critique of Pure Reason*, A820, B848.

| | | SUBJECTIVELY | |
		Insufficient	Sufficient
OBJECTIVELY	Insufficient	Opinion	Belief
	Sufficient	Disbelief	Knowledge

Kant does not give a name to the type of judgment that is subjectively insufficient but objectively sufficient. We might want to call it some form of disbelief, since the evidence is objectively sufficient, yet the person still remains unpersuaded.

Now, let's apply this to the matter of religious faith. If we could have objectively sufficient evidence that God exists, then we could claim that we also have subjective sufficiency for the view that there is a God, and the resulting judgment could be called knowledge. We have already seen in our examination of the arguments for God's existence that no such objectively sufficient evidence is available, so it might be inappropriate to say that we can claim to know that God exists. If the evidence for God's existence is objectively insufficient, then we must look to the types of judgment resulting from evidence that is objectively insufficient. If we are not persuaded that there is a God (or that there is not a God), then our subjective state can only be called opinion. But if we are strongly persuaded of the existence of God even in the face of inadequate evidence, the state of our subjective awareness can be called belief.

No readings from Thomas Aquinas are included in this chapter, but a brief summary of his views will indicate his optimistic and positive attitude toward the relation between faith and reason. The most interesting thing about Thomas's view is that he is convinced that we can have knowledge of God and that faith is required only to lead us to those truths reason alone is incapable of discovering. Not only does Thomas believe that we can have knowledge of God, but he also believes that there are two sources of such knowledge. One of these is reason itself. Thomas believes that God has implanted within us the capacity to learn of His existence and nature through the power of reason. Thomas's massive *Summa Theologica* is an attempt to give reasoned arguments in support of the truth of Christian doctrine. Another path to knowledge of God, Thomas believes, is provided by sacred Scriptures, namely, the Old and New Testaments. If we reason correctly, and if we interpret Scripture correctly, we have two sources of knowledge of God; indeed, if there is ever a conflict between what we can know about God through the power of reason and what Scripture tells us, either we are reasoning incorrectly or we are not understanding Scripture properly. Reason (natural theology) and the Scriptures (revelation) constitute a twofold path to knowledge of God.

The existence of a twofold path to knowledge of God raises two interesting questions. The first is, If we can discover truths about God by the power of reason unaided by revelation, why do we have Scripture? Thomas suggests several answers to this. Without God's self-revelation, few people would possess knowledge of God. Some persons simply do not have the natural disposition to arrive at knowledge of God through the strenuous exercise of reason; not everybody is cut out to be a philosopher. Others are too busy with such matters as earning a living and just don't have the time to think speculatively about divine matters. Still others are just too lazy to think their way to knowledge of God. Besides all this, a trained intellect is not easily attained. It takes time to learn to reason philosophically, and until one's intellect is thoroughly trained, that individual would not have an adequate knowledge of God. And without revelation, young people would be at a disadvantage in spiritual matters, since their minds are on other things. A final reason for the necessity of revelation is that our minds are limited and prone to error, and we can inadvertently fall into falsehood in our thinking. Revelation provides a corrective to errors in our reasoning. So much for the need for revelation.

The second issue is the converse of the first: Why do we need to bother ourselves about natural theology and speculative philosophy if revelation is a sufficient source of truth about God? Thomas answers that, since not everybody accepts the authority of the Scriptures, the power of reason is required to convince them of the truth of Christian doctrine.

Even though Scripture and reason give us a twofold path to knowledge of God, there are some truths about God that are too lofty for human reason alone to discover, and here we need to accept the truth of revelation by faith. The Christian doctrine of the Trinity is an example of something that must be accepted on faith, as are other claims about the divine nature. Here is how Thomas puts it:

> It is also necessary that such truth be proposed to men for belief so that they may have a truer knowledge of God. For then only do we know God truly when we believe Him to be above everything that it is possible for man to think about Him; for, as we have shown, the divine substance surpasses the natural knowledge of which man is capable. Hence, by the fact that some things about God are proposed to man that surpass his reason, there is strengthened in man the view that God is something above what he can think.[2]

In short, faith adds to what we can claim as genuine knowledge about God, and faith is necessary if we are to have the highest awareness of God's nature. Nonetheless, Thomas is convinced that we can gain knowledge of God sufficient for salvation through the power of reason alone, unaided by divine revelation.

At the opposite pole is Søren Kierkegaard, who sees little role for reason in one's quest for faith. For Kierkegaard, faith is essentially commitment involving uncertainty and risk. Faith, as he understands it, is not open to rational analysis,

---

[2] Thomas Aquinas, *On the Truth of the Catholic Faith: Summa Contra Gentiles*, trans. Anton C. Pegis (Garden City, NY: Doubleday-Image, 1955), p. 70, Book 1, 5, 3.

for it involves a relationship with God. Rational theology points to the existence of God, but does not give us much on which to establish a relationship. "I contemplate the order of nature," Kierkegaard says, "in the hope of finding God, and I see omnipotence and wisdom; but I also see much else that disturbs my mind and excites anxiety. The sum of all this is objective uncertainty." We have already seen the inconclusiveness of proofs of the existence of God. We have observed that the debate between those who support the arguments and those who reject them seems endless. While the debate rages on, life slips away, and we must make a decision. This decision Kierkegaard calls the "leap" of faith. Such a leap is risky, to be sure. But, as Kierkegaard puts it, "Without risk, there is no faith." God cannot be grasped objectively because God is an uncertainty, an objective uncertainty. "If I wish to preserve myself in faith," Kierkegaard says, "I must constantly be intent upon holding fast the objective uncertainty, so as to remain out upon the deep, over seven thousand fathoms of water, still preserving my faith."[3]

Few philosophers today would be comfortable with the views of either Thomas Aquinas or Kierkegaard, but debate still centers on the issue of the legitimacy of believing in God. Returning to the distinctions made earlier, a belief is a view that, though subjectively sufficient, is based on objectively insufficient grounds. But just how insufficient can these grounds be? Will we at some point have such objective insufficiency that we are no longer entitled to our belief? If objective sufficiency is not possible for belief, how then are we to distinguish between legitimate beliefs and illegitimate ones? When are we entitled to hold a belief, and when must we abandon it as indefensible? These are the questions raised by the first reading in this chapter.

---

[3] Søren Kierkegaard, *Concluding Unscientific Postscript*, trans. David F. Swenson and Walter Lowrie (Princeton, NJ: Princeton University Press, 1969), p. 182.

Belief and Falsification

One of the characteristics of religious belief is that it rests on evidence that is less than absolutely certain. The distinction between what can legitimately be called *knowledge* and what must be viewed as a matter of *belief* is the objective sufficiency of the evidence for the assertion. If we cannot prove that a religious belief is true, that is, if we cannot verify it, perhaps we can show under what conditions it would be false. If we can neither verify a statement of religious belief nor admit any conditions that would falsify it, then in what sense is a statement of religious belief a genuine assertion?

These are the questions raised in the following article by Antony Flew and central to his attack on the legitimacy of religious belief is his analysis of the conditions under which a sentence or an utterance can properly be viewed as an assertion. An assertion is a particular kind of speech act in which we make a claim that a certain state of affairs is true, or that it is false. When you say, "It is raining outside," you are making an assertion. If you go outside and discover that rain is falling, you have verified the truth of your assertion. But if, on going outside, you discover that the day is bright and sunny and that no rain is falling, you have falsified your assertion. You might think that most of our utterances are assertions, but if you kept track of all the things you say for just an hour, you might be surprised to discover that many of the things you say are not assertions, but other kinds of speech acts. For example, the sentence "Close the door" is not an assertion, but a command. To say "Congratulations on passing the course" is not to make an assertion, but to perform the speech act of congratulating. There are dozens, perhaps hundreds, of speech acts that are not assertions, but since we are dealing here with the question of belief and not the nature of language, we will focus our attention on assertions.[1]

Flew claims that statements of religious beliefs are not genuine assertions. To see how he argues for this view, we must examine more closely the nature of an

---

[1] John Searle gives a partial list of different speech acts and cites J. L. Austin's claim that there are more than one thousand different speech acts in the English language. See John Searle, *Speech Acts* (Cambridge: At the University Press, 1969), p. 23.

assertion. To be an assertion, a statement must make a claim that has a truth value; that is, the assertion is either true or false. Philosophers of language call this the statement's *propositional content*. An assertion, in other words, refers to something and makes a claim about it. In the sentence "God loves us," the refer-ence is to God, and the claim is that of His loving us. The religious believer ac-cepts this statement as true. But how are we to know that it is true? If we could verify its truth, the statement would no longer be a matter of belief, but a matter of knowing. So it seems to be a peculiar quality of statements of religious belief that they cannot, in principle, be *proved* to be true; otherwise they would cease to be beliefs. Flew has no quarrel with this but brings up another interesting ques-tion: What kind of evidence would be required to convince a person who holds a religious belief to be true that in fact it was false? Or, as Flew puts this ques-tion, what would it take to *falsify* the assertion? Even if there is not sufficient evidence to show that the statement is false, we must be prepared to admit that some kind of evidence would be sufficient to falsify the statement. If, however, we insist that there is no evidence whatsoever sufficient to make us give up our belief, then in what sense is it a genuine assertion?

To illustrate how the principle of falsification is applied, Flew borrows the parable of the invisible gardener. Two explorers come upon a clearing in the woods, and one of them attributes it to the work of an invisible gardener. They set up elaborate tests to detect the presence of the gardener, and there is no evi-dence that such an invisible gardener exists. One of the explorers stubbornly re-fuses to abandon belief in the unseen gardener, so he begins to qualify his belief: The gardener is invisible, undetectable, and leaves no traces of his nocturnal vis-its. With each qualification, something of the original belief is lost; the assertion "dies the death of a thousand qualifications." At some point a reasonable person would abandon belief in an unseen gardener, realizing the legitimacy of the ques-tion asked by the skeptic: "Just how does what you call an invisible, intangible, eternally elusive gardener differ from an imaginary gardener or even from no gar-dener at all?" In short, a reasonable person would recognize that the statement that there is an unseen gardener is not a legitimate assertion.

Flew's article originally appeared in a periodical called *University* and was fol-lowed by a written discussion. Two of the responses, with Flew's summation, are included in the readings.

In the first of these responses, R. M. Hare admits that, in a sense, Flew is cor-rect. People do hold certain views so tenaciously that no evidence seems to be sufficient to cause them to abandon these views. But the interesting claim made by Hare is that such beliefs are not uncommon at all, nor are they restricted to matters of religious belief. We all have deeply held convictions that are not ver-ifiable and that likewise do not seem to be falsifiable, which he calls *bliks*. A *blik* is an unverifiable, unfalsifiable presupposition or set of presuppositions in terms of which people orient themselves to the world. It is in the very nature of a *blik* that it also determines what evidence counts against it; and what makes a *blik* a *blik* is that nothing is sufficient to dislodge it. For example, some people have a *blik* about airplanes. They refuse to believe that airplanes are a safe mode of trans-portation. Others may complete hundreds of airplane trips safely, but persons with a *blik* about airplanes are convinced that the moment they board an air-craft, it will be doomed to crash. One could point out statistics which show that the probability of safely completing a journey on a scheduled U.S. airline is 99.99992%, but this evidence would have no effect. Let an aircraft crash, how-ever, and persons with a *blik* about airplanes immediately feel that this is evi-dence in support of their belief about air travel, and their resolve never to take an airplane trip is fortified.

If Hare is correct in saying that all of us have *bliks*, then the position of the religious believer does not seem so strange. But Hare admits that some *bliks* are abnormal; indeed, he suggests that there are sane as well as insane *bliks*, though he does not offer a clear principle for distinguishing between them. The example he offers of an insane *blik* is a college undergraduate who thinks that every professor is a homicidal maniac. His example of a sane *blik* is the confidence most of us have in the reliability of the mechanical linkages of an automobile. There is, of course, evidence that automobiles can experience mechanical difficulty, and that some people die in auto crashes caused by me-chanical malfunction. But most of us have a *blik* about the safety of automo-biles and continue to take auto trips. Hare seems to assume that the difference between a sane or "right" *blik* and an insane or "wrong" *blik* is pri-marily in the number of persons who hold them. A wrong *blik* is one that is clearly a minority viewpoint.

If this is the distinction Hare is making between sane and insane *bliks*, it is hardly a sufficient one, for the question raised by Flew is about the cumulative weight of evidence. If it turned out that most automobiles fell apart while being driven, and most airplanes crashed while in flight, the reasonable conclusion would be that neither is a safe mode of transportation. In other words, the weight of evidence, to use a lawyer's term, is an important consideration. This points up a weakness in Flew's original parable. In the case of the explorers and the unseen gardener, all the evidence seems to point against the existence of an invisible gar-dener who secretly cares for the garden. But let's change the parable somewhat. Suppose that even though the explorers are unsuccessful in detecting the presence of the gardener through their various contrivances—the bloodhounds still smell nothing, and no shrieks are heard from anyone being injured on the electrified barbed-wire fence—there is still evidence that something unusual is happening. Each morning some of the weeds have been pulled. Fresh flowers have been planted. The shrubs have been trimmed, the trees fertilized. The explorers in that case would no doubt be led to mystification but could hardly be faulted for con-cluding that something, or someone, was the cause of the strange phenomena, even though they could detect nothing with their elaborate devices.

This is the point Basil Mitchell makes in the second response to Flew by his parable of the partisans and the mysterious stranger. One of the members of an underground guerrilla band meets a stranger who assures him that he is on the side of the partisans but warns that there will be times when he will seem to be working for the enemy. The partisan is warned not to be deceived on these occasions but to believe that the stranger is indeed on the side of the guerrillas. At times, there is evidence that the stranger is helping the partisans. At other times, the evidence seems to be that the stranger is in the service of their enemy. Although the evidence is ambiguous, so strong is the effect of the stranger on the partisan that he continues to believe that the stranger is on their side even in the face of the contradictory evidence. Unlike Hare's example of the *blik*, against which no evidence really counts, there is evidence that the partisan admits counts against the sincerity of the stranger; yet the partisan continues to trust the stranger.

Now, is the case of the religious believer more like that of the stubborn explorer, the person with a *blik*, or the trusting partisan? This is the question with which you will have to wrestle. Most religious thinkers would admit that there is some evidence that counts against the existence of a loving God—the problem of evil, for example. But there is also evidence, though perhaps not conclusive, *for* the existence of a loving God. The evidence is ambiguous, and it is precisely this ambiguity that makes religious faith possible.

Before turning to the readings, it should be noted that Flew has not had the last word on the principle of falsification as a way of distinguishing between genuine assertions and spurious ones. Flew seems to claim that every assertion, to be genuine, must be either verifiable or falsifiable. But this is not the case. Some assertions are, to be sure, both verifiable and falsifiable, such as the assertion "It is raining outside." There is another type of assertion, however, that has not been verified yet does not seem falsifiable. Failure to verify an assertion of this type does not indicate that it is thereby falsified. John Hick gives as an example of this kind of assertion the claim that "there are three successive sevens in the decimal determination of π." As is well known, the Greek letter *pi* is used as the symbol for the ratio of the circumference of a circle to its diameter. Although the value of *pi* has been computed to several thousand places, and thus far three successive sevens have not occurred, the possibility remains that in some further calculation three successive sevens will occur. Hick observes that "the proposition may one day be verified if it is true, but can never be falsified if it is false."[2] Although Flew's test for the genuineness of assertions is appropriate for some types of assertions, the debate over the principle of falsification as an appropriate test for the acceptability of *all* assertions continues. And disagreement continues to be lively over whether all assertions of religious belief must in principle be falsifiable in order to be accepted as genuine. These are the issues raised by the following readings, and you will have to be the judge of which side presents the most convincing arguments.

---

[2] John Hick, *Faith and Knowledge*, 2d ed. (Ithaca, NY: Cornell University Press, 1966), p. 175.

The Falsification Debate

ANTONY FLEW, R. M. HARE, AND BASIL MITCHELL

ANTONY FLEW

Let us begin with a parable. It is a parable developed from a tale told by John Wisdom in his haunting and revelatory article "Gods."[1] Once upon a time two explorers came upon a clearing in the jungle. In the clearing were growing many flowers and many weeds. One explorer says, "Some gardener must tend this plot." The other disagrees, "There is no gardener." So they pitch their tents and set a watch. No gardener is ever seen. "But perhaps he is an invisible gardener." So they set up a barbed wire fence. They electrify it. They patrol with bloodhounds. (For they remember how H. G. Wells's *The Invisible Man* could be both smelt and touched though he could not be seen.) But no shrieks ever suggest that some intruder has received a shock. No movements of the wire ever betray an invisible climber. The bloodhounds never give cry. Yet still the Believer is not convinced. "But there is a gardener, invisible, intangible, insensible to electric shocks, a gardener who has no scent and makes no sound, a gardener who comes secretly to look after the garden which he loves." At last the Sceptic despairs, "But what remains of your original assertion? Just how does what you call an invisible, intangible, eternally elusive gardener differ from an imaginary gardener or even from no gardener at all?"

In this parable we can see how what starts as an assertion, that something exists or that there is some analogy between certain complexes of phenomena, may be reduced step by step to an altogether different status, to an expression perhaps of a "picture preference."[2] The Sceptic says there is no gardener. The Believer says there is a gardener (but invisible, etc.). One man talks about sexual behavior. Another man prefers to talk of Aphrodite (but knows that there is not really a superhuman person additional to, and somehow responsible for, all sexual

Source: Antony Flew, R. M. Hare, and Basil Mitchell, "Theology and Falsification," in *New Essays in Philosophical Theology*, ed. Antony Flew and Alasdair MacIntyre (London: SCM Press 1955), pp. 96–108. © 1953 by SCM Press Ltd. Used by permission. Published in the United States by Macmillan Publishing Co., 1955, and reprinted with permission of Macmillan Publishing Co., Inc.

1 P.A.S., 1944–5, reprinted as Ch. X of *Logic and Language*, Vol. I (Blackwell, 1951), and in his *Philosophy and Psychoanalysis* (Blackwell, 1953).

2 Cf. J. Wisdom, "Other Minds," *Mind*, 1940; reprinted in his *Other Minds* (Blackwell, 1952).

phenomena).[3] The process of qualification may be checked at any point before the original assertion is completely withdrawn and something of that first assertion will remain (Tautology). Mr. Wells's invisible man could not, admittedly, be seen, but in all other respects he was a man like the rest of us. But though the process of qualification may be, and of course usually is, checked in time, it is not always judiciously so halted. Someone may dissipate his assertion completely without noticing that he has done so. A fine brash hypothesis may thus be killed by inches, the death by a thousand qualifications.

And in this, it seems to me, lies the peculiar danger, the endemic evil, of theological utterance. Take such utterances as "God has a plan," "God created the world," "God loves us as a father loves his children." They look at first sight very much like assertions, vast cosmological assertions. Of course, this is no sure sign that they either are, or are intended to be, assertions. But let us confine ourselves to the cases where those who utter such sentences intend them to express assertions. (Merely remarking parenthetically that those who intend or interpret such utterances as crypto-commands, expressions of wishes, disguised ejaculations, concealed ethics, or as anything else but assertions, are unlikely to succeed in making them either properly orthodox or practically effective.)

Now to assert that such and such is the case is necessarily equivalent to denying that such and such is not the case.[4] Suppose then that we are in doubt as to what someone who gives vent to an utterance is asserting, or suppose that, more radically, we are skeptical as to whether he is really asserting anything at all, one way of trying to understand (or perhaps it will be to expose) his utterance is to attempt to find what he would regard as counting against, or as being incompatible with, its truth. For if the utterance is indeed an assertion, it will necessarily be equivalent to a denial of the negation of that assertion. And anything which would count against the assertion, or which would induce the speaker to withdraw it and to admit that it had been mistaken, must be part of (or the whole of) the meaning of the negation of that assertion. And to know the meaning of the negation of an assertion is as near as makes no matter, to know the meaning of that assertion.[5] And if there is nothing which a putative assertion denies then there is nothing which it asserts either: and so it is not really an assertion. When the Sceptic in the parable asked the Believer, "Just how does what you call an invisible, intangible, eternally elusive gardener differ from an imaginary gardener or even from no gardener at all?" he was suggesting that

[3] Cf. Lucretius, *De Rerum Natura*, II, 655–60,
> Hic siquis mare Neptunum Cereremque vocare
> Constituet fruges et Bacchi nomine abuti
> Mavolat quam laticis proprium proferre vocamen
> Concedamus ut hic terrarum dictitet orbem
> Esse deum matrem dum vera re tamen ipse
> Religione animum turpi contingere parcat.

[4] For those who prefer symbolism: $p \equiv \sim \sim p$.
[5] For by simply negating $\sim p$ we get p: $\sim\sim p \equiv p$.

the Believer's earlier statement had so been eroded by qualification that it was no longer an assertion at all.

Now it often seems to people who are not religious as if there was no conceivable event or series of events the occurrence of which would be admitted by sophisticated religious people to be a sufficient reason for conceding "There wasn't a God after all" or "God does not really love us then." Someone tells us that God loves us as a father loves his children. We are assured. But then we see a child dying of inoperable cancer of the throat. His earthly father is driven frantic in his efforts to help, but his Heavenly Father reveals no obvious sign of concern. Some qualification is made—God's love is "not a merely human love" or it is "an inscrutable love," perhaps—and we realize that such sufferings are quite compatible with the truth of the assertion that "God loves us as a father (but, of course, . .)." We are reassured again. But then perhaps we ask: What is this assurance of God's (appropriately qualified) love worth, what is this apparent guarantee really a guarantee against? Just what would have to happen not merely (morally and wrongly) to tempt but also (logically and rightly) to entitle us to say "God does not love us" or even "God does not exist"? I therefore put to the succeeding symposiasts the simple central questions, "What would have to occur or to have occurred to constitute for you a disproof of the love of, or of the existence of, God?"

R. M. HARE[6]

I wish to make it clear that I shall not try to defend Christianity in particular, but religion in general—not because I do not believe in Christianity, but because you cannot understand what Christianity is until you have understood what religion is.

I must begin by confessing that, on the ground marked out by Flew, he seems to me to be completely victorious. I therefore shift my ground by relating another parable. A certain lunatic is convinced that all dons want to murder him. His friends introduce him to all the mildest and most respectable dons that they can find, and after each of them has retired, they say, "You see, he doesn't really want to murder you; he spoke to you in a most cordial manner; surely you are convinced now?" But the lunatic replies, "Yes, but that was only his diabolical cunning; he's really plotting against me the whole time, like the rest of them; I know it I tell you." However many kindly dons are produced, the reaction is still the same.

Now we say that such a person is deluded. But what is he deluded about? About the truth or falsity of an assertion? Let us apply Flew's test to him. There is no behaviour of dons that can be enacted which he will accept as counting against his theory; and therefore his theory, on this test, asserts nothing. But it does not follow that there is no difference between what he thinks about dons and what most of us think about them—otherwise we should not call him a lunatic

---

6 Some references to intervening discussion have been excised—Editors.

and ourselves sane, and dons would have no reason to feel uneasy about his presence in Oxford.

Let us call that in which we differ from this lunatic, our respective *bliks*. He
has an insane *blik* about dons; we have a sane one. It is important to realize that
we have a sane one, not no *blik* at all; for there must be two sides to any argument—if he has a wrong *blik*, then those who are right about dons must have a
right one. Flew has shown that a *blik* does not consist in an assertion or system of
them; but nevertheless it is very important to have the right *blik*.

Let us try to imagine what it would be like to have different *bliks* about
other things than dons. When I am driving my car, it sometimes occurs to me
to wonder whether my movements of the steering-wheel will always continue
to be followed by corresponding alterations in the direction of the car. I have
never had a steering failure, though I have had skids, which must be similar.
Moreover, I know enough about how the steering of my car is made, to know
the sort of thing that would have to go wrong for the steering to fail—steel
joints would have to part, or steel rods break, or something—but how do I
know that this won't happen? The truth is, I don't know; I just have a *blik*
about steel and its properties, so that normally I trust the steering of my car;
but I find it not at all difficult to imagine what it would be like to lose this
blik and acquire the opposite one. People would say I was silly about steel; but
there would be no mistaking the reality of the difference between our respective *bliks*—for example, I should never go in a motor-car. Yet I should hesitate
to say that the difference between us was the difference between contradictory
assertions. No amount of safe arrivals or bench-tests will remove my *blik* and
restore the normal one: for my *blik* is compatible with any finite number of
such tests.

It was Hume who taught us that our whole commerce with the world depends upon our *blik* about the world; and that differences between *bliks* about
the world cannot be settled by observation of what happens in the world. That
was why, having performed the interesting experiment of doubting the ordinary
man's *blik* about the world, and showing that no proof could be given to make
us adopt one *blik* rather than another, he turned to backgammon to take his
mind off the problem. It seems, indeed, to be impossible even to formulate as
an assertion the normal *blik* about the world which makes me put my confidence
in the future reliability of steel joints, in the continued ability of the road to
support my car, and not gape beneath it revealing nothing below; in the general nonhomicidal tendencies of dons; in my own continued well-being (in some
sense of that word that I may not now fully understand) if I continue to do what
is right according to my lights; in the general likelihood of people like Hitler
coming to a bad end. But perhaps a formulation less inadequate than most is to
be found in the Psalms: "The earth is weak and all the inhabiters thereof: I bear
up the pillars of it."

The mistake of the position which Flew selects for attack is to regard this
kind of talk as some sort of *explanation*, as scientists are accustomed to use the

word. As such, it would obviously be ludicrous. We no longer believe in God as an Atlas—*nous n'avons pas besoin de cette hypothèse.** But it is nevertheless true to say that, as Hume saw, without a *blik* there can be no explanation; for it is by our *bliks* that we decide what is and what is not an explanation. Suppose we believed that everything that happened, happened by pure chance. This would not of course be an assertion; for it is compatible with anything happening or not happening, and so, incidentally, it is contradictory. But if we had this belief, we should not be able to explain or predict or plan anything. Thus, although we should not be *asserting* anything different from those of a more normal belief, there would be a great difference between us; and this is the sort of difference that there is between those who really believe in God and those who really disbelieve in him.

The word "really" is important, and may excite suspicion. I put it in, because when people have had a good Christian upbringing, as have most of those who now profess not to believe in any sort of religion, it is very hard to discover what they really believe. The reason why they find it so easy to think that they are not religious, is that they have never got into the frame of mind of one who suffers from the doubts to which religion is the answer. Not for them the terrors of the primitive jungle. Having abandoned some of the more picturesque fringes of religion, they think that they have abandoned the whole thing—whereas in fact they still have got, and could not live without, a religion of a comfortably substantial, albeit highly sophisticated, kind, which differs from that of many "religious people" in little more than this, that "religious people" like to sing Psalms about theirs—a very natural and proper thing to do. But nevertheless there may be a big difference lying behind—the difference between two people who, though side by side, are walking in different directions. I do not know in what direction Flew is walking; perhaps he does not know either. But we have had some examples recently of various ways in which one can walk away from Christianity, and there are any number of possibilities. After all, man has not changed biologically since primitive times; it is his religion that has changed, and it can easily change again. And if you do not think that such changes make a difference, get acquainted with some Sikhs and some Mussulmans of the same Punjabi stock; you will find them quite different sorts of people.

There is an important difference between Flew's parable and my own which we have not yet noticed. The explorers do not *mind* about their garden; they discuss it with interest, but not with concern. But my lunatic, poor fellow, minds about dons; and I mind about the steering of my car; it often has people in it that I care for. It is because I mind very much about what goes on in the garden in which I find myself, that I am unable to share the explorers' detachment.

*"We have no need of this hypothesis." The French scientist Pierre LaPlace made this reply to the question of why he had not included any reference to God in his book *The System of the World* (ed.).

BASIL MITCHELL

Flew's article is searching and perceptive, but there is, I think, something odd about his conduct of the theologian's case. The theologian surely would not deny that the fact of pain counts against the assertion that God loves men. This very incompatibility generates the most intractable of theological problems—the problem of evil. So the theologian *does* recognize the fact of pain as counting against Christian doctrine. But it is true that he will not allow it—or anything—to count decisively against it; for he is committed by his faith to trust in God. His attitude is not that of the detached observer, but of the believer.

Perhaps this can be brought out by yet another parable. In time of war in an occupied country, a member of the resistance meets one night a stranger who deeply impresses him. They spend that night together in conversation. The Stranger tells the partisan that he himself is on the side of the resistance—indeed that he is in command of it, and urges the partisan to have faith in him no matter what happens. The partisan is utterly convinced at that meeting of the Stranger's sincerity and constancy and undertakes to trust him.

They never meet in conditions of intimacy again. But sometimes the Stranger is seen helping members of the resistance, and the partisan is grateful and says to his friends, "He is on our side."

Sometimes he is seen in the uniform of the police handing over patriots to the occupying power. On these occasions his friends murmur against him: but the partisan still says, "He is on our side." He still believes that, in spite of appearances, the Stranger did not deceive him. Sometimes he asks the Stranger for help and receives it. He is then thankful. Sometimes he asks and does not receive it. Then he says, "The Stranger knows best." Sometimes his friends, in exasperation, say "Well, what *would* he have to do for you to admit that you were wrong and that he is not on our side?" But the partisan refuses to answer. He will not consent to put the Stranger to the test. And sometimes his friends complain, "Well, if *that's* what you mean by his being on our side, the sooner he goes over to the other side the better."

The partisan of the parable does not allow anything to count decisively against the proposition "The Stranger is on our side." This is because he has committed himself to trust the Stranger. But he of course recognizes that the Stranger's ambiguous behaviour *does* count against what he believes about him. It is precisely this situation which constitutes the trial of his faith.

When the partisan asks for help and doesn't get it, what can he do? He can (*a*) conclude that the stranger is not on our side or; (*b*) maintain that he is on our side, but that he has reasons for withholding help.

The first he will refuse to do. How long can he uphold the second position without its becoming just silly?

I don't think one can say in advance. It will depend on the nature of the impression created by the Stranger in the first place. It will depend, too, on the manner in which he takes the Stranger's behaviour. If he blandly dismisses it as of no consequence, as having no bearing upon his belief, it will be assumed that he is thoughtless or insane. And it quite obviously won't do for him to say easily, "Oh, when used of the Stranger the phrase 'is on our side' *means* ambiguous behaviour of this sort." In that case he would be like the religious man who says blandly of a terrible disaster. "It is God's will." No, he will only be regarded as sane and reasonable in his belief, if he experiences in himself the full force of the conflict.

It is here that my parable differs from Hare's. The partisan admits that many things may and do count against his belief: whereas Hare's lunatic who has a *blik* about dons doesn't admit that anything counts against his *blik*. Nothing *can* count against *bliks*. Also the partisan has a reason for having in the first instance committed himself, viz. the character of the Stranger; whereas the lunatic has no reason for his *blik* about dons—because, of course, you can't have reasons for *bliks*.

This means that I agree with Flew that theological utterances must be assertions. The partisan is making an assertion when he says, "The Stranger is on our side."

Do I want to say that the partisan's belief about the Stranger is, in any sense, an explanation? I think I do. It explains and makes sense of the Stranger's behaviour: it helps to explain also the resistance movement in the context of which he appears. In each case it differs from the interpretation which the others put upon the same facts.

"God loves men" resembles "the Stranger is on our side" (and many other significant statements, e.g., historical ones) in not being conclusively falsifiable. They can both be treated in at least three different ways: (1) As provisional hypotheses to be discarded if experience tells against them; (2) As significant articles of faith; (3) As vacuous formulae (expressing, perhaps, a desire for reassurance) to which experience makes no difference and which make no difference to life.

The Christian, once he has committed himself, is precluded by his faith from taking up the first attitude: "Thou shalt not tempt the Lord thy God." He is in constant danger, as Flew has observed, of slipping into the third. But he need not; and, if he does, it is a failure in faith as well as in logic.

ANTONY FLEW

It has been a good discussion: and I am glad to have helped to provoke it. But now—at least in *University*—it must come to an end: and the Editors of *University* have asked me to make some concluding remarks. Since it is impossible to deal with all the issues raised or to comment separately upon each contribution, I will concentrate on Mitchell and Hare, as representative of two very different kinds of response to the challenge made in "Theology and Falsification."

The challenge, it will be remembered, ran like this. Some theological utterances seem to, and are intended to, provide explanations or express assertions. Now an assertion, to be an assertion at all, must claim that things stand thus and thus; *and not otherwise*. Similarly an explanation, to be an explanation at all, must explain why this particular thing occurs; *and not something else*. Those last clauses are crucial. And yet sophisticated religious people—or so it seemed to me—are apt to overlook this, and tend to refuse to allow, not merely that anything actually does occur, but that anything conceivably could occur, which would count against their theological assertions and explanations. But in so far as they do this their supposed explanations are actually bogus, and their seeming assertions are really vacuous.

Mitchell's response to this challenge is admirably direct, straightforward, and understanding. He agrees "that theological utterances must be assertions." He agrees that if they are to be assertions, there must be something that would count against their truth. He agrees, too, that believers are in constant danger of transforming their would-be assertions into "vacuous formulae." But he takes me to task for an oddity in my "conduct of the theologian's case. The theologian surely would not deny that the fact of pain counts against the assertion that God loves men. This very incompatibility generates the most intractable of theological problems, the problem of evil." I think he is right. I should have made a distinction between two very different ways of dealing with what looks like evidence against the love of God: the way I stressed was the expedient of qualifying the original assertion; the way the theologian usually takes, at first, is to admit that it looks bad but to insist that there is—there must be—some explanation which will show that, in spite of appearances, there really is a God who loves us. His difficulty, it seems to me, is that he has given God attributes which rule out all possible saving explanations. In Mitchell's parable of the Stranger it is easy for the believer to find plausible excuses for ambiguous behaviour: for the Stranger is a man. But suppose the Stranger is God. We cannot say that he would like to help but cannot: God is omnipotent. We cannot say that he would help if he only knew: God is omniscient. We cannot say that he is not responsible for the wickedness of others: God creates those others. Indeed, an omnipotent, omniscient God must be an accessory before (and during) the fact to every human misdeed; as well as being responsible for every non-moral defect in the universe. So, though I entirely concede that Mitchell was absolutely right to insist against me that the theologian's first move is to look for an *explanation*, I still think that in the end, if relentlessly pursued, he will have to resort to the avoiding action of *qualification*. And there lies the danger of that death by a thousand qualifications, which would, I agree, constitute "a failure in faith as well as in logic."

Hare's approach is fresh and bold. He confesses that "on the ground marked out by Flew, he seems to me to be completely victorious." He therefore introduces the concept of *blik*. But while I think that there is room for some such concept in philosophy, and that philosophers should be grateful to Hare for his invention, I nevertheless want to insist that any attempt to analyze Christian religious utterances as expressions or affirmations of a *blik* rather than as (at least would-be) assertions about the cosmos is fundamentally misguided. If Hare's religion really is a *blik*, involving no cosmological assertions about the nature and activities of a supposed personal creator, then surely he is not a Christian at all? *Second*, because thus interpreted, they could scarcely do the job they do. If they were not even intended as assertions then many religious activities would become fraudulent, or merely silly. If "You ought *because* it is God's will" asserts no more than "You ought," then the person who prefers the former phraseology is not really giving a reason, but a fraudulent reason for one, a dialectical dud cheque. If "My soul must be immortal *because* God loves his children, etc." asserts no more than "My soul must be immortal," then the man who reassures himself with theological arguments for immortality is being as silly as the man who tries to clear his overdraft by writing his bank a cheque on the same account. (Of course neither of these utterances would be distinctively Christian: but this discussion never pretended to be so confined.) Religious utterances may indeed express false or even bogus assertions: but I simply do not believe that they are not both intended and interpreted to be or at any rate to presuppose assertions, at least in the context of religious practice; whatever shifts may be demanded, in another context, by the exigencies of theological apologetic.

One final suggestion. The philosophers of religion might well draw upon George Orwell's last appalling nightmare *1984* for the concept of *doublethink*. "*Doublethink* means the power of holding two contradictory beliefs simultaneously, and accepting both of them. The party intellectual knows that he is playing tricks with reality, but by the exercise of *doublethink* he also satisfies himself that reality is not violated" (*1984*, p. 220). Perhaps religious intellectuals too are sometimes driven to doublethink in order to retain their faith in a loving God in face of the reality of a heartless and indifferent world. But of this more another time, perhaps.

Discussion Questions

1. In your own words, describe the difference among knowledge, opinion, belief, and unbelief.

2. Do you think that the principle of falsification is an adequate criterion for the genuineness of assertions? Why or why not?

3. What distinction do you think Hare implicitly suggests between sane and insane *bliks*? Do you find this an adequate distinction? Give reasons for your answer.

4. In addition to the examples given in the readings, can you cite other examples of assertions that we would want to consider meaningful even though they do not appear to be falsifiable?

5. Do you find Hare's or Mitchell's response to Flew more adequate? In light of their critique, what is your own assessment of Flew's original proposal?

Will and Belief

Can we really choose to believe whatever we want, regardless of the evidence? Some people have understood Søren Kierkegaard to be saying this. Often compared with Kierkegaard was the brilliant seventeenth-century mathematician and philosopher Blaise Pascal, who argues that we can, and should, simply choose to believe in God. We have an intensely felt need for God, according to Pascal, yet reason is incapable of providing demonstrative certainty of his existence. "The heart has its reasons that reason does not know," Pascal says. So what are we to do in such a situation? Think of it as a wager, Pascal suggests, as a kind of gamble. As in any wager, there is first the matter of what we risk, and second what we stand to gain. In the case of religious belief, we risk very little— only the possibility of being wrong. But we stand to gain an infinite reward—eternal happiness—if our wager for faith turns out to be true. All this sounds somewhat calculating, but let us not forget that Pascal was a mathematician. Suppose someone offered you a chance to participate in a lottery by buying a ticket that cost only 10 cents, and the chances of winning the prize of $5 million were fifty-fifty. Who would reject a chance like that?

Religious faith is precisely this kind of wager, Pascal argues. The terms of the wager are these: Take the risk of believing in God, for the odds are roughly equal for and against the truth of God's existence. If you win your wager, you will receive infinite happiness, an eternal reward. If you lose your wager, you have suffered only a finite loss, and ultimately it will not make any difference anyway. Following through on the terms of your wager will involve going to Mass, receiving communion, and taking holy water (Pascal was a devout Catholic), and participating in these activities will eventually stifle your doubts. And what is the loss of a few hours' time each week in comparison to the possible infinite rewards that will accrue to you if your wager turns out to be true?

In the following selection, William James rejects all such deliberate calculations. To view religious belief in such terms seems, in his opinion, to rob faith of its inner vitality. And who would attribute to God a willingness to accept such a calculating response? Besides, anybody could come along claiming to be the new savior and appeal to us on the basis of Pascal's wager. If we wanted to hedge our bets, we might even be forced into wagering on a multiplicity of such saviors, hoping that at least one of our bets would pay off. Not only is such a possibility insulting to our intelligence; it is simply not the case that we can believe whatever we choose to believe. But the matter is not as simple as this. Are there some issues concerning which "our will either helps or hinders our intellect in its perceptions of the truth"? This is James's question, and he answers it in the affirmative. Where we have empirical evidence for a viewpoint, there is no rational alternative but to base our conclusions on it. But where empirical evidence is lacking, other factors besides reason enter into our decision procedure, and one of the important considerations is our will.

William James was a psychologist, but today he is known as widely for his philosophical inquiries as for his psychological studies. What is interesting about James is that he began his career as a scientist. He was appointed to teach physiology at Harvard when he was 30. As his interests broadened, he became interested in physiological psychology and, in 1876, established one of the first psychological laboratories in the United States. He stood somewhat alone in the nineteenth century in arguing against the prevailing deterministic theories of human action, insisting instead on human freedom and its correlative, moral responsibility. Consequently, many of James's philosophical writings deal with questions of freedom and morality, and with religion. One of his most famous philosophical works is *Varieties of Religious Experience*, in which he analyzes and describes the various forms of religious consciousness both as a psychologist and as a philosopher. In the selection that follows, James looks carefully at the nature of belief, and although the specific context is religious belief, the principles he outlines can be applied to other forms of belief as well.

In the background of the discussion is the opposition to religious belief known as agnosticism. Agnosticism was a term coined by Thomas Henry Huxley, grandfather of Aldous and Julian Huxley. Huxley reached the conclusion that there was no evidence sufficient to establish faith in God. But Huxley did not advocate atheism, for this would also mean reaching a conclusion without adequate evidence. If neither faith in God nor the denial of God's existence is a rational choice, the only alternative, according to Huxley, is complete suspension of belief. Huxley justifies this tactic by claiming that, not only do we not know whether God exists, but we cannot claim knowledge in this matter. How Huxley arrives at the term *agnosticism* to characterize this position he explains in the following way:

> When I reached intellectual maturity and began to ask myself whether I was an atheist, a theist, or a pantheist; a materialist or an idealist; a Christian or a freethinker; I found that the more I learned and reflected, the less ready was the answer; until, at last, I came to the conclusion that I had neither art nor part with any of these denominations, except the last. The one thing in which most of these good people were agreed was the one thing in which I differed from them. They were quite sure they had attained a certain "gnosis,"—had, more or

less successfully, solved the problem of existence; while I was quite sure I had not, and had a pretty strong conviction that the problem was insoluble. . . . So I took thought, and invented what I conceived to be the appropriate title of "agnostic." It came into my head as suggestively antithetic to the "gnostic" of Church history, who professed to know so much about the very things of which I was ignorant.[1]

Huxley's position also reflected the view of one of his contemporaries, William Kingdon Clifford, who, in 1877, published a paper entitled "The Ethics of Belief." Clifford argues that not only is it illogical to believe in the face of insufficient evidence, but it is positively immoral to do so. He gives an example of a shipowner sending a vessel to sea without knowing whether the ship is seaworthy. In Clifford's parable, the vessel founders, and all lives on board are lost. Could the owner avoid moral responsibility by saying that, since there was no evidence that the vessel would sink on that particular voyage, there was every justification for believing that the ship would successfully complete the trip? Not at all, Clifford says:

It is admitted that he did sincerely believe in the soundness of his ship; but the sincerity of his conviction can in no wise help him, because *he had no right to believe on such evidence as was before him.* He had acquired his belief not by honestly earning it in patient investigation, but by stifling his doubts.[2]

The owner could have found out whether the ship was seaworthy; he could have had the vessel inspected to determine whether confidence in its ability to make the voyage safely was warranted. Instead, the owner stifled his doubts, but to hold such a belief without sufficient evidence is immoral, and the owner was guilty of what we might call negligent homicide. A belief not supported by sufficient evidence is, to use Clifford's phrase, a "stolen belief."

Clifford's example is interesting, and doubtless most of us would agree that the shipowner's conduct is an example of criminal negligence. But is this example parallel to religious belief? Hardly, since belief in God cannot be based on sufficient evidence—as Kierkegaard points out—and we could equally well apply Clifford's principle to disbelief. What right have we to disbelieve in God when the evidence against there being a God is also insufficient?

As a matter of fact, neither Huxley nor Clifford had really suspended belief at all; for them the issue was clear: There is no God. All their talk about suspending belief and "stolen beliefs" was, James came to see, a clever smoke screen to hide their atheistic views. In short, James argues that there is no middle choice between belief and unbelief; agnosticism is a phony position. Where

[1] Thomas Henry Huxley, "Agnosticism," in *Science and Christian Tradition* (New York: D. Appleton and Company, 1894), pp. 237–239.
[2] William Kingdon Clifford, "The Ethics of Belief," in *Lectures and Essays*, ed. Leslie Stephens and Sir Frederick Pollock (New York: The Macmillan Company, 1901), II, 164.

evidence is lacking, and we are forced to make a decision, we cannot ignore the function of will in the decision process. But we cannot will ourselves to believe anything. The choice that confronts us must be between live hypotheses; by *hypotheses*, James means things that are posed to us for belief, and a hypothesis can be, for us, either live or dead. There is nothing about hypotheses per se that determines whether they are live or dead; this depends on the individual. For a Christian living in Baltimore, belief in the *Mahdi* (the word used by some Moslems for an anticipated worldwide spiritual ruler) is hardly a live hypothesis; for a Moslem however, this hypothesis may indeed be a live one. James calls the decision between hypotheses an option, and he distinguishes several kinds of options:

Living Option: Both hypotheses are live.

Dead Option: Neither hypothesis is live.

Forced Option: No alternative to the option exists.

Avoidable Option: There is an alternative to the option.

Trivial Option: Nothing of consequence is at stake.

Momentous Option: The opportunity is *unique*, the issue *significant*, or the results *irreversible*.

JAMES'S DECISION PROCEDURE

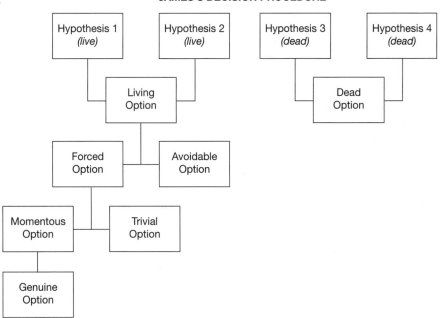

James calls an option *genuine* when it is of the living, forced, momentous kind. The preceding diagram indicates the relationships among these various terms.

For the convenience of our discussion, we will refer to the foregoing flow chart as *James's decision procedure*, and to illustrate how it works, we will trace out several decisions, each time going a little further in the decision procedure. If at any point an option turns out to be dead, avoidable, or trivial, the decision procedure stops. The examples we use will also illustrate that James's analysis can apply to matters other than religious belief, although religious belief is obviously his main concern in his essay.

The first example follows the decision procedure only to the first level and deals with a question dear to the hearts of most undergraduates: Where should I spend spring break?

WHERE SHOULD I SPEND SPRING BREAK?

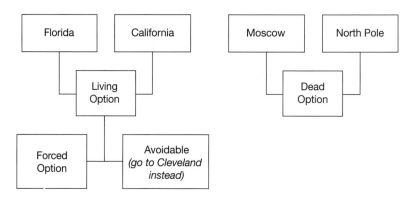

Note that the decision procedure terminates when we find that the living option that faces us is not forced; there is a third alternative. And to use James's language, this option was not genuine, since it was not forced, nor was it momentous.

The next example goes one step further and gives us a forced option. Five minutes before closing time, on the last day of the spring sale, you discover a suit you would like to buy. The decision is forced because there is no more time left in the sale. You must decide "to buy or not to buy"; that is the question.

Even though the option is forced, it does not qualify as a momentous decision, since it is not *unique* (there will be other sales), the issue is not *significant* (you do have other clothes to wear), and the decision is not *irreversible* (you can always find a suit like this one). You might be tempted to conclude that in this example the decision was not forced, for you could always walk out of the store and refuse to decide one way or the other. But it is clear that in this case, not to decide is to decide against buying the suit.

TO BUY OR NOT TO BUY?

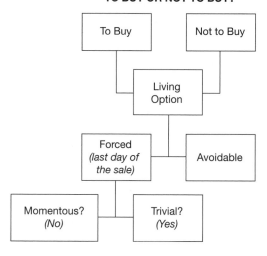

Now let us trace the decision procedure one step further by relating it to a life-and-death decision, the kind that frequently must be made by persons contemplating major surgery. Suppose that you are told by your physician that you probably have cancer of the spleen and that the malignant organ must be removed. The

SHALL I HAVE THE OPERATION?

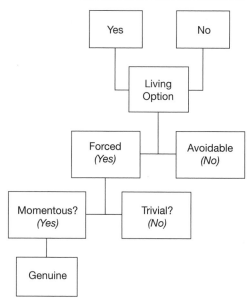

physician also informs you that the evidence is ambiguous, and it is not certain that your spleen is cancerous, but the only way to know is to operate. You are also told that it is a risky operation, and there is no certainty of success. Not only that, but removal of the spleen is irreversible. You must decide now, since every day's delay will only allow the malignancy to spread. To postpone the choice is, in effect, to decide against the operation.

This decision qualifies as a genuine option on all three criteria. The opportunity is unique (it may be the only chance to prevent the spread of the malignancy), the issue is significant (the possible saving of your life), and the results are irreversible (once taken out, your spleen cannot be replaced).

Now apply the decision procedure to the question of faith in God. If the choice between belief and nonbelief in God is not a living option for you, then James has nothing more to say. James does not think that a person can believe just anything at all merely through the force of will. But James disagrees with Clifford and Huxley concerning the possibility of suspending belief. Not to decide, in this case, is to decide, for there is no third possibility; the issue is not avoidable for those to whom the choice between belief and unbelief is a living option. The upshot of James's analysis is to show the defensibility of believing when the evidence is insufficient to provide grounds for a decision. A rule that says we cannot believe because of the risk of error is an illogical rule; not to believe is also to risk missing the truth. As James puts it, "A rule of thinking which would absolutely prevent me from acknowledging certain kinds of truth if those kinds of truth were really there, would be an irrational rule."

TO BELIEVE OR NOT TO BELIEVE?

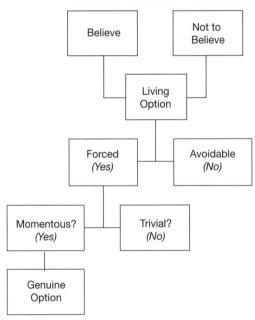

The Will to Believe

WILLIAM JAMES

Let us give the name of *hypothesis* to anything that may be proposed to our be-lief; and just as the electricians speak of live and dead wires, let us speak of any hypothesis as either *live* or *dead*. A live hypothesis is one which appeals as a real possibility to him to whom it is proposed. If I ask you to believe in the Mahdi, the notion makes no electric connection with your nature,—it refuses to scintil-late with any credibility at all. As an hypothesis it is completely dead. To an Arab, however (even if he be not one of the Mahdi's followers), the hypothesis is among the mind's possibilities: it is alive. This shows that deadness and liveness in an hy-pothesis are not intrinsic properties, but relations to the individual thinker. They are measured by his willingness to act. The maximum of liveness in an hypothe-sis means willingness to act irrevocably. Practically, that means belief; but there is some believing tendency wherever there is willingness to act at all.

Next, let us call the decision between two hypotheses an *option*. Options may be of several kinds. They may be: (1) *living* or *dead*; (2) *forced* or *avoidable*; (3) *mo-mentous* or *trivial*; and for our purposes we may call an option a *genuine* option when it is of the forced, living, and momentous kind.

1. A living option is one in which both hypotheses are live ones. If I say to you: "Be a theosophist or be a Mohammedan," it is probably a dead option, be-cause for you neither hypothesis is likely to be alive. But if I say: "Be an agnostic or be a Christian," it is otherwise: trained as you are, each hypothesis makes some appeal, however small, to your belief.

2. Next, if I say to you: "Choose between going out with your umbrella or without it," I do not offer you a genuine option, for it is not forced. You can eas-ily avoid it by not going out at all. Similarly, if I say, "Either love me or hate me," "Either call my theory true or call it false," your option is avoidable. You may re-main indifferent to me, neither loving nor hating, and you may decline to offer any judgment as to my theory. But if I say, "Either accept this truth or go with-out it," I put on you a forced option, for there is no standing place outside of the alternative. Every dilemma based on a complete logical disjunction, with no pos-sibility of not choosing, is an option of this forced kind.

3. Finally, if I were Dr. Nansen and proposed to you to join my North Pole expedition, your option would be momentous; for this would probably be your

Source: From William James, "The Will to Believe," in *The Will to Believe and Other Essays in Popular Philosophy* (New York: Longmans, Green, and Co., 1910), pp. 2–11, 17–30.

only similar opportunity, and your choice now would either exclude you from the North Pole sort of immortality altogether or put at least the chance of it into your hands. He who refuses to embrace a unique opportunity loses the prize as surely as if he tried and failed. *Per contra*, the option is trivial when the opportunity is not unique, when the stake is insignificant, or when the decision is reversible if it later prove unwise. Such trivial options abound in the scientific life. A chemist finds an hypothesis live enough to spend a year in its verification: he believes in it to that extent. But if his experiments prove inconclusive either way, he is quit for his loss of time, no vital harm being done.

It will facilitate our discussion if we keep all these distinctions well in mind.

The next matter to consider is the actual psychology of human opinion. When we look at certain facts, it seems as if our passional and volitional nature lay at the root of all our convictions. When we look at others, it seems as if they could do nothing when the intellect had once said its say. Let us take the latter facts up first.

Does it not seem preposterous on the very face of it to talk of our opinions being modifiable at will? Can our will either help or hinder our intellect in its perceptions of truth? Can we, by just willing it, believe that Abraham Lincoln's existence is a myth, and that the portraits of him in *McClure's* magazine are all of someone else? Can we, by any effort of our will, or by any strength of wish that it were true, believe ourselves well and about when we are roaring with rheumatism in bed, or feel certain that the sum of the two one-dollar bills in our pocket must be a hundred dollars? We can *say* any of these things, but we are absolutely impotent to believe them; and of just such things is the whole fabric of the truths that we do believe in made up,—matters of fact, immediate or remote, as Hume said, and relations between ideas, which are either there or not there for us if we see them so, and which if not there cannot be put there by any action of our own.

In Pascal's *Thoughts* there is a celebrated passage known in literature as Pascal's wager. In it he tries to force us into Christianity by reasoning as if our concern with truth resembled our concern with the stakes in a game of chance. Translated freely his words are these: You must either believe or not believe that God is—which will you do? Your human reason cannot say. A game is going on between you and the nature of things which at the day of judgment will bring out either heads or tails. Weigh what your gains and your losses would be if you should stake all you have on heads, or God's existence; if you win in such case, you gain eternal beatitude; if you lose, you lose nothing at all. If there were an infinity of chances, and only one for God in this wager, still you ought to stake your all on God; for though you surely risk a finite loss by this procedure, any finite loss is reasonable, even a certain one is reasonable, if there is but the possibility of infinite gain. Go, then, and take holy water, and have masses said; belief will come and stupefy your scruples,—*Cela vous fera croire et vous abêtira.** Why should you not? At bottom, what have you to lose?

You probably feel that when religious faith expresses itself thus, in the language of the gaming-table, it is put to its last trumps. Surely Pascal's own personal belief in masses and holy water had far other springs; and this celebrated page of his is but an argument for others, a last desperate snatch at a weapon against the hardness of the unbelieving heart. We feel that a faith in masses and holy water adopted willfully after such a mechanical calculation would lack the inner soul of faith's reality; and if we were ourselves in the place of the Deity, we should probably take particular pleasure in cutting off believers of this pattern from their infinite reward. It is evident that unless there be some pre-existing tendency to believe in masses and holy water, the option offered to the will by Pascal is not a living option. Certainly no Turk ever took to masses and holy water on this account; and even to us Protestants these means of salvation seem such foregone impossibilities that Pascal's logic, invoked for them specifically, leaves us unmoved. As well might the Mahdi write to us, saying, "I am the Expected One whom God has created in his effulgence. You shall be infinitely happy if you confess me; otherwise you shall be cut off from the light of the sun. Weigh, then, your infinite gain if I am genuine against your finite sacrifice if I am not!" His logic would be that of Pascal; but he would vainly use it on us, for the hypothesis he offers us is dead. No tendency to act on it exists in us to any degree.

The talk of believing by our volition seems, then, from one point of view, simply silly. From another point of view it is worse than silly, it is vile. When one turns to the magnificent edifice of the physical sciences, and sees how it was reared; what thousands of disinterested moral lives of men lie buried in its mere foundations; what patience and postponement, what choking down of preference, what submission to the icy laws of outer fact are wrought into its very stones and mortar; how absolutely impersonal it stands in its vast augustness,—then how besotted and contemptible seems every little sentimentalist who comes blowing his voluntary smoke-wreaths, and pretending to decide things from out of his private dream! Can we wonder if those bred in the rugged and manly school of science should feel like spewing such subjectivism out of their mouths? The whole system of loyalties which grow up in the schools of science go dead against its toleration; so that it is only natural that those who have caught the scientific fever should pass over to the opposite extreme, and write sometimes as if the incorruptibly truthful intellect ought positively to prefer bitterness and unacceptableness to the heart in its cup.

*It fortifies my soul to know
That, though I perish, Truth is so—*

---

*That will make you believe without letting reason intervene (*ed.*).

sings Clough, while Huxley exclaims: "My only consolation lies in the reflection that, however bad our posterity may become, so far as they hold by the plain rule of not pretending to believe what they have no reason to believe, because it may be to their advantage so to pretend [the word 'pretend' is surely here redundant], they will not have reached the lowest depth of immorality." And that delicious *enfant terrible* Clifford writes: "Belief is desecrated when given to unproved and unquestioned statements for the solace and private pleasure of the believer.... Who so would deserve well of his fellows in this matter will guard the purity of his belief with a very fanaticism of jealous care, lest at any time it should rest on an unworthy object, and catch a stain which can never be wiped away.... If [a] belief has been accepted on insufficient evidence [even though the belief be true, as Clifford on the same page explains] the pleasure is a stolen one. . . . It is sinful because it is stolen in defiance of our duty to mankind. That duty is to guard ourselves from such beliefs as from a pestilence which may shortly master our own body and then spread to the rest of the town. . . . It is wrong always, everywhere, and for every one, to believe anything upon insufficient evidence."

All this strikes one as healthy, even when expressed, as by Clifford, with somewhat too much of robustious pathos in the voice. Free-will and simple wishing do seem, in the matter of our credences, to be only fifth wheels to the coach. Yet if any one should thereupon assume that intellectual insight is what remains after wish and will and sentimental preference have taken wing, or that pure reason is what then settles our opinions, he would fly quite as directly in the teeth of the facts.

It is only our already dead hypotheses that our willing nature is unable to bring to life again. But what has made them dead for us is for the most part a previous action of our willing nature of an antagonistic kind. When I say "willing nature," I do not mean only such deliberate volitions as may have set up habits of belief that we cannot now escape from,—I mean all such factors of belief as fear and hope, prejudice and passion, imitation and partisanship, the circumpressure of our caste and set. As a matter of fact we find ourselves believing, we hardly know how or why. Mr. Balfour gives the name of "authority" to all those influences, born of the intellectual climate, that make hypotheses possible or impossible for us, alive or dead. Here in this room, we all of us believe in molecules and the conservation of energy, in democracy and necessary progress, in Protestant Christianity and the duty of fighting for "the doctrine of the immortal Monroe," all for no reasons worthy of the name. We see into these matters with no more inner clearness, and probably with much less, than any disbeliever in them might possess. His unconventionality would probably have some grounds to show for its conclusions; but for us, not insight, but the *prestige* of the opinions, is what makes the spark shoot from them and light up our sleeping magazines of faith. Our reason is quite satisfied, in nine hundred and ninety-nine cases out of every thousand of us, if it can find a few arguments that will do to recite in case our credulity is criticized by some one else. Our faith is faith in some one else's faith, and in the greatest matters this is most the case. Our belief in truth itself, for instance, that there is a truth, and that our minds and it are made for each other,—what is it but a passionate affirmation of desire, in which our social system backs us up? We want to have a truth; we want to believe that our experiments and studies and discussions must put us in a continually better and better position towards it; and on this line we agree to fight out our thinking lives. But if a pyrrhonistic sceptic asks us *how we know* all this, can our logic find a reply? No! certainly it cannot. It is just one volition against another,—we willing to go in for life upon a trust or assumption which he, for his part, does not care to make.[1]

As a rule we disbelieve all facts and theories for which we have no use. Clifford's cosmic emotions find no use for Christian feelings. Huxley belabors the bishops because there is no use for sacerdotalism in his scheme of life. Newman, on the contrary, goes over to Romanism, and finds all sorts of reasons good for staying there, because a priestly system is for him an organic need and delight. Why do so few "scientists" even look at the evidence for telepathy, so called? Because they think, as a leading biologist, now dead, once said to me, that even if such a thing were true, scientists ought to band together to keep it suppressed and concealed. It would undo the uniformity of Nature and all sorts of other things without which scientists cannot carry on their pursuits. But if this very man had been shown something which as a scientist he might *do* with telepathy, he might not only have examined the evidence, but even have found it good enough. This very law which the logicians would impose upon us—if I may give the name of logicians to those who would rule out our willing nature here—is based on nothing but their own natural wish to exclude all elements for which they, in their professional quality of logicians, can find no use.

Evidently, then, our non-intellectual nature does influence our convictions. There are passed tendencies and volitions which run before and others which come after belief, and it is only the latter that are too late for the fair; and they are not too late when the previous passional work has been already in their own direction. Pascal's argument, instead of being powerless, then seems a regular clincher, and is the last stroke needed to make our faith in masses and holy water complete. The state of things is evidently far from simple; and pure insight and logic, whatever they might do ideally, are not the only things that really do produce our creeds. . . .

One more point, small but important, and our preliminaries are done. There are two ways of looking at our duty in the matter of opinion,—ways entirely different, and yet ways about whose difference the theory of knowledge seems hitherto to have shown very little concern. *We must know the truth*; and *we must avoid error*,—these are our first and great commandments as would-be knowers; but they are not two ways of stating an identical commandment, they are two separable laws. Although it may indeed happen that when we believe the truth A,

[1] Compare the admirable page 310 in S. H. Hodgson's "Time and Space," London, 1865.

we escape as an incidental consequence from believing the falsehood B, it hardly ever happens that by merely disbelieving B we necessarily believe A. We may in escaping B fall into believing other falsehoods, C or D, just as bad as B; or we may escape B by not believing anything at all, not even A.

Believe truth! Shun error!—these, we see, are two materially different laws; and by choosing between them we may end by coloring differently our whole intellectual life. We may regard the chase for truth as paramount, and the avoidance of error as secondary; or we may, on the other hand, treat the avoidance of error as more imperative, and let truth take its chance. Clifford, in the instructive passage which I have quoted, exhorts us to the latter course. Believe nothing, he tells us, keep your mind in suspense forever, rather than by closing it on insufficient evidence incur the awful risk of believing lies. You, on the other hand, may think that the risk of being in error is a very small matter when compared with the blessings of real knowledge, and be ready to be duped many times in your investigation rather than postpone indefinitely the chance of guessing true. I myself find it impossible to go with Clifford. We must remember that these feelings of our duty about either truth or error are in any case only expressions of our passional life. Biologically considered, our minds are as ready to grind out falsehood as veracity, and he who says, "Better go without belief forever than believe a lie!" merely shows his own preponderant private horror of becoming a dupe. He may be critical of many of his desires and fears, but this fear he slavishly obeys. He cannot imagine any one questioning its binding force. For my own part, I have a horror of being duped; but I can believe that worse things than being duped may happen to a man in this world: so Clifford's exhortation has to my ears a thoroughly fantastic sound. . . . Wherever the option between losing truth and gaining it is not momentous, we can throw the chance of *gaining truth* away, and at any rate save ourselves from any chance of *believing falsehood*, by not making up our minds at all till objective evidence has come. In scientific questions, this is almost always the case; and even in human affairs in general, the need of acting is seldom so urgent that a false belief to act on is better than no belief at all. Law courts, indeed, have to decide on the best evidence attainable for the moment, because a judge's duty is to make law as well as to ascertain it, and (as a learned judge once said to me) few cases are worth spending much time over: the great thing is to have them decided on *any* acceptable principle, and got out of the way. But in our dealings with objective nature we obviously are recorders, not makers, of the truth. . . . The questions here are always trivial options, the hypotheses are hardly living (at any rate not living for us spectators), the choice between believing truth or falsehood is seldom forced. The attitude of skeptical balance is therefore the absolutely wise one if we would escape mistakes. What difference, indeed, does it make to most of us whether we have or have not a theory of the Röntgen rays, whether we believe or not in mind-stuff, or have a conviction about the causality of conscious states? It makes no difference. Such options are not forced on us. On every account it is better not to make them, but still keep weighing reasons *pro et contra* with an indifferent hand.

I speak, of course, here of the purely judging mind. For purposes of discovery such indifference is to be less highly recommended, and science would be far less advanced than she is if the passionate desires of individuals to get their own faiths confirmed had been kept out of the game. See for example the sagacity which Spencer and Weismann now display. On the other hand, if you want an absolute duffer in an investigation, you must, after all, take the man who has no interest whatever in its results: he is the warranted incapable, the positive fool. The most useful investigator, because the most sensitive observer, is always he whose eager interest in one side of the question is balanced by an equally keen nervousness lest he become deceived.[2] Science has organized this nervousness into a regular *technique*, her so-called method of verification; and she has fallen so deeply in love with the method that one may even say she has ceased to care for truth by itself at all. It is only truth as technically verified that interests her. The truth of truths might come in merely affirmative form, and she would decline to touch it. Such truth as that, she might repeat with Clifford, would be stolen in defiance of her duty to mankind. Human passions, however, are stronger than technical rules. "Le coeur a ses raisons," as Pascal says, "que la raison ne connaît pas;"* and however indifferent to all but the bare rules of the game the umpire, the abstract intellect, may be, the concrete players who furnish him the materials to judge of are usually, each one of them, in love with some pet "live hypothesis" of his own. Let us agree, however, that wherever there is no forced option, the dispassionately judicial intellect with no pet hypothesis, saving us, as it does, from dupery at any rate, ought to be our ideal.

The question next arises: Are there not somewhere forced options in our speculative questions, and can we (as men who may be interested at least as much in positively gaining truth as in merely escaping dupery) always wait with impunity till the coercive evidence shall have arrived? It seems *a priori* improbable that the truth should be so nicely adjusted to our needs and powers as that. In the great boarding-house of nature, the cakes and the butter and the syrup seldom come out so even and leave the plates so clean. Indeed, we should view them with scientific suspicion if they did.

Moral questions immediately present themselves as questions whose solution cannot wait for sensible proof. A moral question is a question not of what sensibly exists, but of what is good, or would be good if it did exist. Science can tell us what exists; but to compare the *worths*, both of what exists and of what does not exist, we must consult not science, but what Pascal calls our heart. Science herself consults her heart when she lays it down that the infinite ascertainment of fact and correction of false belief are the supreme goods for man. Challenge the statement, and science can only repeat it oracularly, or else prove it by showing that such ascertainment and correction bring man all sorts of other goods which

---

[2] Compare Wilfrid Ward's Essay, "The Wish to Believe," in his *Witnesses to the Unseen*, Macmillan & Co., 1893.

* The heart has its reasons that reason does not know (*ed.*).

man's heart in turn declares. The question of having moral beliefs at all or not having them is decided by our will. Are our moral preferences true or false, or are they only odd biological phenomena, making things good or bad for *us*, but in themselves indifferent? How can your pure intellect decide? If your heart does not *want* a world of moral reality, your head will assuredly never make you believe in one. Mephistophelian scepticism, indeed, will satisfy the head's play-instincts much better than any rigorous idealism can. Some men (even at the student age) are so naturally cool-hearted that the moralistic hypothesis never has for them any pungent life, and in their supercilious presence the hot young moralist always feels strangely ill at ease. The appearance of knowingness is on their side, of *naïveté* and gullibility on his. Yet, in the inarticulate heart of him, he clings to it that he is not a dupe, and that there is a realm in which (as Emerson says) all their wit and intellectual superiority is no better than the cunning of a fox. Moral scepticism can no more be refuted or proved by logic than intellectual scepticism can. When we stick to it that there *is* truth (be it of either kind), we do so with our whole nature, and resolve to stand or fall by the results. The sceptic with his whole nature adopts the doubting attitude; but which of us is the wiser, Omniscience only knows.

Turn now from these wide questions of good to a certain class of questions of fact, questions concerning personal relations, states of mind between one man and another. *Do you like me or not?*—for example. Whether you do or not depends, in countless instances, on whether I meet you half-way, am willing to assume that you must like me, and show you trust and expectation. The previous faith on my part in your liking's existence is in such cases what makes your liking come. But if I stand aloof, and refuse to budge an inch until I have objective evidence, until you shall have done something apt, as the absolutists say, *ad extorquendum assensum meum*,* ten to one your liking never comes. How many women's hearts are vanquished by the mere sanguine insistence of some man that they *must* love him! he will not consent to the hypothesis that they cannot. The desire for a certain kind of truth here brings about that special truth's existence; and so it is in innumerable cases of other sorts. Who gains promotions, boons, appointments, but the man in whose life they are seen to play the part of live hypotheses, who discounts them, sacrifices other things for their sake before they have come, and takes risks for them in advance? His faith acts on the powers above him as a claim, and creates its own verification.

A social organism of any sort whatever, large or small, is what it is because each member proceeds to his own duty with a trust that the other members will simultaneously do theirs. Wherever the desired result is achieved by the cooperation of many independent persons, its existence as a fact is a pure consequence of the precursive faith in one another of those immediately concerned. A government, an army, a commercial system, a ship, a college, an athletic team, all exist on this condition, without which not only is nothing achieved, but nothing

---

* Extracting assent by torture (*ed.*).

is even attempted. A whole train of passengers (individually brave enough) will be looted by a few highwaymen, simply because the latter can count on one another, while each passenger fears that if he makes a movement of resistance, he will be shot before any one else backs him up. If we believed that the whole carfull would rise at once with us, we should each severally rise, and train-robbing would never even be attempted. There are, then, cases where a fact cannot come at all unless a preliminary faith exists in its coming. *And where faith in a fact can help create the fact,* that would be an insane logic which should say that faith running ahead of scientific evidence is the "lowest kind of immorality" into which a thinking being can fall. Yet such is the logic by which our scientific absolutists pretend to regulate our lives!

In truths dependent on our personal action, then, faith based on desire is certainly a lawful and possibly an indispensable thing.

But now, it will be said, these are all childish human cases, and have nothing to do with great cosmical matters, like the question of religious faith. Let us then pass on to that. Religions differ so much in their accidents that in discussing the religious question we must make it very generic and broad. What then do we now mean by the religious hypothesis? Science says things are: morality says some things are better than other things; and religion says essentially two things.

First, she says that the best things are the more eternal things, the overlapping things, the things in the universe that throw the last stone, so to speak, and say the final word. "Perfection is eternal"—his phrase of Charles Secrétan seems a good way of putting this first affirmation of religion, an affirmation which obviously cannot yet be verified scientifically at all.

The second affirmation of religion is that we are better off now if we believe her first affirmation to be true.

Now, let us consider what the logical elements of this situation are *in case the religious hypothesis in both its branches be really true.* (Of course, we must admit that possibility at the outset. If we are to discuss the question at all, it must involve a living option. If for any of you religion be a hypothesis that cannot, by any living possibility be true, then you need go no farther. I speak to the "saving remnant" alone.) So proceeding, we see, first, that religion offers itself as a *momentous* option. We are supposed to gain, even now, by our belief, and to lose by our nonbelief, a certain vital good. Secondly, religion is a *forced* option, so far as that good goes. We cannot escape the issue by remaining skeptical and waiting for more light, because, although we do avoid error in that way *if religion be untrue,* we lose the good, *if it be true,* just as certainly as if we positively chose to disbelieve. It is as if a man should hesitate indefinitely to ask a certain woman to marry him because he was not perfectly sure that she would prove an angel after he brought her home. Would he not cut himself off from that particular angel-possibility as decisively as if he went and married some one else? Scepticism, then, is not avoidance of option; it is option of a certain particular kind of risk. *Better risk loss of truth than chance of error,*—that is your faith-vetoer's exact position. He is actively playing his stake as much as the believer is; he is backing the field against the religious hypothesis, just as the believer is backing the religious hypothesis against the field. To preach scepticism to us as a duty until "sufficient evidence" for religion be found, is tantamount therefore to telling us, when in presence of the religious hypothesis, that to yield to our fear of its being error is wiser and better than to yield to our hope that it may be true. It is not intellect against all passions, then; it is only intellect with one passion laying down its law. And by what, forsooth, is the supreme wisdom of this passion warranted? Dupery for dupery, what proof is there that dupery through hope is so much worse than dupery through fear? I, for one, can see no proof; and I simply refuse obedience to the scientist's command to imitate his kind of option, in a case where my own stake is important enough to give me the right to choose my own form of risk. If religion be true and the evidence for it be still insufficient, I do not wish, by putting your extinguisher upon my nature (which feels to me as if it had after all some business in this matter), to forfeit my sole chance in life of getting upon the winning side,—that chance depending, of course, on my willingness to run the risk of acting as if my passional need of taking the world religiously might be prophetic and right.

All this is on the supposition that it really may be prophetic and right, and that, even to us who are discussing the matter, religion is a live hypothesis which may be true. Now, to most of us religion comes in a still further way that makes a veto on our active faith even more illogical. The more perfect and more eternal aspect of the universe is represented in our religions as having personal form. The universe is no longer a mere *It* to us, but a *Thou*, if we are religious; and any relation that may be possible from person to person might be possible here. For instance, although in one sense we are passive portions of the universe, in another we show a curious autonomy, as if we were small active centres on our own account. We feel, too, as if the appeal of religion to us were made to our own active good-will, as if evidence might be forever withheld from us unless we met the hypothesis half-way. To take a trivial illustration: just as a man who in a company of gentlemen made no advances, asked a warrant for every concession, and believed no one's word without proof, would cut himself off by such churlishness from all the social rewards that a more trusting spirit would earn,—so here, one who should shut himself up in snarling logicality and try to make the gods extort his recognition willy-nilly, or not get it at all, might cut himself off forever from his only opportunity of making the gods' acquaintance. This feeling, forced on us we know not whence, that by obstinately believing that there are gods (although not to do so would be so easy both for our logic and our life) we are doing the universe the deepest service we can, seems part of the living essence of the religious hypothesis. If the hypothesis *were* true in all its parts, including this one, then pure intellectualism, with its veto on our making willing advances, would be an absurdity; and some participation of our sympathetic nature would be logically required. I, therefore, for one, cannot see my way to accepting the agnostic rules for truth-seeking, or willfully agree to keep my willing nature out of the game. I cannot do so for this plain reason, that *a rule of thinking which would absolutely prevent me from acknowledging certain kinds of truth if those kinds of truth were really there, would be an irrational rule.* That for me is the long and short of the formal logic of the situation, no matter what the kinds of truth might materially be.

I confess I do not see how this logic can be escaped. But sad experience makes me fear that some of you may still shrink from radically saying with me, *in abstracto,* that we have the right to believe at our own risk any hypothesis that is live enough to tempt our will. I suspect, however, that if this is so, it is because you have got away from the abstract logical point of view altogether, and are thinking (perhaps without realizing it) of some particular religious hypothesis which for you is dead. The freedom to "believe what we will" you apply to the case of some patent superstition; and the faith you think of is the faith defined by the schoolboy when he said, "Faith is when you believe something that you know ain't true." I can only repeat that this is misapprehension. *In concreto,* the freedom to believe can only cover living options which the intellect of the individual cannot by itself resolve; and living options never seem absurdities to him who has them to consider. When I look at the religious question as it really puts itself to concrete men, and when I think of all the possibilities which both practically and theoretically it involves, then this command that we shall put a stopper on our heart, instincts, and courage, and *wait*—acting of course meanwhile more or less as if religion were *not* true[3]—till doomsday, or till such time as our intellect and senses working together may have raked in evidence enough,—this command, I say, seems to me the queerest idol ever manufactured in the philosophic cave. Were we scholastic absolutists, there might be more excuse. If we had an infallible intellect with its objective certitudes, we might feel ourselves disloyal to such a perfect organ of knowledge in not trusting to it exclusively, in not waiting for its releasing word. But if we are empiricists, if we believe that no bell in us tolls to let us know for certain when truth is in our grasp, then it seems a piece of idle fantasticality to preach so solemnly our duty of waiting for the bell. Indeed we *may* wait if we will,—I hope you do not think I am denying that— but if we do so, we do so at our peril as much as if we believed. In either case we *act,* taking our life in our hands. No one of us ought to issue vetoes to the other, nor should we bandy words of abuse. We ought, on the contrary, delicately and profoundly to respect one another's mental freedom: then only shall

---

[3] Since belief is measured by action, he who forbids us to believe religion to be true, necessarily also forbids us to act as we should if we did believe it to be true. The whole defense of religious faith hinges upon action. If the action required or inspired by the religious hypothesis is in no way different from that dictated by the naturalistic hypothesis, then religious faith is a pure superfluity, better pruned away, and controversy about its legitimacy is a piece of idle trifling, unworthy of serious minds. I myself believe, of course, that the religious hypothesis gives to the world an expression which specifically determines our reactions, and makes them in a large part unlike what they might be on a purely naturalistic scheme of belief.

we bring about the intellectual republic; then only shall we have that spirit of inner tolerance without which all our outer tolerance is soulless, and which is empiricism's glory; then only shall we live and let live, in speculative as well as in practical things. . . .

Discussion Questions

1. Do you think Pascal's wager is an acceptable way to resolve the question of belief versus nonbelief? Why or why not?

2. Do you agree with James's claim that agnosticism is not a viable alternative? What are the reasons for your answer?

3. What are the conditions under which James thought it was appropriate to apply his decision procedure? Do you agree that, given these conditions, it is rationally acceptable to make a decision on the basis that James suggests? Give reasons for your answer.

4. James obviously thought his approach to the question of faith was different from that of Pascal. Do you agree? Why or why not?

5. Do you think a person could have a satisfactory religious life if the person's initial faith commitment was made on the basis that James suggests?

The Leap of Faith

Probably no philosopher has ever come out on the side of faith against reason as strongly as did Søren Kierkegaard, the moody Dane of the nineteenth century whose writings provided impetus for the existential philosophers of the twentieth century. Kierkegaard proposed that we should not expect to understand human existence completely by means of reason's philosophical analysis. The foolishness of philosophers is that they build elaborate systems and then think they have actually done something significant. For Kierkegaard, the important question is what it means to be an existing, human being, and this is a concern that cannot be addressed by abstract analysis and philosophical system building.

To be human is to exist. What does it mean to exist as a human being? It is first a matter of living in time for a brief period. One is born, lives a few years, and then dies, without ever having any choice in the matter. Seen from our limited perspective, life does not make much sense, and reason is of little help in guiding us through the tangle of human concerns that confront us.

In his attack on philosophical system building, Kierkegaard faces something of a methodological problem. He is opposed to philosophical system building and logical analysis because it distorts the question of human existence. But how can one attack system building in philosophy? Certainly not systematically. It is a curious contradiction to argue against argument and systematically attack system building. So Kierkegaard chooses forms of indirect discourse. Many of his books were written under pseudonyms, and he uses irony, analogy, veiled metaphors, and lyric description in an attempt to help his readers think about the important concerns that face each existing individual.

The following selection, for example, comes from a book entitled *Concluding Unscientific Postscript*, which has as its subtitle *A Mimic-Pathetic-Dialectic Composition, an Existential Contribution*. Is the title a joke? Maybe. But the real joke is that Kierkegaard had previously written a small book—93 pages in English translation—entitled *Philosophical Fragments* (although *Philosophical Scraps* would probably be a better translation of the title). And the *Postscript* is over five times as long as that to which it is a postscript. It is hard to imagine any other nineteenth-century philosopher writing a book entitled *Philosophical Fragments*. Certainly,

Hegel, the most systematic of all nineteenth-century thinkers, would never consider such a title. Kierkegaard's title itself shows his disdain for the prevailing type of philosophy. To this book of fragments or scraps he added a sequel called, not a scientific postscript, but an *un*scientific postscript, whose length exceeds the former book's size substantially.

Central to the theme of the *Postscript* is the distinction between the objective and the subjective thinker. This mirrors the difference between reason and faith. The objective thinker adopts an intellectual, detached, scientific attitude toward life and views life from the perspective of an observer. The most extreme example of this kind of thinker in Kierkegaard's estimation is that of a professor (Hegel?) who produces a "system" of philosophy with little thought about whether such a system applies to the existing individual, including the philosopher developing the system. The objective thinker feels no personal commitment to the topic under investigation. The paradigm of objective thinking is the scientist in a laboratory. A scientific investigator approaches the search for truth in a detached manner and is mainly concerned with confirming or disproving a hypothesis. If the research confirms only one aspect of the hypothesis, the rest of it is discarded, and a new hypothesis is formed which incorporates that which survives from the old one. By this *approximation-process*, to use Kierkegaard's term, the objective thinker gradually moves closer and closer to the truth, but it is a truth to which the scientist feels no intense attachment or passionate commitment. Indeed, a scientist who is passionately committed to a disproved hypothesis is a bad scientist.

The subjective thinker, in contrast, is passionately and intensely involved with truth. For the subjective thinker, truth is not just a process of accumulating evidence to justify a view, but a matter of intense personal concern. Sometimes Kierkegaard calls the subjective thinker an *existential* thinker, for the questions of life and death, the meaning of human existence, and a person's ultimate destiny are issues in which the person raising them is intensely involved. For the subjective thinker, the *approximation-process* of objective thinking is insufficient. The truth of what is under consideration matters enormously to the subjective thinker, and one either accepts it or rejects it.

There is certainly a place for objective thinking, and even though Kierkegaard's concern is primarily with the subjective thinker, he never denies that objective thinking has its place. He insists, however, that not all of life's concerns are open to objective analysis. One could even say, in the spirit of Kierkegaard, that life's most important questions are not open to objective analysis. Consider, for example, falling in love. Romantic love is essentially a relationship between two persons that, at its most intense, produces a lifelong relationship in marriage. We can see the difference between the way an objective and subjective thinker would approach love and marriage relationships. The objective thinker would say, "Here I am at that point in my life where social obligations demand that I have a mate." *Mate* is an appropriate word here, since the objective thinker's concern is not love, but being married, perhaps even producing progeny, in order to satisfy the social demands of life. So the objective thinker creates a list of ideal traits that a spouse should have and evaluates each potential marriage partner accordingly. As each falls short of the ideal, the objective thinker finally decides to look for the one who most closely approximates the objective standards. Through this approximation process, the objective thinker finally finds someone who most closely meets all the criteria. Then the objective thinker proposes a relationship.

The subjective thinker, in contrast, falls in love. There may not be much rational thinking behind this act; in fact, there is a certain nonrational quality about love. A person in love is seized by an intense attraction to another individual. "I can't live without you," the subjective thinker says to the beloved. "My life will be meaningless without you. I can't bear to let you out of my sight." Here is inwardness and passion in the extreme. No rational calculation, no systematic elimination of less fit candidates, no approximation-process is ever considered. Being in love is an intense, inward experience, and the lover is concerned not with the objective analysis of the qualities of the other person, but with establishing a relationship with another individual.

Religious faith, in the sense that Kierkegaard considers it, is not open to objective thinking, for it involves a relationship with God. The accent falls not on *what* is said, that is, on the content of religious doctrines, but *how* it is said, that is, on a relationship of a creature with the Creator. Rational theology, or natural theology, as we have been calling it, points to the existence of God but does not give us much on which to establish a relationship. "I contemplate the order of nature," Kierkegaard says, "in the hope of finding God, and I see omnipotence and wisdom; but I also see much else that disturbs my mind and excites anxiety. The sum of all this is objective uncertainty." We have already seen the inconclusiveness of proofs of the existence of God. We have observed that the debate between those who support the arguments and those who reject them seems endless, with each claiming to make a little further progress in the approximation-process that constitutes objective analysis and rational debate. While the debate goes on, life slips away, and we must make a decision. This decision is the *leap of faith*. To be sure, such a leap is risky, but Kierkegaard observes that "without risk there is no faith."

Look back to the introduction to this section and review the analysis offered by Kant of the different modes of human awareness. If there is objective insufficiency, or "objective uncertainty," to use Kierkegaard's phrase, then two modes of awareness can result, either *opinion* or *belief*. Opinion is appropriate to the objective thinker who views the existence of God as a problem to be rationally analyzed. The objective thinker views the question whether God exists as a problem to be approached from a detached viewpoint. Since God's existence cannot be proved, the objective thinker is left only with an opinion on the question. For the subjective thinker, in contrast, the question of God is not an intellectual problem, but a matter of intense inwardness, and faith is commitment to a relationship that defies objective analysis. An appeal to scripture, after the fashion of Thomas Aquinas, will not give us much help, for Kierkegaard finds the content of

Christian doctrine to be paradoxical in the extreme: that the eternal God was born as a human being, lived and died, and by this death brings salvation for all. No amount of objective analysis can make this rationally acceptable, and if we are to establish a relationship with the Creator, it will have to be based on faith.

The brief selection from Kierkegaard that follows highlights these themes, but it does not show the disdain Kierkegaard had for those for whom religious faith made little difference. His disdain was directed not just toward unbelievers, but toward many of the religious, churchgoing population of his native Denmark. He parodies the figure of the parson who preaches endlessly about a biblical text and is congratulated by the parishioners for preaching a fine sermon while, in fact, neither the preacher nor the congregation feels the intensity of the experiences of Abraham grappling with the demands of faith. Churches are filled with persons, Kierkegaard claims, for whom the question of faith has never really arisen. Being a Christian is not merely a matter of accepting a few doctrines, going to church, and reciting the creeds. Kierkegaard holds that it is not even correct to say that one *is* a Christian, only that one is *becoming* a Christian, for establishing a relationship with the Creator is a lifelong task. All this is Kierkegaard's way of underscoring his central theme: Faith is a matter of intense commitment, a subjective relationship with God of the most passionate inwardness. What matters for the subjective thinker is not an objective analysis, but being in a true relationship, and this is equivalent to faith.

Objective and Subjective Reflection

SØREN KIERKEGAARD

In an attempt to make clear the difference of way that exists between an objective and a subjective reflection, I shall now proceed to show how a subjective reflection makes its way inwardly in inwardness. Inwardness in an existing subject culminates in passion; corresponding to passion in the subject the truth becomes

Source: Excerpts from Søren Kierkegaard, *Concluding Unscientific Postscript,* trans. David F. Swenson and Walter Lowrie. Copyright © 1992 by Howard Hong. Reprinted by permission of Princeton University Press.

a paradox; and the fact that the truth becomes a paradox is rooted precisely in its having a relationship to an existing subject. Thus the one corresponds to the other. By forgetting that one is an existing subject, passion goes by the board and the truth is no longer a paradox; the knowing subject becomes a fantastic entity rather than a human being, and the truth becomes a fantastic object for the knowledge of this fantastic entity.

When the question of truth is raised in an objective manner, reflection is directed objectively to the truth, as an object to which the knower is related. Reflection is not focused upon the relationship, however, but upon the question of whether it is the truth to which the knower is related. If only the object to which he is related is the truth, the subject is accounted to be in the truth. When the question of the truth is raised subjectively, reflection is directed subjectively to the nature of the individual's relationship; if only the mode of this relationship is in the truth, the individual is in the truth even if he should happen to be thus related to what is not true.[1] Let us take as an example the knowledge of God. Objectively, reflection is directed to the problem of whether this object is the true God; subjectively, reflection is directed to the question whether the individual is related to a something *in such a manner* that his relationship is in truth a God-relationship. On which side is the truth now to be found? Ah, may we not here resort to a mediation, and say: It is on neither side, but in the mediation of both? Excellently well said, provided we might have it explained how an existing individual manages to be in a state of mediation. For to be in a state of mediation is to be finished, while to exist is to become. Nor can an existing individual be in two places at the same time—he cannot be an identity of subject and object. When he is nearest to being in two places at the same time he is in passion; but passion is momentary, and passion is also the highest expression of subjectivity.

The existing individual who chooses to pursue the objective way enters upon the entire approximation-process by which it is proposed to bring God to light objectively. But this is in all eternity impossible, because God is a subject, and therefore exists only for subjectivity in inwardness. The existing individual who chooses the subjective way apprehends instantly the entire dialectical difficulty involved in having to use some time, perhaps a long time, in finding God objectively; and he feels this dialectical difficulty in all its painfulness, because every moment is wasted in which he does not have God.[2] That very instant he has God, not by virtue of any objective deliberation, but by virtue of the finite passion of inwardness. The objective inquirer, on the other hand, is not embarrassed by such dialectical difficulties as are involved in devoting an entire period of investigation to finding God—since it is possible that the inquirer may die tomorrow; and if he lives he can scarcely regard God as something to be taken along if convenient, since God is precisely that which one takes *a tout prix,* which in the understanding of passion constitutes the true inward relationship to God.

It is at this point, so difficult dialectically, that the way swings off for everyone who knows what it means to think, and to think existentially; which is something very different from sitting at a desk and writing about what one has never done, something very different from writing *de omnibus dubitandum* and at the same time being as credulous existentially as the most sensuous of men. Here is where the way swings off, and the change is marked by the fact that while objective knowledge rambles comfortably on by way of the long road of approximation without being impelled by the urge of passion, subjective knowledge counts every delay a deadly peril, and the decision so infinitely important and so instantly pressing that it is as if the opportunity has already passed.

Now when the problem is to reckon up on which side there is most truth, whether on the side of one who seeks the true God objectively, and pursues the approximate truth of the God-idea; or on the side of one who, driven by the infinite passion of his need of God, feels an infinite concern for his own relationship to God in truth (and to be at one and the same time on both sides equally, is as we have noted not possible for an existing individual, but is merely the happy delusion of an imaginary I-am-I): the answer cannot be in doubt for anyone who has not been demoralized with the aid of science. If one who lives in the midst of Christendom goes up to the house of God, the house of the true God, with the true conception of God in his knowledge, and prays, but prays in a false spirit; and one who lives in an idolatrous community prays with the entire passion of the infinite, although his eyes rest upon the image of an idol: where is there most truth? The one prays in truth to God though he worships an idol; the other prays falsely to the true God, and hence worships in fact an idol. . . .

The objective accent falls on WHAT is said, the subjective accent on HOW it is said. This distinction holds even in the aesthetic realm, and receives definite expression in the principle that what is in itself true may in the mouth of such and such a person become untrue. In these times this distinction is particularly worthy of notice, for if we wish to express in a single sentence the difference between ancient times and our own, we should doubtless have to say: "In ancient times only an individual here and there knew the truth; now all know it, except that the inwardness of its appropriation stands in an inverse relationship to the extent of its dissemination."[3] Aesthetically the contradiction that truth becomes untruth in this or that person's mouth, is best construed comically: In the ethico-religious sphere, accent is again on the "how." But this is not to be understood as referring to demeanor, expression, or the life; rather it refers to the relationship sustained by the existing individual, in his own existence, to the content of his utterance. Objectively the interest is focussed merely on the thought-content, subjectively on the inwardness. At its maximum this inward "how" is the passion of the infinite, and the passion of the infinite is the truth. But the passion of the infinite is precisely subjectivity, and thus subjectivity becomes the truth. Objectively there is no infinite decisiveness, and hence it is objectively in order to annul the difference between good and evil; together with the principle of contradiction, and therewith also the infinite difference between the true and the false. Only in subjectivity is there decisiveness, to seek objectivity is to be in error. It is the passion of the infinite that is the decisive factor and not its content, for its content is precisely itself. In this manner subjectivity and the subjective "how" constitute the truth.

But the "how" which is thus subjectively accentuated precisely because the subject is an existing individual, is also subject to a dialectic with respect to time. In the passionate moment of decision, where the road swings away from objective knowledge, it seems as if the infinite decision were thereby realized. But in the same moment the existing individual finds himself in the temporal order, and the subjective "how" is transformed into a striving, a striving which receives indeed its impulse and a repeated renewal from the decisive passion of the infinite, but is nevertheless a striving.

When subjectivity is the truth, the conceptual determination of the truth must include an expression for the antithesis to objectivity, a memento of the fork in the road where the way swings off; this expression will at the same time serve as an indication of the tension of the subjective inwardness. Here is such a definition of truth: *An objective uncertainty held fast in an appropriation-process of the most passionate inwardness is the truth*, the highest truth attainable for an *existing* individual. At the point where the way swings off (and where this is cannot be specified objectively, since it is a matter of subjectivity), there objective knowledge is placed in abeyance. Thus the subject merely has, objectively, the uncertainty; but it is this which precisely increases the tension of that infinite passion which constitutes his inwardness. The truth is precisely the venture which chooses an objective uncertainty with the passion of the infinite. I contemplate the order of nature in the hope of finding God, and I see omnipotence and wisdom; but I also see much else that disturbs my mind and excites anxiety. The sum of all this is an objective uncertainty. But it is for this very reason that the inwardness becomes as intense as it is, for it embraces this objective uncertainty with the entire passion of the infinite. In the case of a mathematical proposition the objectivity is given, but for this reason the truth of such a proposition is also an indifferent truth.

But the above definition of truth is an equivalent expression for faith. Without risk there is no faith. Faith is precisely the contradiction between the infinite passion of the individual's inwardness and the objective uncertainty. If I am capable of grasping God objectively, I do not believe, but precisely because I cannot do this I must believe. If I wish to preserve myself in faith I must constantly be intent upon holding fast the objective uncertainty, so as to remain out upon the deep, over seventy thousand fathoms of water, still preserving my faith.

Notes

1. The reader will observe that the question here is about essential truth, or about the truth which is essentially related to existence, and that it is precisely for the sake of clarifying it as inwardness or as subjectivity that this contrast is drawn.

2. In this manner God certainly becomes a postulate, but not in the otiose manner in which this word is commonly understood. It becomes clear rather that the only way in which an existing individual comes into relation with God, is when the dialectical contradiction brings his passion to the point of despair, and helps him to embrace God with the "category of despair" (faith). Then the postulate is so far from being arbitrary that it is precisely a life necessity. It is then not so much that God is a postulate, as that the existing individual's postulation of God is a necessity.

3. *Stages of Life's Way*, Note on p. 426. Though ordinarily not wishing an expression of opinion on the part of reviewers, I might at this point almost desire it, provided such opinions, so far from flattering me, amounted to an assertion of the daring truth that what I say is something that everybody knows, even every child, and that the cultured know infinitely much better. If it only stands fast that everyone knows it, my standpoint is in order, and I shall doubtless make shift to manage with the unity of the comic and the tragic. If there were anyone who did not know it I might perhaps be in danger of being dislodged from my position of equilibrium by the thought that I might be in a position to communicate to someone the needful preliminary knowledge. It is just this which engages my interest so much, this that the cultured are accustomed to say: that everyone knows what the highest is. This was not the case in paganism, nor in Judaism, nor in the seventeen centuries of Christianity. Hail to the nineteenth century! Everyone knows it. What progress has been made since the time when only a few knew it. To make up for this, perhaps, we must assume that no one nowadays does it.

Discussion Questions

1. What is the difference between the claim that truth is subjectivity and the claim that truth is objectivity?

2. Can you cite nonreligious examples of the difference between objective and subjective thinking?

3. What is the relation between truth and faith as Kierkegaard understands these terms?

4. What is the significance of Kierkegaard's reference to God as an objective uncertainty? Do you consider this an adequate way of referring to God? Why or why not?

5. Explain what Kierkegaard means by the following: "The objective accent falls on *what* is said, the subjective accent on *how* it is said."

6. Why does Kierkegaard think that the leap of faith is the only possible way to approach God? Do you agree? What are your reasons?

Faith as Ultimate Concern

The final selection in this chapter is from Paul Tillich, whose identification of faith as *ultimate concern* has entered the theological vocabulary of our time. Religious faith, for Tillich, grows out of those experiences with which we invest ultimate value and to which we give our ultimate allegiance. Behind Tillich's assertion that religious faith is ultimate concern lie two assumptions. The first assumption is that ultimate concern is common to all religions. No matter what their differences, one's faith experience is precisely that which makes an ultimate claim on our loyalties. The second assumption is that no one is without some kind of faith in the sense of an ultimate concern.

Tillich's view enables us to understand the intensity of viewpoints that we would perhaps not ordinarily classify as religious; it also allows us to speak of "gods" of various sorts—power, wealth, ideologies, and "isms" of different kinds. We can speak of an individual consumed with a desire for monetary gain, another person with an almost fanatical desire for power or fame, still another totally consumed with the goal of national liberation or the overthrow of the current political regime. All have in common an intense desire for the success of the cause that claims their ultimate allegiance. To use Tillich's phrase, their "faith" is their ultimate concern, and like all faiths, it makes a total demand of the individual committed to it.

A study of the history of religions reveals that there is such a wide variety of objects to which human beings have attached religious importance at some time or another that virtually nothing has not in some culture been considered worthy of veneration and worship. But as humanity's collective consciousness evolved, it became obvious that stones, trees, and animals were not worthy of ultimate concern. An anthropologist studying this diversity of religious commitments with a value-free method of inquiry would not want to make any normative judgments. Tillich, however, does offer a way of judging rival faith commitments by distinguishing between *true* and *false ultimacy*. That which demands our ultimate concern must indeed be ultimate if it is worthy of our commitment. If the object of faith is not itself ultimate, then such a faith is idolatrous and can give rise to the demonic. The term *demonic* is one Tillich frequently uses to describe an ultimate commitment to that which is not ultimate, as when an individual submits to the demand of a totalitarian state for total allegiance.

It should also be obvious that a person's real faith (in the sense of ultimate concern) may not be the same as the religion to which lip service is given. A professing Christian's real faith (that is, ultimate concern) may be something quite different from the Christian religion. When we give our ultimate allegiance to something that is not ultimate, we take the risk of being disappointed, perhaps even destroyed, by the failure of our faith. It is only when we commit ourselves ultimately to what is truly ultimate that faith can be said to be genuine.

FAITH AS CENTERED ACT

Not only is it the case for Tillich that every act of faith is an act of ultimate concern; it is also apparent in his view that faith provides unity and focus to the human personality. A corollary to this is that without some sort of faith, one would be without any core of meaning to provide coherence to one's personality. Camus's absurd hero is a literary example of this sort of breakdown of human purpose. In Camus's novel *The Stranger*, Mersault is precisely the sort of individual without authentic faith commitments of any kind who is caught up in an existential vacuum from which there is no escape. It is important to note, however, that Tillich does not view faith as purely rational but rather as a response of the whole person, which includes feelings as well as reason.

FAITH AS ECSTATIC

We commonly speak of ecstasy as an intense and positive emotional experience. Certainly Tillich does not rule out the emotional element in religion, for as a response of the whole person, faith contains an emotional element. To speak of faith as ecstatic implies that faith leads the individual beyond the limitations of one aspect of the human personality. The term *ecstasy* literally means *standing outside*. An ecstatic experience is one that leads beyond the immediacy of the moment or, to use a parallel term, an experience that transcends the selfish tendencies of our nature.

A good example of the experience of ecstasy would be that of the person in love. Like faith, love has an emotional element but is more than an emotion; indeed it embraces the totality of the human personality. To experience the ecstasy of love means that an individual is led by the love experience to be directed toward something other than selfish concerns, namely, the beloved. The ecstasy of love calls the lover beyond the immediacy of self-centeredness to a someone who demands loyalty and allegiance and to whom such dedication is gladly given.

FAITH AS UNITY OF OBJECTIVE AND SUBJECTIVE

This is one of the most difficult of all the notions that Tillich discusses, but using the example just given of being in love will show how ecstasy is closely related to overcoming the distinction between the objective and the subjective. The ecstasy of being "in love" means that the individual has gone beyond self to a sense of unity with and belonging to another person. The lover's entire being takes on a new significance when in the presence of the beloved, so much so that the absence of the beloved leads to feelings of incompleteness on the lover's part. Such feelings are perhaps best expressed in poetry. Love poetry frequently speaks of the emptiness of the self when the beloved is absent. No longer does the lover feel like an independent subject distinct from an object. Indeed, the lover's whole being is encompassed by the relationship with another person; in a sense the lover is swallowed up in love and in the person loved. Being "in love," in the truest sense, is an act of commitment, though it cannot be an ultimate commitment in Tillich's sense without becoming idolatrous.

In an analogous way an individual can be swallowed up in an ideology, a nationalistic movement, desire for success, or some other finite goal, and treat this commitment with all the ultimacy that faith implies. But if the object of one's faith is not ultimate, the ultimacy attached to it not only risks becoming demonic, but will finally fail and be a disappointment. By being caught up in the ultimacy of the cause, or whatever one's ultimate concern is directed to, the individual feels at one with that to which ultimate concern is given. Like love, faith—even in its perverted form—erases the distinction between the subject and the object of faith.

FAITH AS EMBRACING THE NONRATIONAL

The Western philosophical and religious traditions have emphasized the rational aspects of our nature to such an extent that reason, argument, and logic are considered by many to be the only guarantee of truth. We tend to identify rationality as the hallmark of our humanness, and coupled with this is a parallel tendency to downplay the nonrational aspects of our nature as unable to provide any useful information about the world. To be sure, we would agree that there is a place for the emotional and noncognitive, but it is thought by many to be a small place, especially if we are concerned with defending our commitments by appealing to logical proofs. Perhaps part of our distrust of the nonrational aspects of our nature stems from our feeling that we are on much less firm ground when we leave the security of logical argument. Freud opened the pathway for psychology to explore the nonrational aspects of our psyche, but we do not have to wander in the labyrinths of the unconscious to be convinced that there is more to our humanness than merely our ability to construct logical arguments or rational proofs.

In summary, Tillich's point is that within human experience there arises something that calls for an act of ultimate commitment. In this sense, then, religious experience for Tillich is not some mystical vision of God but an experience within the ordinary world of something that elicits our ultimate concern, something to which the individual is devoted with passionate intensity and that, in turn, provides a center and focus to the individual's existence. This is an experience that everyone has, but whether one's ultimate concern is directed toward that which is really ultimate or to something that is not ultimate but falsely claims ultimacy determines whether this faith is genuine or idolatrous.

What Faith Is

PAUL TILLICH

FAITH AS ULTIMATE CONCERN

Faith is the state of being ultimately concerned: the dynamics of faith are the dynamics of man's ultimate concern. Man, like every living being, is concerned about many things, above all about those which condition his very existence, such as food and shelter. But man, in contrast to other living beings, has spiritual concerns—cognitive, aesthetic, social, political. Some of them are urgent, often extremely urgent, and each of them as well as the vital concerns can claim ultimacy for a human life or the life of a social group. If it claims ultimacy it demands the total surrender of him who accepts this claim, and it promises total fulfillment even if all other claims have to be subjected to it or rejected in its name. If a national group makes the life and growth of the nation its ultimate concern, it demands that all other concerns, economic well-being, health and life, family, aesthetic and cognitive truth, justice and humanity, be sacrificed. The extreme nationalisms of our century are laboratories for the study of what ultimate concern means in all aspects of human existence, including the smallest concern of one's daily life. Everything is centered in the only god, the nation—a god who

Source: Abridged from pp. 1–12 in *Dynamics of Faith* by Paul Tillich. Volume 10 of the World Perspective Series, ed. Ruth Nanda Anshen. Copyright © 1957 by Paul Tillich. Reprinted with permission of Harper & Row Publishers, Inc.

certainly proves to be a demon, but who shows clearly the unconditional character of an ultimate concern.

But it is not only the unconditional demand made by that which is one's ultimate concern, it is also the promise of ultimate fulfillment which is accepted in the act of faith. The content of this promise is not necessarily defined. It can be expressed in indefinite symbols or in concrete symbols which cannot be taken literally, like the "greatness" of one's nation in which one participates even if one has died for it, or the conquest of mankind by the "saving race," etc. In each of these cases it is "ultimate fulfillment" that is promised, and it is exclusion from such fulfillment which is threatened if the unconditional demand is not obeyed.

An example—and more than an example—is the faith manifest in the religion of the Old Testament. It also has the character of ultimate concern in demand, threat and promise. The content of this concern is not the nation—although Jewish nationalism has sometimes tried to distort it into that—but the content is the God of justice, who, because he represents justice for everybody and every nation, is called the universal God, the God of the universe. He is the ultimate concern of every pious Jew, and therefore in his name the great commandment is given: "You shall love the Lord your God with all your heart, and with all your soul, and with all your might" (Deut. 6:5). This is what ultimate concern means and from these words the term "ultimate concern" is derived. They state unambiguously the character of genuine faith, the demand of total surrender to the subject of ultimate concern. The Old Testament is full of commands which make the nature of this surrender concrete, and it is full of promises and threats in relation to it. Here also are the promises of symbolic indefiniteness, although they center around fulfillment of the national and individual life, and the threat is the exclusion from such fulfillment through national extinction and individual catastrophe. Faith, for the men of the Old Testament, is the state of being ultimately and unconditionally concerned about Jahweh and about what he represents in demand, threat and promise.

Another example, almost a counter-example, yet nevertheless equally revealing—is the ultimate concern with "success" and with social standing and economic power. It is the god of many people in the highly competitive Western culture and it does what every ultimate concern must do: it demands unconditional surrender to its laws even if the price is the sacrifice of genuine human relations, personal conviction, and creative *eros*. Its threat is social and economic defeat, and its promise—indefinite as all such promises—the fulfillment of one's being. It is the breakdown of this kind of faith which characterizes and makes religiously important most contemporary literature. Not false calculations but a misplaced faith is revealed in novels like *Point of No Return*. When fulfilled, the promise of this faith proves to be empty.

Faith is the state of being ultimately concerned. The content matters infinitely for the life of the believer, but it does not matter for the formal definition of faith. And this is the first step we have to make in order to understand the dynamics of faith.

FAITH AS A CENTERED ACT

Faith as ultimate concern is an act of the total personality. It happens in the center of the personal life and includes all its elements. Faith is the most centered
act of the human mind. It is not a movement of a special section or a special function of man's total being. They all are united in the act of faith. But faith is not
the sum total of their impacts. It transcends every special impact as well as the
totality of them and it has itself a decisive impact on each of them.

Since faith is an act of the personality as a whole, it participates in the dynamics of personal life. These dynamics have been described in many ways, especially in the recent developments of analytic psychology. Thinking in polarities,
their tensions and their possible conflicts, is a common characteristic of most of
them. This makes the psychology of personality highly dynamic and requires a dynamic theory of faith as the most personal of all personal acts. The first and decisive polarity in analytic psychology is that between the so-called unconscious and
the conscious. Faith as an act of the total personality is not imaginable without the
participation of the unconscious elements in the personality structure. They are always present and decide largely about the content of faith. But, on the other hand,
faith is a conscious act and the unconscious elements participate in the creation of
faith only if they are taken into the personal center which transcends each of
them. If this does not happen, if unconscious forces determine the mental status
without a centered act, faith does not occur, and compulsions take its place. For
faith is a matter of freedom. Freedom is nothing more than the possibility of centered personal acts. The frequent discussion in which faith and freedom are contrasted could be helped by the insight that faith is a free, namely, centered act of
the personality. In this respect freedom and faith are identical. . . .

This leads to the question of how faith as a personal, centered act is related
to the rational structure of man's personality which is manifest in his meaningful
language, in his ability to know the true and to do the good, in his sense of beauty
and justice. All this, and not only his possibility to analyze, to calculate and to
argue, makes him a rational being. But in spite of this larger concept of reason we
must deny that man's essential nature is identical with the rational character of
his mind. Man is able to decide for or against reason, he is able to create beyond
reason or to destroy below reason. This power is the power of his self, the center
of self-relatedness in which all elements of his being are united. Faith is not an
act of any of his rational functions, as it is not an act of the unconscious, but it
is an act in which both the rational and the nonrational elements of his being are
transcended.

Faith as the embracing and centered act of the personality is "ecstatic." It
transcends both the drives of the nonrational unconscious and the structures of
the rational conscious. It transcends them, but it does not destroy them. The
ecstatic character of faith does not exclude its rational character although it is
not identical with it, and it includes nonrational strivings without being identical with them. In the ecstasy of faith there is an awareness of truth and of ethical value; there are also past loves and hates, conflicts and reunions, individual

and collective influences. "Ecstasy" means "standing outside of oneself"—without ceasing to be oneself—with all the elements which are united in the personal center.

A further polarity in these elements, relevant for the understanding of faith, is the tension between the cognitive function of man's personal life, on the one hand, and emotion and will, on the other hand. In a later discussion I will try to show that many distortions of the meaning of faith are rooted in the attempt to subsume faith to the one or the other of these functions. At this point it must be stated as sharply and insistently as possible that in every act of faith there is cognitive affirmation, not as the result of an independent process of inquiry but as an inseparable element in a total act of acceptance and surrender. This also excludes the idea that faith is the result of an independent act of "will to believe." There is certainly affirmation by the will of what concerns one ultimately, but faith is not a creation of the will. In the ecstasy of faith the will to accept and to surrender is an element, but not the cause. And this is true also of feeling. Faith is not an emotional outburst: this is not the meaning of ecstasy. Certainly, emotion is in it, as in every act of man's spiritual life. But emotion does not produce faith. Faith has a cognitive content and is an act of the will. It is the unity of every element in the centered self. Of course, the unity of all elements in the act of faith does not prevent one or the other element from dominating in a special form of faith. It dominates the character of faith but it does not create the act of faith.

This also answers the question of a possible psychology of faith. Everything that happens in man's personal being can become an object of psychology. And it is rather important for both the philosopher of religion and the practical minister to know how the act of faith is embedded in the totality of psychological processes. But in contrast to this justified and desirable form of a psychology of faith there is another one which tries to derive faith from something that is not faith but is most frequently fear. The presupposition of this method is that fear or something else from which faith is derived is more original and basic than faith. But this presupposition cannot be proved. On the contrary, one can prove that in the scientific method which leads to such consequences faith is already effective. Faith precedes all attempts to derive it from something else, because these attempts are themselves based on faith.

THE SOURCE OF FAITH

We have described the act of faith and its relation to the dynamics of personality. Faith is a total and centered act of the personal self, the act of unconditional, infinite and ultimate concern. The question now arises: what is the source of this all-embracing and all-transcending concern? The word "concern" points to two sides of a relationship, the relation between the one who is concerned and his concern. In both respects we have to imagine man's situation in itself and in his world. The reality of man's ultimate concern reveals something about his being, namely, that he is able to transcend the flux of relative and transitory experiences

of his ordinary life. Man's experiences, feelings, thoughts are conditioned and finite. They not only come and go, but their content is of finite and conditional
concern—unless they are elevated to unconditional validity. But this presupposes
the general possibility of doing so; it presupposes the element of infinity in man.
Man is able to understand in an immediate personal and central act the meaning
of the ultimate, the unconditional, the absolute, the infinite. This alone makes
faith a human potentiality.

Human potentialities are powers that drive toward actualization. Man is driven toward faith by his awareness of the infinite to which he belongs, but which
he does not own like a possession. This is in abstract terms what concretely appears as the "restlessness of the heart" within the flux of life.

The unconditional concern which is faith is the concern about the unconditional. The infinite passion, as faith has been described, is the passion for the
infinite. Or, to use our first term, the ultimate concern is concern about what is
experienced as ultimate. In this way we have turned from the subjective meaning
of faith as a centered act of the personality to its objective meaning, to what is
meant in the act of faith. It would not help at this point of our analysis to call
that which is meant in the act of faith "God" or "a god." For at this step we ask:
What in the idea of God constitutes divinity? The answer is: It is the element of
the unconditional and of ultimacy. This carries the quality of divinity. If this is
seen, one can understand why almost every thing "in heaven and on earth" has
received ultimacy in the history of human religion. But we also can understand
that a critical principle was and is at work in man's religious consciousness,
namely, that which is really ultimate over against what claims to be ultimate but
is only preliminary, transitory, finite.

The term "ultimate concern" unites the subjective and the objective side of
the act of faith—the *fides qua creditur* (the faith through which one believes) and
the *fides quae creditur* (the faith which is believed). The first is the classical term
for the centered act of the personality, the ultimate concern. The second is the
classical term for that toward which this act is directed, the ultimate itself, expressed in symbols of the divine. This distinction is very important, but not ultimately so, for the one side cannot be without the other. There is no faith without
a content toward which it is directed. There is always something meant in the act
of faith. And there is no way of having the content of faith except in the act of
faith. All speaking about divine matters which is not done in the state of ultimate
concern is meaningless. Because that which is meant in the act of faith cannot
be approached in any other way than through an act of faith.

In terms like ultimate, unconditional, infinite, absolute, the difference between subjectivity and objectivity is overcome. The ultimate of the act of faith
and the ultimate that is meant in the act of faith are one and the same. This is
symbolically expressed by the mystics when they say that their knowledge of
God is the knowledge God has of himself; and it is expressed by Paul when he
says (I Cor. 13) that he will know as he is known, namely, by God. God never
can be object without being at the same time subject. Even a successful prayer

is, according to Paul (Rom. 8), not possible without God as Spirit praying within us. The same experience expressed in abstract language is the disappearance of the ordinary subject-object scheme in the experience of the ultimate, the unconditional. In the act of faith that which is the source of this act is present beyond the cleavage of subject and object. It is present as both and beyond both.

This character of faith gives an additional criterion for distinguishing true and false ultimacy. The finite which claims infinity without having it (as, e.g., a nation or success) is not able to transcend the subject-object scheme. It remains an object which the believer looks at as a subject. He can approach it with ordinary knowledge and subject it to ordinary handling. There are, of course, many degrees in the endless realm of false ultimacies. The nation is nearer to true intimacy than is success. Nationalistic ecstasy can produce a state in which the subject is almost swallowed by the object. But after a period the subject emerges again, disappointed radically and totally, and by looking at the nation in a skeptical and calculating way does injustice even to its justified claims. The more idolatrous a faith the less it is able to overcome the cleavage between subject and object. For that is the difference between true and idolatrous faith. In true faith the ultimate concern is a concern about the truly ultimate; while in idolatrous faith preliminary, finite realities are elevated to the rank of ultimacy. The inescapable consequence of idolatrous faith is "existential disappointment," a disappointment which penetrates into the very existence of man! This is the dynamics of idolatrous faith: that it is faith, and as such, the centered act of a personality; that the centering point is something which is more or less on the periphery; and that, therefore, the act of faith leads to a loss of the center and to a disruption of the personality. The ecstatic character of even an idolatrous faith can hide this consequence only for a certain time. But finally it breaks into the open.

Discussion Questions

1. In identifying faith with a person's ultimate concern, Tillich seems to be saying that everyone has a faith of some kind. Do you find this way of defining faith so broadly that everyone has it a good thing or not? Give reasons for your answer.

2. Do you agree that without the centering act that faith is thought to be, one's personality will have no focus and will be in danger of collapse in the face of trial and hardship? What are your reasons?

3. On the basis of Tillich's analysis, would you agree that human beings have a basic need for religion? If your answer is yes, how is one to distinguish between good and bad religious commitments?

4. Given Tillich's analysis, do you find that the term *idolatry* can be useful in understanding the appeal that many secular movements seem to have? If not, why not? If your answer is yes, can you give some examples?

5. If you were to apply Tillich's analysis to your own experience, what would you say it is that has a specifically religious meaning for you?

RETROSPECTIVE

Faith and Reason

We have looked at several different attitudes toward the relation between faith and reason. Antony Flew suggests that in the face of insufficient evidence, a person must give up the religious hypothesis. There is just too much about the world that seems to count against belief in a loving God, and if the believer persists in faith in spite of the preponderance of evidence by repeatedly qualifying the original belief, then it "dies the death of a thousand qualifications." Stubborn refusal to abandon a belief is evidence of a refusal to be rational about such matters.

William James explores both the logical and the psychological dimensions of faith and points out that faith in God, or the denial of God's existence, is a forced option. This leads him to reject the agnostic position of Huxley and Clifford as really atheism in disguise. James holds that in matters of both faith and morals we have to make decisions without completely adequate evidence, and it is simply the nature of our human situation that in these cases our will guides us when reason cannot.

Kierkegaard takes an even stronger position: Faith is essentially a risk, and as long as a person persists in believing, there is risk. "If I wish to preserve myself in faith," Kierkegaard says, "I must constantly be intent upon holding fast the objective uncertainty, so as to remain out upon the deep, over seventy thousand fathoms of water, still preserving my faith."

It should now be obvious to you that two different attitudes have emerged, reflecting the two poles of the reason-faith question. On the one hand is *rationalism*, the view that truth in religion (or in all matters) must be based on reason and not on faith. On the other hand is *fideism*, which is the view that truth in religion is based on faith rather than on reasoning and evidence.

The force of James's analysis is to insist that we cannot avoid the issue of faith or unbelief, and that showing a skeptical attitude toward religious belief is no proof that one acts any more rationally than those who believe. "To preach skepticism to us as a duty until 'sufficient evidence' for religion be found," he observes, "is tantamount therefore to telling us that to yield to our fear of its being error is wiser and better than to yield to our hope that it may be true." Finally we see in Tillich's identification of faith as ultimate concern the impossibility of avoiding the issue. Each of us has a "faith," whether religious or not.

Another problem raised by our study of faith and reason is the language of religion. This issue is addressed in the Flew-Hare-Mitchell discussion when Flew claims that statements of religious belief are not really assertions at all, but pseudoassertions, a kind of "doublethink" to which the ordinary standards of meaningfulness do not apply. So there is a cluster of concerns about language that have to be faced: Do we use language in the same way when speaking about God as when speaking of things in the world? If not, how is religious language different from ordinary language? Is religious language a kind of poetry? How do we distinguish meaningful religious statements from nonsense? These are just some of the issues that we will consider in the next section.

ADDITIONAL READINGS

The problem of both verification and falsification of religious statements is discussed in nontechnical terms in Chapter 6 of John Hick, *Philosophy of Religion*, 4th ed., Foundations of Philosophy Series (Upper Saddle River, NJ: Prentice Hall, 1990). Two other excellent sources also by Hick are his *Faith and Knowledge*, 2d ed. (Ithaca, NY: Cornell University Press, 1966), and the article on "Faith," *The Encyclopedia of Philosophy* (1967), 3, 165–69.

A general source for information on all religious topics is William H. Gentz, ed., *The Dictionary of Bible and Religion* (Nashville, TN: Abingdon Press, 1986). Twenty philosophers give accounts of their own personal journey to religious belief and, in the process, address the role of arguments and reason in the development of faith in a work edited by Thomas V. Morris, *God and the Philosophers: The Reconciliation of Faith and Reason* (New York: Oxford University Press, 1994). Paul Tillich's thought is comprehensively displayed in *The Essential Tillich: An Anthology of the Writings of Paul Tillich*, edited by F. Forrester Church (Chicago: University of Chicago Press, 1999).

CHAPTER SEVEN

RELIGIOUS LANGUAGE

INTRODUCTION

Religion and Language

Ordinary language is pretty messy, and philosophers tend to want to tidy things up. The reason for this is not just a desire for neatness, but the conviction that language is reason's tool, and the misuse of language can lead to faulty thinking. Philosophers therefore include in their concerns the study of language—its nature, its function, and its limitations. All this concern has had implications for the language of religion, for the question is whether language functions in a special way when applied to religious matters, a way different from its ordinary function.

Just as our investigation of the arguments for the existence of God led to a consideration of the relation between faith and reason, the question of faith and reason leads to a consideration of the nature of religious language. The close relation between reason and language is seen even in the origin of the terms. In Greek—the language of the earliest Western philosophers—*logos* meant *word* but was also extended to include the rational function of speech and the rational element in thought. Hence the term *logos* came to mean both *reason* and *word*, and from this Greek root we get the English term *logic*. One of the important functions of philosophy is to investigate the structure of correct reasoning, and this leads to a study of the way language should function in order to reflect the logical modes of thought.

Why is there a problem of specifically *religious* language? We have already glimpsed something of the nature of the problem in Antony Flew's suggestion that statements of religious belief are not genuine assertions at all, but a kind of "double-think." Flew's views reflect a tradition going back to Immanuel Kant, who thinks that such concepts as *cause*, *substance*, and *relation* function perfectly well when we are dealing with matters of sense experience, but that we have no justification for applying these concepts to transcendent realities. Kant concludes that when we use language that is not tied directly to sense experience, we are dealing only with a kind of speculative thought, most of which cannot be said to be knowledge. The question of the meaningfulness of religious language is raised squarely in the discussion between A. J. Ayer and F. C. Copleston, the first selection in this chapter. Ayer doubts the legitimacy of the language used in traditional metaphysical inquiry, and this includes all religious discourse as well. Copleston, in turn, attacks Ayer's conception of philosophy as being too narrow and defends the use of language referring to realities that lie beyond the bounds of sense.

Those who defend the meaningfulness of religious language recognize that there are problems to be resolved, for there are two separate, though related, issues that emerge from the consideration of religious language: First, does language function differently when it is used to make statements about God? Second, how are we to distinguish false statements about God from true ones? In a sense, the answer to the first question is both yes and no. Certainly, we use the same language in speaking of religious matters that we use in referring to human experience, since it is the only language we have at our disposal. But it is also apparent that statements made about God, for example, do not use ordinary language in ordinary ways. One traditional affirmation is that God is incorporeal, that is, God does not have a body or bodily form. To use the language of Scripture, God is spirit. But biblical writers also claim that God is loving and that God is the source of knowledge and wisdom, and they even speak of God in terms of bodily parts—the "arm" of the Lord is sure, the "eye" of God is steadfast, and so forth. How can such language, when used in reference to a pure spirit, mean anything? Or if it does have meaning, what sort of meaning does this language have?

The term used to describe this function of language when applied beyond its literal meaning is *anthropomorphism*, from the Greek words *anthropos* (man) and *morphe* (form). In general, anthropomorphic language speaks in human terms of that which is not human. To speak of the "arm" of God, or the "finger" of God, or the "eye" of the Lord is to speak anthropomorphically, as is to speak of God's being jealous, angry, or possessing knowledge and wisdom. All these mental and physical characteristics are derived from human experience and are applied to God in a nonliteral way. It is important to note that anthropomorphism is not limited to religious discourse but is also present in the literature of imagination and fantasy. Part of the delight of Tolkien's Hobbit stories is the attractiveness of intelligent, talking animals with human form, as is also the case with C. S. Lewis's *Chronicles of Narnia*. And, of course, there would be no poetry if we were limited to merely the literal use of language, for the stock-in-trade of poets is simile, metaphor, symbol, and analogy, those special uses of language that enrich our discourse and enliven our sensibilities.

We might include all these nonliteral uses of language under the rubric *poetic function of language*. This sort of language is the concern of literary critics and rhetoricians, but the old Greek rhetorical tradition took the view that all such nonliteral uses of language are merely ornaments, and that the *meaning* of poetic discourse could perfectly well be translated into ordinary language. This has also been argued by those who view the symbolic and poetic aspects of language as simply a delight to the emotions that adds nothing to our understanding. Thus, the line "My love is like a red, red rose" literally means something like "My love is pleasing to me as a beautiful flower is pleasing to me." You might test this theory yourself by taking your favorite poem, translating it into ordinary language, and then judging whether you have actually captured the meaning the poet had in mind.

Most philosophers who defend the meaningfulness of religious language have nonetheless concluded that language used to talk about God is different from language used literally. If religious language is nonliteral, can there be truth in religious discourse, and if so, how do we determine it? This is the second of our questions. If we are to be philosophical about the question, we cannot ignore the issue of the truth of language, regardless of the context in which it is used. But how are we to determine the truth of nonliteral discourse? To put the question back into the context of poetry, can a poem be true or false? If so, how do we determine it? Or to state the matter even more boldly, who gives the "true" description of a rainbow, the poet who writes a poem about it or the physicist who explains that the various colors, the wavelengths of which can be measured exactly, are due to the refraction of light caused by water particles in the air?

A simple answer to this question, and one that might at first appear attractive, is that the poet does not extend our knowledge at all, but only appeals to our feelings, whereas the physicist extends our knowledge of physical reality. But is it really the case that poets do not expand our awareness—indeed, our knowledge—of reality? It could be argued that a poet makes us aware of levels of reality of which we were previously unaware by calling our attention to things in a new and significant way. The physicist, to be sure, deals with reality, too, but only in a limited and partial way with talk about observable and measurable quantities.

This is the constellation of questions around which the readings in this chapter revolve. The first reading is a discussion between F. C. Copleston, who defends the meaningfulness of religious language, and A. J. Ayer, who argues that religious language, while perhaps providing emotional satisfaction, cannot be cognitively meaningful.

The Verification
of Religious Language

In the Middle Ages, philosophy was viewed as the "handmaiden of theology." Its principal function was thought to be the elucidation and examination of theological statements, and its usefulness was defended only insofar as it was applicable to theological concerns. Although our world view has changed since the Middle Ages, there are still philosophers who defend philosophy's handmaidenly role, no longer to theology, but to science. Early in the twentieth century the view became prevalent that, insofar as it claims to deal with truth, philosophy has no independent method of its own distinct from that of the natural sciences. Philosophy's role was thought to be mainly that of analyzing various concepts in science, and if it had an independent contribution to make, it would be in the area of logic and logical analysis.

This view has its roots in the thought of the philosopher Auguste Comte, who suggests that in the development of thought there have been three discernible stages. The first he calls the *theological* stage, in which explanations of natural occurrences are made in terms of divine or supernatural forces. The next stage is the *metaphysical*, in which abstract principles replace divine forces as principles of explanation. The third and final stage Comte calls the *positive* stage, and he argues that the modern age has squarely entered into it. Today the method of inquiry is that of science, and all natural occurrences are explained by observation, without appeal to either supernatural forces or abstract metaphysical principles. Adopting this Comtian language, the term *positivism* is applied to the view that rejects religion and metaphysics in favor of a scientific model of philosophy. Though there are different forms of positivism, all positivists reject religious language as being unscientific and having no place within philosophy.

In *Language, Truth and Logic*, A. J. Ayer outlines a form of positivism that he calls *logical positivism*, intending by this label to include within the scope of his method the substantial advances made in the discipline of symbolic logic as a tool of analysis. Sometimes the philosophical approach Ayer represents is referred to as *logical empiricism*, which underscores the empiricist approach to truth. Ayer stresses as a central tenet the principle of verification. According to this principle, a statement is meaningful if and only if it is verifiable. As Ayer developed his view, it turned out that there are only two classes of statements that can be verified: logical truths, including mathematical statements; and empirical statements, sometimes called observation statements.

In the discussion that follows, the term *proposition* is used frequently, a term we previously encountered in the discussion of Flew's falsifiability principle. A proposition is an assertion that has a truth value; that is, a statement asserts a proposition if the statement can be shown to be either true or false. The method for determining the truth value of a proposition, according to Ayer, is based on the principle of verification. The first class of propositions that can be verified is those that depend for their truth on the conventions of a logical system. Mathematical statements, such as, "Triangles have three sides," are of this kind. Those statements in ordinary language, the truth of which can be determined solely by analysis of the meaning of the terms in the statement, also qualify as propositions. Examples are such statements as "All bachelors are males," and "Every father is a parent." In each of these statements, truth or falsity is determined solely by an analysis of the meaning of the terms.

Empirical statements, or observation statements, are the second class of verifiable statements. Empirical statements, unlike analytic statements, are contingently true or false, and the only way to discover their truth value is by means of observation. If someone says, "The temperature is 70°F in this room," the only way to determine whether the statement is true or false is to look at a reliable thermometer. If we say, "Caesar crossed the Rubicon," we cannot verify the truth of this statement directly, but by appealing to the records of antiquity, we can examine the observation statements of others. And since crossing a river is a perfectly ordinary human activity that does not defy the normal workings of nature, there is no added barrier to accepting the historical evidence supporting this statement. According to Ayer, these two classes of statements—analytic statements and empirically testable statements—exhaust the range of what is meaningful. If a statement cannot be shown to be of either type, it is meaningless.

The implication of the principle of verification for religious language is that, since the usual range of utterances in religion are not analytic or empirically testable, they must be dismissed as being without meaning. We can also see how Ayer's view differs from those of the traditional atheist or theist. Consider the statement "God exists." The atheist would deny the truth of this statement and claim that it is false. The theist claims that it is true. Ayer's response to both is that neither can prove the truth or falsity of the statement, since it deals with a reality beyond human experience. The statement, therefore, has no meaning at all. The agnostic's position is hardly any more defensible, in Ayer's view, than those of the theist and atheist. The agnostic errs in not simply rejecting the statement as having no meaning; to suspend judgment is to treat a religious statement as meaningful, which Ayer refuses to do.

There is a certain tidiness about Ayer's view. Immediately dismissed are all the metaphysical wrangles that have occurred in the history of philosophy. Also dismissed as meaningless is much of the language of ethics and esthetics. Philosophy would have a narrowed function—dealing principally with logical analysis—but at least a defensible function, and one that shares the respectable aura of science as well.

The following discussion makes it evident that one of the main disagreements between the two participants is over the nature of philosophy, and philosophy is perhaps unique among human disciplines in that one of the central items of philosophical concern is its own nature. F. C. Copleston rejects Ayer's narrowed definition of philosophy and argues that philosophy should include metaphysical inquiry as well as logical analysis. The issue of metaphysical analysis pinpoints a fundamental difference between the two. Copleston understands "metaphysical reality" as referring to a "being which in principle (and not merely in fact) transcends the sphere of what can be sensibly experienced." Ayer, in contrast, defines metaphysics as "an attempt to gain knowledge about the world by non-scientific means." If we accept Ayer's definition of metaphysics, and if philosophy has no method different from that of the natural sciences, then obviously metaphysics is excluded from philosophical investigation. Copleston even suggests that the principle of verification "seems to have been formulated to rule out metaphysics." Ayer's response is that acceptance of his principle of verification rescues philosophical statements from becoming either meaningless or trivial.

As the discussion unfolds, you will be able to see clearly the difference between the two views of the nature of philosophy. But there are other issues that arise as well, such as the status of the principle of verification. Since proposed by Ayer, the principle itself has undergone considerable philosophical scrutiny and has been attacked by other philosophers as an inadequate criterion of meaningfulness.[1] Copleston mentions two of the usual sorts of attacks made against the principle. The first has to do with a class of statements that are not verifiable under the criteria of the principle of verification, but would be considered by most persons as meaningful. The example Copleston gives is the statement "Atomic warfare will take place and it will blot out the entire human race." The statement seems to be perfectly meaningful, but it is not in principle verifiable, since were it true, there would be no one around to verify it. Ayer admits that this statement is not "practically" verifiable, although he insists that it describes "a possible situation." This response underscores a fundamental disagreement between Ayer and Copleston. Ayer assumes that unless something is capable of being experienced, it is meaningless to attempt to talk about it. This, of course,

---

[1] For a rigorous critique of both the principle of verification and the principle of falsification, see Carl Hempel, "The Empiricist Criterion of Meaning," in *Classics of Analytic Philosophy*, ed. Robert Ammerman (New York: McGraw-Hill, 1965), pp. 218–221.

is precisely what Copleston denies. God, by definition, is beyond the reach of our senses, and talk about God cannot even in principle be verified by means of the criteria used for verifying statements about the world of the senses.

The second criticism of the verification principle leveled by Copleston is the status of the principle itself. Let's take Ayer's formulation of the principle of verification: "to be significant a statement must be either on the one hand a formal statement . . . or on the other hand empirically testable." Is this statement verifiable by its own criteria? Let's see. Is it an analytic truth? Hardly. There is nothing in the meaning of the terms used in this statement that shows it to be necessarily true. Then, is it empirically testable? It is difficult to see just how it could be tested. Accordingly, Copleston charges that the principle of verification cannot be verified by its own criteria and therefore must be considered meaningless. Ayer responds that the principle has the status of a "persuasive definition," but a person who sees philosophy's task as broader than Ayer does is not likely to be persuaded by it. By limiting the range of philosophical inquiry, the principle of verification makes philosophy's task less formidable, but for Copleston such a move eliminates many of philosophy's important concerns.

Copleston admits that logical analysis, in Ayer's sense of the term, is a valuable role for philosophy, but maintains that it is not philosophy's only task. Copleston would also admit that some metaphysical statements are meaningless, and he would add that if we are to talk meaningfully about God, we must begin with human experience—with the world—and argue from this to God as its cause. We will also be forced to use language analogically and be prepared to defend the use of this kind of language with well-argued principles. All this seems too vague and sloppy for Ayer, and he rejects any kind of philosophical inquiry that cuts itself loose from logic and analysis of obervational statements.

Few philosophers today would accept the title *logical positivist* with its principle of verification, for subsequent analysis of this criterion of meaningfulness has shown it to be inadequate.[2] On the other hand, the view persists among some philosophers that metaphysics in the sense that Copleston defends it is not a legitimate area of inquiry. Part of the reason for this may be due to the prestige of science and to the fact that many philosophers feel more comfortable devoting their attention to logical analysis than to traditional metaphysical speculation. Regardless of their views on the nature of philosophical inquiry, most philosophers would agree that an investigation into the nature and function of language is a fruitful—indeed, a necessary—task if religious discourse is to be shown to be meaningful. It is for this reason that the other readings in this chapter will investigate the precise nature of religious discourse in an effort to understand better how the language of religion functions.

---

[2] John Passmore gives an excellent summary of the background and present status of logical positivism in his article "Logical Positivism," *The Encyclopedia of Philosophy* (1967), 5, pp. 52–57.

A Discussion
on Religious Language

A. J. AYER AND F. C. COPLESTON

AYER: Well, Father Copleston, you've asked me to summarize logical positivism for you, and it's not very easy. For one thing, as I understand it, logical positivism isn't a system of philosophy; it consists, rather, in a certain technique, a certain kind of attitude towards philosophical problems. Perhaps one thing which those of us who are called logical positivists tend to have in common is that we deny the possibility of philosophy as a speculative discipline. We should say that if philosophy was to be a branch of knowledge as distinct from the sciences it would have to consist in logic or in some form of analysis; and our reason for this would be somewhat as follows.

We maintain that you can divide propositions into two classes—formal and empirical. Formal propositions, like those of logic and mathematics, depend for their validity on the conventions of a symbol system. Empirical propositions, on the other hand, are statements of observation—actual or possible—or hypotheses from which such statements can be logically derived; and it is they that constitute science insofar as science isn't purely mathematical. Now our contention is that this exhausts the field of what we may call speculative knowledge. Consequently we reject metaphysics, if this be understood—and I think it commonly has been—as an attempt to gain knowledge about the world by non-scientific means. Inasmuch as metaphysical statements are not testable by observation, we hold they're not descriptive of anything; and from this we should conclude that if philosophy is to be a cognitive activity, it must be purely critical. It would take the form of trying to elucidate the concepts that were used in science and mathematics or in everyday language.

COPLESTON: Well, Professor Ayer, I can quite understand, of course, philosophers confining themselves to logical analysis if they wish to do so, and I shouldn't dream of denying or of belittling in any way its utility; I think it's obviously an extremely useful thing to do, to analyze and clarify the concepts used in science. In everyday life, too, there are many terms used that practically have taken on an emotional connotation—"progressive," or "reactionary," or "freedom," or "the modern mind." To make clear to people what's meant—or what *they* mean—by

Source: This discussion was transcribed from a broadcast by the British Broadcasting Corporation and is used by permission of Professor Sir Alfred Ayer and Father Frederick Copleston, S.J.

those terms, or the various possible meanings, is a very useful thing. But if the logical positivist means that logical analysis is the *only* function of philosophy, that's the point at which I should disagree with him; and so would many other philosophers disagree, especially, I think, on the Continent.

Don't you think that by saying what philosophy is one presupposes a philosophy or takes up a position as a philosopher? For example, if one divides significant propositions into two classes—namely, purely formal propositions and statements of observation—one is adopting a philosophical position, one is claiming that there are no necessary propositions which are not purely formal. Moreover, to claim that metaphysical propositions to be significant should be verifiable as scientific hypotheses are verifiable is to claim that metaphysics—to be significant—should not be metaphysics.

AYER: Oh, I agree that my position is philosophical, though not that it's metaphysical, as I hope to show later. To say what philosophy is is certainly a philosophical act, but this I mean is itself a question of philosophical analysis. We have to decide, among other things, what it is we're going to call philosophy—and I've given you my answer. It is not, perhaps, an obvious answer, but it at least has the merit that it rescues philosophical statements from becoming either meaningless or trivial. . . .

COPLESTON: . . . Well, perhaps we'd better attend to your principle of verifiability. You mentioned the principle of verification earlier. I thought possibly you'd state it. Professor, would you?

AYER: Yes, I'll state it in a very loose form; namely that to be significant a statement must be either on the one hand a formal statement—one that I should call analytic—or on the other hand empirically testable. I should try to derive this principle by an analysis of understanding. I should say that understanding a statement meant knowing what would be the case if it were true. Knowing what would be the case if it were true means knowing what observations would verify it. And this in turn means being disposed to accept some situations as warranting the acceptance or rejection of the statement in question. From which there are two corollaries. One—which we've been talking about to some extent—: The statements to which no situations are relevant one way or the other are ruled out as nonfactual. And, secondly, the contents of the statement, the cash value, to use James's term, consists of a range of situations, experiences, that would substantiate or refute it.

COPLESTON: Thank you. Now I don't want to misinterpret your position, but it does seem to me that we're supposing a certain philosophical position. What I mean is this. If you say that any factual statement, in order to be meaningful, must be verifiable, and if you mean, by verifiable, verifiable by sense experience, then surely you are presupposing that all reality is given in sense experience. If you are presupposing this, you are presupposing that there can be no such thing as metaphysical reality, and if you presuppose this you are presupposing a philosophical position which cannot be demonstrated by the principle of verification. It seems to me that logical positivism claims to be what I might call a neutral technique, whereas in reality it presupposes the truth of positivism. And please pardon my saying so, but it looks to me as though the principle of verifiability was cogitated partly in order to exclude metaphysical propositions from the range of meaningful propositions.

AYER: Even if that were so it doesn't prove anything, really. But to go back. I certainly shouldn't make any statement about all reality. That's precisely the kind of statement I use my principle in order not to make. Nor do I wish to restrict experience to sense experience. I shouldn't at all mind counting what might be called introspectable experiences or feelings; mystical experiences, if you like.

It would be true then that people who haven't had certain experiences won't understand propositions which refer to them, but that I don't mind either. I can quite well believe that your experience is different from mine. Let's assume, which is after all an empirical assumption, that you even have a sense difference from mine. I should then be in the position of a blind man, and I should admit that statements that are unintelligible to me might be meaningful to you. But I should then go on to say that the factual content of your statement was determined by your experiences—which contents are verifiers or falsifiers.

COPLESTON: Yes, you include introspection, and just assumed it, but my point is that you assumed that a factually informative statement is significant only if it is verifiable—at least in principle—by direct observation. Now obviously the existence of a metaphysical reality is not verifiable by direct observation unless you're willing to recognize a purely intellectual intuition as observation. I'm not very keen on appealing to intuition, though I see no compelling reason to rule it out from the beginning. However, if you mean, by verifiable, verifiable by direct sense observation, and/or by introspection, you seem to me to be ruling out metaphysics from the start. In other words, I suggest that acceptance of the principle of verification, as you appear to understand it, implies the acceptance of philosophical positivism. I think I should probably be prepared to accept the principle if it were understood in a very wide sense—that is, if verifiable by experience is understood as including intellectual intuition, and also as meaning simply that some experience, actual or conceivable, is relevant to the truth or falsity of the proposition concerned. But what I object to is any statement of the principle which tacitly assumes the validity of the definite philosophical position. Now you've made a distinction, I think, between the analytic statements, on the one hand, and the empirical statements, and the metaphysical and ethical statements on the other. Or at any rate the metaphysical statements—let's leave ethical out of it. You call the first group cognitive statements and the second emotive. Is that so?

AYER: I think the word "emotive" isn't very happy, though I've used it in the past, and I suggest I make it "emotion," which isn't necessarily the case. But I accept what you say if you mean by emotive simply not cognitive.

COPLESTON: Very well, I accept, of course, your substitution of noncognitive for emotive, but my objection still remains that by cognitive statements I presume that you mean statements which satisfy the criterion of meaning—that is to say, the principle of verifiability; and by noncognitive statements I presume you mean statements which do not satisfy that criterion. If this is so, it seems to me that when you say that metaphysical statements are non-cognitive you are not saying much more than that statements which do not satisfy the principle of verification do not satisfy the principle of verification. In this case, however, no conclusion follows as to the significance or non-significance of metaphysical propositions, unless, indeed, one has previously accepted your philosophical position—that is to say, unless one has assumed that they are non-significant.

AYER: It's not so simple as that. My procedure is this. I shall claim that the account I have given you of what understanding a statement is . . . does apply to ordinary common-sense statements and scientific statements. So I'd give a different account of how a mathematical statement functions, and a different account again of value judgment.

COPLESTON: Yes.

AYER: I then say that statements which don't satisfy these conditions are not significant, not to be understood; and I think you can quite correctly object that by putting my definitions together all I come down to saying is that statements that are not scientific or common-sense statements are not scientific or common-sense statements. But then I want to go further and say that I totally fail to understand—and, again, I'm afraid I'm using my own sense of understanding; what else can I do?—I fail to understand what these other non-scientific statements and non-common-sense statements, which don't satisfy these criteria, propose to be. Someone may say he does understand them, in some sense of understanding other than the one I've defined. I reply: It's not clear to me what that sense of understanding is, nor, a fortiori, what it is he understands, nor how these statements function. But of course you may still say that in making it a question of how these statements function I'm presupposing my own criterion.

COPLESTON: Well, then, in your treatment of metaphysical propositions you are either applying the criterion of verifiability or you are not. If you are, then the significance of metaphysical propositions would seem to be ruled out of court a priori, since the truth of the principle, as it seems to be understood by you, inevitably involves the non-significance of metaphysical propositions. In this case the application of the criterion to concrete metaphysical propositions constitutes a proof neither of the non-significance of metaphysical propositions nor of the truth of the principle. All that is shown, it seems to me, is that metaphysical propositions do not satisfy a definite assumed criterion of meaning. But it does not follow that one has to accept that criterion of meaning. You may legitimately say, if you like, "I will accept as significant factual statements only those statements which satisfy these particular demands or conditions." But it doesn't follow, does it, that I or anybody else has to make those particular demands before we are prepared to accept a statement as meaningful?

AYER: What I do is to give a definition of certain related terms: "understanding," "meaningful," and so on. I can't possibly accept them, either. But I can perhaps make you unhappy about the consequences of not accepting them. What I should do is this. I should take any given proposition, and show how it functions. In the case of a scientific hypothesis, I would show that it had a certain function—namely, that, with other premises, you could deduce certain observational consequences from it. I should then say this is how this proposition works. This is what it does, this is what it amounts to. I then take mathematical propositions and play a slightly different game with them, and show that they function in a certain way, in a calculus, in a symbolic system. You then present me with these other statements, and I say: On the one hand, they have no observational consequences. On the other hand, they aren't statements of logic. All right. So you understand them. I have given a definition of understanding according to which they are not, in my usage of the term, capable of being understood. Nevertheless, you reject my definition; you are perfectly entitled to, because you can give understanding a different meaning if you like. I can't stop you. But now I say: Tell me more about them. In what sense are they understood? They are not understood in my sense. They aren't parts of a symbolic system. You can't do anything with them in the sense of deriving any observational consequences from them. What do you want to say about them? Well, you may just want to say they're facts or something of that sort. Then again I press you on your use of the word "facts."

COPLESTON: You seem to me to be demanding that in order for a factual statement to be significant, one must be able to deduce observational consequences from it. But I don't see why that should be so. If you mean directly observable consequences, you appear to me to be demanding too much. In any case, are there some propositions which are not verifiable, even in principle, but which would yet be considered by most people to have meaning and to be either true or false? Let me give an example. I don't want to assume the mantle of a prophet, and I hope the statement is quite false. But it is this. "Atomic warfare will take place and it will blot out the entire human race." Now, most people would think that this statement has meaning. It means what it says. But how could it possibly be verified empirically? Supposing it were fulfilled; the last man could not say with his last breath, "Copleston's prediction has been verified," because he would not be entitled to say this until he was dead—that is, until he was no longer in a position to verify the statement.

AYER: It is certainly practically unverifiable. You can't be a man surviving all men. On the other hand, there's no doubt it describes a possible situation. Putting the observer outside the story, one knows quite well what it would be like to observe devastation and fail to observe any men. Now it wouldn't necessarily be the case that, in order to do that, one had to observe oneself. Just as, to take the case of the past, there were dinosaurs before there were men. Clearly, no man saw that, and clearly I, if I am the speaker, I can't myself verify it, but one knows what it would be like to have observed animals and not to have observed men.

COPLESTON: The two cases are different. In regard to the past, we have empirical evidence. For example, we have fossils of dinosaurs. But in the case of the prediction I mentioned, there would be nobody to observe the evidence and so to verify the proposition.

AYER: In terms of the evidence, of course, it becomes very much easier for me. That would be too easy a way of getting out of our difficulty, because there is also evidence for the atomic thing.

COPLESTON: Yes, but there would be no evidence for the prediction that it will blot out the human race, even if one can imagine the state of affairs that would verify it. Thus by imagining it, one's imagining oneself into the. . . .

AYER: No, no.

COPLESTON: Yes, yes. One can imagine the evidence and one can imagine oneself verifying it; but in point of fact, if the prediction were fulfilled, there would be no one there to verify it. By importing yourself imaginatively into the picture, you are canceling out the condition of the fulfillment of the prediction. But let us drop the prediction. You have mentioned imagination. Now, what I should prefer to regard as the criterion of the truth or falsity of an existential proposition is simply the presence or absence of the asserted fact or facts, quite irrespective of whether I can know whether there are corresponding facts or not. If I can at least imagine or conceive the facts, the existence of which would verify the proposition, the proposition has significance for me. Whether I can or cannot know that the facts correspond is another matter.

AYER: I don't at all object to your use of the word "facts" so long as you allow it to be observable facts. But take the contrary case. Suppose I say, "There's a drogulus over there." And you say, "What?" and I say, "Drogulus," and you say, "What's a drogulus?" "Well," I say, "I can't describe what a drogulus is because it's not the sort of thing you can see or touch; it has no physical effects of any kind; it's a disembodied being." And you say: "Well, how am I to tell if it's there or not?" And I say: "There's no way of telling. Everything's just the same if it's there or it's not there. But the fact is it's there. There's a drogulus there standing just behind you, spiritually behind you." Does that make sense?

COPLESTON: It seems to me to do so. I should say that a drogulus in the room or not is true or false, provided that you can—that you at any rate, I have some idea of what is meant by a drogulus, and if you can say to me it's a disembodied spirit, then I should say that the proposition is either true or false whether one can verify it or not. If you said to me, "By 'drogulus' I merely mean the word 'drogulus' and I attach no other significance to it whatsoever," then I should say that it isn't a proposition any more than if I said "piffle" was in the room.

AYER: That's right. But what is "having some idea" of something? I want to say that having an idea of something is a matter of knowing how to recognize it. And you want to say that you can have ideas of things even though there's no possible situation in which you could recognize it because nothing would count as finding it. I would say that I understand the words "angel," "table," "clock," "drogulus" if I'm disposed to accept certain situations as verifying the presence or absence of what the word is supposed to stand for. But you want to admit these words without any reference to experience, whether the thing they are supposed to stand for exists, and everything is to go on just the same.

COPLESTON: No. I should say that you can have an idea of something if there's some experience that's relevant to the formation of the idea, not so much to its verification. I should say that I can form the idea of a drogulus or a disembodied spirit from the idea of body and the idea of mind. You may say that there's no mind and there's no spirit, but, at any rate, there is, as you'll admit, certain internal experience of thinking and so on which at any rate accounts for the formation of the idea. Therefore I can say I have an idea of a drogulus or whatever it is, even though I'm quite unable to know whether such a thing actually exists or not.

AYER: You would certainly not have to know that it exists, but you would have to know what would count as its existing.

COPLESTON: Yes, well, if you mean by count as its existing that there must be some experience relevant to the formation of the idea, then I should agree.

AYER: Not to the formation of the idea, but to the truth or falsity of the propositions in which it is contained.

COPLESTON: The word "metaphysics" and the phrase "metaphysical reality" can have more than one meaning, but when I refer to a "metaphysical reality" in our present discussion I mean a being which in principle (and not merely in fact) transcends the sphere of what can be sensibly experienced. Thus God is a metaphysical reality. Since God is, *ex hypothesi*, immaterial, he cannot, in principle, be apprehended by the senses.

May I add two remarks? My first remark is that I do not mean to imply that no sense experience is in any way relevant to establishing or discovering. I certainly do believe that metaphysics must be based on experience of some sort, but metaphysics involves intellectual reflection on experience. No amount of immediate sense experience will disclose the existence of a metaphysical reality. In other words, I should say, there is a halfway house between admitting only the immediate data of experience and, on the other hand, leaping to the affirmation of a metaphysical reality without any reference to experience at all. You yourself reflect on the data of experience. The metaphysician carries that reflection a stage further.

My second remark is this. Because one cannot have sense experience of a metaphysical reality it doesn't follow that one couldn't have another type of experience of it, and if anybody had such experience it does not seem to me that the metaphysical reality is deprived, as it were, of its metaphysical character and become non-metaphysical. I think that's an important point.

AYER: Yes, but asking are there metaphysical realities isn't like asking are there still wolves in Asia, is it? It looks as if you've got a clear usage for metaphysical reality and then ask does it occur or not, does it exist or not, as if I'm arbitrarily denying that it exists. My difficulty is not in answering the question—are there or are there not metaphysical realities?—but in understanding what usage is being given to the expression "metaphysical reality." When am I to count a metaphysical reality? What would it be like to come upon a metaphysical reality? That's my problem. It isn't that I arbitrarily say there can't be such things, already admitting the use of the term, but that I'm puzzled about the use of the term. I don't know what people who say there are metaphysical realities mean by it.

COPLESTON: Well, that brings us back to the beginning—the function of philosophy, I think. I should say that one can't simply raise in the abstract the question: Are there metaphysical realities? Rather, one asks: Is the character of observable reality of such a kind that it leads one to postulate a metaphysical reality, a reality beyond the physical sphere? If one grants that it is, even then one can only speak about that metaphysical reality within the framework of human language. And language is, after all, primarily developed to express our immediate experience of surrounding things, and therefore there's bound, I fully admit, to be inadequacy in any statements about a metaphysical reality.

AYER: But you're trying to have it both ways, you see. If it's something that you say doesn't have a meaning in my language, then I don't understand it. It's no good saying: "Oh, well, of course, it really has a meaning," because what meaning could it have except in the language in which it is used?

COPLESTON: Well, let's take a concrete example. If I say, for example, God is intelligent—well, you may very well say to me, "What meaning can you give to the word 'intelligent'?—because the only intelligence you have experienced is the human intelligence, and are you attributing that to God?" and I should have to say no, because I'm not. Therefore, if we agree to use the word "intelligent" simply to mean human intelligence, I should have to say God is not intelligent. But when I say that a stone is not intelligent I mean that a stone is less than intelligent; when I say God is intelligent I mean that God is more than intelligent, even though I can't give an adequate account of what that intelligence is in itself.

AYER: Do you mean simply that he knows more than any given man knows? But to what are you ascribing this property? You haven't begun to make that clear.

COPLESTON: It's a point, of course. But what you are inviting me to do is to describe God in terms which will be as clear to you as the terms in which one might describe a familiar object of experience or an unfamiliar object which is yet so like familiar objects that it can be adequately described in terms of things which are really familiar to you. But God is *ex hypothesi* unique; and it's quite impossible to describe him adequately by using concepts which normally apply to all ordinary objects of experience. If it were possible, then God wouldn't be God. So I think you're really asking me to describe God in a manner possible only if he weren't God.

I freely admit that all human ideas on God are inadequate. I also affirm that this must be so, owing to the finitude of the human intellect and to the fact that we can come to a philosophical knowledge of God only through reflection on the things we experience. But it doesn't follow that we can have no knowledge of God. It does follow, though, that our philosophical knowledge of God cannot be more than analogical.

AYER: Yes, but in the case of an ordinary analogy when you say that something is like something else you understand what both things are. But in this case, if you do say something is analogical I say: Analogical to what? And you don't tell me of what. You merely repeat the first term of analogy. Well, I get no analogy. It's like saying that something is "taller than," and I say, "Taller than?" and you repeat the first thing you say. Then I understand it's taller than itself, which is nonsense.

COPLESTON: I think that one must distinguish physical analogy and metaphysical analogy. If I say that God is intelligent, I don't say so simply because I want to call God intelligent, but either because I think that the world is such that it must be ascribed, in certain aspects at least, to a Being which can be described in human terms only as intelligent or because I am satisfied by some argument that there exists an absolute Being and then deduce that that Being must be described as intelligent. I am perfectly well aware that I have no adequate idea of what that intelligence is in itself. I am ascribing to God an attribute which, translated into human terms, must be called intelligence. After all, if you speak of your dog as intelligent, you are using the word in an analogous sense, and it has some meaning for you, even though you don't observe the dog's physical operations. Mathematicians who speak of multidimensional space have never observed, I suppose, such a space, but presumably they attach some meaning to the term. Or when we speak of "extrasensory perception" we are using the word "perception" analogously.

AYER: Yes, but mathematical physicists do test their statements by observation, and I know what would count as a case of extrasensory perception. In the case of your statement I don't know what counts. Of course, you might give it an empirical meaning; you might say that by "God is 'intelligent,'" you meant that the world had certain features. Then we'd inspect it to see if it had the features or not.

COPLESTON: Well, of course I do argue from the world to God. I must start from the world to God. I wouldn't wish to argue from God to the features of the world. But to keep within your terms of reference of empiricism, I should say that if God is personal then he's capable, for example, of entering into relationship with human beings. Then it's possible to find human beings who claim at any rate they have a personal intercourse with God.

AYER: Then you've given your statement a perfectly good empirical meaning. But it would then be like a scientific theory, and you would be using it in exactly the same way as you might use a concept like "electron"—to account for, explain, predict a certain range of human experience—namely, that certain people did have these experiences which they described as "entering into communion with God." Then one would try to analyze it scientifically, find out in what conditions these things happened. Then you might put it up as a theory. What you'd done would be psychology.

COPLESTON: Well, as I said, I was entering into your terms of reference. I wouldn't admit that when I was saying God is personal I merely meant that God could enter into intercourse with human beings. But I should be prepared to say that he was personal even if I had no reason for supposing that he entered into intercourse with human beings.

AYER: No, but it's only in that case one has anything one can control. The facts are that these human beings have these experiences. They describe these experiences in a way which implies more than that they're merely having them. But if one asks what more, then what answer does one get? Only, I'm afraid, repetition of the statement that was questioned in the first place.

COPLESTON: Well, let's come back to this religious experience. However you subsequently interpret the religious experience, you'd admit, then, that it was relevant to the truth or falsity of the proposition that God existed.

AYER: Relevant only insofar as the proposition that God existed is taken as a prediction or description of the occurrence of their experiences. But not, of course, that one has any inference you might want to draw, such as that the world was created, or anything of that kind.

COPLESTON: No. We'll leave that out. What I'm trying to get at is that you'd admit the proposition "God exists" could be a meaningful form of metaphysical proposition.

AYER: No, it wouldn't then be a meaningful metaphysical proposition. It'd be a perfectly good empirical proposition, like the proposition that the unconscious mind exists.

COPLESTON: The proposition that people have religious experience would be an empirical proposition. I quite agree. And the proposition that God exists would also be an empirical proposition, provided that all I meant by saying that God exists was that some people have a certain type of experience. But actually that's not all I mean by it. All I originally said was that if God is personal then one of the consequences would be that he could enter into communication with human beings. If he does so that doesn't make God an empirical reality in the sense of not being a metaphysical reality, but God can perfectly well be a metaphysical reality—that is, independent of physics or nature even if intelligent creatures have a non-sensible experience of him. However, if you wish to call metaphysical propositions empirical propositions, by all means do so. It then becomes a question of terminology, I think.

AYER: Oh, no. I suggest that you're again trying to have it both ways. You see, you allow me to give these words, these shapes, or noises an empirical meaning. You allow me to say that the test . . . [of whether] what you call God exists or not is to be that certain people have certain experiences, just as the test whether the table exists or not is that certain people have experiences. Only the experiences are a different sort. Having got that admission, you then shift the meaning of the words "God exists"; you no longer make them refer simply to the possibility of having these experiences, and so argue that I have admitted a metaphysical proposition, but of course I haven't. All I've admitted is an empirical proposition, which you've chosen to express in the same words as you also want to use to express your metaphysical proposition.

COPLESTON: Pardon me. I didn't say that the test . . . [of whether] what I call God exists or not is that certain people have certain experiences. I said that if God exists one consequence would be that people could have certain experiences. However, even if I accept your requirements, it follows that in one case at least you are prepared to recognize the word "God" as meaningful.

AYER: Of course I recognize it as meaningful if you give it an empirical meaning, but it doesn't follow there's any empirical evidence for the truth of your metaphysical proposition.

COPLESTON: But then I don't claim that metaphysical propositions are not in some way founded on reflection on experience. In a certain sense I should call myself an empiricist, but I think that your empiricism is too narrow.

AYER: My quarrel with you is not that you take a wider view of experience than I do, but that you fail to supply any rules for the use of your expressions. Let me try to summarize. I'm not asking you for explicit definitions: All that I require is that some indication be given of the way in which the expression relates to some possible experience. It's only when a statement can't be interpreted as referring even indirectly to anything observable that I wish to dismiss it as metaphysical. It's not necessary that the observation should actually be made; there are cases, as you've pointed out, where for practical, or even for theoretical, reasons, the observation couldn't, in fact, be made, but one knows what it would be like to make it. The statements which refer to it would be said to be verifiable in principle, if not in fact. To put the point more simply, I understand a statement of fact, I know what to look for on the supposition that it's true. My knowing what to look for is itself a matter of my being able to interpret the statement as referring, at least, to some possible experience.

Now you may say—indeed, you have said—that this is all entirely arbitrary. The principle of verifiability is not itself a descriptive statement; its status is that of a persuasive definition. I am persuaded by it, but why should you be? Can I prove it? Yes—on the basis of other definitions. I have in fact tried to show you how it can be derived from an analysis of understanding. But if you're really obstinate you'll reject these other definitions, too, so it looks as if we reach a deadlock. . . . I claim for my method that it does yield valuable results in the way of analysis, and with this you seem disposed to agree. You don't deny the importance of the analytic method in philosophy, nor do you reject all the uses to which I put it; therefore you accept in the main the account that I give of empirical propositions. You have indeed objected to my treatment of the propositions of logic, but there I think that I'm in the right. At least I'm able to account for their validity, whereas on your view it is utterly mysterious.

The main difference between us is that *you* want to leave room for metaphysics. But now look at the result that you get. You put forward your metaphysical statements as ultimate explanations of fact, yet you admit that they're not explanations in any accepted sense of the term, and you can't say in what sense they *are* explanations. You can't show me how they're to be tested, and you seem to have no criterion for deciding whether they are true or false. This being so, I say they're unintelligible. You say no, you understand them; but for all the good they do you—I mean cognitively, not emotionally—you might just as well abandon them.

This is my case against your metaphysical statements. You may decline to be persuaded by it, but what sort of case can you make *for* them? I leave the last word to you.

COPLESTON: Well, I've enjoyed our discussion very much. I've contended that a metaphysical idea has meaning if some experience is relevant to the formation of that idea, and that a rational metaphysic is possible if there are—as I still think there are—principles which can express an intellectual apprehension and a nature of being. I think that one *can* have an intellectual experience—or intuition, if you like—of being. A metaphysical proposition is testable by rational discussion, but not by purely empirical means. When you say that metaphysical propositions are meaningless because they are unverifiable in your sense, I don't really think that this amounts to more than saying that metaphysics are not the same thing as empirical science.

In short, I consider that logical positivism, apart from its theory of analytic propositions, really embodies the notion of nineteenth-century positivism; that the terms "rational" and "scientific" have the same extension. This notion certainly corresponds to a popularly held prejudice, but I don't see any adequate reason for accepting it. I still find it difficult to understand the status of the principle of verification. It must be, I should have thought, either a proposition or not a proposition. If it is a proposition it must be, on your premises, either a tautology or an empirical hypothesis. If it's a tautology, then no conclusion follows as to metaphysics; if it's an empirical hypothesis, then the principle itself would require verification. But the principle of verification cannot itself be verified. If, however, the principle is not a proposition, it should be, on your premises, meaningless. In any case, if the meaning of an existential proposition consists, according to the principle, in its verifiability, it is impossible, I think, to escape an infinite regress, since the verification will itself need verification, and so on indefinitely; and if that is so, then all propositions, including scientific propositions, are meaningless.

Discussion Questions

1. What is your own evaluation of the principle of verification as a criterion of the meaningfulness of statements? Give reasons for your answer.

2. Do you see any similarities between Ayer's principle of verification as a criterion for the meaningfulness of language and Flew's principle of falsification?

3. Do you find Ayer's or Copleston's view of the nature of religious language more acceptable? Why?

4. The positions espoused by Ayer and Copleston each presuppose a certain view of the nature of philosophy. What are these presuppositions, and which do you think is the more defensible view of the nature of philosophy?

5. In what ways do you think that religious language is different from other uses of language?

Models
for Theological Discourse

In a marvelously inventive fable called *Flatland*, Edwin A. Abbott describes a country in which there are only two dimensions—length and breadth. Nothing in Flatland has height. Into this two-dimensional world comes a sphere from Spaceland that tries to communicate to an inhabitant of Flatland that it is a solid having height. All this is too much for the Flatlander to understand, so the Spaceland sphere has to resort to analogy, using the only thing within the Flatlander's experience that is appropriate: a circle. Although the sphere is not literally a circle, it must try to explain to the Flatlander what a sphere is by using the notion of a circle: "I am not a plane Figure, but a Solid. You call me a Circle; but in reality I am not a Circle, but an infinite number of Circles . . . your country of Two Dimensions is not spacious enough to represent me, a being of Three, but can only exhibit a slice or section of me, which is what you call a Circle."[1]

With respect to God, we are like the Flatlander. Limited as we are in intelligence, bound as we are to finite experience, we are unable to think or speak of God as God really is, and nothing we can say about God is literally true in the same sense as when applied to finite human experience. We are forced to use human language and images drawn from human experience when we talk about God. Like the Flatlander attempting to understand a sphere, we must resort to analogy when speaking of God.

No treatment of the topic of religious language would be complete without a consideration of analogy, for one of the oldest defenses of the legitimacy of religious language is to analyze it in terms of the analogical function of language. The basic distinctions go all the way back to Aristotle, and the analogical use of language in religious discourse was thoroughly explored by Thomas Aquinas in the

---

[1] Edwin A. Abbott, *Flatland: A Romance of Many Dimensions*, 6th ed. (New York: Dover Publications Inc., 1952), p. 73.

293

thirteenth century. The topic is no mere medieval curiosity, however, for contemporary authors continue to explore these issues.[2]

The problem is basically this: How can the concepts and images that we draw from our experience be applicable to God? One response is to adopt the *via negativa* (the negative way) of theological discourse. Recognizing that nothing we can say of God means quite the same thing as it does when applied to objects within human experience, we should only refer to the divine attributes in terms of what God is *not*: God is *not* finite, God is *not* evil, God is *not* material, and so forth. Though the *via negativa* remains a valuable corrective to sloppily made statements about God, by itself it is not a sufficient mode of religious discourse. Among the objections to the *via negativa* is that a negative utterance does not have the same connotation as does a positive one. If you were to say of a friend, "Susan is not untruthful," and someone asked, "Do you mean to say that Susan always tells the truth?" and you replied, "I didn't say that; I mean only that she is not untruthful," your response would be perceived as casting doubt on Susan's truthfulness. You did not mean to do this at all, yet your negative utterance had this connotation. The second objection to the *via negativa* is that it simply is not compatible with the language of Scripture and devotion. Try to recast the Lord's Prayer into the language of the *via negativa*, and see just how unsatisfactory this sort of language is. Additionally, it is difficult to be consistent in the use of the *via negativa*, for we want to speak positively of God, not just negatively.

We have inherited from the ancient Greek philosophers several basic distinctions in the way language functions, and one of these important distinctions is the difference between the univocal and equivocal use of language. A word is used *univocally* when it has more or less the same meaning when applied to different objects. We can speak of a beautiful day, a beautiful painting, a beautiful automobile, a beautiful person, and so forth, with generally the same meaning attached to the word *beautiful*. There is some difference in meaning, depending on the context, but there is no major shift of meaning in the various uses. When such a major shift of meaning occurs, a term is said to be used *equivocally*, and when words are used equivocally in an argument, the argument becomes invalid. Consider the following: John is poor (i.e., has no money) and is a student; thus, John must be a poor (i.e., incompetent) student. There is no valid inference here, since *poor* has two different meanings in this sentence, and the shift in meaning from its first use to its second use renders the argument fallacious.

The problem for religious language emerges because neither the univocal nor the equivocal use of language seems to allow us to speak positively about God. We cannot claim that positive statements about God are univocal, since the nature of God is such that no terms applied to God have the same meaning as when they are applied to us. Yet we would not want to say that language used of God is equivocal, that is, has totally different meanings than when it is applied to finite beings,

[2] Examples of the debate about analogical language are represented by the following books: Frederick Ferré, *Language, Logic and God* (New York: Harper & Row, 1961) and E. L. Mascall, *Existence and Analogy* (London: Longmans, Green, 1949).

for this would make theological utterances meaningless. We must find a third way of using language to speak of God, and this third way is analogy.

An analogy is basically a comparison of two or more things in terms of their likeness, in a way that also recognizes their differences. Analogy does not ignore the differences between the things being compared but instead focuses on their similarities. Analogies are frequently used in various kinds of achievement tests, and there the form is usually "A is to B as C is to?" and the test taker is asked to supply the missing analogue. There is nothing strange about the analogical use of language, and we resort to it more frequently than you may at first think. For example, if you say that your cat is intelligent, you are speaking analogically. What you mean is that even though you are different from your cat, there is a resemblance between your nature and your intelligence and your cat's nature and its intelligence. The following diagram will illustrate these relations:

Intelligence   Intelligence
(*fuller meaning*) :: (*limited meaning*)
Your Nature   Cat's Nature

We can call this a downward analogy, since you are going from a fuller understanding of the term intelligence to a limited application of the term to your cat. The value of the analogical way of speaking is that it recognizes that human beings are different from cats but also recognizes the similar meanings of intelligence when applied to different kinds of creatures. In this example human intelligence supplies the fuller meaning of the term, which is only partially applicable to feline intelligence.

Now reverse the process. We will begin with a limited sense of the term and apply it analogously to God in a fuller sense:

Intelligence   Intelligence
(*limited meaning*) :: (*fuller meaning*)
Your Nature   God's Nature

Since God's nature is so much greater than ours, God's intelligence is correspondingly greater than our own limited intelligence. The attribution of intelligence to God is an upward analogy in that human intelligence supplies only the partial, and limited, sense of the term.

FROM ANALOGIES TO MODELS

Today the use of the doctrine of analogy to describe religious language can seem a bit dated. In the selection that follows, Ian Ramsey gives us a more contemporary way of approaching this issue by using the term "model." We are familiar with the notion of models in science: There, they function as a way of helping us understand complex phenomena that are not easily described in ordinary language. We may think of an atom as a miniature solar system, though physicists find such a model extremely crude. We might think of light as traveling in little packets of energy called photons, although the use of the term "packet" here does not give a literal description of what light is really like.

Interesting in Ramsey's discussion is the multiplicity of models in both Jewish and Christian Scriptures. They range from the unusual—laundress, metalworker, and vine—to the commonplace—friend, farmer, builder. All the lists of models that Ramsey discusses come from the everyday life of those with whom Scripture originated. It was a rural, even nomadic society, strongly patriarchal and undemocratic in form of government. How can we translate these pastoral and autocratic models into language to which twenty-first-century democratic citizens can more easily relate? Ramsey suggests that perhaps the models of "protector" and "guide" will prove to be more apt for our culture than the older ones of "shepherd" and "potter," or perhaps we will find in contemporary professions replacements for models derived from older societies. But this is more easily said than done, for reasons that Ramsey explores in some detail.

It is the case, he points out, that some models are more fertile than others; that is, they provoke additional insights and seem to have a longer life than others. "Some models may take us a long way in theological talking," Ramsey points out, "but eventually even they must grind to a halt." An additional point he offers is that we should not become too attached to a single model or even a cluster of models, for no model of theological discussion will ever be adequate for all changes in all societies. The reason for this, Ramsey argues, is that "theology must always have some fit with the world around us." His concluding comment is that the believer must always be committed to "an endless exploration of countless models" in order to understand better the God who confronts us in many cosmic disclosures.

Talking of God:
Models, Ancient and Modern

IAN RAMSEY

In this paper[1] I hope to show how talk about God arises around, and derives from, what I shall call models. I shall then consider some of the problems raised by this view, and finally glance at some of its wider implications.

Let me start by recalling that at one time, and in the Old Testament in particular, people made free use of all kinds of pictures, images, metaphors, models[2] in their talk about God. No one has illustrated this more plainly than Eric Heaton in his book *His Servants the Prophets* where he remarks that, in the Old Testament, 'Yahweh's relationship to his people is represented under the figures of a father, mother, nurse, brother, husband, friend, warrior, shepherd, farmer, metal-worker, builder, potter, fuller, physician, judge, tradesman, King, fisherman, and scribe—to mention, almost at random, only a few of the activities of the community' (p. 71).

Let us remind ourselves of how and where these pictures, these models, occur in the Bible by taking up references which for the most part are those which Mr Heaton gives us.

First, God is talked of in terms of phrases which spread from, and presuppose, a family model:

1. *Father.* There is the promise in Jer. 3.19, 'Ye shall call me "My father" and shall not turn away from following me.'

2. *Mother.* In Deut. 32.18 the Hebrews are accused of forgetting 'God that gave thee birth,' or rather more explicitly in Isa. 66.13 God promises Jerusalem: 'As one whom his mother comforteth so will I comfort you.'

Source: Ian Ramsey, *Christian Empiricism* (Grand Rapids, MI: William B. Eerdmans Publishing Company, 1974). Used with permission of SPCK.

[1] The paper incorporates, in a revised form, most of the paper given to the Modern Churchmen's Conference in August 1964 and subsequently printed in *The Modern Churchman*, Vol. VIII, No. 1 (New Series), October 1964; but it has been enlarged by the addition of a new section dealing with various difficulties raised by the views which are set out in what is now the earlier part of the paper.

[2] My preference is for the word 'model' because, by virtue of its wider use in contemporary philosophical discussion, it carries with it natural logical overtones and takes us at once into a logical context. By contrast with 'model', 'image' seems to me to have too strong a psychological ancestry, and to beg or to by-pass too many epistemological and ontological questions. For the close relation between model and metaphor see my *Models and Mystery*, Chap. III. I choose 'model', then, because it is least likely to prejudice discussion and most likely to direct our attention to logical, epistemological, and ontological issues.

3. *Husband.* Not surprisingly in Hosea—the book which, as is well known, more than any other uses the model of personal relationship in its discourse about God—we find an express preference for the picture of God as husband instead of God as an overlord, a distinction which was as novel in a secular context as in reference to God: 'It shall be at that day, saith the Lord, that thou shalt call me Ishi [= My husband] and shalt call me no more Baali [= My Master]' (Hos. 2.16).

4. *Friend.* In Jer. 3.4 'the companion of my youth' is used as an appropriate phrase for God, though the verse also speaks of God as 'My father.' Here God is spoken of at one and the same time as father and friend, a point to which I will return later.

But God is also pictured more widely in terms of men's work and crafts and professions; and again, for the most part with the help of Mr Heaton, we may recall many verses with phrases which point back to such pictures as these twelve I will now mention.

1. *The shepherd.* God is a shepherd whose sheep are men: 'Ye are my sheep, the sheep of my pasture are many . . . saith the Lord God' (Ezek. 34.31).

2. *The farmer.* 'I will sift the house of Israel . . . like as corn is sifted in a sieve; yet shall not the least grain fall on the earth' (Amos 9.9).

3. *The dairymaid.* Job speaks of God as one who has 'poured me out as milk, and curdled me like cheese' (Job 10.10).

4. *The fuller—the laundress.* In Mal. 3.2 God is said to be 'like fuller's soap,' a theme further developed in Isa. 4.4 which speaks of a time when God will have 'washed away the filth of the daughters of Zion.'

5. *The builder.* In Amos 7.7 we read that 'the Lord stood beside (or upon) a wall made by a plumbline, with a plumbline in his hand.'

6. *The potter.* 'Behold, as the clay in the potter's hand, so are ye in mine hand O house of Israel' (Jer. 18.6)—and the verse has echoes in Isaiah where as with the 'father and friend' of Jeremiah, we now have God as 'father and potter': 'O Lord, thou art our father: we are the clay, and thou our potter' (Isa. 64.8).

7. *The fisherman.* In Hab. 1.14, 15 men are 'as the fishes of the sea' and God 'taketh up all of them with his angle, he catcheth them in his net, and gathereth them in his drag: therefore he rejoiceth and is glad.'

8. *The tradesman.* The well-known opening verse of Isa. 55 comes readily to mind: 'Ho, everyone that thirsteth, come ye to the waters, and he that hath no money; come ye, buy, and eat: yea, come, buy wine and milk without money and without price.'

9. *The physician.* Jer. 30 says of Israel and Judah that their 'hurt is incurable,' their 'wound grievous', that they have no 'healing medicines'. But in verse 17 we read that God will restore their health: 'I will restore health unto thee, and I will heal thee of thy wounds, saith the Lord."

10. *The teacher and scribe.* The well-known verse from Jer. 31: 'I will put my law (my teaching) in their inward parts, and in their hearts will I write it.'

11. *The nurse.* 'I have nursed (nourished) and brought up children, and they have rebelled against me' (Isa. 1.2).
12. *The metal worker.* In Mal. 3.2.3 God is 'like a refiner's fire . . . and he shall sit as a refiner and purifier of silver.'

Finally, pictures from a national setting are also used in the Old Testament to enable man to be articulate about God. We have, for example, the models of the King, the warrior, and the judge:

1. *The King.* In Jer. 10.7: 'Who would not fear thee, O King of the nations . . . forasmuch as among all the wise men of the nations, and in all their royal estate there is none like unto thee', and verse 10 'The Lord is the true God . . . and an everlasting King.'
2. *The warrior.* We read in Isa. 63.1 how God comes 'marching in the greatness of his strength', and the theme is developed in the next few verses.
3. *The judge.* 'The Lord is our judge, the Lord is our lawgiver,' says Isa. 33.22, and the verse continues: 'The Lord is our King: he will save us.' The verse combines all the national models.

Here is theological language directly related, as Mr Heaton said, 'to the world of experience': here are religious situations linked with 'secular' situations; here is talk about God which has plain links with the discourse of ordinary life. Here is religious life and theological language linked with the life and talk of home and family and friends: linked with man's work and talk whether it be in the fields or in the city, whether it be the work and talk of the craftsman or that of a profession; linked with the life and talk of the nation. The same could also be said about the characterization of God as 'my rock, and my fortress . . . my strong rock . . . my shield, and the horn of my salvation my high tower' (Ps. 18.2). Here is language about God gaining its relevance by means of what I have called 'models.' Now, what is involved when models are used in this way? Let us answer this question by reference in turn to each of the three groups I have mentioned above.

First then, those models associated with home and friends. How do they come to be used in talk about God? Let us begin by recognizing that on occasion circumstances all 'go our way,' as it is often said. On these occasions, the world displays predominantly favourable features, features which give rise to a sense of dependence, but dependence on what is reliable and secure. Such features are those, for example, which characterize the changing seasons in such a way that the farmer ploughs hopefully and harvests thankfully. Or it may happen that when we are faced with some major problem as to vocation, or emigration, or the suffering of an aged relative, or marriage, there occurs a complex set of circumstances, too complex and too diversified to be the result of any one man's design, which helps us to resolve the problem as well for those around us as for ourselves. Or it may be that we are walking in remote, mountainous country, and as night comes on we are filled with all kinds of uncertainties and anxieties. But then we refresh ourselves at a mountain stream, look up to the stars as symbols of stability, and find our path illuminated by the moon. A sense of kinship with nature strikes us; the Universe is reliable after all.

But, it might be asked, how do situations like this lead to homely phrases—what I have called models—being used in discourse about God? My answer begins by reminding ourselves that there are patterns of behaviour characteristically associated with a father, mother, husband, or friend which are reminiscent of the patterns of these natural circumstances—that there are, for example, features of a friend's behaviour—his reliability and trustworthiness—whose pattern resembles in an important way the pattern of seed-time and harvest. Moreover, in the personal case it is in and through such patterns that we see certain men and women—a husband, mother, father, friend—as more than what they plainly and obviously are, namely human organisms in specialized relationships. Around such patterns occurs what we may call a 'disclosure,' as when we 'see' twelve lines on a blackboard as a box; as when a cluster of lines called more technically an 'envelope' discloses an ellipse to us; as when two images take on another dimension and become a scene with 'depth,' looking (as we say) 'very real' in a 3-D viewer. When such a disclosure occurs around a human pattern we speak of knowing people as they 'really are,' of there being 'deep' affection between us, of loving them 'for themselves.' You may recall the 'pop' song: 'I love you for a hundred thousand reasons'—these reasons no doubt ranging from purely verifiable features and behaviour—hair, eyes, shape, tone of voice—to more distinctively personal reasons—trustfulness against the evidence—until as the climax: 'But most of all I love you 'cos you're you'—someone whose uniqueness and transcendence is disclosed in, and through these patterns of behaviour. 'Husband,' 'mother', 'father', 'friend'—these are words which while they are undoubtedly associated with certain characteristic behaviour patterns have a transcendent reference as well—and are grounded in disclosures.

Building on these reflections, my next suggestion is that the human case acts as a catalyst for the cosmic case, to generate a cosmic disclosure. The cosmic pattern chimes in with the human pattern; the human pattern has already led to a finite disclosure—of persons—and their matching then evokes a cosmic disclosure around natural events such as seed-time and harvest. It is as and when a cosmic disclosure is thereby evoked that we are able to speak of God—what the cosmic disclosure discloses—in terms of the models with which the finite situations have supplied us. It is on these occasions that we speak of a 'sense of kinship' with the Universe, of a 'friendly' valley—so friendly that, as Ps. 65 would express it, 'the valley laughs and sings with us.'[3]

To turn now to the second group of phrases—those which originate in models taken from man's work and crafts. Once again there must have been, at least in the case of Israel, a correspondence of patterns. There must, for example, be

---

[3] I have of course tried to set out the exercise in its logical order; but it may well be that in appropriate circumstances we immediately talk of the world being 'friendly' and 'cooperative.'

some pattern discernible in the behaviour of sheep which was repeated in the social behaviour of the Israelites. Alternatively, the events of the nation must be such that words like 'straining' and 'sifting' become appropriate, so that it becomes possible to speak of the nation going through a severe period of testing, or through trying times, or being wounded or hurt. In all this no religious phrases are begged. Even the most secular man might speak of Germany smarting from the grievous wounds of Versailles, or France being incurably hurt by the war of 1870–1. Or we might speak of the life of a nation being strained or soured, of its public representatives being no longer upright, of our lives being moulded by current events or caught in the net of circumstances.

The phrases might be used, and no doubt often are used, without any religious overtones whatever. That indeed, so far, is my point, namely that these phrases relate to patterns of events recognizable by all, believers or not. What further conditions are wanted for theological language to arise? If genuine theological language is to arise, the characteristic behaviour of what the Income Tax Schedules call a 'trade, profession, or vocation', i.e. shepherd, farmer, dairymaid, fuller, builder, potter, metal-worker, fisherman, tradesman, physician, teacher must, as in our own case, disclose an activity which gives to the overt 'professional' behaviour a distinctively personal and transcendent backing. We ourselves may then be used as catalysts to evoke a cosmic disclosure around the national pattern.

So once again—and this time when national events display patterns which, having their counterparts in human activity, become at the next move occasions of a cosmic disclosure—a corresponding pattern in the universe may lead to a cosmic disclosure, reveal God, and make possible the use of an appropriate model.

The third case—the case of those models which originate in the context of national or international politics—King, warrior, judge—is different again. Here the model carries within itself the possibility of limitless development, and so the possibility arises of evoking a cosmic disclosure by developing a pattern whose range is unlimited.[4] Let me illustrate from the case of King. Each King, as the old Bidding Prayer phrases it, is over all persons and in all causes as well ecclesiastical as temporal within his dominions supreme. So why in principle impose any limit on the concept—any restriction of power in space and time? Then, as the King-pattern is developed, at some point or other a cosmic disclosure may occur, when (as we would say) the God of all power and might, the King of the whole earth will be disclosed. The model of warrior likewise embodies in itself the possibility of limitless inclusion, through victory, until the same kind of buildup of power pattern leads to a cosmic disclosure. Or the Judge—easily universalized by the concept of justice he embodies—points to yet another limitless pattern which can generate a cosmic disclosure, and so become another model for God.

Now it is in terms of these models that we become theologically articulate, that we talk about God. Sometimes this discourse is well developed as it is already in some of the verses we quoted; on other occasions it is hardly developed at all

4 See, for example, my *Religious Language*, esp. Chap. II.

though the *prima facie* possibility of considerable development is always implicit. Let us recall some examples.

The model of a father gives rise to talk about 'backsliding children' who if they but turn and are faithful will inherit a pleasant land and enjoy a distinguished heritage (Jer. 3.18, 19); talk of a husband leads to talk of a betrothal 'in righteousness, and in judgement, and in lovingkindness, and in mercies' and in 'faithfulness' (Hos. 2.19, 20). The shepherd is one of the most developed models, as we may see in Ezek. 34, for example, verses 12, 13, 14, 'As a shepherd seeketh out his flock in the day that he is amongst his sheep that are scattered abroad, so will I seek out my sheep . . . and I will feed them upon the mountains of Israel by the watercourses . . . I will feed them with good pasture . . . there shall they lie down in a good fold.' Again the potter leads the religious man to say as of God that 'when the vessel that he made of the clay was marred in the hand of the potter, he made it again another vessel' (Jer. 18.4). We have seen already from Jer. 30 how the physician, like the shepherd, model is prolific in its articulation possibilities, and the same could be said about King, or warrior, or judge. For example, God is the King who reigns for ever, gives his people the blessings of peace (Ps. 10.16; 39.11)—and (Dan. 4.34, 39) his dominion is everlasting, he doeth according to his will . . . among the inhabitants of the earth. The theme of God as judge characterizes many psalms, for example, 7. 8–11; 58.11; 135.14, to take three almost at random. God as the powerful warrior is epitomized in Ps. 68. 'Let God arise, and let his enemies be scattered,' a psalm which has led many a soldier from Cromwell to Montgomery to be theologically articulate—perhaps indeed too articulate, though that is to anticipate difficulties to which I shall now very soon turn.

In these ways, then, in terms of a model set in a cosmic disclosure, we talk about God, and our theology contrives to be relevant. But such articulation is no free-for-all; it develops under checks and balances. There are cautions to be exercised, and problems to be faced, and to these various difficulties we now turn.

In the first place, it is clear that while undoubtedly, and as we have seen, some models are much more fertile than others, giving rise much more quickly to much more discourse, every model is sooner or later inadequate. Models like father, shepherd, physician, King may be much more fertile than builder or tradesman, but even discourse about fathers, shepherds, physicians, and Kings must sooner or later be incongruous. No one is so captivated by the physician model that he is emboldened to ask whether God will benefit from the new deal to be given to consultants by the Ministry of Health. Some models may take us a long way in theological talking, but eventually even they must grind to a halt. While therefore a model gives us relevance, and there will be a high or a low degree of relevance depending on the fertility of the model, we must be alert to the solecisms it will sooner or later produce.

There will be at least two cautions which we shall always observe. First we shall not remain content with any one model. Already we have seen how God was spoken of as King and judge; as father and friend; as father and potter. So the language that is most reliable will be that discourse which is licensed by, and consistent with, the widest possible range of models. We can already see in broad outline the character of this multimodel discourse. It will speak of God as caring for, providing for, as guiding, testing, healing, and cleansing, as possessing a moral authority and calling forth a total devotion and response; and something of this same discourse might well be derived from impersonal models, for example, rock, fortress, shield. Because a model like Protector or Guide by being more fertile for providing discourse is more 'dominant' than models such as Shepherd and Potter, God will be more reliably spoken of as Protector and Guide than as Shepherd or even as both Shepherd and Potter. But we shall need to see the limitations of even these strands of discourse, and if we look for discourse which harmonizes these dominant strands in such a way as to exclude the limitations of each, we may well arrive at discourse about love or perhaps activity; when we shall conclude that God is spoken of most reliably as 'Love' or perhaps as just 'the living God.' The important point to recognize is that such characterizations of God as these are utterly valueless and positively misleading unless they are suitably contextualized in a multimodel discourse. It is a point which Professor Flew overlooked—or worse, parodied—in his criticisms of talk about God's love in the Falsification controversy,[5] and it is a point which few of his critics explicitly recognized. So the first caution to be observed in talking about God is: use as many models as possible, and from these develop the most consistent discourse possible. Never suppose the supply of models has been exhausted.

The second caution we shall need to observe is this. If we are to talk reliably about God we must be alert to the need to fit our discourse at all points to patterns of events in the world around us. The discourse is, as we have seen, derived from models, by no matter how complex a route, and there will always be the possibility—nay more, the necessity—of relating our discourse to events of the world around us. We must always give our language the kind of empirical fit which is exemplified in our earlier illustrations of seed-time and harvest, the moor-land walk, national events, or a monarchical constitution. Talk about God will not be related to the world around us as a scientific hypothesis is related to it. But meaning and relevance is no prerogative of scientific assertions.

* * *

What now have these reflections taught us as we seek to explicate theological language today?

1. Theological language, and talk about God in particular, often passes men by because it brings with it no cosmic disclosures. Its models have been drained of their disclosure possibilities by the vast sociological, psychological, and cultural changes which separate us from the Biblical, and not least the Old Testament, world.

[5]See, for example, *New Essays in Philosophical Theology*, ed. A. G. N. Flew and A. MacIntyre (S.C.M. Press), p. 99.

Kings and judges are contextualized in an oppressive, insensitive Establishment; warriors vary between bawling sergeant majors and brass-hatted dunderheads; trades, and even professions, are irritating frustrations from which a man escapes as frequently as possible and with as much money as possible in order to 'live.' In our present society, human relations within a family are perhaps the only group of traditional models which continues to offer any hope for relevant theological language.

In order to instil talk about God with new relevance, we must seek to discover where in the world and where in man's life and work, disclosures are most likely to occur. A relevant theology must learn new occasions for moments of vision.

Perhaps scientific discourse may not be unhelpful. In particular, if (as we have suggested) activity is a central theological concept, it may be that we shall discover new models amongst whatever represents the scientific concept of energy. More particularly, the Principle of the Conservation of Energy may be a means of pointing to a cosmic disclosure by mounting a series of energy considerations. Again, we may recall Ralph Waldo Trine's implicit use of the phenomenon of resonance in the title of his well-known book *In Tune with the Infinite*.

On a still wider canvas, may we hope that sleek sports cars will replace strong towers; or personnel manager replace the good shepherd? If these or any similar suggestions seem fantastic, it is either because sleek sports cars and personnel managers evoke no disclosures whatever or, if they do, which may be more likely, it is because we cannot discern reminiscent patterns in the universe which can thereafter lead to cosmic disclosures.

Our Victorian great-grandfathers did not hesitate to write theological discourses entitled 'Railways to heaven.' But for them railways were opening up a world which was itself evolving with a wonderful novelty and with apparently limitless possibilities: a cosmic disclosure justified railways as a theological model. But there is little about British Rail to generate cosmic disclosures. If we look for transport parallel in our own day, let it be granted that for some—and I believe Professor Coulson is amongst them—Heath Row, like kings and judges of old, can be set in an ever-widening cosmic perspective which surveys aircraft, airlines, languages, nationalities . . . until a cosmic disclosure is evolved. If that is so, there is no reason why some should not speak of God in the Control Tower bringing men to the arrival gate where they would be. If that language jars, let us be sure to ask ourselves why it does.

Meanwhile, the philosopher of religion finds unexpected significance in the girl who screamed at the Beatles because (she said) they seemed so much bigger than herself and for whom, quite consistently, Liverpool was heaven. Here, in so far as there was a sense of finitude, was a cosmic disclosure: Beatle-language was virtually theological language. If we wish to coin a relevant theology it is our duty to learn, not to scoff.

But I have roamed enough in an area where prejudices flourish, where men can be blinkered and insensitive, and where words are contextually hazardous; and those are only some of the difficulties which confront us as we try to make our theology meaningful.

2. Whether our models are old or new they must be developed with circum-spection. It is significant that Mr Heaton in the very sentence where he praises the Old Testament writers for their relevance—acknowledges that 'it was occasionally a crude tradition' (p. 73). Sometimes, models were developed in the Old Testament without adequate circumspection. We must learn our lesson. Models have to be developed with an eye both to other models, and to what we want to say about the universe in terms of the history and science and sociology and moral insights of the times.

A reliable theology will need to be in constant dialogue and conversation with other disciplines, as much to listen as to speak.

3. Further, all models in theology must be accompanied by *qualifiers*, those words in theological language which preserve the mystery and transcendence of God, for example, 'perfect,' 'infinite,' 'all,' 'only,' and so forth. Mr Heaton, after granting that on occasion Old Testament theology issues in crudities, remarks that nevertheless 'the prophets knew how to discriminate and were acutely aware of the seven limitations of all human language for conveying the full richness of their knowledge of Yahweh,' and when they discriminated it was to exclude 'everything which suggested that [God] was capricious and [like the deities of Canaan] unworthy of man at his best.' It is the purpose of qualifiers to remind us of the need for this discrimination. So, in relation to 2, qualifiers might well help us to be cautious about developing a model. But in helping us to discriminate and to be cautious they have another and more characteristic purpose as well.

This purpose is to point us unmistakably to the cosmic disclosures in which all talk about God must be grounded. Take, for instance, the qualifier 'infinitely' in 'God is infinitely loving.' It may be thought to be merely a formal courtesy phrase or even a disingenuous addition to by-pass intellectual difficulties.[6] It might be supposed that 'God is loving' says all that is important to preserve—something which is clear and relevant. But 'God is loving' is just as inadequate and as incomplete a theological assertion as 'God is infinite'—though both are relevant. The first generates discourse which (as we have seen) enables theology to be intelligible and to fit the world, and the second points us to the transcendence and mystery of a cosmic disclosure.

It is true that by themselves qualifiers *describe* nothing, and for that reason may be thought to be utterly irrelevant theological jargon. But they are in fact words or phrases whose relevance is to be found in the cosmic disclosure to which, when they have models to qualify, they point. Prayers and hymns of adoration are largely catenae of qualifiers and it entirely accords with these philosophical reflections that for their relevance they depend on a meditation which, in supplying the models, relates the prayers and hymns to the life of the world.

4. We are thus brought naturally to my fourth point. Theologians have far too often supposed, and mistakenly, that the most generalized doctrines were most

---

[6] Cf. again A. G. N. Flew and the Falsification controversy, *New Essays in Philosophical Theology* (S.C.M. Press), pp. 98–99.

free from all contamination (as it would have been judged) with metaphor, or as I would say, models. But none of us must ever despise the models whence our theological discourse is hewn, for without these we have no way to the cosmic disclosure and no way back to relevance. Without its models, theology will always run the risk of being no more than word-spinning. There is a theological sophistication which, as Mr Heaton remarks, is 'pitiful self-deception.' He continues: 'Metaphor—*mere* metaphor—is all we have to help us understand God, no matter how discreetly we try to disguise the fact by thinning out a selection of images into pseudo-philosophical "doctrines." The "fatherhood" of God, the "Kingship" of God, the "love" of God, the "wrath" of God and the rest remain metaphorical because they were and still are attached at some point to human experience. They would be incomprehensible (and therefore useless) if they were not.' Only when we remember that will our preaching 'become at once more personal, more imaginative and more intelligible.' He concludes: 'At the moment it really does seem that we are all desperately afraid of leaving the well-trodden path of theological jargon and of claiming that measure of imaginative freedom which all the great preachers from Amos to St Paul assumed—not as a right, but as a pastoral necessity.'

5. Presented with some theological phrase, then, of whose meaning (if meaning it has) we are doubtful or even inclined to deny, my recipe for understanding it is:

(a) Do not be content to take the phrase in isolation, but search for its appropriate context, verbal and nonverbal.

(b) At this point try to pick out the model(s) from which the context is derived; these should help us to discover that 'basis in fact' for the theological assertion—its bearing on the world around us.

(c) At the same time no model will ever be a picturing model; if that occurred the language might seem to be relevant but it could not be *theological*. See, then, how any particular model has been qualified to generate that cosmic disclosure in which I am bound to think that the ultimate ground of all theological assertions will be found.

Theology must always have some fit with the world around us—that is true and a point which it is important to emphasize. Further, this 'fit' arises in virtue of the language to which the different models collectively give rise. But those models originate in a cosmic disclosure, and here is the basis for all talk about God.

This I would say is even true of doctrines such as those of the future life, of creation, and of angels. Which means that in all theological assertions the logical stress is always on God. In this sense there is something that we may call a logical imbalance about theological assertions, and this is what the qualifiers help to exhibit. Theological assertions are not flat or uniform as we might say 'The cat is on the mat' is flat and uniform. If we speak of God catching men in his net, and gathering them in his drag, do not let us have such an interest in fishing that we revel in developing discourse of the net and drag, and forget that it is not necessarily theology at all. If this seems an incredible mistake, think of those who have lavished time and thought on the details of the Last Assize or the temperature of hell in a way which denied the very character of the God of whom they were talking.

Talk about God, and theological assertions in general, then, point us in two directions: in the one direction to that cosmic disclosure where God reveals himself; and in the other direction to some particular models into whose discourse they fit, discourse which relates to patterns in the world around us. Talk about God must combine understanding and mystery; it must relate to models and disclosures. Meanwhile, the believer is committed to an endless exploration of countless models, in this way constantly improving his understanding of the one God who confronts him in any and every cosmic disclosure.

Discussion Questions

1. What are the advantages and the disadvantages of the *via negativa* as a way of talking about God?

2. Make a list of the "models" of God used in devotional language. Why are some biblical models not widely used in such contexts?

3. How do you explain the fact that some biblical models have survived in general usage whereas others have not?

4. Can you think of any contemporary models that evoke what Ramsey calls a "cosmic disclosure"?

5. Discuss the role of what Ramsey calls "qualifiers" in all theological models. Make a list of the most commonly used qualifiers.

The Metaphorical Use of Language

Language bears on everything we do. Whether in religion, art, science, literature, or any other human activity, language is in the forefront. And for this reason, a discussion of religious language quickly leads into the more general problems of the nature and function of language. The discipline known as semantics is the systematic investigation of the development and changes in the meaning and form of language, and the semantic question addressed by the following selection is how we are able to create new meanings in language.

Paul Ricoeur, a contemporary French philosopher, explores the role of metaphor as a way new meanings emerge in language. He begins by acknowledging that the question of language and the study of metaphor are ancient philosophic concerns. The Greek philosophers recognized that language is a powerful tool that can be used to prove the truth of a claim or to persuade an opponent to abandon a position. They called the study of correct reasoning *logic* and the study of the art of persuasion *rhetoric*. From the earliest times, the art of rhetoric was not held in high esteem by philosophers. Philosophers are interested in truth; rhetoricians are concerned only to sway their audiences with persuasive discourse. During Plato's time, there was a group of professional teachers called the Sophists who, for a fee—usually quite substantial—taught young Greek gentlemen how to be persuasive in speech. Never mind the question of truth; in the view of rhetoricians, it is more important to win one's day in debate, a court of law, or a political contest. The silver-tongued orator is the ideal of the Sophists, not the careful, reasoned thinker.

In the rhetorical tradition, the use of metaphor is principally a device for ornamenting speech and embellishing discourse for the purpose of persuasion. Metaphor is considered one of the *tropes*, a trope being a rhetorical use of words in other than their literal senses. For rhetoricians, the function of metaphor is purely to embellish discourse, not to add new meanings to what is being said. Since metaphor does not introduce any new meanings into discourse, rhetoricians think that the literal meaning can always be substituted for the metaphorical use of language without changing the meaning of what is being said.

Drawing on numerous writers, Paul Ricoeur calls all the assumptions of the traditional rhetorical tradition into question and offers a different theory of metaphor. He sees metaphor not just as an embellishment of discourse, but as a way new meanings enter language. Consider the statement "Time is a beggar." Taken literally, this statement is an absurdity. But as a metaphor, it expresses something new about time. Or consider the statement "A mighty fortress is our God." Taken literally, the statement is absurd. We had enough trouble justifying the use of anthropomorphic language about God in terms of the analogical function of language. Here, however, we have gone beyond analogy to a metaphor that cannot possibly make sense if the words are taken literally. Religious literature is filled with metaphor, and if we are to have an adequate view of religious language, we must give some attention to the metaphorical process.

The dictionary defines a metaphor as a word applied to an object in a non-literal way in order to suggest a comparison between two objects. But this definition does not tell us how metaphors function. Ricoeur argues that metaphors arise from a tension between two words when they are used together in an unusual way, a way that does not reflect their ordinary, literal meanings. There is a clash of literal meanings in a metaphor that has a kind of shock value and stimulates the reader or the hearer into new ways of understanding. Time cannot literally be a beggar, but this metaphor is a semantic innovation that enables us to understand time in a new way.

If a metaphor is a good one, it is a living metaphor. When metaphors become dead, they lose their metaphorical function and end up in the dictionary as one of the multiple meanings of a word, a feature of language Ricoeur refers to as *polysemy*. The first person to refer to a table's "leg" was speaking metaphorically, but the metaphor is so common that we no longer consider it a metaphorical use of language. Two conclusions emerge from Ricoeur's analysis: First, a true metaphor in his sense—not just a substitution of one word for another—is untranslatable because the metaphor *creates* meaning. Second, a true metaphor is not just an ornamentation in language, but includes new information—new ways of speaking about reality.

Another important distinction in the philosophy of language is the difference between sense and reference. Sense refers to what the statement says; reference, to what the statement is about. Ricoeur's theory allows us to make sense of metaphors, but what is the reference of metaphors, that is, what are they about? A structuralist view of language would say that metaphors simply refer to other words in language. Whole theories of literary interpretation have been developed along this view, in terms of which poetry, for example, refers not to reality, but only to language. This clearly won't do for Ricoeur; he argues that metaphors have reference; not the ordinary, literal reference of their words, but reference to a new experience of reality. In this sense, his view of metaphor is closer to Aristotle's than to some current theories of literary criticism. Aristotle holds that the poet does not merely describe reality, but redescribes it and allows new meanings to emerge in language.

Ricoeur also claims that the metaphorical process is at work not only in religious discourse, but in poetry, art, and even science. It may be easier to see the process at work in poetry than in the other two endeavors, for the poet is attempting to describe reality in new and insightful ways. The artist, too, is redescribing reality, whether in a painting, a sculpture, or a musical composition. An artistic work does not merely copy reality, but interprets it in a new way, and if the artist is a good one, the work enables us to understand reality better than we could have been able to without the artwork. Even the scientist, when constructing a theoretical model, is redescribing reality in order to understand it better. In all these cases the metaphorical process operates as a heuristic device, *heuristic* being taken from the Greek word for discovery and meaning that which stimulates interest and furthers investigation. Living metaphors, good works of art, and inventive theoretical models all stimulate us to discover new realities and to bring these discoveries to the level of expression and understanding.

But what is this reality that metaphor allows to emerge into language? Not the world of objects, things manipulable by scientific technique, but the life world (*Lebenswelt*), the world of persons, beauty, love, feelings, and values. All these realities would remain inexpressible unless the metaphorical process were at work. The claim being made by the defenders of religious language in opposition to the positivists is that reality is not limited to that which can be described by the literal meanings of words. Religious statements are not verifiable in the same way as empirical statements are, for if they were, they would not be dealing with the religious dimension of human experience, the ultimate human concern.

Ricoeur's work on metaphor is part of a vaster project of developing a theory of interpretation, a hermeneutics, applicable to religious language. One of the difficulties facing us when we attempt to understand religious texts is that they often were written a long time ago by persons who lived in a vastly different situation from ours. This distance that separates us from the origin of the text is one of the difficulties to be overcome in the process of interpretation, but we cannot be content with re-creating the meaning the words had for their author. Great religious texts, good poetry, and significant works of art can all bridge this distance because they speak directly to us and open up new insights into reality for us. This is what Ricoeur means when he says that the question of reference is still important, for the world of poetic discourse is a world "in front of the text," a world that will open up a new world for us, in the sense of new levels of reality. Religious language is possible only if the literal meaning of words is surpassed so that the metaphorical process can take place, a process that brings new levels of reality and self-understanding to expression.

The Metaphorical Process

PAUL RICOEUR

THE SEMANTICS OF METAPHOR

The first part of this study will take us from a rhetoric to a semantics. Or, more precisely, as we shall see in a moment, from a rhetoric of the *word* to a semantics of *discourse* or of the sentence.

In the rhetorical tradition, metaphor is classed among the tropes, that is, among those figures which concern variations of meaning in the use of words, and more precisely in the process of naming. The concerns of rhetoric are of the following sort. Words themselves have their own meanings, that is to say, meanings common to a speaking community, fixed by the norms of usage in this community and inscribed in a lexical code. Rhetoric begins where this lexical code ends. It deals with the figurative meanings of a word, i.e., those meanings which deviate from ordinary use. Why these variations, these deviations, these figures of speech? The ancient rhetoricians generally answered in this way: It is either to fill a semantical lacuna, or to ornament discourse. It is because we have more ideas than we have words that we need to extend the meaning of those words which we do have beyond their ordinary usage. Or, we may have a correct word, but we prefer to use a figurative word to please and seduce. This strategy is a part of the function of rhetoric, which is persuasion, i.e., influencing people by means of discourse which is neither the means of proof nor of violence, but rather the means of rendering the probable more acceptable.

Metaphor is one of these figures, the one in which resemblance serves as a reason for the substitution of a figurative word for a literal word which is either lacking or omitted. Metaphor is distinguished from other figures of style, such as metonymy, where contiguity plays the role which resemblance plays in metaphor.

This is a very schematic summary of a long history which begins with the Greek sophists, moves through Aristotle, Cicero and Quintilian, and which ends with the last treatises on rhetoric of the nineteenth century. What remains constant in this tradition can be summarized in the following six propositions: (1) Metaphor is a trope, i.e., a figure of discourse which concerns naming. (2) Metaphor is an extension of naming by a deviation from the literal sense of words. (3) The reason for this deviation in metaphor is resemblance. (4) The function

Source: Paul Ricoeur, "Biblical Hermeneutics," *Semeia* 4, ed. John Dominic Crossan (Missoula, MT: Scholars Press, 1975), pp. 75–78. © 1975 by the Society of Biblical Literature. Used by permission.

of resemblance is to ground the substitution of the figurative meaning of a word borrowed from the literal sense of a word which could have been used in the same place. (5) The substituted meaning does not include any semantic innovation; we can thus translate a metaphor by restoring the literal word for the figurative word which was substituted. (6) Since it admits of no innovation, metaphor gives no information about reality; it is only an ornament of discourse, and therefore can be categorized as an emotional function of discourse.

All of these presuppositions of rhetoric are called into question by a modern semantics of metaphor.

The first presupposition which should be combatted is that metaphor is only an accident of naming, a displacement, a shift in the meaning, that is, the impact of the word on a production of meaning which involves a complete statement. This is in effect the first discovery of a semantics of metaphor. Metaphor depends on a semantics of the sentence before it concerns a semantics of the word. Metaphor is only meaningful in a statement; it is a phenomenon of predication. When a poet speaks of a "blue angelus," or of a "white twilight" or a "green night," he places two terms in tension, which we may call with I. A. Richards the *tenor* and the *vehicle*, and of which only the whole constitutes the metaphor. In this sense we must not speak of words used metaphorically, but of metaphorical *statements. Metaphor proceeds from the tension between all the terms in a metaphorical statement.*

This first thesis implies a second. If metaphor concerns words only because it first happens on the level of an entire sentence, then the first phenomenon is not the deviation from the literal or proper meaning of words, but the very functioning of predication at the level of the whole statement. What we have called a tension is not just something which occurs between the two terms of the statement, but between the two complete interpretations of the statement. The strategy of discourse by which the metaphorical statement obtains its meaning is absurdity. This absurdity is revealed as an absurdity for a literal interpretation. The angelus is not blue, if blue is a color. Thus metaphor does not exist in itself, but in an interpretation. Metaphorical interpretation presupposes a literal interpretation which is destroyed. Metaphorical interpretation consists in transforming a self-defeating, sudden contradiction into a meaningful contradiction. It is this transformation which imposes on the word a sort of "twist." We are forced to give a new meaning to the word, an extension of meaning which allows it to *make* sense where a literal interpretation does not make sense: So metaphor appears as an answer to a certain inconsistency of the statement interpreted literally. We might call this inconsistency a "semantic impertinence," to use an expression more supple and comprehensive than that of contradiction or absurdity. Because in using only the ordinary lexical value of words I can make sense only by saving the entire statement, I make the words undergo a sort of labor of meaning, a twist by which the metaphorical statement obtains its meaning. We can thus say that metaphor, considered only as its words, consists in a shift of meaning. But the effect of this shift is to reduce another shift at the level of the whole statement, this shift which we just called a semantic impertinence, and which consists in the mutual unsuitability of the terms when interpreted literally.

It is now possible to return to the third theme of the rhetorical conception of metaphor, the role of resemblance. This has very often been misunderstood. It has been reduced to the role of images in poetic discourse. For many literary critics, especially among the ancients, to study the metaphors of an author is to study the nomenclature of the images which illustrate his ideas. But if metaphor does not consist in clothing an idea with an image, if it consists rather in the reduction of the shock between two incompatible ideas, it is in this reduction of the shift, in this rapprochement, that we must look for the play of resemblance. What is at stake in a metaphorical statement is making a "kinship" appear where ordinary vision perceives no mutual appropriateness at all. Here metaphor operates in a way which is very close to what Gilbert Ryle has called a "category-mistake." It is a calculated error. It consists in assimilating things which do not go together. But precisely by means of this calculated error, metaphor discloses a relationship of meaning hitherto unnoticed between terms which were prevented from communicating by former classifications. When the poet says that "time is a beggar," he teaches us to "see as if. . . ," to see time *as*, or like, a beggar. Two categorical classes which were hitherto distant suddenly become close. To render close what was "distant" is the work of resemblance. Aristotle, in this sense, was correct when he said that "to make good metaphors is to perceive likenesses." But this seeing is at the same time a construction: good metaphors are those which institute a resemblance more than those which simply register one.

From this description of the labor or resemblance in a metaphorical statement results yet another opposition to the purely rhetorical conception of metaphor. For rhetoric, you will remember, the trope was a simple substitution of one word for another. Now, substitution is a sterile operation, but in metaphor, on the contrary, the tension between the words and especially the tension between two interpretations, one literal and one metaphorical, in the whole sentence, gives rise to a veritable creation of meaning of which rhetoric perceived only the end result. In a theory of tension, which I am here opposing to a theory of substitution, a new signification emerges which deals with the whole statement. In this respect, metaphor is an instantaneous creation, a *semantic innovation* which has no status in established language and which exists only in the attribution of unusual predicates. In this way metaphor is closer to the active resolution of an enigma than to simple association by resemblance. It is the resolution of a semantic dissonance. We do not recognize the specificity of the phenomenon if we only consider dead metaphors which are no longer true metaphors, for example, the foot of a chair, or the leg of a table. True metaphors are *metaphors of invention* in which a new extension of the meaning of the words answers a novel discordance in the sentence. It is true that the metaphor of invention tends through repetition to become a dead metaphor. Then the extension of meaning is noted in the lexicon and becomes part of the polysemy of the word which is thereby simply augmented. But there are no living metaphors in the dictionary.

Two conclusions follow from this analysis which will be of great importance for the second and third parts of this section. And these two conclusions are opposed to the themes drawn from the rhetorical model. First, *true metaphors are untranslatable*. Only metaphors of substitution are capable of a translation which restores the proper meaning. Tension metaphors are untranslatable because they create meaning. To say that they are untranslatable does not mean that they cannot be paraphrased, but the paraphrase is infinite and does not exhaust the innovation in meaning.

The second consequence is that metaphor is not an ornament of discourse. Metaphor has more than an emotional value. It includes *new information*. In effect, by means of a "category-mistake," new semantic fields are born from novel rapprochements. In short, metaphor says something new about reality.

It is this last conclusion which will serve as the basis for the second step in this section, which will be devoted to the function of *reference* or the denotative power of metaphorical statements.

METAPHOR AND REALITY

To investigate the referential or denotative function of metaphor is to bring to bear a number of general hypotheses about language which I would like to lay out, although I cannot justify them here.

First, we must admit that it is possible to distinguish in every statement between sense and reference. We owe this distinction to Frege who postulated it as a logician. *Sinn* is the ideal objective content of a proposition; *Bedeutung* is its claim to truth. My hypothesis is that this distinction is of interest not only to the logician, but concerns the functioning of discourse in its whole scope. Meaning is *what* a statement says, reference is *that about which* it says it. What a statement says is immanent within it—it is its internal arrangement. That with which it deals is extra-linguistic. It is the real insofar as it is conveyed in language; it is what is said about the world.

The extension of Frege's distinction to the whole of discourse implies a conception of the whole of language close to that of Humboldt and Cassirer, for whom the function of language is to articulate our experience of the world, to give form to this experience. This hypothesis marks our complete break with structuralism where language functions purely internally or immanently, where an element refers only to another element of the same system. This vision is perfectly legitimate as long as we can treat the facts of speech and of discourse as being homogeneous with the phenomena of language, and consequently as different only in the dimension of the units at stake—phonemes, lexemes, sentences, discourse, texts, works. And in fact certain discourses, certain texts, certain works function like a language, that is, on the basis of structures closed in upon themselves, like the interplay of differences and oppositions homologous to the differences that the phonological schema presents with a sort of crystalline purity. But this homology ought not to make us forget a trait fundamental to discourse, namely, that discourse is based on a unit of genre completely different from the units of language which are signs. This unit is the sentence. Now, the sentence has characteristics which are in no way a repetition of those of language. Among these characteristics the difference between reference and meaning is fundamental. If language is closed in upon itself, discourse is open and turned toward a world which it wishes to express and to convey in language. If this general hypothesis holds and is significant, the ultimate problem raised by metaphor is to know in what respects the transposition of meaning which defines it contributes to the articulation of experience, to the forming of the world.

Furthermore, the conception of the whole of language implied by the distinction of logical origin between meaning and reference implies a hermeneutical conception which I laid out in the preceding section. If we admit that the hermeneutical task is to conceptualize the principles of interpretation for works of language, the distinction between meaning and reference has as its consequence that interpretation does not stop at a structuralist analysis of works, that is, at their immanent meaning, but that it aims at unfolding the sort of world that a work projects. This hermeneutical implication of the distinction between meaning and reference becomes completely striking if we contrast it with the romantic conception of hermeneutics in which interpretation aimed at recovering the intention of an author *behind* the text. The Fregeian distinction invites us rather to follow the movement which conveys meaning, that is, the movement of the internal structure of the work toward its reference, toward the sort of world which the work opens up *in front of* the text.

These are the sort of semantic hypotheses of the philosophy of language and of hermeneutics which are at the basis of the present reflections on the referential scope of metaphorical statements.

That metaphorical statements can make a claim to truth must meet serious objections which cannot be reduced to prejudices issuing from the purely rhetorical conception discussed above; the claim that metaphor contains no new information and is purely ornamental. To that sort of objection I shall not return. But to those prejudices of rhetorical origin is added an objection which concerns the functioning of poetic language itself. It is not surprising that an objection should come from this direction, since metaphor is traditionally tied to the functioning of poetic language.

Here we run up against a very strong tendency in contemporary literary criticism to deny that poetic language aims at reality or that it says anything whatsoever about something exterior to itself, since the suppression of reference, the abolition of reality seems to be the very law for the functioning of poetic language. Thus Roman Jakobson in a famous essay on "Linguistics and Poetics" claims that the poetic function of language consists in accentuating the message for its own sake at the expense of the referential function of ordinary language. "This function," he says, "by promoting the palpability of signs, deepens the fundamental dichotomy of signs and objects" (356). There are numerous literary critiques from this point of view. The conjunction of meaning and sound in poetry seems to make a poem a solid object closed upon itself, where words become the material for the shaping of the poem as stone does for sculpture. In poetry, say the most extreme of these critics, it is a question of nothing outside of language itself. Thus we might oppose the centripetal movement of poetic language to the centrifugal movement of descriptive discourse, as Northrop Frye does, and say that poetry is a "self-contained" language. From this perspective metaphor is a privileged instrument for suspending reality by means of the displacement of the ordinary meaning of words. If a descriptive claim is tied together with the ordinary meaning, the abolition of the reference is equally tied to the abolition of the ordinary meaning.

I would like to oppose to this conception of poetic function another hypothesis, namely, that the suspension of the referential function of ordinary language does not mean the abolition of all reference, but, on the contrary, that this suspension is the negative condition for the liberation of another referential dimension of language and another dimension of reality itself.

Jakobson himself, referred to above, invites us to explore this direction. "The supremacy of the poetic function over the referential function," he says, "does not obliterate the reference (the denotation), but renders it ambiguous." Again, he says that poetry is "reference split in two."

Let us take our point of departure from the earlier thesis that the meaning of a metaphorical statement is produced by the failure of the literal interpretation of the statement. In a literal interpretation, the meaning destroys itself, and so does the ordinary reference. The abolition of the reference of poetic language is thus related to the self-destruction of meaning for a literal interpretation of metaphorical statements. But this self-destruction of meaning, by means of absurdity, that is, by means of the semantic impertinence or the inconsistency of the statement, is only the reverse side of an innovation of meaning on the level of the entire sentence. From this point onward can we not say that the metaphorical interpretation gives rise to a re-interpretation of reality itself, in spite of, and thanks to, the abolition of the reference which corresponds to the literal interpretation of the statement?

Thus I propose to extend to reference what I said about meaning. I said that the metaphorical meaning instituted a "proximity" between significations which were hitherto distant. I will say now that it is from this proximity that a new vision of reality springs up, one which is resisted by ordinary vision tied to the ordinary use of words. Then it is the function of poetic language to weaken the first-order reference of ordinary language in order to allow this second-order reference to come forth.

But reference to what? Here I propose two detours in order to prepare an answer to this question.

I will follow a first suggestion which comes from the relationship between metaphor and models. I owe this to Max Black in his *Models and Metaphors* and to Mary B. Hesse in her *Models and Analogies in Science*. The general idea is that metaphor is to poetic language as model is to scientific language. In scientific language a model is essentially a heuristic device which serves to break up an inadequate interpretation and to blaze a trail toward a new, more adequate interpretation. In Mary Hesse's terms, it is an instrument of "re-description." This is the expression I will retain for the following analysis. But it is important to understand the meaning of this term in its strictly epistemological use.

The power of *redescription* of models can only be understood if we, along with Max Black, carefully distinguish three sorts of models: scale models, which materially resemble the specimen, for example, a model boat; analogical models, which conserve only the structural identities, for example, a diagram; and theoretical models, which consist in constructing an imaginary object more accessible to description and in transposing the properties of this object into a domain of more complex reality. Now, says Max Black, to describe a domain of reality in terms of an imaginary theoretical model is a certain manner of seeing things "otherwise," by changing our language on the subject of these things. And the change of language goes through the construction of a *heuristic fiction* and the transposition of this heuristic fiction to reality itself.

Let us now apply to metaphor this world of the model. Our guiding thread will be the connection between the two notions of heuristic fiction and of redescription by transference of the fiction to reality itself. It is this double movement which we find in metaphor. "A memorable metaphor has the power to bring two separate domains into cognitive and emotional relation by using language directly appropriate to the one as a lens for seeing the other."[1] Through this detour of heuristic fiction, we perceive new connections in things.[2] The rationale for this is the presumed isomorphism between the model and a domain of application. It is this isomorphism which grounds the "analogical transfer of a vocabulary"[3] and which allows metaphor, like the model, to "reveal new relations."[4]

A second detour in the direction of a theory of metaphor consists in showing that a *language of the arts* exists and does not differ fundamentally from the general language. The first detour passed through the comparison between poetry and science, the second passes through the comparison between plastic art and ordinary language. This detour is proposed by Nelson Goodman in his *Languages of Art*. In this work, he opposes the facile solution which consists in saying that only scientific language denotes reality and that art is limited to adding purely subjective and emotional connotations to "denotation." A painting represents reality no less than a discourse on reality does. Not that the painting imitates what it represents; on the contrary, like all description, the pictorial representation organizes reality. And its organizing power is all the greater when the denotation is the more fictional, that is, in logical language, when the denotation is of zero quantity. But multiple denotation, unique denotation, and null denotation are equally denotations, that is, they refer to, or in the last analysis, they organize the real.

---

[1] Max Black, *Models and Metaphors* (Ithaca, NY: Cornell University Press, 1962), p. 236.

[2] *Ibid.*, p. 237.

[3] *Ibid.*, p. 238.

[4] *Ibid.*

Nelson Goodman places this analysis under a title which is shocking at first glance: *Reality Remade*. This title applies to all symbolic functioning.

Then what is metaphor? It is an extension of denotation by a transference of labels to new objects which resist the transfer. Thus a painting can literally be said to be grey and metaphorically to be sad. Metaphor is nothing other than the application of a familiar label to a new object which first resists and then surrenders to its application. Here we recognize an essential point of the earlier analysis which compared metaphor with a calculated error. But this point is now inserted into the framework of a theory of denotation. This calculated error untracks the literal application of the predicate. In effect, paintings are literally neither happy nor sad because they are not feeling beings. Literal falsity is thus an ingredient of metaphorical truth. A counter-indicated application puts us on the track of a transferred application. I will retain in what follows this strong expression of Nelson Goodman, "literal falsity and metaphorical truth." Literal falsity consists in the misassignment of a label; metaphorical truth, in the reassignment of the same label by transference.

After these two detours through the notion of model and that of a transfer of labels, we can return to the question which we left in suspense, that of the "ambiguous reference," or the "split" reference of poetic language.

Poetic language also speaks of reality, but it does so at another level than does scientific language. It does not show us a world already there, as does descriptive or didactic language. In effect, as we have seen, the ordinary reference of language is abolished by the natural strategy of poetic discourse. But in the very measure that this first-order reference is abolished, another power of speaking the world is liberated, although at another level of reality. This level is that which Husserlian phenomenology has designated as the *Lebenswelt* and which Heidegger has called "being-in-the-world." It is an eclipsing of the objective manipulable world, an illuminating of the life-world, of non-manipulable being-in-the-world, which seems to me to be the fundamental ontological import of poetic language.

Here I rejoin the great idea of Aristotle in his *Poetics*. There poetry is depicted as a *mimesis* of human action. (Aristotle has tragedy in mind.) But this *mimesis* passes through the creation, through the *poiesis* of a fable or a myth which is the very work of the poet. In the language which I have adopted here, I would say that poetry imitates reality only by recreating it at a mythical level of discourse. Here fiction and redescription go hand in hand. It is the heuristic fiction which bears the function of discovery in poetic language.

I will conclude this second part of the section with three remarks: (1) The rhetorical and the poetic function of language are reciprocally inverse. The first aims at persuading men by giving to discourse pleasing ornaments; the second aims at redescribing reality by the twisting pathway of heuristic fiction. (2) Metaphor is that strategy of discourse by which language divests itself of its ordinary descriptive function in order to serve its extraordinary function of re-description. (3) We can speak cautiously of metaphorical truth to designate the claim of attaining reality which is attached to the power of redescription of poetic language.

When the poet says, "Nature is a temple where living columns . . . ," the verb "is" is not limited to relating the predicate "temple" to the subject "nature." The copula is not only relational. It implies that this relation redescribes *what* is in a certain way. It says that such is the case.

Are we thereby falling into the trap which language holds out for us by confusing two senses of the verb "to be," the relational and the existential senses? This would be the case if we took the verb "to be" in a literal sense. But there is also a metaphorical sense of the verb in which the tension we have found between words (nature and temple) is retained, as well as the tension between interpretations (literal and metaphorical). The same tension resides in the verb "to be" in metaphorical statements. The "is" is both a literal "is not" and a metaphorical "is like." The ambiguity, the splitting, is thus extended from sense to reference and across the latter to the "is" of metaphorical truth. Poetic language does not say literally what things are, but what they are like. It is in this oblique fashion that it says what they are.

Discussion Questions

1. Do you find convincing Ricoeur's claim that metaphor is the way we create new meanings in language? Why or why not?

2. Explain what is meant by saying that a metaphor is a kind of deliberate category mistake.

3. Ricoeur claims that the metaphorical process is at work not only in religious discourse, but also in art and science. Do you agree? Why or why not?

4. What points does Ricoeur's view of metaphor share with Ramsey's use of models?

5. Do you find acceptable Ricoeur's claims about the referential function of metaphor? Give reasons for your answer.

6. Find an example of recent religious writing and make a list of all the metaphors it exhibits. Which of these do you think are best? Do you think that many people fail to see some metaphors as actually being metaphorical? What would this tell you about the stage of the metaphorical process that those particular metaphors are in?

Religious Language
and Gender

Probably no issue has thrust the discussion of religious language back into the forefront than has debate about the appropriateness of gender-specific language in Scripture and liturgy. Propelled by the emergence of feminist theology, the apparent exclusiveness of religious language and models, to use Ramsey's term, has generated a vast literature exploring the issue of gender-specific language used in liturgy and theological discussion.

Given that most of the societies from which Scripture emerged were patriarchal, both Jewish and Christian Scriptures contain predominantly masculine models, although, as Ramsey has shown, this is not universally the case. Relevant to this point are several feminine models used to speak about God in Jewish Scriptures (the Old Testament): mother (Deut. 32:18), dairymaid (John 10:10), laundress (Mal. 3:2), and nursemaid (Isa. 1:2). Language that refers to God as father is not a predominant model in Jewish Scripture, but it is the dominant one in the New Testament. Indeed, the term *Abba* (the familiar form of address used by an infant to its father), introduced by Jesus as the intimate form of address to God, becomes the mark of the indwelling of God's spirit in the life of believers: "When we cry, 'Abba! Father!' it is that very Spirit bearing witness with our spirit that we are children of God" (Romans 8:15–16). Given the movement toward sexual equality and the quest for gender-inclusive language in both speech and formal writing, how are we to deal with such masculine models in theological talk?

This issue was a concern in the revision of the Revised Standard Version of the Bible (New RSV). The original RSV translators followed the then-accepted English grammatical norms of using masculine forms for indefinite pronouns and employing such terms as "men" to mean "people." Now that these usages are understood by some as exclusive rather than inclusive, the revisers followed the principle of removing the masculine-dominated language from the English translation when it was there only because the earlier translators had introduced it even though it was not in the Hebrew or Greek texts. For example, the old RSV of John 2:10 was, "Every man serves the good wine first; and when men have drunk freely, then the poor wine." The New RSV translates the same passage as, "Every-one serves the good wine first, and then the inferior wine after the guests have become drunk." Another example is found in Romans 2:16: "God judges the secrets of men . . ." (old RSV); "God . . . will judge the secret thoughts of all . . ." (New RSV).

A stronger approach to the issue of inclusive language is offered by the *In-clusive-Language Lectionary*, a project sponsored by the Division of Education and Ministry of the National Council of the Churches of Christ in the United States. A lectionary is a collection of scriptures selected to harmonize with the Christian year, and this project takes the added step of changing the terms in Scripture to inclusive language. Instead of "God the Father," the *Inclusive-Language Lectionary* uses "God the Father and Mother." In explaining the reason for this change, the editors say, "The image of God as Father has been misused to support the exces-sive authority of earthly fathers in a patriarchal social structure. The metaphor 'God the Father and Mother' points to the close relationship between language about God and language about the human community."[1] In the *Inclusive-Language Lectionary*, Romans 8:15–16 therefore becomes, "When we cry, '[God! my *Mother and*] Father!' it is the Spirit bearing witness with our spirit that we are children of God."

Critics of the inclusive-language approach argue that it is one thing to *remove* gender-specific language introduced into translations of Scripture by translators, but it is quite another thing to *change* the language of Scripture to conform to prevailing norms for language. To be sure, the editors of the *Inclusive-Language Lectionary* always put their changes in brackets to indicate that they are additions to the text, but it is clear that these additions are intended to be read in public worship. Those who take Scripture as divine revelation are even less enthusiastic about the inclusive-language project, since their view is that the terminology of Scripture itself is part of that revelation and should not be arbitrarily changed. In defending their changes, the editors of the *Inclusive-Language Lectionary* see the fa-ther-language of the Bible as metaphorical—and, indeed, a metaphor in need of reexamination. According to the editors, "Although 'God the Father' has been a powerful metaphor for communicating the nature of God, like any metaphor it can become worn. It may even be interpreted literally, that is, as describing ex-actly. The dissimilar become similar. The metaphor becomes a proposition."[2]

Some critics are convinced that such metaphors can be readily changed. They maintain that the issue here is not language, but ideology, namely, that the sub-jection of women is encouraged by male-dominated metaphors. Opponents ques-tion the evidence for this and point out that religions of the ancient Near East, for example, were dominated by feminine deities, with a strong emphasis on na-ture worship, which was anathema to the religion of Israel. In such religions there

---

[1] *An Inclusive-Language Lectionary* (published for The Cooperative Publication Association by John Knox Press, the Pilgrim Press, and the Westminster Press, 1986), p. 270.

[2] Ibid., p. 269.

was no improvement in the status of women, so the link between gender-specific language and the status of women is questionable. Inclusivists make clear that a parental relationship to God is a special one made possible because of the relationship between Jesus and God, and just as father-language does not imply that God is Father of the world, so neither should God as Father-Mother be misinterpreted as justification for nature worship. Other examples of inclusive language used in the lectionary are *sovereign* instead of Lord; *ruler, sovereign,* or *monarch* rather than King; *realm of God,* not kingdom of God; *sisters and brothers, friends,* or *neighbors* as a substitute for brother and brethren; *the Human One* for Son of Man; and *child of God* instead of Son of God.

In the reading that follows Rosemary Radford Ruether explores the female images of God in Scripture and offers an analysis of their significance, noting that "God is not always described as a male." According to Ruether, not only are the feminine images important for a fuller understanding of God, but also the suppression of them only encourages the revitalization of nonbiblical religions that more prominently feature the feminine. For Ruether the issue is not an either/or choice: not male or female images. Both are needed to expand our understanding of God and in so doing "expanding human potential."

The Female Nature of God

ROSEMARY RADFORD RUETHER

The exclusively male image of God in the Judaeo-Christian tradition has become a critical issue of contemporary religious life. This question does not originate first of all in theology or in hermeneutics. It originates in the experience of alienation from this male image of God experienced by feminist women. It is only when this alienation is taken seriously that the theological and exegetical questions begin to be raised.

1. WHAT IS THE PROBLEM?

The problem of the male image of God cannot be treated as trivial or an accidental question of linguistics. It must be understood first of all as an ideological

Source: Reprinted from Rosemary Ruether, "The Female Nature of God," *Concilium,* vol. 143, 1981. Published by SCM Press. Reprinted by permission.

bias that reflects the sociology of patriarchal societies; that is, those societies dominated by male, property-holding heads of families. Although not all patriarchal societies have male monotheist religions, in those patriarchal societies which have this view of God, the God-image serves as the central reinforcement of the structure of patriarchal rule. The subordinate status of women in the social and legal order is reflected in the subordinate status of women in the cultus. The single male God is seen not only as creator and lawgiver of this secondary status of women. The very structure of spirituality in relation to this God enforces her secondary status.

What this means quite simply is the following. When God is projected in the image of one sex, rather than both sexes, and in the image of the ruling class of this sex, then this class of males is seen as consisting in the ones who possess the image of God primarily. Women are regarded as relating to God only secondarily and through inclusion in the male as their "head." This is stated very specifically by St. Augustine in his treatise *On the Trinity* (7, 7, 10).

The male monotheist image of God dictates a certain structure of divine-human relationship. God addresses directly only the patriarchal ruling class. All other groups—women, children, slaves—are addressed by God only indirectly and through the mediation of the patriarchal class. This hierarchal order of God/Man/Woman appears throughout Hebrew law. But it also reappears as a theological principle in the New Testament. Thus Paul (despite Gal. 3:28) in I Cor. 11:3 and 7 reaffirms this patriarchal order of relationships:

> But I want you to understand that the head of every man is Christ, the head of a woman is her husband, and the head of Christ is God. . . . For a man ought not to cover his head, since he is the image and glory of God; but the woman is the glory of man.

Thus the woman is seen as lacking the image of God or direct relation to God, in herself, but only secondarily, as mediated through the male.

2. THE SUPPRESSED "FEMININE" IN PATRIARCHAL THEOLOGY

Recognising the fundamentally ideological, and even idolatrous, nature of this male-dominant image of God, some recent scholars have sought to show that this was never the whole story. God is not always described as a male. There is a small number of cases where God is described as a female. These texts occur in the Scriptures, particularly in the context of describing God's faithfulness to Israel and suffering on behalf of Israel. Here the labours of a woman in travail, giving birth to a child, and the fidelity of a mother who loves the child unconditionally, seemed to be more striking human analogies for these attributes of God than anything to be found in male activity. Thus in Isaiah we find:

> Yahweh goes forth, now I will cry out like a woman in travail, I will gasp and pant. (Isa. 42:13, 14).

For Zion said, "Yahweh has forsaken me; my Lord has forgotten me. Can a woman forget her suckling child, that she should have no compassion on the son of her womb? Even these may forget, yet I will not forget you." (Isa. 49:14, 15).

These analogies of God as female in Scripture have been collected in Leonard Swidler's *Biblical Affirmation of Woman* (Philadelphia: Westminster 1979).

There is a second use of the female image for God in Scripture. The female image also appears as a secondary *persona* of God in the work of mediation to creation. In biblical thought this is found primarily in the Wisdom tradition. Here Holy Wisdom is described as a daughter of God through whom God mediates the work of creation, providential guidance, revelation, and reconciliation to God. In relation to the Solomon, the paradigmatic royal person, Wisdom is described as a "bride of his soul." Of her Solomon says:

I loved her and sought after her from my youth, and I desired to take her for my bride, and I became enamoured of her beauty. . . . Therefore I determined to take her to live with me, knowing that she would give me good counsel (Wisd. of Sol. 8:2, 9).

The same view of Wisdom as mediating creatrix is found in Proverbs (8:23–31). Here she is imaged as the mother who mediates wisdom to her sons.

Behind this powerful image of Divine Wisdom undoubtedly lies remnants of the ancient Near Eastern Goddess, Isis or Astarte. These Goddesses were imaged as creators and redeemers. They are linked particularly with Wisdom, defined as both social justice and harmony in nature, over against the threatening powers of Chaos. Raphael Patai, in his book, *The Hebrew Goddess* (Ktav 1967), has delineated the heritage of this ancient Near Eastern Goddess as she appeared in suppressed form in Hebrew theology.

Although the Sophia image disappears in rabbinic thought after the advent of the Christian era, possibly because of its use in gnosticism, a new image of God's mediating presence as female appears in the form of the *Shekinah*. The *Shekinah* is both the mediating presence of God in the midst of Israel, but also the reconciler of Israel with God. In rabbinic mystical speculation on the *galut* (exile), the *Shekinah* is seen as going into exile with Israel when God-as-father has turned away his face in anger. Each Shabbat celebration is seen as a mystical connubial embrace of God with his *Shekinah*, anticipating the final reuniting of God with creation in the messianic age. The exile of Israel from the land is seen ultimately as an exile within God, divorcing the masculine from the feminine "side" of God.

In Christianity this possibility of the immanence of God as feminine was eliminated. Christianity translated the Sophia concept into the Logos concept of Philo, defined as "son of God." It related this masculine mediating *persona* of God to the human person, Jesus. Thus the maleness of Jesus as a human person is correlated (or even fused into) the maleness of the Logos as "son of God." All possible speculation on a "female side" of God within trinitarian imagery was thus cut off from the beginning.

Some Sophia speculation does get revived in the Greek Orthodox tradition in relation to creation, the Church and Mariology. One somewhat maverick modern Orthodox thinker (Sergius Bulgakov, *The Wisdom of God*, London 1937) even relates this sophiological aspect of God to the *ousia* or Being of God. Sophia is the matrix or ground of Being of the three (male) persons of God! But it is doubtful if most Orthodox thinkers would be comfortable with that idea.

In western thought speculation on feminine aspects of God were probably rejected early because of links with gnosticism. Some recent Catholic thinkers (i.e., Leonard Swidler) have tried to revive the Sophia/*Shekinah* idea and link it with the Holy Spirit. But this does not have roots in western trinitarian thought. Basically the Spirit is imaged as a "male" but nonanthropomorphic principle. As the power of God that "fecundates" the waters at creation and the womb of Mary, its human referent would seem to be closer to the male semen as medium of male power.

This means that in western Christian theology, the female image is expelled from any place within the doctrine of God. It appears instead on the creaturely side of the God/creation relation. The female is used as the image of that which is created by God, that which is the recipient of God's creation; namely, Nature, Church, the soul, and, finally, Mary as the paradigmatic image of the redeemed humanity.

One partial exception to this rule is found in the Jesus mysticism of the middle ages that finds its culmination in Juliana of Norwich. Here Jesus, as the one who feeds us with his body, is portrayed as both mother and father. Eucharistic spirituality particularly seems to foster this mothering, nurturing image of Jesus. However since both the divine and the human person of Jesus is firmly established in the orthodox theological tradition as male, this feminine reference to Jesus remains an attribute of a male person. Female-identified qualities, such as mothering and nurturing, are taken over by the male. But the female is not allowed "male" or "headship" capacities.

What I wish to argue then is that all of these suppressed feminine aspects of God in patriarchal theology still remain fundamentally within the context of the male-dominant structure of patriarchal relationships. The female can never appear as the icon of God in all divine fullness, parallel to the male image of God. It is allowed in certain limited references to God's faithfulness and suffering for Israel. Or it appears as a clearly subordinate principle that mediates the work and power of the Father, much as the mother in the family mediates to the children (sons) the dictates of the father. She can be daughter of the divine king; bride of the human king; mother of his sons; but never an autonomous person in her own right.

The "feminine" in patriarchal theology is basically allowed to act only within the same limited, subordinate or mediating roles that women are allowed to act in the patriarchal social order. The feminine is the recipient and mediator of male power to subordinate persons; i.e., sons, servants. In Christianity even these covert and marginal roles of the feminine as aspects of God disappear. Here the feminine is only allowed as image of the human recipient or mediator of divine grace, not as an aspect of the divine. In every relationship in which this "feminine" aspect appears in patriarchal theology, the dominant sovereign principle is always male; the female operating only as delegate of the male.

3. "PAGAN FEMINISM": THE REVOLT AGAINST THE BIBLICAL PATRIARCHAL GOD

In the 1970s the feminist movement, particularly in the United States, began to develop an increasingly militant wing that identified patriarchal religion as the root of the problem of women's subordination. These women saw that efforts to create a more "androgynous" God within the biblical tradition would be insufficient. The female aspect of God would always be placed within this fundamentally male-centred perspective. They concluded that biblical religion must be rejected altogether.

In its place they would substitute a Goddess and nature religion that they believe to be the original human cult of matriarchal society before the rise of patriarchy. They believe that the witches of the European middle ages preserved this Goddess-centred nature religion. They were persecuted for this faith by the Christian Church who falsely accused them of malevolence and "devil worship." Feminist Wicca (or witchcraft) believes itself to be reviving this ancient Goddess religion. The book by Starhawk (Miriam Simos), *The Spiral Dance* (New York 1979), is a good expression of this feminist Goddess movement.

It is possible that we are witnessing in this movement the first strings of what may become a new stage of human religious consciousness. This possibility cannot be ruled out by the critical Christian. It may be that we have allowed divine revelation through the prophets and through Jesus to be so corrupted by an idolatrous androcentrism, that a fuller understanding of God that truly includes the female as person must come as superseding and judging patriarchal religion. However, Goddess religion in its present form manifests a number of immaturities that are open to criticism, even from the point of view of feminism.

Following outdated matriarchal anthropology from the nineteenth century, much of the pedigree claimed by this movement is of doubtful historicity. In fact, the patterns of Goddess religion reveal very clearly their roots in nineteenth-century European romanticism. The dualistic world view that sets the feminine, nature and immanence on one side, and the masculine, history and transcendence on the other, is fundamentally preserved in this movement. It simply exalts the feminine pole of the dualism and repudiates the masculine side. One must ask whether this does not entrap women in precisely the traditional stereotypes. The dualisms are not overcome, but merely given a reverse valuation. But, in practice, this still means that women, even in "rebellion," are confined to a powerless Utopianism in which males own and run "the world."

Moreover, within their own community, instead of transforming the male monotheist model, they have reversed it. Now the great Goddess is the predominant image of the Divine. Woman then becomes the one who fully images the

Goddess and communicates directly with her. Males are either excluded or given a subordinate position that is analogous to the position traditionally accorded women in the patriarchal cult. This *coup d'etat* may feel satisfying in the short run, but in the long run would seem to reproduce the same fundamental pathology.

4. DOES THE ANCIENT GODDESS REPRESENT THE FEMININE?

Both biblical feminists, who search for the suppressed feminine in the Judaeo-Christian tradition, and Goddess worshipers, who wish to exalt the feminine at the expense of the masculine, share a common assumption. Both assume that the recovery of the female as icon of the divine means the vindication of the "feminine." Neither ask the more fundamental question of whether the concept of the feminine itself is not a patriarchal creation. Thus the vindication of the "feminine," as we have inherited that concept from patriarchy, will always be set within a dualistic scheme of complementary principles that segregate women on one side and men on the other. Even if this scheme is given a reversed valuation, the same dualism remains.

A recent study by Judith Ochshorn, *The Female Experience and the Nature of the Divine* (Indiana University Press 1980) raises some important questions about the appropriateness of identifying this patriarchally-defined feminine with the ancient goddesses of polytheistic cultures. What Ochshorn has discovered is that, in polytheistic cultures of the Ancient Near East, gods and goddesses do not fall into these stereotyped patterns of masculinity and femininity. A God or Goddess, when addressed in the context of their own cult, represents a fullness of divine attributes. The Goddess represents sovereignty, wisdom, justice, as well as aspects of sexual and natural fecundity. Likewise the God operates as a sexual and natural principle, as well as a principle for social relations. The Goddess displays all the fullness of divine power in a female image. She is not the expression of the "feminine." Ochshorn also believes that this more pluralistic schema allows women to play more equalitarian and even leading roles in the cultus.

The subordinate status of women, in which relation to God is mediated only through the patriarchal class, is absent from religions which have a plurality of divine foci in male and female forms. Although such a lost religious world is probably not revivable as an option today, such studies may help to point us to the relativity of our patriarchally-defined patterns of masculine or feminine. They alert us to the dangers of simply surfacing the suppressed "feminine side" of that dualism as part of the image of God, without further criticism.

5. TOWARDS AN IMAGE OF GOD BEYOND PATRIARCHY

If we are to seek an image of God(ess) beyond patriarchy, certain basic principles must be acknowledged. First we must acknowledge that the male has no special priority in imaging God(ess). If male roles and functions; i.e., fathering, are only analogies for God, then those analogies are in no way superior to the parallel analogies drawn from female experience; i.e., mothering. God(ess) as Parent is as much Mother as Father.

But even the Parent image must be recognised as a limited analogy for God(ess), often reinforcing patterns of permanent spiritual infantilism and cutting off moral maturity and responsibility. God(ess) as creator must be seen as the Ground of the full personhood of men and women equally. A God(ess) who is a good parent, and not a neurotic parent, is one that promotes our growth towards responsible personhood, not one who sanctions dependency. The whole concept of our relation to God(ess) must be reimaged.

If God(ess) is not only creator, but also redeemer of the world from sin, then God(ess) cannot be seen as the sanctioner of the priority of male over female. To do so is to make God the creator and sanctioner of patriarchy. God becomes the architect of injustice. The image of God as predominantly male is fundamentally idolatrous. The same can be said of an image of God(ess) as predominantly female.

The God(ess) who can be imaged through the experience of men and women alike does not simply embrace these experiences and validate them in their traditional historical form. We cannot simply add the "mothering" to the "fathering" God, while preserving the same hierarchal patterns of male activity and female passivity. To vindicate the "feminine" in this form is merely to make God the sanctioner of patriarchy in new form.

God(ess) must be seen as beyond maleness and femaleness. Encompassing the full humanity of both men and women, God(ess) also speaks as judge and redeemer from the stereotyped roles in which men as "masculine" and women as "feminine" have been cast in patriarchal society. God(ess) restores both men and women to full humanity. This means not only a new humanity, but a new society, new personal and social patterns of human relationships. The God(ess) who is both male and female, and neither male or female, points us to an unrealised new humanity. In this expanding image of God(ess) we glimpse our own expanding human potential, as selves and as social beings, that have remained truncated and confined in patriarchal, hierarchal relationships. We begin to give new content to the vision of the messianic humanity that is neither "Jew nor Greek, that is neither slave nor free, that is neither male nor female" (Gal. 3:28) in which God(ess) has "broken down the dividing wall of hostility" (Eph. 2:14).

Discussion Questions

1. One of the arguments for changing to inclusive language in Scripture is that patriarchal images have lost their metaphorical function. Do you agree?

2. What are the best arguments you can formulate in favor of inclusive language? What are the best arguments against it? Is there a middle ground?

3. What specifically does Ruether think has been lost as a result of the "ideological" commitment to exclusively patriarchal images when speaking of God?

4. Another argument against exclusionary language is that it leads to the subjection of women. Do you agree?

5. If religious metaphors and symbols cannot be changed arbitrarily but arise from the cultural situation itself, has the contemporary cultural situation changed sufficiently to warrant a change in religious language such as Ruether proposes?

RETROSPECTIVE

Religious Language

This chapter on religious language points out that, in spite of the often complex analysis required in a study of language, an investigation of the nature and function of language is an important concern, for language is intimately tied up with all cognitive activity. It therefore remains an important and ongoing area for philosophical investigation, and a great deal of the work of philosophy has been directed toward a study of language. Since the language of religious discourse is a part of the overall concern of language, it is important to note several of the general conclusions that the contemporary philosophical study of language has reached.

First, it is generally agreed that ordinary language cannot be reduced to a formal system, such as logic, that would capture the multiple meanings expressible in language in a logical system free from ambiguity. The ideal for some philosophers has always been a language that is perfectly exact, precise, and free from equivocation. Symbolic logic seemed to be precisely such an ambiguity-free language. But it is now recognized that ordinary language cannot be completely translated into symbolic logic. Anyone who has studied logic knows how difficult it is to translate even a simple sentence into symbolic notation; this says nothing of the difficulty of translating complex statements from ordinary language into logical form. This is not the fault of symbolic logic, which remains a valuable tool of analysis and has many practical applications, not only in the analysis of traditional philosophical arguments, but also in the development of artificial languages for computer programs. Still, symbolic logic captures only a part of the range of meanings expressible in ordinary language, and it is a mistake to think that a statement is not meaningful unless translatable into symbolic form.

A second conclusion of contemporary philosophy of language is that no single theory of meaningfulness is adequate to cover all the uses of language. Within the scope of certain narrowly defined limits, such principles are useful, but they cannot be shown to apply to all the functions of language. The principle of verification has had its defenders, but the weight of philosophical scholarship is against its being an adequate principle of meaning for all uses of language. It excludes many of the principles of science that even defenders of the principle agree are meaningful. It must be seen in the historical context of the desire for precise and exact criteria of meaningfulness that reflect the precision of scientific investigation.

Finally, it is generally recognized today that it is probably not possible to develop a theory of language that is adequate for all uses of language—what philosophers would call "necessary and sufficient conditions for language." What confronts us when we turn to an examination of language is an almost bewildering variety of uses of language. Ludwig Wittgenstein suggests the analogy of games to describe this apparent chaotic situation in language. If you were to attempt to give a complete description of what constitutes the activity known as a "game," you would find a similar bewildering variety of activities. There are many different kinds of games—board games, ball games, card games, games that involve teams, games for single players, games with fixed rules, other games with flexible rules, and so forth. This variety of games can be grouped into classifications having certain "family resemblances," but some features of one family of games might be missing from a different family of games. Even though families of games share common characteristics with other families of games, these family resemblances are missing from other families. Something like this confronts us when we examine language: There are many different language games, including the language of science, the language of art, the language of poetry, and the language of religion. The error of logical positivism is the attempt to impose on all "language games," to use Wittgenstein's phrase, the criteria relevant only to the language of science. The selection from Paul Ricoeur shows that there are some common features among the language of religion, the languages of art and poetry, and scientific models, but this does not mean that any one of these particuliar language games can be totally reduced to any other.

In short, language seems to break all artificial boundaries that are set for it. And it is simply not convincing to say that certain kinds of discourse are not meaningful because they do not fit into a prescribed theory of meaningfulness. Not all areas of human investigation admit of the same degree of precision as one finds in natural science and mathematics, and it would be foolish to dismiss all language that does not fit a scientific model of language. Aristotle recognizes this when he says, "It is the mark of an educated man to look for precision in each class of things just so far as the nature of the subject admits; it is evidently equally foolish to accept probable reasoning from a mathematician and to demand from a rhetorician scientific proofs."[1]

If religious language constitutes a distinct "language game," to continue using Wittgenstein's phrase, it is also possible to distinguish *within* religious language many different forms of discourse. We have considered only a few ways in which language functions to express religious matters. When we examine the many different religions that have existed during human history, we see many different types of religious language: legends, myths (narratives involving symbolic elements), poetry, chronicles, oracles, and so on. Even within the confines of Christian Scripture, there is a rich variety of uses of language: parables, sayings, prayers, proverbs, pronouncements, hymnic material, and apocalyptic literature with its

---

[1] Aristotle, *Nicomachean Ethics* 1094b25, W. D. Ross translation.

often exaggerated symbolism. Each of these distinct types of religious language raises its own questions for a theory of interpretation, and a great deal of attention is being given by philosophers and theologians to developing a theory of interpretation that does justice to the rich variety of religious linguistic materials. Our survey of some of the main problems in religious language must stop here, but the preceding has shown that a great deal of attention has been given to the questions arising from a study of the nature of religious language. It is also evident that there is still much work yet to be done.

ADDITIONAL READINGS

Since much of the philosophy of the twentieth century has been devoted to an analysis of the nature and function of language, the amount of literature dealing with language and religion is enormous. A collection of essays spanning much of the diversity of this discussion is the volume edited by Ronald E. Santoni, *Religious Language and the Problem of Religious Knowledge* (Bloomington: Indiana University Press, 1968). A. J. Ayer advances his views on the nature of religious statements in his *Language, Truth and Logic,* which was published in a second edition in 1946 (New York: Dover Publications). Copleston discusses Ayer in volume 9 of his *History of Western Philosophy* (Garden City, NY: Doubleday-Anchor, 1976). A defense of the meaningfulness of religious utterances and an analysis of their various forms can be found in Ian Ramsey, *Religious Language* (New York: Macmillan, 1963), and in a shortened form in part 2, "The Meaning of God Talk," in his *Christian Empiricism,* ed. Jerry H. Gill (Grand Rapids, MI: Eerdmans, 1974). An overall discussion of the many aspects of this topic, with a good bibliography, is William P. Alston, "Religious Language," *The Encyclopedia of Philosophy* (1967), 7, 168–74. A new lectionary of the Bible containing sexually inclusive language is entitled *An Inclusive Language Lectionary* and is available from the John Knox/Westminster Press in Louisville or the Pilgrim Press in New York, 1986.

A work highly critical of the changes proposed by those advocating inclusive religious language is a collection of eighteen articles edited by Alvin F. Kimel, Jr., *Speaking the Christian God: The Holy Trinity and the Challenge of Feminism* (Grand Rapids, MI: Eerdmans, 1992). A collection of 13 essays in support of feminist theological themes, or what some of the writers call "thealogy," is a work edited by Ursula King, *Religion and Gender* (Oxford: Blackwell, 1995). Rosemary Radford Ruether argues in *Gaia & God: An Ecofeminist Theology of Earth Healing* (New York: Harper Collins, 1992) that we need a new set of language and symbols to help us deal with our ecological crisis.

BIOGRAPHICAL SUMMARIES

AL-GHAZZALI ABU HAMID MUHAMMAD (1058?–1111): Persian philosopher and Islamic theologian. He abandoned his life as a teacher in a university for ten years of wandering as a pilgrim. He is author of several treatises on philosophy, including "The Intentions of Philosophers" and "Autodestruction of the Philosophers."

ARISTOTLE (384–322 B.C.E.): Greek philosopher whose influence on the development of Christian philosophy in the Middle Ages was effected through the thought of Thomas Aquinas. Aristotle's writings embrace virtually every topic, but his work in logic and metaphysics was especially influential in the medieval period. The arguments for the existence of God used by St. Thomas were variations of arguments originated by Aristotle.

AUGUSTINE (354–430): Philosopher, theologian, and bishop of the north African city of Hippo. Considered one of the greatest theologians of the first millennium of the Christian era, Augustine successfully used the categories of Greek philosophical thought, especially that of Plato, as a vehicle for expressing Christian doctrine.

AYER, A. J. (1910–1989): British philosopher whose book *Language, Truth and Logic* introduced logical positivism to English-speaking philosophers. Ayer was knighted and elected to the prestigious British Academy. Among his many books are *The Problem of Knowledge*, *The Concept of a Person*, and *Philosophy in the Twentieth Century*.

BUBER, MARTIN (1878–1965): Viennese-born philosopher who was professor of the philosophy of Jewish religion and ethics at Frankfurt-am-Main University from 1924 to 1933; in 1938 he emigrated to Palestine, where he was professor of the sociology of religion at the Hebrew University. In addition to *I and Thou*, he wrote *Between Man and Man*, *The Prophetic Faith*, and *The Eclipse of God*.

COPLESTON, FREDERICK C. (1907–1994): Philosopher and fellow of the British Academy. A noted Jesuit who taught at universities both in England and in the United States, he wrote the widely used nine-volume *History of Philosophy*. Other works include *Philosophers and Philosophies* and *Contemporary Philosophy*.

DESCARTES, RENÉ (1596–1650): French philosopher and mathematician who is regarded by many as the thinker who signaled the end of medieval philosophy and the rise of modern philosophy. His *Discourse on Method* and *Meditations on First Philosophy* address many of the problems that have become the concern of modern philosophy.

DONIGER, WENDY [O'Flaherty] (1940–): American theologian who is a member of the faculty of the University of Chicago Divinity School, where she is Mircea Eliade Professor of the History of Religions. She is author of *Hindu Myths: A Sourcebook, Women, Androgynes and Other Mythical Beasts*, and *Dreams, Illusions and Other Realities*.

EPICURUS (341–270 B.C.E.): A younger contemporary of Aristotle who taught that moderation, contemplation, and happiness are important to self-fulfillment. Accepting the atomistic metaphysics of Democritus, Epicurus denied that there was a God or any transcendent reality. In midlife, and at the urging of his students, he moved to Athens and taught there until his death, surrounded by his friends and students in what became a quasi-religious community devoted to his teachings.

FLEW, ANTONY (1923–): British philosopher who has lectured widely in the United States and is the author of many books. Among the best known are *God and Philosophy, Thinking Straight*, and *The Presumption of Atheism*.

GRIFFIN, DAVID RAY (1939–): American theologian who teaches at the School of Theology at Claremont, California. Griffin is a noted authority on Charles Hartshorne and process thought. Among his books are *A Process Christology; God, Power and Evil: A Process Theodicy*; and, with John Cobb, Jr., *Process Theology: An Introduction*.

HARE, R. M. (1929–): British philosopher and professor at Corpus Christi College, Oxford. He is a fellow of the British Academy and has lectured at numerous American universities. His books include *The Language of Morals, Freedom and Reason*, and *Applications of Moral Philosophy*.

HARTSHORNE, CHARLES (1897–): American philosopher and theologian who was an assistant to Whitehead at Harvard and is one of the most influential thinkers in the development of process thought as it applies to theological issues. He taught at the University of Chicago, Emory University, and the University of Texas. Among his books are *Man's Vision of God and the Logic of Theism, Divine Relativity*, and *The Logic of Perfection*.

HICK, JOHN (1922–): British philosopher and professor at Birmingham University. He has taught at universities in the United States, including Cornell and Princeton. Among his many books are *Faith and Knowledge, Evil and the God of Love*, and *Death and Eternal Life*.

JAMES, WILLIAM (1842–1910): American philosopher who developed an approach to philosophy known as pragmatism. Among his books are *Pragmatism* and *Essays in Radical Empiricism*.

KANT, IMMANUEL (1724–1804): Professor of philosophy at the University of Königsberg, Kant developed what he labeled his critical philosophy and concluded that certain questions, such as the nature of ultimate reality, the origins of the cosmos, and the nature and destiny of the human soul, cannot be answered by human reason. He is known for his moral theory and the articulation of the categorical imperative. Among his important works are *Critique of Pure Reason* and *Critique of Practical Reason*.

KIERKEGAARD, SØREN (1813–1855): Danish philosopher and major precursor of existential philosophy. His works, many of which were written under pseudonyms, all stress the importance of becoming an individual. Among his most widely read books are *Either/Or* (2 vols.), *Fear and Trembling*, and *The Sickness Unto Death*.

KOLENDA, KONSTANTIN (1923–1991): American philosopher who was the Fred McManis Professor of Philosophy at Rice University. His books include *The Freedom of Reason, Ethics for the Young, Philosophy's Journey,* and *Cosmic Religion.*

MITCHELL, BASIL (1917–): British philosopher and professor at Oriel College, Oxford. His works dealing with religion include *Faith and Logic, Religion in a Secular Society,* and *The Justification of Religious Belief.*

NIETZSCHE, FRIEDRICH (1844–1900): German philosopher and social historian. Nietzsche was appointed to a professorship of Greek literature and philosophy at Basel when he was only twenty-four. His numerous works include *Thus Spake Zarathustra, The Genealogy of Morals,* and *The Will to Power.*

O'FLAHERTY, WENDY: See Doniger.

OTTO, RUDOLF (1869–1937): German theologian and philosopher of religion. He held positions at Göttingen, Breslau, and Marburg, where he taught from 1917 until his death. In addition to *The Idea of the Holy,* he wrote *Naturalism and Religion* and *Mysticism, East and West.*

PALEY, WILLIAM (1743–1805): English clergyman and philosopher who taught at Cambridge University and whose writings were widely read and used as textbooks. In addition to *Natural Theology,* he wrote *A View of the Evidences of Christianity* and *The Principles of Moral and Political Philosophy.*

PAUL (died 64 CE): Disciple of Jesus and a leading figure in the expansion of Christianity. Originally a persecutor of Christians, he became an apostle to the Gentiles, as he described himself. As many as thirteen of the twenty-seven books of the New Testament have been attributed to him. Undisputed books that clearly show Paul's understanding of Christianity are Romans and Galatians.

PLATO (428/27–348/47 B.C.E.): Greek philosopher and founder, in 388 or 387 B.C.E., of the Academy, in many ways the first university. Much of what we know of early Greek philosophy we learn from Plato, especially the thought of Socrates, Plato's teacher and a person whom many consider to be the father of Western philosophy. Plato's thought had a profound influence on the development of Christian philosophy, and his philosophical categories were used by many early Christian writers as vehicles for expressing Christian doctrine.

RAHULA, WALPOLA (1907–): Born in Sri Lanka, Walpola Rahula is a noted interpreter of Buddhist thought. In addition to being a philosopher, he is a Buddhist monk. He was educated at universities in England, India, and France and has served as chancellor of Kelaniya University of Sri Lanka. He has taught at Northwestern University, Swarthmore College, and the University of California, Los Angeles. Among his books are *Zen and the Taming of the Bull: Towards the Definition of Buddhist Thought, History of Buddhism in Ceylon: The Anuradhapura Period,* and *What the Buddha Taught.*

RAMSEY, IAN (1915–1972): British theologian who was chaplain and fellow of Christ Church, Cambridge, and later taught at Oxford from 1951 until 1966, when he was appointed Bishop of Durham. Among his works dealing with religious language are *Models and Mystery, Christian Discourse,* and *Words About God.*

RICOEUR, PAUL (1913–): French philosopher who has held professorships at the University of Paris and the University of Chicago. His work has focused especially on problems of hermeneutics, the rules for interpreting texts. His many books include *The Symbolism of Evil*, *Freud and Philosophy*, *The Rule of Metaphor*, and *Time and Narrative*.

RUSSELL, BERTRAND (1872–1970): British philosopher and mathematician, Russell was awarded the Order of Merit by the British government in 1949 and received the Nobel prize for literature in 1950. With Alfred North Whitehead, he wrote *Principia Mathematica*, which was a major influence on the development of symbolic logic. Good places for someone unacquainted with his work to begin are *The Problems of Philosophy* and *My Philosophical Development*.

RUETHER, ROSEMARY RADFORD (1936–): American theologian and professor of applied theology at Garrett-Evangelical theological seminary, Evanston. She is author of a number of books on feminist and liberation theology. Among them are *Mary: The Feminine Face of the Church*; *Sexism and God-Talk*; and *Gaia and God: Ecofeminist Theology of Earth Healing*.

TAYLOR, RICHARD (1919–): American philosopher who has taught at the University of Rochester and other American universities. Among his books are *Good and Evil* and *Freedom, Anarchy and the Law*.

TILLICH, PAUL (1866–1965): German theologian who fled Hitler's Germany in 1933. He taught at Union Theological Seminary in New York, the University of Chicago, and Harvard University. His three-volume *Systematic Theology* is the most complete expression of his views; his shorter works include *The Courage to Be* and *The Dynamics of Faith*.

TOLSTOY, LEO (1828–1910): One of the great Russian novelists of the nineteenth century. Born an aristocrat, Tolstoy renounced his position and fortune to seek a simple Christian lifestyle among the peasants. He is perhaps best known for his novels *War and Peace* and *Anna Karenina*.

WHITEHEAD, ALFRED NORTH (1861–1947): British philosopher and mathematician and influential contributor to process thought. Whitehead taught at Cambridge, the University of London, and Harvard University. His best known book, and the one that is formative in developing a metaphysical view compatible with quantum mechanics, is *Process and Reality*. Other influential works by Whitehead are *Science in the Modern World* and *Adventures of Ideas*.

GLOSSARY

Anatman: In Buddhism the doctrine that there is no separate and persisting soul or self; sometimes called the no-soul view.

A priori: Refers to knowledge that is derived solely from reason independently of the senses. The truth of a priori knowledge is claimed to be both necessary and universal.

A posteriori: Literally means *following after* and refers to the kind of knowledge that follows and is dependent upon sense experience, as opposed to the kind of knowledge that human reason can know independently of the senses.

Agnosticism: The view that we do not have, nor is it possible to attain, certain kinds of knowledge. As originated by Thomas Huxley, the term refers to his view that we cannot know whether God does or does not exist. This being the case, Huxley urges the complete suspension of belief. Others have argued that the kind of uncertainty espoused by agnosticism is compatible with faith.

Analogical predication: The use of language to say something that, while not literally true, conveys its sense by comparing one thing with another. For example, one can predicate the quality of intelligence literally to human beings and analogously to animals, as in "I have an intelligent cat." Analogical use of language allows one to speak of two different things by focusing on their similarities without ignoring their differences. To say that "God is loving" is to predicate love of God in an analogous use of the term.

Analytic: A statement is analytic if its truth or falsity can be determined by analysis of the terms in the statement alone. Statements that are analytically true are said to be either true by definition or logically true. Examples are "All bachelors are males" and "A rose is a rose."

Animism: The belief that souls or spirits inhabit animals, plants, even places, such as rivers and mountains. Used in a collective sense with reference to "primitive" religions.

Anthropomorphism: The use of human characteristics to describe nonhuman realities. In religion any description of the divine in terms of human characteristics—for example, the "hand of God"—is an anthropomorphism.

Atheism: The assertion that there is no God.

Atman: Hindu term for the ultimate Self. In Vedanta, Atman is held to be identical with Brahman, the ultimate reality. Buddhism denies that there are substantive and persistent individual souls or selves.

Bhikkhu: A Buddhist monk.

Bios: Greek word meaning "life" and used by John Hick to refer to physical existence.

Blik: A term coined by R. M. Hare to refer to any unverifiable, unfalsifiable assumption or set of assumptions in terms of which we view the world. It is in the nature of a blik to determine what kinds of evidence count against it. Hare thought that we all have bliks, though some bliks are sane and others are insane.

Bodhisattva: In Buddhism a person who has achieved great spiritual wisdom but instead of accepting nirvana chooses to stay behind to assist others in their quest of enlightenment.

Brahman: Literally, "power," especially the power of words. The Hindu term for the ultimate reality.

Buddha: An enlightened being; also used to refer to the historical Buddha, Siddhartha Gautama.

Buddhism: A way of thought and practice that emphasizes moral practice, meditation, and enlightenment founded by Siddhartha Gautama, the Buddha, in India during the sixth century B.C.E.

Category mistake: A term used by Gilbert Ryle to refer to those cases when words are taken to belong to a different category than their true one.

Compensation: A psychological term that refers to the human tendency to substitute an area of strength for an area of weakness. Some people argue that belief in God is compensation for human finitude and limitation.

Confucianism: Chinese tradition based on the teachings of Confucius and his followers, particularly Mencius and Xun Zi.

Contingent: Dependent, not having the characteristic of necessity.

Contradiction: A statement that is internally inconsistent so that on any interpretation it comes out false. Contradictions are false on logical grounds.

Cosmological: A term derived from the Greek word meaning *order*. *Cosmological* pertains to nature as a cosmos or ordered system. Applied to a type of argument for the existence of God, it refers to the kind of reasoning that proceeds from the apparent order and regularity of the world to God as the best explanation for this order.

Deism: Derived from the Latin word *deus* (god). Refers to the specific view that God is creator of the world but has no ongoing involvement with the world and does not intervene in the natural order. Some interpreters of the cosmological argument have concluded that the deistic conception of God is all that the argument can prove.

Demiurge: Derived from a Greek word for handyman or tinkerer who fashioned articles out of materials supplied by customers. When applied to the notion of a creator-god, it refers to the view that the creator fashioned a cosmos out of available materials but did not create those materials. This kind of creator was suggested by the ancient Greek philosopher Plato and by John Stuart Mill in the nineteenth century.

Dharma: A term derived from Sanskrit that refers to one's social situation and its duties. It can sometimes have the sense of moral and social law, even natural law considered in the moral sense of the term, and refers to the law of truth, virtue, and righteousness.

Dualism: Any explanation offered in terms of two equal but opposed powers, principles, or beings. A religious view is dualistic when it suggests that there are two equal but opposed deities, one evil and one good. Such a view is found in Zoroastrian religion. A metaphysical dualism is that of body and soul or matter and spirit.

Dukkha: The term used in Buddhism for life's inevitable suffering.

Dysteleological suffering: Suffering that is pointless and does not produce any good outcome; unmerited and unjust suffering. See *teleological suffering.*

Enlightenment: The realization of truth that liberates.

Epistemic distance: Has to do with the remoteness of the knower from the thing known. It is said that we have epistemic distance from God—that is, God is not known to us in the usual ways of knowing—so we cannot claim to have certainty about things we say of God.

Epistemology: The theory of knowledge; an inquiry into the origin, validity, and limits of knowledge.

Equivocal: The use of language in which a term has two or more different meanings. When language is used equivocally in an argument, the fallacy of equivocation results.

Eschatological: Literally pertaining to the doctrine of last things; in religious thought, the events surrounding the end of the world. Sometimes in a religious context it refers only to doctrines concerning future occurrences.

Ethics: The philosophical investigation of the principles governing human actions in terms of their goodness, badness, rightness, and wrongness.

Falsifiability: A principle appealed to by Antony Flew that says that in order to be a genuine assertion, a statement must in principle be capable of being proved false, or falsified. If nothing will count against the statement to falsify it, then, according to Flew, it is not a genuine assertion.

Fideism: Derived from the Latin word for faith, fideism is the view that truth in religion is based solely on faith rather than on reasoning and evidence. Fideism is the opposite of *rationalism.*

Genuine option: Technical term introduced by William James to refer to an option that is living, forced, and momentous.

Hermeneutics: The analysis of principles for interpreting a written text. The term has in recent years been extended to include more than written texts and can refer to the principles for interpreting any human action in order to proceed with rigorous philosophical analysis of that action.

Heuristic: From the Greek word for discovery; refers to that which stimulates interest in, and furthers investigation of, a topic.

Holy: Originally meant that which is separate and wholly other; gradually the term took on the sense of moral perfection. The word is used by Rudolf Otto in its original sense to refer to the Wholly Other, the *mysterium tremendum.* See *numinous.*

Immanent: Refers to that which is found within, as opposed to transcendent. To speak of God as immanent is to say that God is to be found within, which can mean either within the human soul or within the created order as the inner purpose of the universe.

Karma: In Hindu and Buddhist thought, a law of cause and effect in terms of which one's future existence is affected by the ethical nature of one's present actions; conversely, one's present situation is the result of deeds done in a previous existence.

Lex naturale: See *natural law*.

Logical positivism: The view that philosophy has no method independent of that of science and that philosophy's only task is logical analysis. According to the principle of verifiability, which was defended by logical positivists as a way of distinguishing meaningful statements from nonsense, a statement is meaningful if and only if it is analytic or can be verified empirically.

Master morality: Nietzsche's view that to avoid nihilism the ruling class develops a morality based on strength and creativity in which values such as pride and nobility are paramount. He considers it the opposite of *slave morality*.

Maya: A term in Hinduism meaning illusion. According to this Hindu doctrine, the physical, visible world has no real permanent existence but is temporary.

Metaphysics: The philosophical inquiry into the nature of ultimate reality. The term can also refer to the analysis of fundamental principles used in philosophical analysis.

Moksha: Term used in Hinduism to refer to liberation from the cycle of birth, death, and rebirth. See *samsara*.

Monotheism: Belief that there exists only one god, usually conceived to be personal; the opposite of *polytheism*.

Moral evil: Suffering in the world caused by human perversity, in contrast to that caused by the processes of nature. See *natural evil*.

Mores: A term used by anthropologists to refer to the customs or folkways of a people that have taken on moral significance and have the force of law.

Mystery: That which is beyond human understanding. In contrast to a problem, which can be solved by an increase in knowledge, no amount of additional knowledge can dispel a mystery. Used by Gabriel Marcel to discuss that which finite human beings cannot understand.

Mysticism: An experience is mystical if it is characterized by a sense of unity and oneness with the divine. One variation is union mysticism, characterized by loss of individuality and transportation beyond time and space into an experience that is ineffable. Another variation is communion mysticism, in which the individual experiences a sense of unity of purpose and communion with the divine but does not lose a sense of individuality. Communion mysticism is more characteristic of both Jewish and Christian mystical experiences than is union mysticism, although the latter does have its representatives within both traditions.

Natural evil: The suffering in the world due to the processes of nature, in contrast with suffering caused by human perversity. Floods, hurricanes, earthquakes, and disease are examples of natural evil.

Natural law: The universally valid principles of conduct known by reason alone and therefore accessible to all people, as opposed to the *positive law* of a state or society. Originating in ancient Greek philosophy, natural law theories were used by philosophers of the Middle Ages as another proof of the existence of God, who was thought to be the author of the natural law.

Natural theology: That which can be known about God purely by the power of human reason unaided by revelation. Natural theology claims to be able to provide proofs of God's existence either completely a priori, and therefore independent of the senses, or a posteriori, that is, based on certain facts about the natural order.

Naturalism: The view that nature is the totality of reality and needs no supernatural cause or explanation.

Nihilism: In ethics the view that there are no principles of morality. The term can also refer to a situation in which there is a complete breakdown of all previous ethical systems and the collapse of moral principles.

Nirvana: In Buddhist thought, the goal of life is to reach nirvana, a loss of individuality and the cessation of suffering. The term is also found in Hinduism.

Nonrational: Refers to those beliefs which, while not derived from reason, are nonetheless not irrational. Such beliefs stem from a source other than reason, such as feelings of utter dependence (Schleiermacher).

Numinous: A term coined by Rudolf Otto and derived from the Latin term *numen,* meaning divine power. It refers to that which is experienced as the "wholly other" or as the *mysterium tremendum.* Otto also referred to the *numinous* as *the holy.* See *holy.*

Objectivism: In ethics the view that there are objective principles that are true or false independent of people's feelings about them. Regarding ethical statements, objectivism holds that such statements have a truth value, that is, they can be true or false. The opposite of *subjectivism.*

Omnipotence: Having all power; a characteristic of the traditional Jewish, Christian, and Islamic views of God.

Omniscience: Having knowledge of all things, or perfect knowledge; a characteristic traditionally attributed to God.

Ontological: Derived from the Greek word for *being,* the term relates to the question of being. The ontological argument is an argument for God's existence based solely on an analysis of the concept of the being of God. Ontology is the metaphysical inquiry into the nature of being in general.

Panentheism: God is not identified with the world as in *pantheism,* but though distinct from the world, God nonetheless interpenetrates everything that is. Panentheism is the view championed by process thought.

Panexperientalism: A term found in process thought to describe reality as occasions of experience rather than static objects. It is preferred by process philosophers to the comparable term *panpsychism.*

Panpsychism: The view that all reality is mental, not physical, in nature. A form of metaphysical idealism.

Pantheism: The view that identifies God with the visible universe; derived from two Greek words, *theos* ("God") and *pan* ("all"). For pantheism, God is the world, the world is God.

Polysemy: A term used in semantics to refer to the feature of a word whereby it has many meanings. Ricoeur uses the term in his discussion of metaphor, which is a kind of polysemy.

Polytheism: Belief that there are many gods; opposite of *monotheism*.

Positive law: Laws enacted by the state or by society to regulate behavior. Such laws are not required to be the same for all people but may reflect societal differences, such as the speed limits in various countries. See *natural law*.

Positivism: In general a view that rejects the possibility of metaphysics. Auguste Comte suggests that the history of thought has proceeded through three stages: the religious, the metaphysical, and the positive. The latter stage is characterized by a rejection of all religious and metaphysical thinking. See *logical positivism*.

Process theology: A theological view that sees the universe as made of dynamic, interrelated processes, not static, substantial beings. God as conceived of by process thought is not immutable and unchanging but is interdependent with the world and is affected by other entitites of the world. Process theologians tend to identify God with the principle of value, rather than with the principle of reality, and conceive of God as savior of the world rather than as its creator.

Proposition: A proposition is expressed by a sentence that has a truth value, that is, it can be either true or false. The sentence "The book is blue" expresses a proposition. The sentence "Close the door" does not express a proposition. To express a proposition, a statement must have propositional content, which means that it refers to something and predicates a quality of it.

Radiance: Term used by Thomas Aquinas to refer to a property of beautiful objects whereby they call attention to themselves. Konstantin Kolenda adopts the term to refer to those features of life that bring delight and satisfaction.

Rationalism: In religion it is the view that truth must be based on reason and not on faith; the opposite of *fideism*.

Reincarnation: A belief that one is reborn in successive lives.

Relativism: Any view that denies there are objective principles. In ethics it is the view that there are no objective principles of ethics and no values that hold for all people at all times and all places. Instead, it sees values as arising either from human cultures or as legislated by human agreement.

Samsara: Used in Hinduism and Buddhism to refer to the cycle of birth, death, and rebirth.

Semantics: The systematic investigation of the development, and changes in the meaning and form, of language.

Slave morality: Nietzsche's term for moralities that exalt values based on weakness, such as forgiveness and humility. Such moralities, he thought, do not allow for the development of great cultures.

Subjectivism: In ethics the view that ethical statements are descriptions of the way people feel about certain actions. According to subjectivism, there are no moral standards independent of human feelings.

Sufficient reason: The principle that holds that things do not happen without a cause or without some reason sufficient to explain their happening. The principle of sufficient reason cannot be proved but has been suggested as a basic presupposition of all thought.

Synthetic: Refers to those kinds of statements in which the predicate adds something not already contained in the subject. The truth or falsity of synthetic statements is determined by observation and sense experience.

Tautology: A statement that is logically or trivially true by virtue of its meaning.

Teleological: From the Greek word for *end* or *purpose*; refers to that which is purposive. Teleological arguments for God's existence are based on the claim that the world exhibits order and purpose, which can best be explained with reference to God.

Teleological suffering: Suffering that accomplishes some purpose, as opposed to *dysteleological suffering*, which is suffering with no apparent purpose.

Theodicy: An attempt to justify the goodness of an omnipotent God in spite of the presence of evil in the world.

Theophany: A manifestation or appearance of the divine at a definite time and a definite place. Moses' experience of the burning bush was an example of a theophany.

Transcendent: Literally means that which goes beyond; in religion the transcendent refers to that which lies beyond the physical or natural order. The traditional Jewish, Christian, and Islamic view is that God is a transcendent being.

Transmigration: Belief in a form of reincarnation wherein souls may be reborn in animal as well as human forms.

Univocal: The use of language in which a term has one and only one meaning, or at least one central meaning in terms of which its various usages can be understood.

Upanishads: Concluding portions of the Vedas containing discussions of sacred knowledge of reality.

Verification principle: A principle suggested by A. J. Ayer by means of which to distinguish meaningful statements from nonsense. According to the verification principle, a statement is meaningful if, and only if, it is analytic or can in principle be verified empirically.

Via negativa: Literally means the negative way; a use of language wherein one makes only negative statements, not positive ones, in order to avoid possible equivocation in language usage. Examples would be to say that God is not finite, or God is not evil.

Weltanschauung: The German term for worldview.

Zoe: Greek word meaning "life" that is used by John Hick to refer to spiritual existence. He argues that "soul making" is the transition from *bios* to zoe.

INDEX

A

A *posteriori* arguments, 119-20, 132ff
A *priori* arguments, 119-20
Abbott, Edwin A., 293
Abe, Masao, 42
Abraham, 119, 256
Actual entities, 182
Adam and Eve myth, 172-73
Agnosticism, 235-36
    and Ayer, 277
Al-Ghazzali, Abu Hamid Muhammad, 55-
    57
Amos, 306
Analogy, 287-88
    arguments based on, 145-46
    downward, 295
    and religious language, 293-95
    upward, 295
Analytic statements, 277ff
Anaxagoras, 94-95
Anselm, Saint, 118
    and ontological argument, 119, 122ff
Anthropomorphism, 274
Approximation-process, 254
Aquinas, Saint Thomas, 105, 220, 255
    and analogy, 293-94
    and cosmological arguments, 132ff
    and design argument, 145
    and faith and reason, 216

and God's omniscience, 211
and radiance, 75, 80
twofold path, 218-19
Argument from contingency
    notion of contingency, 133
    Richard Taylor's version of, 136ff
    weaknesses of, 135
Arguments
    from analogy, 145-46
    from contingency, 136ff
    cosmological, 120, 131ff
    deductive, 131
    from design, 145ff
    for God's existence, 117ff
    for God's existence, and natural
        theology, 120
    from morality, 120, 154ff
    inductive, 132
    ontological, 120, 122ff
    superontological, 77, 79
    teleological, 120, 132, 145ff
Aristotle, 159, 184, 310, 311, 330
    and analogy, 293
    Thomas Aquinas' familiarity with
        terminology of, 133
    compatibility of metaphysical and
        ethical views, 52
    on humans and society, 30
    and metaphor, 313
    and *mimesis*, 318